21ST CENTURY FUNERAL DIRECTING

AND

FUNERAL SERVICE MANAGEMENT

RALPH L. KLICKER, Ph.D.

Ralph L. Klicker, Ph.D.
Thanos Institute
P.O. Box 1928
Buffalo, NY 14231-1928
rk@anubus.net

Previous Edition 2008, Printed in the U.S.A.

ISBN: 978-1-7344805-0-4

Published by:
Thanos Institute
P.O. Box 1928
Buffalo, NY 14231-1928
Phone: 716-636-0383
Toll Free: 1-800-742-8257
Fax: 716-689-2821
Email: mrizzo@thanosinstitute.com
Website: http://www.thanosinstitute.com

Ralph L. Klicker's Other Books Include:

A Walk Through Time: A History of Funeral Service

Funeral Service Psychology and Counseling

Restorative Art and Science

Ethics in Funeral Service

Kolie and the Funeral

A Student Dies, A School Mourns

Leaderships According to St. Peter

Don't Wait Until You Are 6 Feet Under: It's too Late to Change Your Life When You Hear the Dirt Being Thrown on Your Casket

Unexpected, Traumatic Death and the Funeral Director

From the Author:

I have wanted to be a funeral director since I was in the eighth grade. While in high school, I started working at a funeral home cutting grass and doing general maintenance work. Within six months, I was assisting on removals, calling hours, funerals, and helping in the embalming room. I thought I had died and gone to heaven. The funeral directors who took me under their wings were consummate professionals. Much of what I know about being a funeral director came from their example. They let me make mistakes and treated me as one of the team. They taught me that you could work in a serious business and still have fun.

Since then I have worked as a funeral director, embalmer, mortuary science educator, continuing education provider, and a grief counselor. I give you this background only to help you understand where I am coming from when I talk about the profession. I believe in the value of post-death rituals and ceremonies more than any other belief I have ever had. I also believe that as society's view of the funeral changes, the profession must also change to meet the needs of our grieving families.

This book provides you with the most up-to-date information available from around the country. The suggestions are not the only way to conduct service and operate a funeral home but are ways that have been proven successful.

Any mistakes or omission in the citations or references were not intentional. If you know of a correction, please notify us so that we can make the necessary addition or correction.

Some of the references in this book may seem outdated. They have been included, however, because the issues they address and the recommendations they provide are still relevant in funeral service today.

If you have questions or comments, please feel free to contact me at rk@anubus.net.

Ralph L. Klicker, Ph.D.

DEDICATION

This book is dedicated to those funeral directors and educators who were influential in getting me started in the profession.

Louis Nagel (deceased) and **Richard McCready** (deceased) took the interest of a 12-year-old boy and treated it with respect. They were my family's funeral directors when I was a child, and it was at their funeral home that my interests in the profession began.

Anthony P. Amigone Sr. gave me my first job in a funeral home when I was 15 years old. He has remained a trusted advisor, mentor, friend, and employer throughout my career. There will never be another funeral director like him.

Frederick R. Henderson taught me most of what I know about embalming. He is a great funeral director, embalmer, and friend, one who I am proud to have learned under.

Dan D. Amigone Jr. was a willing and patient teacher in the embalming room and on funerals.

Carmen A Paolini has taught me much about embalming and funeral directing without ever knowing he was doing it. I treasure his friendship.

The **San Francisco College of Mortuary Science** gave me a great educational experience.

Leander Coles for hiring me for my first teaching position at the University of the District of Columbia.

The **State University of NY at Canton** for hiring me as Director of their program twice.

ACKNOWLEDGEMENTS

Candice Giles: A special thank you to for all of the formatting, proofing, editing, and many other contributions that made this book possible.

Tanya Biscardi: Thank you for all the initial work that got this book off to a great start!

Thank you to the following individuals and companies for their contributions:

Contributing Authors

• Alice Adams	*Photographing at a Funeral*
• Emily Albrecht	*Federal Trade Commission (FTC)* *Third Party Crematories*
• Mark Allen	*Nine Tips for Connecting with Funeral Shoppers*
• Angela Berwald	*Top 10 Things to Consider When Dealing with Funeral Shipping*
• Bill Bates	*Personalization*
• Barb Bloomquist	*4 Ways Aftercare Can Help Grow Your Funeral Home Business*
• Beverly Brown	*6 Tips for an Effective Community Outreach Program*
• CANA	*Asking the Right Questions: Interviewing Families with an Event Planner Mindset*
• A. Creedy	*Narrow Your Focus, Broaden Your Market*
• S. Cronin	*The Dual Licensure Debate*
• Frank Dawson	*Example of Hours Spent on a Funeral Call*
• Ellis Funeral Homes	*Funerals vs. Celebrations of Life*
• Barb Garrison	*Watch Out for Bedbugs!*
• Candice Giles	*Funeral Service Technology in the 21st Century*
• Glen Gould	*Brand Loyalty*
• Adele Haas	*Life is for Sharing, Beginning-to-End*
• Robin Heppell	*Funeral Home Ad Checklist*
• Welton Hong	*Blogging 101: What to Write, How Much and How Often*
• Carolyn Hyams & Joe Troxler	*Behave Yourself on LinkedIn*
• L. Howard-Fusco	*Crowd Funding: The Future of Funeral Financing*
• Cole Imperi	*Death Doulas and Funeral Service*
• Daniel Isard	*Tips on Pricing* *The Past, Present, and Future of Cremation*
• Michael Kubasak	*Customer Service*
• Christopher Kuhnen	*Who Make the Best Pre-Need Buyers? Women?*
• PlanningaFuneral.com	*After Funeral or Cremation Gathering*
• Poul Lemasters	*Knowing Who has Final Control of Disposition* *What Does Supreme Court Ruling on Same-Sex Marriage Mean for Death Care Providers*
• Live Oak Bank	*Funeral Home Buying Guide*

ACKNOWLEDGEMENTS (cont.)

• Sara J. Marsden	*Funeral Poverty in the 21st Century*
• Patti Martin-Bartsche	*Casket Personalization: Making Your Mark* *Cremation Language*
• Patrick McGowan	*What is a Cemetery?*
• Quincy Memorials	*8 Reasons to Memorialize with a Monument*
• National Cemetery Administration	*Burial Benefits*
• Patch Spotlights	*Funeral Director Jeffrey M. Dames Discusses Traditional Funerals*
• David Penepent	*Domestic Shipping*
• Chris Raymond	*The Pros and Cons of Funeral Webcasting*
• Gail Rubin	*Funeral Insurance Pros, Cons, and Differences*
• Eric D. Ruggeri	*Forensic Removal*
• Mary Ann Schueble	*Suggestions for Improving Customer Service*
• Joseph Shay	*Becoming a Certified Shipper*
• Cas Skretny	*Merchandising Pricing*
• Gary Sokoll	*Caskets, Vaults, & Urns*
• Darci Swisher	*How to Show off Your Best Self to a Potential Employer on Social Media*
• David Tackett	*Clergy-Funeral Director Relations*
• Majorie Todd & Richard Best	*Health and Safety in the Funeral Home*
• U.S. Department of Veterans Affairs	*Burial and Plot-Internment Allowances*
• U.S. Navy Mortuary Affairs	*Burial at Sea Program*
• Veterans Flag Depot	*How to Fold the Flag*
• Todd W. Van Beck	*Multiple Contributions*
• Jamie Watts	*Code of Ethical Cremation Practices*
• Lee Webster	*Defining Home Funeral Guides*
• Joe Weigel	*10 Tips to Create Press Releases that Get Published*
• Melissa Johnson Williams	*Shipping Human Remains to Foreign Countries* *Receiving Remains from Abroad*
• William York	*Dangerous Synthetic Opioids and the First Call*

Batesville Casket Company, Clark Grave Vault Company, Ensure-A-Seal, Goliath Casket Company, Vantage Products Company, and **York Casket Company** for supplying photographs.

Adfinity for supplying advertisement samples.

The Director for supplying graphics and articles.

American Funeral Director, The Dodge Magazine, Funeral Service Insider, Mortuary Management Magazine, Southern Funeral Director*, *and Texas Funeral Director for permission to reprint articles.

Amigone Funeral Home, Inc. for supplying photographs and the use of staff in photographs.

Buszka Funeral Home for digital photo examples.

EMBALMING

In writing this book, I chose not to include a chapter on embalming. This does not mean that I do not see a value in embalming. On the contrary, I believe that embalming can be one of the most important aspects of our profession. Embalming allows us to offer our client families the opportunity to view their deceased loved one. This viewing can have a profoundly positive impact on their adjustment to the death. Embalming is so important and technical that I would rather you refer to the following excellent embalming text that is available:

Embalming History, Theory, and Practice by Robert G. Mayer

Even though this book discusses funeral directing and the management aspects of funeral service, there is one important fact that we must never forget. That fact is: ***We are in the business of taking care of the dead.***

Granted, we also care for those grieving people who come to us for help, but if it were not for the need to provide some final disposition for a dead human body, there would be no need for us. Embalming is why we are licensed in most states. Our professional license is not required because we operate a business; it is required because we perform medical-type procedures on dead human remains. It is required because of the public health aspects of embalming.

Embalming is what differentiates us from everyone else in the death care fields. Hospice cares for the dying and bereaved; grief counselors help those who are grieving; cemeteries provide a final resting place. We in the funeral profession care for both the living and the dead.

Embalming has a history dating back 6,000 years to the Egyptian priests who cared for the dead. Our techniques are different now than they were 6,000 years ago and they will be different 6,000 years from now. But as long as people receive comfort from viewing their deceased loves ones, there will be a need for embalming.

I would like to acknowledge Dennis Gospodarski for recommending that I mention the above information. Dennis has embalmed more bodies than any other embalmer I know. Dennis also served his country proudly as an Airborne Ranger in the U.S. Army.

KLICKER'S FUNERAL SERVICE CONTINUUM

Funeral Director's Prayer

Our Father grant me the knowledge to wisely counsel the grieving people I serve.

Grant me the skill to professionally care for their loved ones who have died.

Grant me the sensitivity and awareness to understand the depth of their pain and sorrow.

Grant me the strength to care, without my heart breaking, so I can be of help.

And yes God, **grant** me a sense of humor, so at the appropriate time and in a sensitive way, I can give these mourners a moment's rest.

Amen.

Ralph L. Klicker, Ph.D.

TABLE OF CONTENTS

SECTION 2 – Cremation

SECTION 3 – Management

Section 4 – Marketing

Section 5 – Starting or Buying a Business

Section 6 – Government Agencies

Section 7 – Technology & The Future

Section 8 – Supportive Readings

INTRODUCTION

Why We have Post-Death Ceremonies/Rituals

- **Final Disposition for the body of the deceased.** One of the harsh realities of death is the necessity for the final disposition of the physical body of the deceased. This final disposition, whether it is burial, cremation, or entombment, can be accomplished with as much or as little ceremony as desired.

- **Religious Ritual**. Although religious affiliation is decreasing across the country, religion has a prominent position in many people's lives. They receive comfort and reassurance from religious beliefs and ceremonies. For many people, funerals are primarily a religious ceremony that allows them to fulfill the final phase of their spiritual life. For others this is not important.

- **Social Support**. The pain of grief is never more intense than when it is experienced alone. The coming together of friends and family to pay tribute to the deceased provides support for the survivors and comfort to all that experience it. Although some people feel awkward or frightened when attending a funeral, almost everyone feels a sense of belonging when expressing condolences, offering acts of concern and supporting the survivors. This same sense of community and caring is felt by the survivors along with a sense of pride that others respected the deceased enough to attend the visitation, gathering, or funeral.

- **Recognition of a life lived**. Everyone, no matter how famous or unknown, rich or poor, young or old, affects the lives of others in some way. The funeral may be the only opportunity for an organized reflection and recognition.

- **Acceptable environment to express feelings**. Many people find it difficult to express their feelings in public. They worry about appearances or feel embarrassed. The post-death ceremony is the one place and time where all are encouraged to openly express their feelings. Mourners are in an atmosphere where everyone is experiencing similar feelings and where the social taboo of crying in public does not apply.

Alternative 21st Century Terminology

Starks (2017) Dawson (2015)

1. **Instead of coffin, consider casket.**

2. **Instead of morgue or embalming room, consider preparation room or care center.**

3. **Instead of showroom, consider selection room.**

4. **Instead of hearse, consider funeral coach.**

5. **Instead of shipped, consider "Mr. Smith's remains are to be sent out of town."**

6. **Instead of service, consider commemoration.**

7. **Instead of stillborn, consider infant.**

8. **Instead of laying out room, consider "Williamsburg Room," "Lakeview Room," or another name.**

9. **Instead of embalming, consider preparation.**

10. **Instead of pick-up or removal, consider transfer or "bringing Mr./Mrs. ---- into our care**

11. **Instead of obituary, consider editorial tribute.**

12. **Instead of visitation, consider "time for sharing" or a gathering.**

13. **Instead of "Mr. Smith's body," consider "Mr. Smith's remains or just "Mr. Smith."**

14. **Instead of ashes or cremains, consider cremated remains or use their name.**

15. **Instead of rental casket, consider ceremonial casket.**

16. **Instead of direct cremation, consider nonceremonial cremation.**

17. **Instead of products, consider choices.**

18. **Instead of arrangements, consider planning.**

19. **Instead of Funeral Director for cremation planning, consider Cremation Specialist.**

20. **Instead of final viewing, consider final goodbye.**

21. **Instead of vault, consider protective outer container.**

22. **Instead of saying "placed in a niche," consider saying "placed in a permanent memorial."**

These alternative terms are suggestions to bring our terminology into the 21st Century. I know they will not be accepted by everyone. They are simply presented for your consideration.

21st Century Funeral Service

For thousands of years in hundreds of cultures the dead body was the center of importance in death-related rituals. This custom spanned the continents. **"Seeing is believing"** visual confrontation with the body reinforced the fact that death was real and could not be psychologically denied. Funeral directors' thoughts on embalming and viewing the deceased were based on this premise. It was why we had funerals.

For years we believed this was true for everyone. However, in the 21st century most enlightened funeral directors have altered this belief to be that **embalming and viewing the deceased CAN be helpful to SOME grieving loved ones.** We have now learned that there is an increasing number of individuals who do not need this visual confrontation to proceed healthily through the grieving process. Some do request a short, unembalmed identification viewing while others have no desire to see the deceased at all. Aside from the viewing aspect of a death ritual, new cultural ceremonies are developing. Some people are gathering together at the funeral home or other venue to celebrate the life of the deceased. It has become known as a "Celebration of Life" and focuses on the person's life rather than his/her death. As a 21st century funeral director you will need to be flexible, creative, and adaptable to meet the needs of all who request your services, no matter how different they may be.

Remember our job is to help families at this time of need. We must provide them with professional, sensitive, and honest service. Also remember that we must treat the dead body and the family with respect and dignity whether they select a service or not, the type of casket or container selected, or what the final disposition is for the deceased.

PROFESSIONAL, SENSITIVE, HONEST SERVICE TO THE LIVING.

RESPECTFUL AND DIGNIFIED CARE OF THE DEAD.

**IF YOU CANNOT ABIDE BY THESE PRINCIPLES,
YOU SHOULD NOT BE IN THE PROFESSION!**

Traditional Funerals

Excerpt From: Patchwork Spotlights (2018)

Confronting death head-on is often difficult and unpleasant for many, as society has veered toward the social surrogacy of a Smartphone instead of the things that enrich the quality of life such as personal human connection. Attending the funeral of a loved one is never an experience to look forward to. However, it is an essential step on the path toward complete and healthy grief recovery.

At a funeral, the deepest emotions often rise to the surface. One is able to confront these emotions in the company of friends and family with the guidance of an experienced, caring funeral service professional. Individuals witness with their own eyes that someone has truly died, and everyone around them witnesses the same thing, making it impossible to deny. This forces people to truly accept the death and creates an opportunity for them to purge emotions and start to heal.

The traditional funeral is a time-tested method of allowing people to begin healing and avoid keeping their emotions bottled up inside. For countless generations, people have relied on this practice to help them grieve. Sadly though, there has lately been a shift away from traditional funerals. When planning for death, a growing number of people are choosing to forgo a funeral service entirely, and instead they look to memorial services, celebration of life services, and even cremation with nothing after. Of course, some families find solace in these kinds of tributes. After all, when people come together for a shared remembrance it can be therapeutic. With that being said, circumstances for any final earthly tribute should be carefully considered by all who it will affect.

Some people make the decision to avoid a traditional funeral for economic reasons. This is a time when some people are struggling to find stable jobs with opportunities for advancement. When meeting basic needs becomes an everyday struggle, they are likely to reduce spending wherever they can. This means that even in times of loss, these people are likely to put financial concerns ahead of the need to cope with grief. Many people also believe they will spare their family and friends from pain and suffering by avoiding a traditional funeral. They think the loved ones they leave behind will simply be able to move on with their lives as if nothing had happened.

Despite the good intentions of the people seeking alternatives to traditional funerals, they could be unknowingly doing a disservice to the family and friends they leave behind. Without the chance to gather with others in the presence of the deceased's body, people in some cases are unable to fully process the death of their loved ones. The loss may not be fully realized, and survivors are left to carry these feelings deep inside. Many mental health professionals believe that whether the surviving family's preference is cremation, burial, or donation to science, it is the gathering with the deceased present that reaches the deepest emotions within everyone. People who express their feelings and truly deal with them, in any situation, do better in life than those who keep their emotions repressed.

Negative and Positive Views of Funerals

The Good

In 2015, FAMIC, The Funeral and Memorial Information Council, conducted a survey of 1,238 Americans over 40 on the value of funerals and memorialization.

Results:

- 82% of those surveyed responded that a funeral service was helpful in paying tribute to the deceased — down from 95% in 2010.
- 65% felt that funeral homes were the best source for information on funerals.
- 86% felt that funeral directors were important in making funeral arrangements – down from 93% in 2010.
- 82% felt funeral directors provided valuable services – down from 94% in 2010.

Young adults ages 20-39 are more apt to visit online memorial sites and hear about funeral and obituary information through social media.

There are three types of consumers living within your service area:

1. Those that will use your firm no matter what.
2. Those that will NOT use your firm no matter what.
3. Those that do not know what firm to use. (Isard, 2014)

WHY SELECTED FUNERAL HOME	CONSIDERED ONLY ONE FUNERAL HOME	CONSIDERED TWO OR MORE FUNERAL HOMES
Family/friend used it before	**27%**	**11%**
Closest location	**17%**	**24%**
More familiar with it	14%	8%
Good reputation	**10%**	**17%**
Know the owner	10%	4%
Preferred by the deceased	9%	4%
Seemed most caring	3%	11%
Faith/religion	1%	2%
Cost/Price	**0%**	**10%**
Appearance	0%	4%
Other	14%	11%

Source: The Director (January 2015).

The Bad

Joe Joachim (2014) reports that the Funeral Service Foundation and Olson Zaltman Associates teamed up to study baby boomers and their feelings about traditional funeral service. Below are some of the negative views that were received:

> *"Traditional funerals are mindless. You just go through the motions. I think, 'Is this all this person was worth? **Didn't anybody think any more of that person** to want to really show what that person's life was about or why they loved that person or what they liked about that person?' It's kind of sad to think they didn't put any energy into their supposed 'celebration' of life ... we just have to bury the old broad and let's get on with our lives."*

> *"...when you go to a traditional funeral it's just about death and death is depressing and sad and it's just about broken relationships and there is just **nothing positive about it**."*

> *"When I go to a funeral, **I feel like I'm alone**. It's not a group. You're just there as an individual to say goodbye to this person ... you're not there to reminisce. You're just there to say goodbye. It's depressing and lonely."*

> *"They're cold. Kind of intimidating. It's pretty formal ... sometimes **not real inviting**. Like art museums or galleries."*

> *"Traditional services are almost a lecture of sorts. Some people who preside over death ceremonies don't allow for any release of sorrow. In fact, the ceremony itself makes participants more sorrowful. It's almost like we are **being forced to feel sorrowful** instead of being able to celebrate. I almost think of traditional funerals as puppetry with someone in control manipulating the people in attendance to act the way they feel is appropriate."*

> *"There is so much that has happened in a person's life that you don't really get to know and express during traditional [services]. There are so many things that in a traditional funeral get overlooked. **You don't get a chance to see the total person**."*

> *"The non-traditional [services] that I have experienced tend to get you balanced, taken away from that sad, pensive state. I don't know many traditional funerals that do that as well as the non-traditional [ones]. They quite often just **leave you sad at the end like you were in the middle**."*

Funeral Service from the Heart

De Leon (2012) believes that "**funeral service from the heart**, should be **the heart of funeral service**." As funeral directors, we have opportunities on a daily basis to deliver service from the heart. Service that is delivered with care, empathy, and yes, even with love. As funeral directors, we have seen some who have come and gone from our profession because they were never able to get their arms around how to provide this "service from the heart," this ability to empathize – to put themselves in the other's shoes and walk a mile.

Service from the heart is the ability to imagine what it might be like to experience what the family sitting across the table from you has experienced. When you express feelings of empathy for an angry or upset family, your empathy absorbs their emotions allowing them to think more logically. This makes it possible for your arrangement conference to go more smoothly. Ibid.

Service from the heart also takes strong commitment on your part, each time you see or speak with the families you serve or the people you work with. Let us remember, as funeral directors, that service from the heart will make a difference to families we serve as they journey through their loss. Ibid.

De Leon suggests the following goals as a reminder that may help you fulfill this commitment to service from the heart:

- **Focus** – I promise not only to hear but to listen.
- **Passion** – I promise to focus on meaningful ways in which I can enrich the lives of others.
- **Respect** – I promise to treat each family member as an individual who is deserving of my respect, attention, and highest level of professionalism.
- **Teamwork** – I promise to work as a team player for the maximum benefit of each family.
- **Sensitivity** – I promise to treat every problem as an important issue in a caring and timely manner.
- **Loyalty** – I promise to make earning the loyalty of each family my goal in every encounter.
- **Compassion** – I promise to communicate sincere concern and to express appreciation for the opportunity to help each family, share their burdens, and lighten their load.
- **Communication** – I promise to carefully explain the options of services we provide during each arrangement conference.
- **Value** – I promise to look for ways to give each family more than they ask for and to create value for them with every service we provide.

We must remember that we must provide the service from the heart within the context of making profit in order to stay in business.

Best Practices in Explaining Funeral Service

A number of years ago, I heard a quote I liked and have often used: "If you don't toot your own horn, someone will use it as a spittoon." More, shall I say, mature readers will know what a spittoon is, but the younger funeral directors might have to look it up. I did not take this quote to mean bragging or boasting. Rather, in regard to funeral service, I believe it could be interpreted to mean truthfully explaining or educating a person, group, community, or the public in general about:

1. The value of the funeral.

2. The many (and I emphasize "many") services a funeral home provides.

3. Differentiating yourself and your funeral home from your competitor (in other words, why a family should select your funeral home and not your competitor's firm).

When funeral directors are asked to explain what they do, thc general answer goes something like this: "We transfer the deceased from the place of death to the funeral home and prepare it according to the family's wishes. We meet with the family to arrange the funeral and then, according to the family's instructions, we provide visitation and funeral service. We also offer pre-need planning."

I will agree that this does describe what we do, in a nutshell. However, we need to break out of that shell and do a better job of educating people about the countless services funeral directors provide. We must give enough information for the public to realize that we do more than drive around in expensive cars and help them to understand the value they receive for the price they pay.

Funeral Directing

Klicker's 150 Services a Funeral Director Provides

1. Available 24 hours a day, 365 days a year.
2. No extra charges for holidays, weekends, or after normal business hours.
3. Provide and maintain facilities necessary for all services.
4. Provide for security for deceased.
5. Keep all information confidential.
6. Receive death calls.
7. Provide details of steps to be taken after death notification.
8. Obtain release of remains.
9. Transfer deceased from place of death to funeral home.
10. Take custody and inventory personal effects of deceased.
11. Embalm remains when requested.
12. Perform restorative art procedures when necessary.
13. Perform alternative preparation when no embalming.
14. Hold body without any preparation when required.
15. Coordinate with organ/tissue bank for donation.
16. Meet with physician or hospital to obtain signed death certificate.
17. File death certificate with proper government agency.
18. Obtain burial, cremation, or transit permit.
19. Provide family with transportation to funeral home to make arrangements.
20. Meet with family at home to make arrangements if requested.
21. Return deceased's personal effects to family.
22. Provide family with governmental forms required for arrangement conference.

23. Obtain vital statistics needed for legal documents.
24. Advise family on any legal decision that must be considered.
25. Maintain funeral records as required by law.
26. Explain and provide final disposition options.
27. Explain religious and cultural options and requirements.
28. Explain and provide service and funeral options.
29. Assist family in planning meaningful funeral.
30. Assist family in planning meaningful memorial service.
31. Assist family in planning alternative service.
32. Contact and coordinate with clergy.
33. Explain military options.
34. Contact and coordinate with military.
35. Explain service options for fraternal/special group.
36. Contact and coordinate with fraternal/special group.
37. Obtain information for death notice.
38. Write death notice and submit to newspaper.
39. Obtain information and photograph for obituary.
40. Write and submit obituary to newspaper.
41. Advance or guarantee cost of death notice/obituary.
42. Assist family with flower selection.
43. Order flowers for family, if requested.
44. Provide guidance for writing eulogy.
45. Provide photo board/easels.
46. Assist family in arranging photo board.
47. Offer video tribute option.
48. Receive photos and music requests for tribute video.
49. Produce tribute video/DVD with music.
50. Provide equipment to play tribute video.
51. Ensure video is played at proper time.
52. Provide casket display.
53. Assist family in casket selection.
54. Provide vault display.
55. Assist family in vault selection.
56. Provide and display urn selection.
57. Assist family in urn selection.
58. Provide register book and memorial card selection.
59. Assist family in selection of register books/memorial cards.
60. Print memorial card and register book information pages.
61. Restock memorial card and register book pages during service.
62. Provide memorial donation envelopes for charities.
63. Provide Mass cards.
64. Provide Mass card and donation envelopes.
65. Assist guests in filling out donation and Mass cards.
66. Print extra memorial cards, if necessary.
67. Provide religious symbols.
68. Explain cemetery options and rules.
69. Assist family with cemetery selection.
70. Contact and coordinate with cemetery.
71. Order last-minute items, such as a tent.
72. Explain crematory options and rules.
73. Contact and coordinate with crematory.
74. Explain Veterans benefits.
75. Complete Veterans forms for death benefits.

76. Obtain flag for Veterans.
77. Complete and send forms for Social Security benefits.
78. Complete insurance forms, when required.
79. Provide clothing for deceased.
80. Clean and press clothing provided by family.
81. Dress deceased.
82. Cosmetize deceased.
83. Provide dressing of hair for deceased.
84. Provide nail care for deceased.
85. Place deceased in casket and make presentable for visitation.
86. Place casket in visitation room in proper manner.
87. Arrange visitation room for wake, calling hours.
88. Meet with families for first visitation.
89. Make adjustments after first visitation.
90. Greet and direct guests to visitation room.
91. Assist guests with questions and special requests.
92. Provide guests with documentation of funeral attendance as needed for work time off.
93. Answer telephone inquiries about visitation and/or funeral.
94. Receive and arrange flowers.
95. Photograph flowers, if requested. Give family flower cards.
96. Provide music system.
97. Provide selection of music.
98. Play music selected by family during visitation and funeral.
99. Complete automobile list for funeral procession.
100. Provide assistance to special groups holding service.
101. Make arrangements for funeral brunch, if requested.
102. Prepare visitation room for funeral or move deceased to chapel.
103. Arrange for police or private funeral procession escort.
104. Implement funeral service according to family wishes.
105. Re-cosmetize deceased on day of funeral, if necessary.
106. Meet with family before funeral to finalize details.
107. Arrange cars for funeral procession.
108. Coordinate with and assist clergy before funeral.
109. Coordinate with and assist special groups before funeral.
110. Coordinate with escort on day of funeral.
111. Supervise pallbearers.
112. Coordinate music for funeral service.
113. Provide transportation for pallbearers, if necessary.
114. Provide transportation for clergy, if necessary.
115. Close casket, ensuring family's requests for items left in or removed from casket.
116. Provide transportation for family to church and cemetery.
117. Provide transportation for deceased.
118. Lead procession to church.
119. Ensure proper parking at church.
120. Coordinate church service.
121. Ensure correct grave or crypt is opened.
122. Ensure vault is delivered and installed at cemetery.
123. Transport and arrange flowers at cemetery/crematory.
124. Lead procession to cemetery/crematory.
125. Fulfill special family requests for procession, such as passing by home or workplace.
126. Supervise cemetery/crematory service.
127. Present flag if military detail is not present.
128. Act in place of clergy, if necessary.

129. Ensure that vault cover is sealed correctly.
130. Provide cemetery with burial/cremation permit.
131. Deliver cash advances to church/cemetery.
132. Provide transportation to funeral breakfast, if necessary.
133. Deliver flowers not used in service to location designated by family.
134. Provide thank-you cards to family.
135. Assist family with monument purchase or inscription.
136. Secure initial certified copies of death certificate, as requested.
137. Secure additional certified copies of death certificate, as requested.
138. Retrieve cremated remains from crematory.
139. Retain cremated remains until family picks up.
140. Deliver cremated remains to family when requested.
141. Assist family with final disposition of cremated remains.
142. Provide pre-need planning.
143. Provide options for pre-need funding.
144. Ensure security of pre-need funds.
145. Provide long-term security for pre-need records.
146. Assist with Medical spend-down details.
147. Facilitate returns of deceased from out of town.
148. Facilitate transportation of deceased to out-of-town location.
149. Provide aftercare support.
150. Provide payment options.

What It Takes to Be a Funeral Director in the 21st Century

It is often said that working in the funeral industry is a vocation rather than a job. The staff employed need to have a variety of skills and a genuine desire to offer as much help, guidance, and assistance as is required by those they are called upon to serve. The funeral industry is by no means an easy career option; however, it can be one of the most fulfilling and rewarding of the service careers.

The work environment for a funeral director can be both physically and emotionally challenging and sometimes stressful. Funeral directors work irregular hours, including evenings, weekends, and holidays. They are often "on call" and need to be available when their clients need them. In many businesses, particularly small businesses, a variety of tasks may be performed by one person and the skills needed for these various tasks may need to be acquired.

What qualities will I need to work in the funeral industry?

The death of a loved one is often a difficult and traumatic time for the family and friends of the deceased. An important role of the funeral director is to provide emotional support. There are also many cultural differences in how people deal with death which need to be treated with sensitivity.

Funeral directors have to be able to put their own emotions aside in order to fully support the relatives and friends of the deceased person. Everybody grieves in different ways, and funeral directors need to be flexible and open in how they offer emotional support. It is important that they develop ways of dealing with emotional demands of the job to be able to continue to perform their role effectively.

Employees in the funeral industry need a mature and responsible attitude, given the sensitive situations they deal with. They are generally working with clients who are emotionally vulnerable, hence a need for excellent communication skills and an understanding of how people deal with grief.

What skills do I need to be a funeral director?

According to the Australian Funeral Directors Association (2018), the following ***skills*** are necessary to be a funeral director:

- An interest in helping people.
- Maturity and self-confidence.
- Empathy, sensitivity, and tact.
- Ability to work with grieving and distressed clients.
- A driver's license with good driving record.
- Physical strength for manual handling. You may be required to pass a physical examination.
- A well-groomed appearance.
- Ability to work according to fixed procedures and legal requirements.
- Flexibility to work evenings, weekends, and extended hours.
- Willingness to take responsibility and have confidence in own decisions.
- Excellent written and oral communication skills.
- Good practical and organizational skills.
- An ability to put people at ease.
- An ability to remain calm and maintain composure under stressful circumstances.

Work Styles and Skills

According to MyMajors (2019), the ***work styles*** of Morticians, Undertakers, and Funeral Directors are:

- **Dependability** – Being reliable, responsible, and dependable, and fulfilling obligations.
- **Integrity** – Being honest and ethical.
- **Attention to Detail** – Being careful about detail and thorough in completing work tasks.
- **Concern for Others** – Being sensitive to others' needs and feelings and being understanding and helpful on the job.
- **Stress Tolerance** – Accepting criticism and dealing calmly and effectively with high-stress situations.
- **Cooperation** – Being pleasant with others on the job; displaying a good-natured, cooperative attitude.
- **Leadership** – Having a willingness to lead, take charge, and offer opinions and direction.
- **Self-Control** – Maintaining composure, keeping emotions in check, controlling anger, and avoiding aggressive behavior, even in difficult situations.
- **Adaptability/Flexibility** – Being open to change (positive or negative) and to variety in the workplace.
- **Social Orientation** – Preferring to work with others rather; being connected with others on the job.
- **Initiative** – A willingness to take on responsibilities and challenges.
- **Innovation** – Having the ability to think creatively and have alternative thinking to develop new ideas for and answers to work-related problems.

Some of the ***skills and knowledge*** required for Morticians, Undertakers, and Funeral Directors as listed by the O*NET (2019) are:

- **Active Listening** – Giving full attention to what other people are saying, taking time to understand the points being made, asking questions as appropriate, and not interrupting at inappropriate times.
- **Writing** – Communicating effectively in writing as appropriate for the needs of the audience.
- **Reading Comprehension** – Understanding written sentences/paragraphs in work-related documents.
- **English Language** – Knowledge of the structure and content of the English language, including the meaning and spelling of words, rules of composition, and grammar.
- **Chemistry** – Knowledge of the chemical composition, structure, and properties of substances and of the chemical process and transformation that they undergo. This includes uses of chemicals and their interactions, danger signs, production techniques, and disposal methods.
- **Psychology** – Knowledge of human behaviors and performance, individual differences in ability, personality, and interests; learning and motivation; psychological research methods; and the assessment and treatment of behavior and affective disorders.

O*Net (2019) also lists the following as some of the ***abilities*** needed to be a Mortician, Undertaker, or Funeral Director:

- **Deductive Reasoning** – The ability to apply general rules to specific problems to produce answers that make sense.
- **Inductive Reasoning** – The ability to combine pieces of information to form general rules or conclusions (includes finding a relationship among seemingly unrelated events).
- **Oral Comprehension** – The ability to listen to and understand information and ideas presented through spoken words and sentences.
- **Oral Expression** – The ability to communicate information and ideas in speaking so others will understand.
- **Written Comprehension** – The ability to read and understand information/ideas presented in writing.
- **Written Expression** – The ability to communicate information/ideas in writing so others understand.
- **Speech Clarity** – The ability to speak clearly so others can understand you.
- **Speech Recognition** – The ability to identify and understand the speech of another person.
- **Information Ordering** – The ability to arrange things or actions in a certain order or pattern according to a specific rule or set of rules (e.g. patterns of numbers, letters, words, pictures, mathematical operations).

Example of Hours Spent on a Funeral Call

Excerpt Example From: Dawson (2015)

Although the example below is a fictitious example of a case, it's a perfect illustration of how many hours can be devoted by a funeral director and staff, despite never handling the actual remains.

Time	Staff	06/12/20_ _	Hours/Min.
10:00 a.m.	Bev	Received call from Mary Jones, who reported that her father, John Jones, had died while on vacation in Fairbanks, AK.	7 min
10:07 a.m.	Bev	Called Coroner's office in Fairbanks to determine situation (not certain).	5 min
2:00 p.m.	Bev	Coroner's Office returned call; Mr. Jones was found in his hotel room; an autopsy will be conducted on 6/13.	6 min
2:06 p.m.	FDD	Called Mary to inform her of autopsy & to begin some preliminary arrangements. Mary wanted options.	30 min
3:07 p.m.	FCD	Called recommended firm in Alaska for fee and distance from Fairbanks, also fee for immediate cremation.	5 min
3:15 p.m.	FCD	Called second firm in Alaska, closer and more reasonable. Requested removal and wait for instructions.	5 min
		Total Time for 6/12/20_ _	**58 min**
Time	**Staff**	**06/13/20_ _**	**Hours/Min.**
3:00 a.m.	BDD	Received call from Coroner's Office that remains were released.	4 min
3:05 a.m.	BDD	Notified shipping funeral home to make removal, but delay embalming — possible cremation.	7 min
10:00 a.m.	DTI	Face-to-face meeting with local family who expressed wish for direct cremation & urn placement at Arlington	60 min
11:00 a.m.	DTI	Faxed vital stats to shipping firm and notified them of cremation decision and Arlington National Cemetery.	15 min
11:15 a.m.	DTI	Made call to Arlington National Cemetery to obtain basic information and requirements for placement.	10 min
11:25 a.m.	DTI	Recorded as much information as possible, including details from Alaska service providers & coroner.	15 min
1:30 p.m.	FDD	Spoke with widow in Alaska and discussed the need for her to meet with the funeral home there.	30 min
		Total time 6/13/20_ _	**141 min**

Time	Staff	06/14/20_ _	Hours/Min.
9:00 a.m.	TWM	Funeral home in Alaska met with Mrs. Jones. ID made; cremation authorization signed. Awaiting instruction.	20 min
2:00 p.m.	FDD	Meeting with family, takes obit info notes, and military information. Explained options.	120 min
2:15 p.m.	BDD	Received obit notes from FDD and composed obituary for final proof by family (corrections made).	30 min
3:30 p.m.	BDW	Scanned photographs of deceased, sent obituary to media, and began entering information into computer system.	45 min
4:00 p.m.	FDD	Completed meeting with local family and began working on logistics with Arlington for day and time of service.	60 min
5:00 p.m.	FDD	Discussed service time and all details by phone with local family and Mrs. Jones in Alaska. Faxed VA forms.	120 min
		Total Time for 6/14/20_ _	**395 min**

Time	Staff	06/15/20_ _	Hours/Min.
8:30 a.m.	TWM	Discussed forwarding of cremains from Alaska to Arlington and travel plans of family.	90 min
10:00 a.m.	TWM	Informed shipping funeral home of plan to have cremains sent directly to Arlington.	60 min
10:15 a.m.	ERA	Ordered death certificates from shipping firm and began completing insurance forms.	50 min
11:00 a.m.	BDW	Completed all personal and financial information in computer. Received photo for newspaper release.	45 min
11:00 a.m.	FDD	Reviewed cemetery arrangements with Mrs. Jones and details of service at Arlington.	30 min
11:30 a.m.	FDD	Called local family to assure them that cremains had been received by Arlington. Set day and time of service.	30 min
7:00 p.m.	FDD	Sorted photographs and began production of video tribute.	90 min
		Total Time 6/15/20 _ _	**395 min**
		Total Time to Date: 989 minutes = 16 hours 29 minutes	

Life is for Sharing, Beginning-to-End
Excerpt From: Adele Haas (2018)

Until Dad passed away, I had dreaded going to wakes. What could words to do help? But I found out first-hand that there is a reason for ritual, which can bring healing and comfort to loved ones. And when you don't know what to do, there is a precedent to follow.

At Dad's wake, it was so helpful to learn about his early years. During the Depression, times were hard for many, jobs were scarce, and money was even more so. I heard from neighbors who described a young man starting out in his own business. Dad would put food purchases "on the books" when these people had no cash and slip something extra in the bag (at no charge) knowing that there were hungry youngsters at home. He was a generous man of compassion. But he was someone I had taken for granted because he was just Dad.

Those who came to the wake came to honor a man who helped so many. I only knew him as a father. He was 37 when I was born; he had experience and a life before. Visitors spoke of a young, eager, hardworking, good neighbor, a jokester, a talented tenor in the choral group, an eager student, a whiz with numbers, a conscientious business man, a loyal son, brother, cousin, best man at a wedding, and a good friend with a teasing sense of humor who just loved to laugh. Wow, my dad.

I was so pleased to know these sides of him. I was proud and grateful. When I think of him, those stories warm my heart. I finally knew then how comforting a wake could be. It can be a time of discovery and sharing, not just gloom and sadness.

NOTES

Section I

Funeral Directing

- First Call & Price Shopping
- Transfer/Removal of Remains
- Arrangement Conference
- Visitation
- The Funeral
- Procession
- Aftercare
- Memorialization
- Personalization
- Memorial Service, Life Celebration & Gatherings
- Pre-Need
- Caskets & Vaults
- Merchandising
- Shipping Human Remains
- Disasters
- Cemetery/Mausoleum
- Clergy/Celebrant-Funeral Director Relations

Chapter 1

FIRST CALL & PRICE SHOPPING

> ***First Call*** – *The request, usually made by a surviving family member, for a funeral home to transfer a deceased from the place of death to the funeral home; and then for the funeral home to carry out the wishes of the next of kin regarding funeral services and disposition.*

The importance of the notification of a death cannot be understated. This call is a bereaved family's cry for help to a funeral home. It is more than a grieving family's request that the deceased be transferred from the place of death to the care and custody of the funeral home. It is a statement of trust and confidence in a funeral home's ability to meet their needs in a professional and sensitive manner. **98% of initial contacts are made by telephone**, the remainder are made in person or online.

No two notifications are ever the same. Some callers will be efficient, quick, and businesslike; while others may be crying, upset, in a state of shock, or even unable to speak clearly. Be prepared to respond to any type of caller. A bereaved caller is looking for someone who understands his situation, knows what must be done, can immediately take charge, and perform all the necessary activities to meet the family's needs in a caring and efficient manner. The ability to do this must be conveyed during this first call.

Good funeral service starts with this first call no matter who the caller is speaking to, whether it is an answering service, secretary, non-licensed attendant, or the funeral director. The caller will decide in the first couple of minutes how compassionate and professional the staff is, and if this is the type of firm with which he or she wants to do business.

You only have one opportunity to make a good first impression. In the funeral profession, this opportunity often comes through a phone call. This call can be a request for information about a service, directions to the funeral home, price shopping, or to request services to handle funeral arrangement for a person who has died. First impressions are everything! When a family member calls a funeral home, they are at their most vulnerable (Martin Bartsche, 2016).

The following factors contribute to the caller's evaluation of the image of the funeral home.

- **Salutation** – The person answering the phone should:
  - Give the name of the funeral home.
  - Give His/her name (how he/she would like to be addressed, e.g. Mr. Smith, David Smith).
  - Ask "May I help you?" This is optional but leaves a good first impression.
  - Avoid using "good morning" and "good evening." Some people may feel that this is out of place if a loved one has just died.
- **Tone of Voice** – The funeral director's tone of voice should be sympathetic yet professional, not overly sad, forlorn, or cheerful. It should have some inflection to avoid sounding monotonous or bored.
- **Speed of Questions and Pronunciation** – The speed of the funeral director's conversation should be slightly slower than that of a normal telephone conversation.
- **Diction** – The voice should be clear and crisp. The telephone should not be answered if the person answering is eating, drinking, or chewing gum.
- **Volume** – The voice should not be so loud that it is offensive or disturbing to the caller, yet it should not be so quiet or soft that the caller has to strain to hear or frequently ask the funeral director to repeat herself.
- **Phone Image** – It is just as important to project a professional, sensitive, and empathetic image over the phone as it is in person. You want the caller to feel secure and comforted. The beginning of a relationship of trust starts with the image you project during the telephone call.
- It is important to get the name of the caller and phone number first. If you get cut off, you will have the number and be able to reconnect with the person.

Information Needed from Caller (1st Call Form)

The First Call or Notification Form will assist you in asking the necessary questions and allows you to have a written record of the call. These forms should be located near every phone. The following information is necessary to proceed with the transfer of the deceased from a home:

Notification Form

1. Name of deceased ______________________________
2. Location of the deceased ______________________________
3. Name & Relationship of caller ______________________________
4. Phone number of caller ______________________________
5. Name of next of kin, if not caller ______________________________
6. Phone number of next of kin ______________________________
7. Name of attending physician ______________________________

   7A. Has the Physician or Medical Examiner been notified? _____ YES _____ NO
8. Age of the deceased ______________________________
9. Permission to embalm obtained? _____YES _____ NO

If the deceased is at a hospital, nursing home, or hospice, the following questions should also be asked:

10. Has a release form been signed? ___YES ___ NO

    10A. By Whom? ______________________________
11. Is there going to be an autopsy performed? ___YES ___NO
12. Organ or Tissue Donation? ___YES ___NO

    12A. Have you been in contact with the donation agency? ___YES ___NO

Comments:

One copy of the notification form should be taken by the person making the removal, and at least one copy should remain at the funeral home.

Why the Following Questions Are Asked?

- **Age of Deceased:** The age should be asked to avoid any misunderstanding. The author was told of an instance when a funeral director received a first call. The woman calling said, "My baby died." The director never asked the age. He went to the removal expecting to transfer an infant. The deceased, however, was an adult whose mother just referred to her adult child as her "baby."

- **Release**: Most hospitals will not allow the funeral home to transfer the deceased without a signed "release of deceased" form. If the family did not sign one at the health care facility, the funeral director may have to take one to the family to sign before the removal is made. In some areas this may be achieved by email.

- **Permission to Embalm**: The law requires that permission to embalm must be received before embalming can begin. This is often done during the first call. Each person has his or her own unique way of asking for permission. Most directors just state, "Do we have your permission to embalm?" You should be prepared with an explanation of what embalming is, why you want to do it, and to answer any questions the family may have.

- **Organ and Tissue Donation**: The Routine Referral Act requires that hospitals contact the local organ procurement organization (OPO) and tissue and eye banks about each death, or pending death, that occurs in the hospital. The OPO must offer the family the opportunity to donate, if the person is eligible for donation. In some areas the OPO has the authority to place a hold on the release of the deceased until the family has been contacted. In these instances, the funeral home will have to contact the organ or tissue agency to check on when the deceased body will be released. **For more information on this subject, see Supportive Readings page 465.**

If the caller is someone other than the family member:

Occasionally , the family will ask someone else to call the funeral home with the information about the death. Oftentimes this will be a nurse in the hospital, nursing home, or hospice. Points to consider are:

- Treat the caller as if she was the NOK (next of kin). The respect, empathy, and professionalism you show the person may get back to the family and give them a feeling of comfort and security.

- If the caller is not the NOK, it is important to clarify that the next of kin gave the caller permission to contact the funeral home. The name and phone number of the NOK should be obtained.

- A 2015 landmark Supreme Court ruling legalized same-sex marriage in all 50 states in the U.S. (Neptune Society, 2015). This ruling guarantees same-sex couples the same rights as married heterosexual couples. The surviving spouse, whether same-sex or heterosexual, is considered the next of kin for disposition of remains.

- Get the name, phone number, and relationship of the person in charge of the arrangement and tell the caller you will be calling that person unless the family has said not to call them back.

When the Informant is not Next of Kin:

If the informant caller tells the director the family does not want to be called back, do not call them back. If the family has not stated this, it is a good idea to contact them for the following reasons:

- Some people take comfort in talking with the funeral director to be reassured that their loved one will be taken care of with respect and dignity.
- Arranging the time for the family to come to the funeral home may require some planning because of previous appointments the funeral home or family may have.
- It is difficult to give messages to the caller who is not next of kin, a nurse for example, about what the family should bring with them to the funeral home.
- It can be comforting to a family to know that they have someone specific at the funeral home to contact with any questions or concerns that might arise before the arranged meeting.

Every effort should be made to speak directly to the person with the definitive legal right to control in the 1st call. If the initial person you are speaking with does not have that right (which you have figured out by having an artful conversation with the caller after expressing your condolences), then you need to try and speak to the person that does. The necessity for this is easily explained. Circumstances do not always make it possible to speak right then and there to a spouse (for instance). So, if you are not talking to the person with the actual right to control, you must connect with at least one immediate family member who can reasonably represent that they speak for the wishes of the person with the right to control.

Are you afraid that asking these questions will cause you to lose the call? It is better to find a family dispute now, rather than later. Under no circumstances should you accept a third party's representation concerning the authorization to remove or as to who has the right to control. Not a nursing home administrator. Not the admitting desk at the hospital. Not a "friend." Most State Board rules have a statement such as:

> *"No person shall remove human remains from any residence or institution without first securing authorization consenting to the removal from the next of kin or a person legally entitled to grant said authorization"* (Beebe, 2016).

For more information on legal control, see Supportive Readings, page 444.

When the first call is from another funeral director

The call for service from another funeral director is usually for one of three reasons:

1. The out-of-town director will need you to send the deceased to her funeral home. This request will usually involve:

    - Removal of deceased.
    - Preparation of the body.
    - Filing all necessary paperwork for death notice and transfer permit.
    - Transfer the deceased to the requesting funeral home by funeral home vehicle, plane, or train.

2. The out-of-town funeral director is informing you that a family has requested that he ship a deceased to your funeral home. All the duties above are incumbent on the calling funeral home.

3. The out-of-town funeral director requests that you make the transfer from the place of death to your funeral home. He plans on driving to your location to pick up the deceased. You may or may not be asked to embalm the remains and secure any necessary paperwork.

You are ethically obligated to provide honest, professional services. You must not unduly pressure the family into purchasing any merchandise, such as a casket, unless the family requests it.

Concluding the Call

Consideration must be given for closing the conversation. At the conclusion of the initial contact, carefully summarize the call, repeat all the information from the First Call form, give an attitude of confidence, and convey assurance as to the implementation of the arrangements. Be aware that often the caller will pass on reactions to others involved.

As the call concludes:

1. Review all information received for accuracy and completeness.

2. Inform the caller of the items he should bring to the arrangement conference, if he will not be talking with you again before that time. These items may include:

   - Clothing
   - Photo(s)
   - Military discharge papers
   - Social security number
   - Cemetery deed
   - Life insurance policy (if it is being used to pay for the funeral)

   If you will be seeing the family at the removal, this information can be given to them at that time.

3. Assure the caller that they can be confident that they will be served adequately and well.

4. Assure the caller that their request for service will be implemented at once. Give the caller the approximate time of arrival at the place of transfer. Do not say, "We will be right there."

5. Leave the caller with the feeling that for the next few days she will be assisted competently and given the support and counsel that is necessary. Use a question and statement such as:

   "Mrs. Smith, I have all the information I need for now. Do you have any additional questions or requests from me? We should be at your home within an hour. If you need to contact me, you can call me at ____."

6. Avoid saying "Thank you," since this may seem out of place to some. Some funeral directors have developed ways to say thank you that have been successful for them. The following is an example:

   "Mrs. Smith, I would like to thank you for the confidence you have placed in our funeral home. We will do everything necessary to live up to it."

Phone inquiries/Price Shoppers

Information on the topic of phone inquiry and price shopping was not provided in the earlier edition of this book. Newest reports from the profession, however, indicate that phone requests for price information have become an everyday event. I vacillated between placing this material in general phone etiquette or in the section on cremation. Most inquiry calls have to do with requests for the least expensive price for cremation, hence the term price shoppers. I chose to place this information in the beginning of the book because the phone inquiry call could be a request for any type of services and could turn into a first call request to handle a funeral. This information may help funeral directors turn this phone conversation into a call to service.

Some information calls are not a request for the funeral home to serve a family. A caller may have questions regarding costs before they decide. This is becoming more common as people are being encouraged by consumer groups to "shop around" before making a final decision on which funeral home to use. A funeral director's openness and honesty in responding to financial questions and concerns may be the deciding factor as to whether a family will choose a funeral home.

Most businesses view receiving price inquiries positively because it means that the caller is considering using their business. Many funeral directors feel the opposite; they view these calls as a nuisance. I would hope that all funeral directors learn to look at these calls as an opportunity, not an inconvenience. They provide an opportunity to develop a relationship with the caller by educating them and clarifying any misconceptions they may have. Christopher Kuhnen (2016) explains that the caller may start the conversation with questions about prices, because they do not know what else to ask to begin the conversation.

Johnson Consulting Group conducted the first-ever survey on this topic and found the following data on what price shoppers are typically asking for:

Direct cremation pricing	91%	
Traditional burial pricing	13%	
Price for least expensive funeral	54%	
Price of caskets	9%	
What does a funeral cost?	48%	
Do you have packages?	22%	(Funeral Service Insider, 2014)

The purpose of the price-related conversation is important to keep in mind. Is the caller:

Price-shopping only – They will use the funeral home with the cheapest price regardless of any other factor.

People-shopping – These callers will select the funeral director with whom they were able to bond with and they feel will treat them right.

Solution-shopping – This caller is looking for a funeral home that will provide the best solution to their pressing need.

The best outcome for the caller is that they will find a funeral home they feel comfortable working with, that can be the solution to their need, at a price they feel is a value for what they will receive. About 10% of the price shoppers you speak with will decide on the funeral home with the lowest price. The other 90% choose a funeral home based on emotion and value (Adams, 2012).

The following suggestions will help you conduct a meaningful conversation:

- The funeral home that keeps the caller on the line the longest usually gets the funeral.
- Start the convesation with a supportive statement such as:

  "I will be happy to answer all of your questions. My name is Ralph, may I ask your first name?"

- **Ask a probing question such as:**

  "Have you had experience with funeral or cremation before or is this your first time?"

- **Next ask a permission question to build rapport.**

  "May I explain to you the options that are available with cremation or burial?"

- **Explain the options.**

  Some callers are more comfortable hearing a range of prices such as:

  "Our caskets range in price from ____ to ____."

  When offering a price range on any services or merchandise, your low end should be your lowest price. You must be willing to sell it for that price (Kuhnen, 2016)

- **After explaining the options, ask a closing question.**

  "Do you have any other questions I can assist you with?"

- **Then make a closing statement.**

  "We are proud to be known as the funeral home that has the most reasonable prices along with exceptional service. We would be proud to be the funeral home you select. We treat every deceased person with the same respect and dignity as someone purchasing our most expensive funeral."

You will not turn every price shopper into a customer. Some will choose another funeral home for a number of reasons, including:

- Your price was higher than another funeral home they contacted. You must have the "commercial courage" to walk away.
- Your telephone manner was not inviting or informative.
- You were not able to make a personal connection with the caller.

Nine Tips for Connecting with Funeral Shoppers

By: Mark Allen (2017)

Phone shoppers get a bad rap. But let's face it – they're simply trying to educate themselves about something they most likely know little about. Pricing is something everyone is familiar with, so it makes sense that most people will start in that area. Your job as a funeral professional is to get them curious about how different funerals can be from what they've experienced in the past. Granted, some phone shoppers will shut you down. That's okay. Let them go. The worst they can say about your funeral home is that you tried to offer suggestions for an amazing and meaningful memorial experience.

1. Set expectations among all staff

Anyone who represents your funeral home should know what the expectations are for communicating with members of the public in person or otherwise. If it's possible that a staff member will answer the phone, train them to answer the phone in a way that puts your funeral home's best foot forward.

2. End your greeting with your name

Not so many years ago, funeral directors thought that answering the phone with "Hello, this is XYZ Funeral Home" was insensitive because it indicated that a funeral home was a business. People are well aware that funeral homes are businesses. Include the funeral home's name, but begin establishing a personal connection from the start. *The Telephone Doctor,* a business communication expert, recommends the following greeting:

"Hello, XYZ Funeral Home. This is Mary."

People are more likely to remember your name if it's the last word in your greeting. If the caller fails to mention his or her name, ask,

"And I'm speaking with...?" or "May I ask your first name?"

3. Be an expert

People want assurance that the person they speak with has the expertise they need. Taking control of the conversation will let them know you have what it takes to guide them through an unfamiliar experience. Communicate that helping families arrange meaningful and appropriate tributes to people they love is what you do every day. Include your title if it reflects the information the price shopper needs.

4. If you have to transfer a call, do it warmly

Everyone hates repeating the reason they are calling each time they are transferred. If it's necessary to transfer a call, first ask the caller for permission to transfer them and provide an explanation.

"Mr. Johnson is the funeral director who will be able to answer your questions. May I put you on hold while I see if he is available?"

If you transfer a call, make sure you pass along any information the caller told you. If a call is transferred to you, begin with something like:

> ***"Hello, this is Barney. I'm sorry to hear the sad news about your grandfather. I'll be glad to tell you how I can help your family plan a wonderful tribute to him."***

5. Respond! Respond! Respond!

With the dawning of the Internet, people are accustomed to getting answers to their questions almost instantaneously. If you're the person a caller needs to talk to and were unavailable when he or she called, call them back as soon as possible, but never longer than two hours. Respond as soon as possible to general questions sent by email, but never longer than 12 hours.

6. Never say "I don't know"

People may perceive "I don't know" as a sign of indifference, or worse, as incompetence. If you don't know the answer to a question, say "I'll check on that for you." It assures callers that they will receive the information they need because you accepted the responsibility of providing it to them. It works the same with email communications.

7. Choose your words wisely

The #1 rule of word selection is to avoid professional jargon such as "GPL," "cremains," and "basic service fee." Instead, use descriptive words such as "list of our prices," "your mother" and "our fee for handling the details of funeral arrangements." Use inclusive words like "our" and "we" that imply the caller is already connected to the funeral home's team. When talking to or emailing someone who has lost a loved one or who recently received bad news, never end the conversation with "have a nice day."

8. Answer the question with a question – But *answer* it!

Price shoppers are notorious for demanding to know "the price" of "a funeral." Avoid responding with, "I can't answer that question without more information." Instead, counter with something like, "I'll be happy to give you that information. ***To help me provide the most accurate information, can you first tell me…"*** Never divert the caller to another topic or pretend he or she didn't ask a question you don't want to answer.

9. Ask for more information

You would be surprised at how many funeral professionals end a conversation with a prospective client without offering to send him or her more information or asking for their contact information. This is your permission to follow up. So, do it!

NOTES

OSHA: Occupational safety and health administration

NOTES

FTC: Funeral Rule

↳ gives consumers the right to a price list

Chapter 2 TRANSFER/REMOVAL OF REMAINS

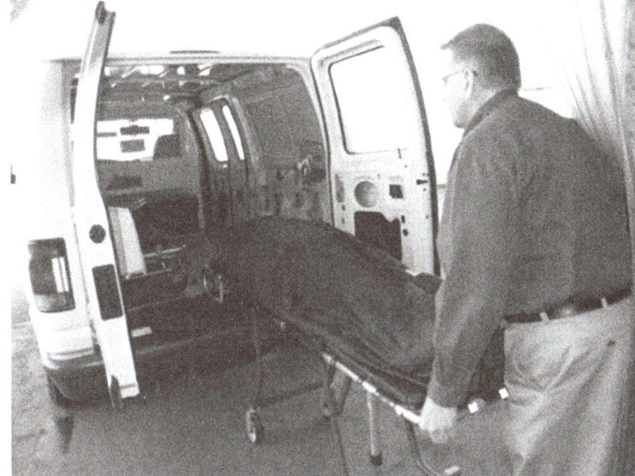

Source: http://blog.sevenponds.com

***Transfer/Removal**: The moving of the deceased from the place of death to the funeral home.*

Author's Note: I will be using both "transfer" and "removal." Transfer seems to be the more accepted term in the 21st century, but removal is still commonly used.

There is not much written in our professional literature about **the transfer of the deceased from the place of death to the funeral home**. Yet, this transfer can be the only opportunity a funeral director has to make a good first face-to-face impression on a family at a home, healthcare workers at a hospital or facility, or on first responders at an accident scene.

A transfer can be a private event from a secluded location in a hospital or nursing home late at night or out the front door of a family home with a dozen neighbors gathered outside watching. It may be seen by thousands of people watching it as a homicide or crime scene filmed by a news crew on the 11 o'clock news. No matter the location, or the time of day, the funeral director must proceed in a dignified and professional manner. Remember almost everyone has a cell phone that can take pictures and video. Photo or video of your transfer can be on social media, such as Facebook, in a matter of minutes. (Stark, 2017).

Ensuring each transfer is completed professionally includes making sure each employee knows what they're doing and how to operate all equipment. For example, everyone must know how to operate the stretcher, including using features such as lowering to different levels or dropping one end to make it shorter to make turns in a room. Making these maneuvers with practiced ease shows professionalism. It is important for firms to have the proper equipment for every transfer. Americans are not getting any smaller. While oversize stretchers are expensive, they are a necessary business expense to ensure the safety of your staff and proper care of the deceased. Ibid.

Even the government gets involved with the transfer of a deceased. Firms may be fined if OSHA and FTC requirements are not met. For example, the FTC Funeral Rule is triggered if the family asks about funeral costs and you do not have copies of a price list with your transfer equipment. Your staff must know what triggers the FTC Funeral Rule on a transfer. Ibid.

Transfer Vehicles

There are several factors to consider before leaving the funeral home to make a transfer. The first of these is choosing which vehicle to use. Throughout the country there are a variety of different vehicles used but the most common are:

- **Hearse (also known as a funeral coach)**
- **Mini van**
- **Utility Van**
- **SUV**

There has been some discussion in funeral service about the professionalism of making a removal in a vehicle other than a hearse, such as a converted minivan that looks like a small hearse. The author believes that the use of such conversion vans is an acceptable alternative to a traditional hearse. However, the author does not endorse using a plain utility type van such as those used by commercial companies, home repair, or delivery services. Ask yourself, would you want a loved one transferred in a utility truck?

The decision on which vehicle to use is determined by such factors as:

In some areas, it is becoming more common for funeral homes to use a minivan or utility vehicle to make transfers from institutions, but to use a funeral coach for a transfer from a home. In other areas, the same vehicle is used for all transfers. There are times when a funeral director may make a transfer at the scene of an accident, such as on the highway or desolate wooded area, which requires a four-wheel drive vehicle or even a snowmobile to move the decedent from the place of death to the transfer vehicle.

Factors to Consider

- **Age of deceased** – Some funeral directors prefer not to use a hearse for an infant transfer.

- **Location of the deceased** – Some institutions, such as hospitals or nursing homes, prefer that transfers be made using a vehicle other than a hearse. Their job is to help keep people alive, and a hearse is an obvious sign that they did not do what they were supposed to have done. The presence of a hearse can also make some patients or residents feel uncomfortable.

- **Local Custom** – In many areas of the country funeral directors follow similar procedures for the various aspects of the funeral. This is relevant in the type of transfer vehicle to be used. Local customs can change with the times. Years ago, hearses were used for all transfers because people expected to see a hearse. The change from using a hearse to some other type of vehicle developed slowly over time. The reasons behind this change can be attributed to:

    - **Economics** – The cost of a hearse is so high that funeral directors wanted to use it as little as possible, so it lasts longer. The first alternative is the station wagon, then the utility van, followed by the minivan or suburban.

    - **Societal Change** – As the country became more death-denying, a hearse no longer was considered a status symbol. Instead, the hearse was considered morbid. As a result, people became more accepting of the mini and conversion vans.

No matter which type of vehicle a funeral director decides to use for a transfer, it must be **clean**, in **good repair**, **professional looking**, and be **driven safely** and **professionally**.

Equipment

The transfer vehicle should be equipped with the following equipment to meet any situation the funeral director might encounter.

Adult Transfer:

Cot – Most funeral homes use what is called a one-man cot. This cot can usually be taken from, or placed in, a transfer vehicle by just one person. A head rest or pillow and clean sheets should be included.

Flexible Stretcher – Often a funeral director will place a small collapsible stretcher on top of the one-man cot. If the transfer is from an inaccessible area with narrow doors and stairs, it is easier to place the deceased on the stretcher, secure them with straps, and carry them to the cot.

It is common to cover the deceased with a sheet, blanket, or cot cover, with the head placed on a pillow or headrest. Some directors prefer to use a transfer pouch, which is vinyl or rubber on the inside and fabric on the outside. The pouch is opened and closed by a zipper. If such a pouch isn't used, it is recommended that a rubber or plastic sheet be placed under the deceased for ease in cleaning in case any fluid leaks from the deceased during the transfer.

The late Ron Hast, publisher of *Mortuary Management*, once commented,

> "I have noticed a decline in the condition, maintenance, and appearance of the transfer cot. This is the one visible item other than the personnel to come into the house or healthcare facility. I'll bet no metal polish has ever touched the majority of this important and visible equipment. Center zipper pouches have become commonplace. As we leave the home or facility all that has been observed, heard, and taken place has quite likely become the impression of the funeral itself."

The transfer vehicle should also contain:

- **Rubber gloves**
- **Towels**
- **Cotton**
- **Spray deodorant and disinfectant**
- **Some form of disposable apron or surgical type gowns in case there is the danger of the director's clothing being soiled**
- **The funeral home's General Price List and information sheets**

Infant Transfer

During an infant transfer, the director may prefer to use a bassinet to carry the infant. There should also be a small rubber or plastic sheet placed under the infant, and the infant should be covered with a baby blanket. No matter what vehicle you use for the infant transfer, it is recommended that the infant not be placed on the front seat. If placed in the rear seat, a seat belt should be used to secure the infant.

Infant Removal at a Hospital

In the case of an infant removal, some firms still use the older black suitcase carrier. Throw that thing out and use a bassinet or even a car seat device. Regardless, in order not to upset other families in the obstetrics waiting room, some have the switchboard operator at the main office contact the OB Floor.

Arrange to meet a nurse or assistant from the floor with the infant in the downstairs morgue area or other secluded place, thus avoiding entrance to the maternity area with the removal equipment.

If the family is present, bypass the previous instructions. Instead, move to the maternity area and talk with the family. Inform them of the options for the transfer and ask if they would prefer to carry the infant to your vehicle. Allow them to assist with any or all of the above procedures.

The black box was traditionally used for infant removal.

Source: Dennis Gospodarski

The bassinet is modern and preferred for infant removal.

Director's Attire during Transfer

There is no one type of attire that is used by all funeral directors during a transfer. Most directors will wear conservative business clothing, such as a suit or sport coat with a tie for men and similar business clothing for women. There are some areas of the country where a more casual style of clothing is used. No matter which style is used, clothing should always be neat, clean, and conform to local customs.

The author has had two experiences with attire on transfers that have left an impression. My early experience in funeral service was in metropolitan cities where suits were required for transfers. I then moved to a rural town in Northern New York to teach funeral service at a local state university. I made myself available to the local funeral homes. One called me to assist on a home transfer. I dressed in my usual attire of a dark suit, white shirt, tie, and dress shoes. When I arrived at the funeral home, the director looked at me and said, "What the heck are you all decked out for? We don't wear anything special for removal. We go with whatever we have on." His outfit was a ski coat and jeans.

Another time I was visiting a funeral director friend when his removal man came in from making a hospital transfer. He had on jeans with large holes in the knee. My jaw dropped and I said, "I don't believe what I am seeing." He said, "You can't get good help, he's not a funeral director," like that made it okay.

Dennis Dalton, of the Dodge Chemical Company, recommends the following for all transfers:

- **DO NOT slam hearse door.**
- **Use calm and quiet in all activities.**
- **All material on the transfer cot, including the cot itself, must be neat and clean.**
- **If you make a transfer from an airport, train station, or from a distant location, call the family when you arrive back at the funeral home and let them know *"Bill has safely arrived at the funeral home."***

Home Transfers

This is the most unpredictable and delicate form of transfer. Because of this, it is the most interesting, but can also be the most difficult. It involves going into someone's private residence to remove a dead body, often in front of family or friends. One must always be on guard and act professionally when doing a house transfer. You should never forget that you are not only moving a body, but a loved one, and you are doing it in someone's private home making it incredibly personal for most people (Handy, 2012).

A funeral home should always send at least two people on a home transfer. There are some instances when, because of the excess weight of the deceased, it may be necessary to send more than two people.

Two vehicles should be sent to the home if it is the custom of the funeral director to stay and talk with the family for any length of time after the deceased is placed in the transfer vehicle. This allows the transfer vehicle to return to the funeral home, eliminating any anxiety the family may feel by having the deceased parked in the driveway or in the street while they are talking with the director.

A home removal may be the first impression a family has of your funeral home. The removal staff must be well trained, not only in the technical aspects of transferring the deceased, but also in how to talk to the family at this time. They need to know what to say and how to say it, while exuding confidence and professionalism. There may come a time when no matter how professional you are being, a situation occurs that can destroy your image.

The author, an apprentice at the time, and a funeral director had lunch in a diner (these many years later I still remember what we had – Italian sausage subs with onions and peppers). We received a call to make a home removal. When we arrived, two family members and the police were standing outside. As we approached them, the family told us their grandfather had been dead for weeks. The police officer said, "It's pretty bad in there." When we entered the smell was terrible. The deceased was lying face down on the floor. When we went to lift him, the skin on his face stuck to the floor and the smell got worse. I ran out of the house and vomited my lunch over the railing. I felt embarrassed. When I went back inside, the director said, "It happens sometimes."

The Unpredictability:

The driveway is the first issue you may find. Some residences do not have driveways and you will need to 'load up' on the street. Do what you have to do but be quick and discrete. Other times there is a driveway, but it is impractical or difficult to reverse into. Reverse ***in*** if you can. It is easier to load and then you can just pull out. Reversing out is always more difficult than reversing in (Handy, 2012).

Upon Arrival at the House

The funeral director should go to the door without the cot. The director should introduce herself and ask to be taken to where the deceased is located. Refer to everyone, including the deceased as Mr. or Mrs. While walking to the room, the director should be observing:

- **Stairways.** Stairs and doors can be a nightmare. Not only are they difficult to get around, but they are often dangerous. Stairs can be slippery, steep, and have tight corners. Handy (2012) tells a story about how stairs collapsed as he carried a heavy body out of a house. It resulted in him being up to his waist in stairs with a heavy stretcher holding the body on top of him.
- **Size of hallways**
- **Number of turns**
- **Throw rugs**
- **Objects or furniture that will need to be moved**. Furniture can be an issue. It is often in the way of getting the body onto the stretcher or getting the stretcher out of the house. Problematic furniture can be anything from a little table by the door to a washing machine. Move it out of your way. Try to put the furniture back if you can, but this is not always possible. When moving anything electrical, turn it off at the source and unplug it before moving it. Ibid.
- **Doorways**
- **The position, condition, and size of the deceased**
- **Location of the body**. The location of the body is often a hazard in itself. The deceased may be on the floor of a tiny bathroom with water everywhere and not enough room for the stretcher. Or they may be in the middle of a large bed. Beds are surprisingly difficult as you cannot get a solid or stable foot hold to move the body. The deceased will not have been cleaned in most cases. While hospitals and nursing homes will usually clean the body, or at least neaten them up, the residents of houses will not. Be ready for a dirty or messy body. Ibid.

During this observation, the director should be making the determination as to which stretcher or cot should be used. After the director has seen the deceased, she should advise the family that the cot will be brought in. Ask any persons who will be in the way if they would mind moving to a room out of direct view of the actual transfer of the deceased. Most people will not object to this request. If they do object, the director should allow them to stay. Any furniture that is in the way should be moved.

Some funeral directors will ask if anyone would like a last viewing or kiss; or if they would like to observe or assist with the transfer. If you do this, arrange the deceased into a more pleasant position if possible. Doing this shows that you are flexible and willing to address any concern they might have. However, it also puts more pressure on the staff to make sure everything goes perfectly during the transfer.

Transferring the Body & Next Steps:

- The director should return to the transfer vehicle and bring in the other employee, the cot, and any other necessary items into the house. Introduce this employee to the family. The transfer should be made as quickly and quietly as possible. The deceased should be wrapped in a plastic sheet or cloth and/or placed in the transfer pouch. They should then be strapped onto the cot and taken through the house in a quiet and dignified manner. A cot cover, blanket, or sheet can be placed over the pouch to make a softer appearance. Some directors use a flag to cover the pouch during the transfer of a Veteran.

- If the deceased was in bed, some funeral directors will remove soiled bed linens and place them neatly aside or in a pillowcase. Blankets are arranged neatly. The placement of a flower or meaningful note on the bed is a nice touch. If the deceased is wearing any jewelry or valuables, the director should ask the family if they should be removed. After placing the deceased in the transfer vehicle, the director then returns to the house and replaces any furniture that was removed.

- The director should inform the family of information they should bring with them to the arrangement conference. At the same time, the director should **ask for permission to embalm** the deceased and, if possible, have them sign an authorization. If the family has the clothing the deceased will wear, it can be taken at this time. If possible, a time should be set for the arrangement conference if it has not already been made.

- If you offer the option of making arrangement while at the home, be sure to have all necessary technology and paperwork.

- Some directors bring a garment bag for clothing, an envelope for vital papers, and an envelope or smaller bag for jewelry.

A transfer sounds rather simple on paper. The reality is, however, that it is often not an easy task. The potentially excessive weight of a deceased, narrow steep stairs, inaccessible locations, the condition of the individual, or the state of a room in a homicide or suicide can make a transfer exceedingly difficult. No matter what the circumstances, directors should strive to be as dignified, caring, and professional as possible.

Institutional Transfers

There is usually a designated location to park the transfer vehicle when the transfer is being made from a hospital, nursing home, or hospice. Each facility has its own procedure to follow. This procedure usually includes signing a form indicating you are taking possession of the deceased and signing a receipt for any belongings received. If necessary, the director must present a signed body release and her funeral director's license where required.

Release Remains

To Whom It May Concern: Please release the remains of the late,

____

To the ____
Name of Funeral Home, address and phone number.

☐ I give permission for an autopsy.

☐ I do not give permission for an autopsy.

☐ I grant permission to care for, embalm, and otherwise prepare for burial and/or other disposition.

____________________ Witness	____________________ Signature
____________________ Date	____________________ Relationship
	____________________ Address
	____________________ City, State, Zip Code

The facility usually has a route they want taken to get to the location of the deceased and will have a policy that requires a staff member to accompany you to the location. It is good procedure to avoid crowded areas of the hospital or general use elevators if possible. If it is necessary to park in a location that takes you directly through a busy area, such as the emergency room, professional conduct is an absolute necessity.

<u>An embarrassing teachable moment:</u>

The author had an embarrassing situation during a transfer from a nursing home. It was in the early morning, around 3:00 am. I was an apprentice and a funeral director was with me. We arrived at the nursing home. The supervisor met us and said we could take the cot right into the room. We walked in and saw the deceased in the bed by the door. She looked like a typical elderly deceased resident. I went to the feet and the director went to the head. We each put our hands on the decedent to lift her onto the cot. The woman we were lifting, who we thought was the deceased said, "She's in the other bed." Neither of us knew what to do but apologize. We had never checked the name band, we just assumed. As the saying goes, "when you assume, you make an <u>ass</u> out of <u>u</u> and <u>me.</u> I have never assumed again.

Documentation

It is important to have a removal/transfer form that covers all aspects of the transfer because of the litigious society that we live in (Kubasak, 2015). The following is a good example of what should be recorded.

REMOVAL/TRANSFER INFORMATION FORM

1. Time call received: ______________________________
2. Person making transfer: ______________________________
3. Address transfer was made from: ______________________________
4. Who authorized transfer: ______________________________
5. Arrival time at location: ______________________________
6. Conditions of deceased:

   ____

   ____
7. Where deceased was located and condition of location:

   ____

   ____
8. Any problems with transfer:

   ____

   ____
9. Time personnel and deceased left location: ______________________________
10. Time & date of arrival at funeral home: ______________________________
11. The name(s) of the person(s) making the delivery. If an outside 1st call firm, record its name and representative(s): ______________________________
12. Valuables and personal items on or with the deceased's body:

    ____

    ____
13. Where the deceased was placed, such as embalming table, in refrigeration storage, etc.:

    ____

______________________________ Employee Signature

______________________________ Date & Time

Upon arrival at the funeral home, the remains should be placed into a refrigeration unit if you have one. Dawson (2015) suggests the following functions be carried out prior to placement, including:

1. Turn on the cooler if it has not been on.
2. Confirm name tags and identification.
3. Move remains to portable embalming table or gurney.
4. Elevate head and shoulders. Adjust hands, feet, and head.
5. Be certain that the body is properly covered with a sheet over the face and body.
6. Place massage cream on face and hands.

Universal Precautions

The use of universal precautions is important protocol that should not be taken for granted. Protective personal equipment should be used on any transfer of a decedent. If making a transfer where isolation or infectious conditions are indicated, one should use gloves, a mask, hair cover, and, if possible, a gown and shoe covers. While that may appear ridiculous, we must remember how overwhelmed and understaffed medical facilities are today. Due to inadequate sanitizing, various strands of MRSA are active in these settings. They are often not as clean as they should be. It would be dreadful to contaminate the entire mortuary with a disease due to carelessness or inadequate training (Newbern, 2015).

Transfer Identification

The following is a best practice to be implemented when making a transfer of a decedent (Starks, 2017).

- **Before attaching the funeral home identification band, the deceased must be identified.** This can be accomplished by a pre-existing identification band, a relative or a person who knew the deceased, an employee of the hospital or nursing home, etc. It is important that the name of the deceased corresponds with all existing paperwork.

- **Attach the identification band on the deceased at the place of death.** Even if there is other identification on the deceased, the band should still be attached. And, if possible, do not remove the other form of identification.

- **Place the identification band around the deceased's ankle or around the wrist if an ankle cannot be used.** In the event the deceased is in a disaster pouch, securely attach the identification band to the pouch. Never remove the identification band once it has been attached.

- **Use waterproof identification bands made of tear-resistant material.** The band should not be possible to remove by any method other than cutting.

- **Keep identification bands in each transfer vehicle.** If an outside transfer service is used, furnish the service with a supply of identification bands for their transfer vehicles.

- **Write the information on the identification band using a pen with indelible ink (i.e. a Sharpie).** At a minimum, include the full name of the deceased and date of death. This information must be clearly printed. Under no circumstances should the deceased's name or other information be written on the arms, legs, or any other part of the body.

Accidents/Crime Scenes (Forensic Transfers)

For more information on forensic transfers, see Supportive Readings, page 435.

For more information on the issue of bed bugs in removals, see Supportive Readings, page 437.

Family Preparation Time: Before the Arrangement Conference

The time between the transfer of the deceased and the arrangement conference is what the author calls "family preparation time." This is usually a time in which the family and the funeral director have little or no interaction.

Example of Family Preparation Timeline

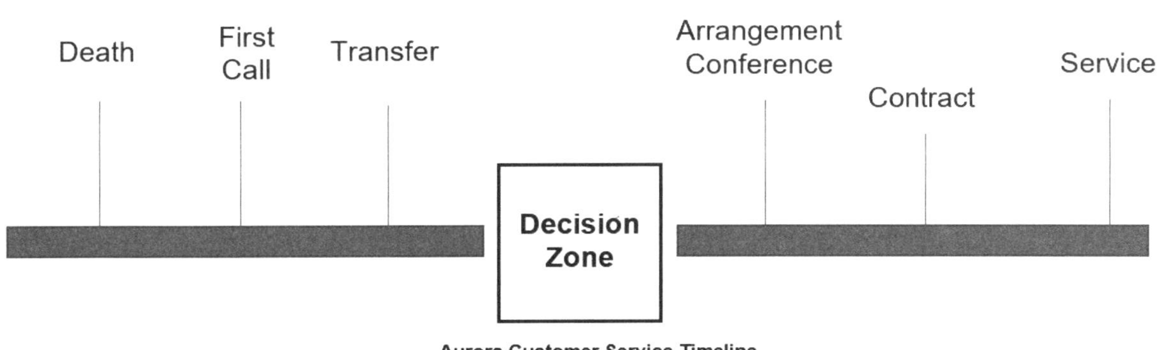

Aurora Customer Service Timeline

(Author acknowledges Aurora Casket's timelines and family connections advice as inspiration for this.)

Family preparation time can be a time where the funeral director helps the family prepare for their upcoming meeting. The funeral director can accomplish this by developing a "Preparation Information Packet." This packet should be given to the family, available in hard copy at the funeral home, and on the funeral home's website. The **Preparation Information Packet** should contain information pertaining to:

- The value of having a funeral, memorial, or life celebration service and a description of each.
- A tasteful explanation of cremation with options available, descriptions of the process, the funeral home's policies for authorization to cremate, holding and returning the cremated remains, and disposition options.
- An explanation of caskets, urns, vaults, and keepsake merchandise.
- A vital statistic form that the family can complete.
- Any paperwork that may be needed, such as social security number or military discharge.
- Any special services or aftercare activities you provide.

This information packet can be introduced with a statement such as:

> *"I have some information that will be helpful to you before we meet to make arrangements. It is available in hard copy, or on our website. Which would you prefer?"*

This system can be a positive experience for the family in many ways:

- In a way, it keeps the family in contact with the funeral home.
- It gives the family something to do during this time.
- It allows the family to be better prepared for the arrangement conference.
- If the family chooses the computer option, they can share information with distant relations.

ELLSWORTH FUNERAL HOME
1221 W. 109th Street
Rumsey, Kentucky 42327

800-555-1212

The Ellsworth Family & Staff would like to express our sincere appreciation for allowing us to serve you. We are thankful that you have placed confidence in our funeral home as we hope to exceed the standard you have come to expect at Ellsworth Funeral Home. We have compiled the list on the back of this card to prepare you for the upcoming funeral arrangement conference. The required items on this card will be fully explained to you during your appointment time.

Your funeral director will assist your family with everything from organizing the funeral service to writing an obituary for the newspaper. If you have any questions, please do not hesitate to contact us.

Appointment Date: _____/_____/_____ **Appointment Time:** ____________

The following information will be required during the funeral arrangement conference. If possible, please bring this information to your appointment:

- Deceased's Social Security Number
- Deceased's father's full name
- Deceased's mother's full name (Maiden)
- Deceased's date of birth
- Deceased's place of birth

The following documents will also be required during the funeral arrangement conference:

- Burial Clothing (Full dress, including all undergarments, shoes are optional)
- Recent photograph (For newspaper obituary)
- Military discharge (Form DD214)
- Any applicable life insurance policies (Ellsworth Funeral Home will help to file the insurance as an added service to your family)

Your arrangement conference will cover many items and will answer any questions you have. You may also want to be thinking about the following items for your service:

- The day and time the funeral service will be conducted.
- A minister for the funeral service.
- Special Music for the funeral service (organ background, tapes, CD's, or live vocal performance).
- A list of casket-bearers and telephone numbers.
- A list of club or civic group memberships.
- A list of activities or hobbies the person enjoyed during their life.

Reprinted with permission of Sam Ellsworth, M.A.

NOTES

Chapter 3 ARRANGEMENT CONFERENCE

<u>Arrangement Conference</u> *- The meeting between the funeral director and the client family during which the funeral arrangements are discussed.*

The arrangement conference is the key to establishing trust and providing families with services that are truly special and meaningful and that meet or exceed their expectation (Cozine, 2017).

It is this interaction that can make the difference between the family experiencing a "Wow" moment or just a "Whatever" moment (Defort, 2017).

The purposes of the funeral arrangement conference are:

1. To build rapport with the family.
2. To help them plan a service that will be meaningful to them and reflect the life of the deceased.
3. To obtain vital statistical information for funeral home records, needed legal documents, and death notices or obituaries.

Importance of the Arrangement Conference

Often a bereaved family's first face-to-face meeting with the funeral director is at the arrangement conference. This meeting is designed to not only collect information and plan funeral details, but also allow the funeral director to develop a relationship of trust and confidence with the family. If done properly, it can also help the family in their grieving process. Canine (2002) observes that the funeral director is usually the first person to hear the death story, the first to observe the acute grief in the family, the first to hear the multiplicity of feelings the family is going through, and the first to offer support.

Funeral professionals can assist in the expression of feelings during this helping interview. When the funeral professional is present, feelings are usually intense. The funeral professional can provide within the safe harbor of the funeral interview, and overall funeral experience, the personal attitude and social atmosphere within which the appropriate deep grief feelings can be expressed, accepted, and understood (Van Beck, 2016).

The arrangement conversation is the rudder of our entire business, and success or failure of our enterprise rises and falls by what does or doesn't happen in this interaction. According to Boxley (2017), however, the arrangement style and process of most funeral directors is:

- 50% what we were shown by our internship supervisor
- 30% lessons of trial and error
- 20% flying by the seat of our pants, hoping to avoid any objection for which we are unprepared

Rarely do we take a purposeful approach to what happens during the arrangement. The whole of funeral service probably spends more time training on what to do with the flower cards or how to park cars than how to engage with families making important decisions on the most difficult day of their lives. But we can change that. Some funeral homes have and are seeing the difference the right arrangement conversation can make. Ibid.

Being proficient at knowing your services and merchandise well is a baseline assumption. Being kind and compassionate is also a minimum standard. To create a better arrangement conversation, we typically need to improve our listening skills, creativity, and ability to think outside of the box. Ibid.

Location of Arrangements

At the Funeral Home

Arrangements can be made anywhere. Most funeral directors prefer to make arrangements at their funeral home because it is their comfort zone. They have everything they need at their fingertips, including their merchandise display room.

Room Style

The style of an arrangement office recommended for a funeral home resembles a small conference room or a dining room in a home, not one with a desk that the director sits behind. A table with chairs can provide a comfortable, non-intimidating seating arrangement. It allows the funeral director space to write on without a formal businesslike atmosphere of a desk. Some funeral homes use a lounge or living-room design with couches, chairs, coffee table, and tables with lamps to try and provide a more comforting setting. This may take the funeral director some time to get used to. Your goal, however, should be to make the room comfortable for the family—not the funeral director.

Alternative Locations

Some locations for the arrangement conference, other than the funeral home, may be more comfortable or convenient for the family. These locations can include:

- Family's home — This may be the family's comfort zone.
- Hospital
- Hospice

In today's digital society, we have the tools at our fingertips to make arrangements anywhere. By using a laptop, tablet, or smart phone, a director can:

- Collect all data needed for files and legal documents.
- Present merchandise.
- Contact clergy, celebrant, cemetery, and vault company.
- Plan personalization and memorialization options.

Arrangements Online

In today's world, statistics prove that many people want to do business online from the convenience of their homes and on their schedule. Record numbers of consumers are now purchasing online as a matter of convenience and in a much less hurried environment. Many people are uncomfortable with dealing with salespeople, and shopping online allows them to avoid them. There are also families that cannot or do not want to visit a funeral home.

During the Covid-19 Pandemic of 2020, many states had "lockdown" or "stay-at-home" orders that required businesses to shut down and people to stay at home. While funeral homes were deemed "essential services" during this time, it was safer and more comfortable for many families to not have to come to the funeral home to make arrangements. As a result, many funeral director's made arrangements over the phone or through video conferencing using online platforms such as Zoom or Google Meet.

Pre-Conference Suggestions at the Funeral Home

- Meet the family at the door. Instead of saying the usual sympathy, ***"I am sorry for your loss,"*** try something more personal, ***"I can't know exactly how you feel, but I do know that this must be a hard time for you."*** This sets the mood that you are there to help and care for them.
- Before entering the arrangement room, give the family a tour of the funeral home. You can present this with a statement such as:

  "Before we start, let me show you some of the special features of our funeral home."

- Have a demonstration tribute video playing in one of the rooms. This feature may be new to the family and may stimulate questions or comments. Point out any other special features you offer such as memorial blankets or quilts and video systems to record or broadcast the service.
- After the family is seated, ask if you can bring them some water, soda, or coffee if your state allows it. Doing so gives you the opportunity to leave the room for a few minutes to let the family get settled.

Beginning the Conference

Old Method

Many new arrangers fear starting the arrangement conference interview the proper way. Some funeral directors get right down to business with a statement such as, *"I'll need to ask you a series of questions that will give me the information necessary for our records and the death certificate."* This method is described as the **1950's model.** Although this method has not been recommended for years, funeral homes are still using it. This type of beginning sets the tone for a business meeting where you are more of a functionary collecting data than a facilitator interacting in concert with the family.

Most funeral directors are more comfortable with this **order-taking model** and use it throughout the entire arrangement conference. The family is asked what they want for service details and the information is recorded with little or no discussion of creative or customized options available to make a uniquely personalized and meaningful service. The result of the meeting is usually what is known in the profession as a **"cookie-cutter"** funeral. This kind of funeral is identical or remarkably similar to every other funeral the funeral home conducts. It is not unusual to hear funeral directors say, *"This is the way we conduct funerals. We have done it this way for 10, 20, 30, or 40 years and our families seem satisfied."*

In defense of those funeral directors, the satisfaction part may be true. Some of their families are satisfied with what these funeral directors provide, and they may always be satisfied. Others are satisfied until they experience a different type of funeral: One that is creative, personalized, individualized, and customized to reflect the true life of the deceased and the desires of the family.

New Method

A creative, personalized, individualized, and customized funeral experience is being requested more often around the country. The trend has been growing because of the changing attitudes of baby boomers (those born between 1946 and 1964). This generation and the millennial generation born between 1982 and 2004 have redefined many cultural issues of the time, just as future generations will institute other changes.

Funeral directors who have adapted to the changing demands of the funeral consumer have changed how they approach the arrangement conference, including a very simple change in style. Instead of beginning the conference with collecting data, they start by putting down their pens and asking a simple question, something such as:

- **"Why don't you tell me about your dad?"**
- **"Was your mother sick for long?"**
- **"Were you with your son when he died?"**

There is a saying **"People don't care what you know until they know that you care."** The first five minutes with a family can be the difference between them feeling like you care or feeling like you are there to just take information and sell them something.

Functionary Aspect – A legal or ethical relationship of trust.

During the arrangement conference the funeral director acts as both a **functionary**, collecting information, and a **facilitator**. As a functionary, the funeral director needs to collect information for:

- Legal documents
- Explanation of expenses
- Explanation of government forms, such as the death certificate, burial or, cremation permits
- The death notice or obituary
- Presenting merchandise for the family to purchase, including caskets, vaults, urns, clothing, flowers, or memorial markers.
- Date and time for visitation
- Date and time for disposition (i.e. interment, cremation, entombment)
- Coordination with clergy or funeral celebrant
- Special requests
- Service details, such as music selections, religious or inspirational readings
- Financial arrangements
- Automobile needs

The director also functions as a **facilitator.** As a facilitator, the director helps the family understand their options and plan a service that meets their needs, all while bringing them comfort and support. Part of this important role is also making the arrangement and planning process easier for families.

Another prearrangement option available to families is to complete all or most of the funeral arrangement on a funeral home's website. A consumer inputs all necessary vital statistics, uses the online merchandise display room to select needed merchandise, and states religious and cemetery requests. Directors at the funeral home can verify the religious and cemetery requests with the appropriate people. A funeral director must ensure that all state and FTC rules are followed before they allow this type of arrangement.

Interviewing Skills

To be able to serve families well, we must ask them a lot of questions. We are good at asking those questions clearly and compassionately, but the most important questions are not those we need for the death certificate and other paperwork. The most important are those that reveal the life story, the memories, and the stories stacked with emotion and importance (Boxley, 2017).

The following suggestions for the arrangement conference have been recommended by leaders in the profession and can help any funeral director improve his/her approach to this vital aspect of the funeral process.

Ask powerful questions about the death that show you are interested in the deceased.

Powerful questions are those that give insight to the life of the deceased and what the needs of the family are. Examples include:

- Tell me what happened.
- Tell me a little something about your dad.
- Was your mom sick for long? Or was her death sudden?
- Was your wife's death expected or unexpected?

After these types of questions, ask questions about the family's experience with funerals such as:

- Have you made funeral arrangements before? When and for whom?
- Have you ever attended a wake or funeral before? When and for whom?
- Is there anything about that funeral that you thought was especially meaningful? What was it?
- Is there anything about that funeral that you did not like? What was it?

After these types of questions, you have an idea of where the family is coming from and their likes/dislikes. These questions show the family your interest in them and may allow them to verbalize something that could otherwise be on their mind throughout the arrangements. Once you have made these connections, built this rapport, you can then state something such as:

> **"I have a number of questions to ask and details to discuss, but I want to answer your most pressing questions first."**

Pre-Need Arrangement

If this is a funeral for someone who has prearranged/prefunded, do the following before the family arrives:

- Remove the prearranged folder from your prearrangement file.
- Make two copies of this folder — One to give to the family, the other to keep yourself.
- Check to be sure selected merchandise is available.

Sayer (2016) suggests that the arranger present a family with an agenda at the beginning of the conference. This agenda should include a list of all aspects that will be covered during the arrangement with space to check off items as they are completed. Additionally, a note at the bottom of the form states that those items already marked with a check mark were taken care of during prearrangement where applicable.

Cremation Arrangement

A. If the family states that they want a cremation, the funeral director should respond with something such as, "*Fine*," or "*That will not be a problem*." Then ask:

   "May I read the cremation options we offer?"
   (A list of options should already be created)

B. The family should be informed of your rules for holding of cremains at the funeral home.

   "Our policy is that we will hold Bill's cremated remains for ______, after which they will be placed in a cremation vault at the cemetery. You will be billed _____."

C. Explain the reasoning behind the policy.

   "We have this policy because we believe that all deceased persons must be treated with respect and dignity. We do not believe that placing an urn of cremated human remains on a shelf at a funeral home for an indefinite time shows dignified respect."

For more information on Cremation Arrangements, see Chapter 18 Cremation.

Explanation of Service Offerings

Visitation

Wolfelt (2014) explains that the more information families are given about each of the elements of the funeral, the more their decisions become true choices. As you bring up each element of the funeral, you should educate the family about:

1. The purpose of the element.
2. How the element fits into the whole funeral experience.
3. Some ways to personalize the element.

Then and only then is the family equipped to make an informed choice about whether to include that element in the unique funeral they are planning.

Music

Wolfelt (2015) discusses the importance of explaining the impact music can have at a service.

> ***"Music can activate feelings of empathy and support. The quiet reflection during musical interludes often stimulate the acknowledgement of the reality of death and touches our hearts. Music that was meaningful to the deceased stimulates our memories of that person. Instead of suggesting suitable music ask the family, "What music reminds you of him/her? What music captures your feeling best about his/her unique life?"***

Pall Bearers

Explain the role of pallbearers and the importance they hold in the service. For example:

> ***"We believe it should be considered an honor to be asked to be a pall bearer. You may want to select family and friends who were close to Bill. Some people will offer their services even before being asked."***

Funeral Options

By allowing the family to talk and by listening carefully, the director can get a sense for the type of funeral that will best meet their needs. There are enough funeral options available to meet the needs of any family.

These options include:

1. A funeral with the body present, with public viewing, service, and committal (burial, entombment, or cremation.)
2. A funeral with the body present, with a private viewing, public or private service, and committal (burial, entombment, or cremation).
3. A funeral with the body present, but everything else is private.
4. A funeral with the body present with no viewing, but a public service and public or private committal.
5. A funeral with the body present with no viewing and everything else private.
6. A public graveside service with the body present to be distinguished from a committal service only.
7. A direct disposition by cremation or interment preceded or followed by a public or private service without the body present.
8. A direct disposition by cremation or interment preceded by identification viewing.
9. A direct disposition by cremation or interment with no viewing or attendant rites or ceremonies.
10. A body donation preceded or followed by a public or private service with the body or cremains present.
11. A body donation without any public or private service.

Cemetery/Crematory

It is necessary for the funeral director to obtain information on the type and location of the final disposition. Will it be burial, cremation, or entombment? If it will be burial or entombment, the family must already have purchased the grave or crypt; or it will have to be done immediately. Assuming the family has pre-purchased the grave, they should present the deed to the funeral director. He/she in turn will call the cemetery to notify them of the death, grave number, and date and time of the service.

For more information on this subject, see Chapter 16 Cemetery-Mausoleum.

Religious Services

It will be necessary for the director and family to decide on a time, place, and type of religious service. Before making any definite plans, the member of the clergy should be called and informed of the death, if he has not already been contacted. He should be consulted on the time, date, and type of service the family wishes. Agreeing on a time and day of the funeral may involve some negotiations among all parties involved. The family's first request may not be able to be filled because of a time conflict with clergy.

Historically, religion has played an important role in funeral services. For some people, a religious service is the culmination of a person's spiritual life. The services may follow a strict dogmatic formula such as a Catholic mass or may be less rigid and more flexible in the rituals. Society has seen a change in the number of people who now consider themselves religious and who follow religious rituals and ceremonies. It is estimated that around 30% of people describe themselves as spiritual, not religious. These people are referred to as "**nones**."

A traditional religious ceremony may be conducted in the church, synagogue, mosque, or funeral home and generally adheres to the church's rules and rituals.

The following four options are adaptive (nontraditional) services:

1. **Non-traditional** - Religious orientated but follows a more modern interpretation, including favorite music, poems, and readings.
2. **Memorial Service** - A service without the body present usually held days or weeks after the disposition.
3. **Humanistic Service** - A service devoid of religion.
4. **Celebration of Life** – A personalized service focused on the life of the person instead of their death.

Funeral Celebrant Services

A growing trend across the country is non-religious funeral services. Today, more people describe themselves as spiritual, not religious. To meet the needs of these families, funeral directors can use a funeral celebrant instead of a member of the clergy to conduct a non-religious service.

Vital Statistics

Once rapport and a foundation of trust have been established in the arrangement conference, the funeral director can proceed with obtaining the vital statistics and service details. These will be needed for the death notice, death certificate, and for the funeral home's records.

The following information is typically gathered by the director:

- Name
- Address
- Date of birth
- Gender
- Place of birth
- Date of death
- Place of death
- Cause of death
- Marital Status
- Spouse – name, age
- Race
- Father's name
- Father's birthplace
- Mother's Name/maiden name
- Mother's birthplace
- Cemetery/Crematory
- Grave #
- Date of funeral
- Time of service
- Doctor's name
- Doctor's contact information
- Informant's name, age
- Informant's contact information
- Veteran
- Rank
- Service #
- Date entered service
- Date discharged
- Type of Business
- Occupation
- Social Security Number
- Name of hospital
- Clergy Person name
- Clergy person contact information
- Church
- Grave owner
- Section
- Service at:

A Sample Arrangement Form

Arrangement Form

Statistical/Service Information

Last Name ________________________ First ________________________ Middle Initial ______

Address ____

City ________________________________ State __________ Zip Code ___________

Date of Death ___________ Time of Death ___________ Sex ___________ Race ___________

Birth Date ______________ City & Country of Birth
____

State & County of Birth ________________________________ Citizen of
____

Marital Status ___________________ Full Maiden Name ______________________________

Employer _____________________________ Social Security Number ______________________

Occupation ___________________________ Business Type ____________________________

Military Service: Veteran? ___Y ___N Branch of Service ____________________________

Dates of Service ___________________ Service Number_____________________________

Years of Education ______

Father's First Name ____________________ Middle _____ Last ___________________________

Birth City & State ________________________ Living ___Y ___N Phone __________________

Mother's First Name ___________________ Middle _____ Last ___________________________

Birth City & State ________________________ Living ___Y ___N Phone __________________

Cause of Death: __________________________________ Location ______________________

City/Town of Death _____________________ County/State of Death ______________________

Autopsy ___Y ___N Organ/Tissue Donation ___Y ___N

Religion _____________________ Church/Synagogue Attended __________________________

Clergy Name _____________________________ Phone _______________________________

Cemetery/Crematory ____________________________ Location ________________________

Date of Disposition ________________ Time ___________

Arrangement Form

Family

Husband/Wife of ______________________________

Address ______________________________

Father/Mother/Other of ______________________________

____

____

Grandfather/Grandmother of ______________________________

____

____

Great-Grandchildren ______________________________

Son/Daughter of ______________________________

Brother/Sister of ______________________________

Visitation

The family will be present (Dates & Days) ______________________________

From (Times) ______________ a.m./p.m. TO ______________ a.m./p.m.

At the ______________________________

Where the funeral services will be held ______________________________

At ______________________ and from ______________ at ______________

Organization(s) belonged to ______________________________

____

Special Instructions

Informant Name ______________________________

Address ______________________________ Phone ______________

Arranging Director ______________________________

Death Notice/Announcements

The following information is gathered during the arrangement conference for the death notice/obituary:

Spouse/Partner	Sisters
Father	Grandchildren
Mother	Organizations
Sons	Visitation
Daughters	Funeral
Brothers	Funeral Home

There are generally two types of death announcements found in newspapers:

1. ***Death Notice*** — A classified notice publicizing the death of a person, listing survivors, and giving those details of the funeral service that the survivors wish to have published. There is usually a charge for this announcement.

Sample Death Notice

URBAN, George A.

URBAN - George A. November 2, 2017, of East Amherst, NY. Best friend and loving husband of Teresa (nee Pasnik) Urban; survived by David and Mark; beloved son of the late Casper and Martha (nee Wolski) Urban; brother of the late Casper (Paula) and late Marcia. Favorite son-in-law of Art and Joan Pasnik. Special brother-in-law of Matthew (Linda), Peggy (late Mark) Henline, Mark (Lisa), Becky (Glenn) Biddlecom, Nadine (Don) O'Connor and the late Simon; also survived by nieces, nephews, cousins and many loving friends. Family and friends may call at the URBAN BROTHERS FUNERAL HOME, 6685 Transit Rd., East Amherst, NY (South of County and N. French Rds.) on Sunday, November 5, 2017 from 2-4 and 6-8 PM. A Mass of Christian Burial will be held on Monday, Nov. 6 at St. Mary's Church, 6919 Transit Rd., Swormville, NY at 10 AM (Please assemble at church). Flowers gratefully declined.

Taken from http://buffalonews.com/2017/11/04/urban-george-a/

2. ***Obituary*** — An announcement of death that has a biographical sketch of the person's life, listing occupation, organizations, and notable information, sometimes with a photograph. There is not usually a charge for an obituary.

Sample Obituary

James R. Loomis Sr., Army vet, third-generation funeral director

Dec. 24, 1931 – Oct. 21, 2017

James R. "Jim" Loomis Sr., who consoled countless grieving failies as a third-generation funeral director, died Saturday at home in Orchard Park after a lengthly illness.
He was 85.
Mr. Loomis was born and raised in South Buffalo. He graduated from School 70, South Park High School, Alfred Agricultural and Technical Institute and the University at Buffalo.
Mr. Loomis was in the Army, and the day after marrying the former Marjorie E. Sleg, he was sent to Germany.
He was discharged from the Army in 1955 and returned home to the funeral home business that his grandfather founded in 1893 on Seneca Street.
Mr. Loomis spent 68 years operating Loomis, Offers & Loomis Inc., where he emphasized dignity for the deceased and compassion for grieving families.
He played piano, organ and the accordion. He was a painter, a voracious reader of poetry, biographies and nonfiction. He read the Bible several times in its entirety.
He enjoyed hiking, skiing and boating and was a lifelong dog owner.
Mr. Loomis belonged to numerous organizations, including the Buffalo Court Royal Order of Jesters, the Hamburg Kiwanis club, Hamburg VFW 1419, the Hamburg America Legion 527, Western Star Lodge #1184, Ismailia Temple AAONMS, Seneca Shrine Club and the national, New York and Erie Niagara Funeral Director's Associations.
Besides his wife of 63 years, Mr. Loomis is survived by two sons, Greg and Jim Jr.; three daughters, Joanne Ryan, Peggy Hillery and Jeannine Higgins; a brother, Roy; a sister, Kate Martin; 15 grandchildren and step-grandchildren; and four great-great-grandchildren and step-great-grandchildren.
A Mass of Christian Burial will be offered at 11:30 a.m. Thursday at Our Lady of Charity Parish, St. Ambrose site, 65 Ridgewood Road

Death Certificate & Burial Permit

Death Certificate *- A legal document containing vital statistics, disposition information, and final medical information pertaining to the cause of death.*

The information obtained during the arrangement conference is used by the funeral director to complete part of the death certificate. It is necessary for an M.D. or coroner to complete the proper section. Once the death certificate is completed, it is filed with proper government agency and a Burial, Cremation, or Transit Permit is issued.

- The vital statistic information is supplied by an informant (one who supplies the information concerning the deceased).
- Funeral Directors/Embalmers Information — Data pertaining to the place of death, the date, and location of the disposition.
- A physician, medical doctor, or coroner is required to complete the cause of death section.
- Registrar's Information - Official signature and data of the legal government agency.

Purposes of the death certificate:

- Shows cause of death for medical or actuarial research
- Is the legal, permanent record of death
- Is a permanent, statistical record of the deceased
- Assists with settling estate/legal affairs

Burial, Cremation, or Transit Permit/Disposition Permit

This legal document, issued by the proper government agency, authorizes transportation and/or disposition of human remains. This permit:

- Is issued upon the filing of the completed death certificate with the proper agency.
- Is the legal permit that allows the funeral director to transport and/or dispose of a dead human body.
- Is the legal record that final disposition has occurred (burial, removal, or cremation).

In some instances, a release from the coroner or medical examiner may be required.

Sample Death Certificate

DEATH CERTIFICATE

DECEDENT

1. NAME: FIRST | MIDDLE | LAST
2. SEX: MALE ☐ 1 FEMALE ☐ 2
3A. DATE OF DEATH: MONTH DAY YEAR
3B. HOUR: m

4A. PLACE OF DEATH: (Check only one) HOSPITAL DOA ☐ 1 ER ☐ 2 HOSPITAL OUTPATIENT ☐ 3 HOSPITAL INPATIENT ☐ 4 NURSING HOME ☐ PRIVATE RESIDENCE ☐ OTHER (Specify)
4B. IF FACILITY, DATE ADMITTED: MONTH DAY YEAR

4C. NAME OF FACILITY: (If not facility give address)
4D. LOCALITY: (Check one and specify) CITY OF ☐ VILLAGE OF ☐ TOWN OF ☐
4E. COUNTY OF DEATH:

4F. MEDICAL RECORD NO.
4G. WAS DECEDENT TRANSFERRED FROM ANOTHER INSTITUTION? (If yes, specify institution name, city or town, county and state) NO ☐ YES ☐

5. DATE OF BIRTH: MONTH DAY YEAR
6. AGE: yrs. | IF UNDER 1 YEAR months days | IF UNDER 1 DAY hours minutes
7A. CITY AND STATE OF BIRTH: (Country if not U.S.A.)
7B. IF AGE UNDER 1 YEAR, NAME OF HOSPITAL OF BIRTH:

8. SERVED IN U.S. ARMED FORCES? NO ☐ 0 YES ☐ 1 (Specify years)
9. RACE: (Black, White, etc.)
10. HISPANIC ORIGIN? (If yes, specify) NO ☐ YES ☐
11. DECEDENT'S EDUCATION (Specify only highest grade completed) Elementary/Secondary (0-12) College (1-4 or 5+)

12. SOCIAL SECURITY NUMBER:
13. MARITAL STATUS: NEVER MARRIED ☐ 1 MARRIED OR SEPARATED ☐ 2 WIDOWED ☐ 3 DIVORCED ☐ 4
14. SURVIVING SPOUSE: (If wife, provide maiden name)

15A. USUAL OCCUPATION: (Do not enter retired)
15B. KIND OF BUSINESS OR INDUSTRY:
15C. NAME AND LOCALITY OF COMPANY OR FIRM:

16A. RESIDENCE, STATE:
16B. COUNTY:
16C. LOCALITY: (Check one and specify) CITY OF ☐ VILLAGE OF ☐ TOWN OF ☐
16F. IF CITY OR VILLAGE, IS RESIDENCE WITHIN CITY OR VILLAGE LIMITS? ☐ YES ☐ NO IF NO, SPECIFY TOWN:
16D. STREET AND NUMBER OF RESIDENCE:
16E. ZIP CODE:

PARENTS

17. NAME OF FATHER: FIRST MI LAST
18. MAIDEN NAME OF MOTHER: FIRST MI LAST

19A. NAME OF INFORMANT:
19B. MAILING ADDRESS: (Include zip code)

DISPOSITION

20A. BURIAL, CREMATION, REMOVAL OR OTHER DISPOSITION: (Specify) MONTH DAY YEAR
20B. PLACE OF BURIAL, CREMATION, REMOVAL OR OTHER DISPOSITION:
20C. LOCATION: (City or town and state)

21A. NAME AND ADDRESS OF FUNERAL HOME:
21B. REGISTRATION NUMBER:

22A. NAME OF FUNERAL DIRECTOR:
22B. SIGNATURE OF FUNERAL DIRECTOR: ▶
22C. REGISTRATION NUMBER:

23A. SIGNATURE OF REGISTRAR: ▶
23B. DATE FILED: MONTH DAY YEAR
24A. BURIAL OR REMOVAL PERMIT ISSUED BY:
24B. DATE ISSUED: MONTH DAY YEAR

CERTIFIER

ITEMS 25 - 33 COMPLETED BY CERTIFYING PHYSICIAN — OR — ITEMS 25 - 33 COMPLETED BY CORONER OR MEDICAL EXAMINER

25A. TO THE BEST OF MY KNOWLEDGE, DEATH OCCURRED AT THE TIME, DATE AND PLACE AND DUE TO THE CAUSES STATED.
SIGNATURE: ▶ MONTH DAY YEAR

25A. ON THE BASIS OF INVESTIGATION AND SUCH EXAMINATIONS, AS I FELT NECESSARY, IN MY OPINION DEATH OCCURRED AT THE TIME, DATE AND PLACE AND DUE TO THE CAUSES STATED.
☐ CORONER ☐ CORONER'S PHYSICIAN ☐ MEDICAL EXAMINER
SIGNATURE AND TITLE: ▶

25B. THE PHYSICIAN ATTENDED THE DECEASED FROM MONTH DAY YEAR TO MONTH DAY YEAR
25C. LAST SEEN ALIVE BY ATTENDANT: MONTH DAY YEAR
25B. PRONOUNCED DEAD ON MONTH DAY YEAR
25C. HOUR: m
25D. DATE SIGNED: MONTH DAY YEAR

25D. NAME OF ATTENDING PHYSICIAN:
25E. SIGNATURE OF CORONER OR CORONER'S PHYSICIAN, IF OTHER THAN CERTIFIER: ▶

25D. ATTENDING PHYSICIAN LICENSE NUMBER
25F. ME/COR. PHYS. LICENSE NUMBER

26. NAME AND ADDRESS OF CERTIFIER WHO SIGNED 25A.

27. MANNER OF DEATH: NATURAL CAUSE ☐ 1 ACCIDENT ☐ 2 HOMICIDE ☐ 3 SUICIDE ☐ 4 UNDETERMINED CIRCUMSTANCES ☐ 5 PENDING INVESTIGATION ☐ 6
28. WAS CASE REFERRED TO CORONER OR MEDICAL EXAMINER? ☐ 0 NO ☐ 1 YES
29A. AUTOPSY? NO ☐ 0 YES ☐ 1 REFUSED ☐ 2
29B. IF YES, WERE FINDINGS USED TO DETERMINE CAUSE OF DEATH? ☐ 0 NO ☐ 1 YES

CAUSE OF DEATH

CONFIDENTIAL | SEE INSTRUCTION SHEET FOR COMPLETING CAUSE OF DEATH | CONFIDENTIAL

30. DEATH WAS CAUSED BY: (ENTER ONLY ONE CAUSE PER LINE FOR (A), (B), AND (C).)
APPROXIMATE INTERVAL BETWEEN ONSET AND DEATH

PART I. IMMEDIATE CAUSE:
(A)
DUE TO OR AS A CONSEQUENCE OF:
(B)
DUE TO OR AS A CONSEQUENCE OF:
(C)
PART II. OTHER SIGNIFICANT CONDITIONS CONTRIBUTING TO DEATH BUT NOT RELATED TO CAUSE GIVEN IN PART I (A):

31A. IF INJURY, DATE: MONTH DAY YEAR
HOUR: m
31B. LOCALITY: (City or town and county and state)
31C. DESCRIBE HOW INJURY OCCURRED:

31D. PLACE OF INJURY:
31E. INJURY AT WORK? NO ☐ 0 YES ☐ 1
32. WAS DECEDENT HOSPITALIZED IN LAST 2 MONTHS? NO ☐ 0 YES ☐ 1
33A. IF FEMALE, WAS DECEDENT PREGNANT IN LAST 6 MONTHS? NO ☐ 0 YES ☐ 1
33B. DATE OF DELIVERY: MONTH DAY YEAR

Sample Burial Permit

Burial Permit

DECEDENT

Name First | Middle | Last | Sex

Date of Death | Age | If Veteran of U.S. Armed Forces War or Dates

Place of Death City, Town or Village | Hospital, Institution or Street Address

Manner of Death ☐ Natural Cause ☐ Accident ☐ Homicide ☐ Suicide ☐ Undetermined Circumstances ☐ Pending Investigation

Medical Certifier Name | Title

Address

Death Certificate Filed City, Town or Village | District Number | Register Number

DISPOSITION

☐ Burial ☐ Cremation | Date | Cemetery or Crematory

Address

☐ Removal and/or Hold | Date | Place Removed and/or Held

Address

☐ Transportation by Common Carrier | Date | Point of Shipment

Destination

☐ Disinterment | Date | Cemetery Address

☐ Reinterment | Date | Cemetery Address

PERMIT

Permit Issued to Name of Funeral Home | Registration Number

Address

Name of Funeral Firm Making Disposition or to Whom Remains are Shipped, If Other than Above

Address

Permission is hereby granted to dispose of the human remains described above as indicated.

Date Issued ____________ Registrar of Vital Statistics ________________________________ (signature)

District Number ____________ Place ________________________________

ENDORSEMENT

I certify that the remains of the decedent identified above were disposed of in accordance with this permit on:

Date of Disposition __________ Place of Disposition ________________________________ (address)

________________________________ (section) (lot number) (grave number)

Name of Sexton or Person in Charge of Premises ________________________________ (please print)

Signature ________________________________ Title ________________________________

Merchandise Options

Presenting the General Price List

Aside from the vital statistics, it is necessary for the family and funeral director to discuss the service and merchandise options that are available to the family. At this time, the funeral director will present the family with the funeral home's "General Price List," or GPL, if he has not already done so. The Federal Trade Commission (FTC) requires that this form be given to the family for their retention. The GPL contains identifying information and itemized prices for goods and services that the funeral home sells and discloses.

The FTC Rule requires that a GPL be presented when a family asks about pricing. The FTC also requires that the funeral home have a Casket Price List and an Outer Burial Container Price List available. These do not have to be given to the family for retention but must be available.

General Price List Example

ABC FUNERAL HOME
100 Main Street
Yourtown, USA 12345
(123) 456-7890

GENERAL PRICE LIST

These prices are effective as of [date].

The goods and services shown below are those we can provide to our customers. You may choose only the items you desire. However, any funeral arrangements you select will include a charge for our basic services and overhead. If legal or other requirements mean you must buy any items you did not specifically ask for, we will explain the reason in writing on the statement we provide describing the funeral goods and services you selected.

Basic Services of Funeral Director and Staff and Overhead.............................. $__________

Our services include: Conducting the arrangements conference; planning the funeral; consulting with family and clergy; shelter of remains; preparing and filing of necessary notices; obtaining necessary authorizations and permits; and coordinating with the cemetery, crematory, or other third parties. In addition, this fee includes a proportionate share of our basic overhead costs.

This fee for our basic services and overhead will be added to the total cost of the funeral arrangements you select. This fee is already included in our charges for direct cremations, immediate burials, and forwarding or receiving remains.

Embalming ....$__________

Except in certain special cases, embalming is not required by law. Embalming may be necessary, however, if you select certain funeral arrangements, such as a funeral with viewing. If you do not want embalming, you usually have the right to choose an arrangement that does not require you to pay for it, such as direct cremation or immediate burial.

Other Preparation of the Body .... $_________

[List individual services and prices]

Transfer of Remains to the Funeral Home (within __ mile radius).............................$_________

(Beyond this radius we charge __ per mile

Use of Facilities and Staff for Viewing at the Funeral Home ....$_________

Use of Facilities and Staff for Funeral Ceremony at Funeral Home .... $_________

Use of Facilities and Staff for Memorial Service at the Funeral Home ....$_________

Use of Equipment and Staff for Graveside Service ....$_________

Hearse ....$_________

Limousine ....$_________

Caskets ....$_______ to ______

A complete price list will be provided at the funeral home.

Outer Burial Containers ....$______ to ______

A complete price list will be provided at the funeral home.

Forwarding of Remains to Another Funeral Home ....$__________

Our charge includes: Basic services of funeral director and staff; a proportionate share of overhead costs; removal of remains; embalming or other preparation of remains, if relevant; and local transportation.

Receiving Remains from Another Funeral Home ....$_________

Our charge includes: Basic services of funeral director and staff; a proportionate share of overhead costs; care of remains; and transportation of remains to funeral home and to cemetery or crematory.

Direct Cremation...$_______ to $_______
Our charge for a direct cremation (without ceremony) includes: Basic services of funeral director and staff; a proportionate share of overhead costs; removal of remains; transportation to crematory; necessary authorizations; and cremation if relevant.

If you want to arrange a direct cremation, you can use an alternative container. Alternative containers encase the body and can be made of materials like fiberboard or composition materials (with or without an outside covering). The containers we provide are a fiberboard container or an unfinished wood box.

A. Direct cremation with container provided by the purchaser...............................$_________

B. Direct cremation with a fiberboard container ....$_________

C. Direct cremation with an unfinished wood box..$_________

Immediate Burial ....$______ to $_______

Our charge for an immediate burial (without ceremony) includes: Basic services of funeral director and staff; a proportionate share of overhead costs; removal of remains; and local transportation to cemetery.

A. Immediate burial with casket provided by purchaser.................................$_________

B. Immediate burial with alternative container [if offered]...........................$_________

C. Immediate burial with cloth covered wood casket..............................$_________

Sample Casket Price List

SAMPLE CASKET PRICE LIST

ABC FUNERAL HOME
CASKET PRICE LIST
These prices are effective as of [date].

Alternative Containers:

1. Fiberboard Box.. $________
2. Plywood Box.. $________
3. Unfinished Pine Box... $________

Caskets:

1. Beige cloth-covered softwood with beige interior........................... $________
2. Oak stained softwood with pleated blue crepe interior.................... $________
3. Mahogany finished softwood with maroon crepe interior................. $________
4. Solid White Pine with eggshell crepe interior................................ $________
5. Solid Mahogany with tufted rosetan velvet interior.......................... $________
6. Hand finished solid Cherry with ivory velvet interior........................ $________
7. 18-gauge rose colored steel with pleated maroon crepe interior......... $________
   (Available in a variety of interiors)
8. 20-gauge bronze colored steel with blue crepe interior..................... $________
9. Solid Bronze (16-gauge) with brushed finish white ivory interior......... $________
10. Solid Copper (32 oz.) with Sealer (Oval Glass) and medium bronze finish with rosetan velvet interior.. $________

Sample Outer Burial Container Price List

SAMPLE
Outer Burial Container Price List

ABC FUNERAL HOME
OUTER BURIAL CONTAINER PRICE LIST

These prices are effective as of [date].

In most areas of the country, state or local law does not require that you buy a container to surround the casket in the grave. However, many cemeteries require that you have such a container so that the grave will not sink in. Either a grave liner or a burial vault will satisfy these requirements.

1. Concrete Grave Liner .... $______
2. Acme Reinforced Concrete Vault (Stainless Steel Lined).................... $______
3. Acme Reinforced Concrete Vault .... $______
4. Acme Solid Copper Vault .... $______
5. Acme Steel Vault (12 gauge) .... $______

Merchandise Selection

After the family selects the services they desire and understands the price for these services, they must select the merchandise to be used. This merchandise may include a casket or container, outside enclosure for grave, an urn or container for cremains if the disposition is cremation, clothing, register book, memorial cards, religious or fraternal symbols, and thank you notes.

Pre-Selection Room Introduction

At this time, the funeral director may show the family items, such as register books and memorial cards, or he may wait until after the family has selected the casket. Before entering the casket display (selection) room, the funeral director should give the family some idea of what to expect when in the room, including:

- Permission to touch
- Number of caskets
- Range of prices
- Explanation of the different types of caskets
- Reason for the large selection
- Explanation of what will occur
- If the funeral director will stay or leave

Sample Statement:

Our casket selection room contains 25 caskets ranging in price from $400 to $6,500 made of both wood and metal. When we enter the room, I will take a few minutes to explain what makes one casket different from another and what affects the price. I will then walk with you through the room explaining individual caskets and answering any questions you may have. With your permission, I will leave you while you make your decision. I'll be sitting at the table by the door. If you wish me to stay with you while you make your decision, I'll be happy to do so.

When you have selected the casket, I will then show you some scale models of burial vaults. The cemetery you selected requires that some form of outer container be used to surround the casket to keep the ground from sinking. When we finish, we'll come back here to the conference room. You will notice that in the packet of information that I gave you, you will find a copy of our casket and outer burial container price lists. You may take those with you along with the General Price List. Do you have any questions before we go to the selection room?

Put a photo of the selected casket and vault in the folder the family takes home with them.

After Merchandise Selection

After the family has selected the merchandise they wish to purchase, they will return to the arrangement room with the funeral director. At this time, the director can discuss prayer cards, register books, and flowers, if they were not discussed in the selection room.

Flowers

The director can contact a florist, for the family, concerning the amount the family wishes to spend and the type and design of the floral piece. If the family wishes to contact a florist themselves, the director can suggest that they inform the florist of the color of the casket interior and exterior as well as the color of the clothing the deceased will be wearing. This will allow the florist to suggest flower and ribbon color that will complement the casket and clothing. The director may even recommend colors to the family. The family may also wish to consider the deceased's favorite color and flower when making their decision. Some funeral homes have a flower shop that can design the pieces for a family. In this instance, the director will usually show the family a catalog of flower designs that are available to them.

Prayer Cards and Register Book

Prayer cards or memorial cards and a register book are also selected by most families.

Statement of Goods and Services Selected Form

Once the services and merchandise have been selected, the funeral director records this information on the Statement of Funeral Goods and Services Selected Form This form is required by the Federal Trade Commission and is to be given to the family at the end of the arrangement conference.

Sample "Statement of Funeral Goods and Services" Form

ABC FUNERAL HOME

STATEMENT OF FUNERAL GOODS AND SERVICES SELECTED

Charges are only for those items that you selected or that are required. If we are required by law, or by a cemetery or crematory to use any items, we will explain the reasons in writing below.

Deceased:____

Purchaser: ____

Address: ____

Tel. No. ____

Date of Death ____________________ Date of Arrangements ____________________

Basic Services of Funeral Director and Staff and Overhead .... $________

Embalming .... $________

If you selected a funeral that may require embalming, such as a funeral with viewing, you may have to pay for embalming. You do not have to pay for embalming you did not approve if you selected arrangements such as a direct cremation or immediate burial. If we charge for embalming, we will explain why below.

Other Preparation of the Body

1. Cosmetic Work for Viewing.. $________
2. Washing and Disinfecting Unembalmed Remains .... $________

Transfer of Remains to the Funeral Home.. $________

Use of Facilities and Staff for Viewing .... $________

Use of Facilities and Staff for Funeral Ceremony .... $________

Use of Facilities and Staff for Memorial Service .... $________

Use of Equipment and Staff for Graveside Service .... $________

Hearse .... $________

Limousine .... $________

Casket .... $________

Outer Burial Container .... $________

Forwarding of Remains to Another Funeral Home .... $________

Receiving Remains from Another Funeral Home .... $________

Direct Cremation .... $________

Immediate Burial .... $________

CASH ADVANCE ITEMS

We charge you for our services in obtaining: [specify relevant cash advance items].

Cemetery charges .... $_______
Crematory charges .... $_______
Flowers .... $_______
Obituary notice .... $_______
Death certificate .... $_______
Music .... $_______

Total Cash Advance Items .... **$_______**

TOTAL COST OF ARRANGEMENTS (including all services, merchandise, and cash advance items) .... **$_______**

If any legal, cemetery, or crematory requirement has required the purchase of any of the items listed above, we will explain the requirement below:

____

____

____

Reason for Embalming:

____

____

____

Payment Options

The funeral director should discuss payment options with the family. **Your payment policy should be prominently displayed in your arrangement room.**

- **Immediate Payment** — Payment for the entire funeral is due at the time of the arrangement or by the day of the funeral. Most funeral directors will offer a discount for selecting this option.

- **Insurance Assignment** — Assigning over the amount of the funeral bill from an insurance policy the deceased had. It is necessary for the funeral director to complete the proper paperwork to send to the insurance company, then wait for the insurance company to send a check. Some funeral directors charge a service fee for this option because of the paperwork and waiting time.

- **Credit Card** — Credit card use is becoming more common. People have become so accustomed to using credit cards that this option will continue to increase in use. With this option, the funeral director is charged a percentage of the total by the credit card company as a user fee. It is sometimes necessary for the credit card holder to request an increase in the credit line available on his/her card to a point where the funeral bill will be covered. The funeral bill can be divided among family members and that amount charged to each of their credit cards.

- **Financial Institution Loan** — Some funeral homes have an arrangement with a bank or lending company to issue loans to the families for the payment of the funeral. It is necessary for the institution to do a credit check on the borrower. This check can usually be completed in a day.

- **Wait Until the Estate is Settled** — This used to be the most common method of payment. However, this is no longer the case. The settling of estates has become a sometimes long and legally complicated affair. It is not unusual for a funeral home to wait six months or more for an estate to be settled. If a funeral home does offer this option, an interest charge should be added to the bill. This is the least favorable option for the funeral home.

Why People Selected the Funeral Home

Every funeral director wants to know why people selected his funeral home. The question is important because it allows the director to analyze how effectively his/her money is being spent to generate business. Is it the location, the advertising, or the personal contacts? This information is vital for future planning and budgeting. Ask families why they selected your funeral home. They won't be offended. It's a compliment that they chose you, so asking will only help you do more of what they like about you.

Explanation of What to Expect in the Next Day or Two

Not everyone has had experience with a funeral. It is a good idea to give the family a brief explanation of what will be occurring during the next day or two. <u>The following should be included in this explanation:</u>

- When to arrive for the first viewing.
- What to expect during the public visitation.
- What will be done with flowers that are received.
- Any items or information they need to bring with them.

Amount of Time for Arrangements

Be patient and kind. Our hurry-up society and bottom-line mentality make speedy transactions a fact of life, but a line must be drawn when it comes to arranging and conducting funerals. The recently bereaved need time, attention, and sympathy — not automatic, mechanical responses.

During the arrangement conference, the director can send a strong message to the family that he cares. Caring is the catalyst in all good relationships. The families you like the best and who like you the best are the ones with whom you have established the most caring relationships.

Empathy, patience, and kindness make strong first impressions and set the tone for everything that follows. The time you take translates into care and concern. The funeral you conduct today may be your 10th, but the family you're serving in this moment views it as the most important. Take the time to do it right. Some families, however, may think the conference is too long. Tailor what you do to each family.

Closing the Conference

Todd Van Beck (2017) addresses options to close the arrangement conference. He explains that closing a human interaction, particularly one as potentially sensitive as this, may sound easy, but it is not always. The novice funeral employee may not be adept at letting the client family know that the sales and service conference is coming to an end. He/she may be fearful that they will make the client family feel that they are being pushed out. Both parties in the interview/conference should be aware of the fact that closing is taking place. Keep in mind that during the closing phase of the interview no new material should be introduced or discussed.

The style of closing used will depend on the particulars of the client family and attitude of the funeral professional. Closing remarks such as "I believe we have the information we need to proceed with your wishes; we know how to get in touch with one another should anything else come up, thank you for your trust. We will make certain all your instructions and wishes are taken care of, don't worry about this, we will take care of it," normally will suffice. When we have nothing else to add, the more we say, the less meaningful what we say becomes and the more drawn out the closing is. Ibid.

Van Beck gives the following sample statements that could be used:

- ***"Now that we've decided on the type of services, I'll make the necessary arrangements."***
- ***"If you have further questions please call my private cell phone number at..."***

Occasionally a more explicit summation is required, such as:

- ***"Before you leave, I just want to make sure I understood you correctly."***

A somewhat different approach is to ask the family if they have questions. The following are examples of this approach:

- ***"We've covered quite a bit of information and I'm wondering if there are any areas which I can further explain?"***
- ***"I know this has been such a difficult time, and it hasn't been easy for you, is there any information you would like to review?"***

Finally, Van Beck points out the importance of briefly recapping when definitive decisions and plans have been made. This is a kind of mutual feedback to verify that both parties understand what they are to do.

- ***"Now let's see. You agree to talk to your mother about the lump sum funeral allowance and I will call the crematory."***
- ***"We have completed the arrangements and we've made quite a lot of decisions, so before we end let's quickly review what is going to happen and who is going to do what."***

There should be enough time left for closing so that it is not rushed. With patience, practice, awareness, and reflection, every professional can develop a style that satisfies him/her and facilitates the arrangement interview.

Death Benefits

The funeral director should be familiar with the most common forms of death benefits available to families. She should make it clear that the final decision is made by the agency involved.

For more information on Social Security Benefits, see Chapter 24 Veteran Benefits, Burial at Sea, & Social Security.

NOTES

NOTES

Chapter 4 VISITATION

Permission for use of photograph granted by family.

Visitation/wake/calling hours - *A scheduled time when the deceased is presented for viewing in a casket so that family and friends may come together in an environment of mutual support to pay their last respects to the deceased. In some instances, the deceased is in a closed casket with photos of on display. A visitation is sometimes held with the cremated remains in an urn on display with one or more photos of the deceased.*

As with many aspects of funeral service, the visitation has changed over the years. Visitations used to receive friends and families from 2-5pm and 7-10pm for three days. Now the average visitation is from 2-4pm and 7-9pm, or 4-7pm for one day. In many instances, it is 1 or 2 hours directly before the funeral.

The once, almost national, custom of everyone having an open casket visitation is also changing. Now we are seeing more closed casket visitations. A growing trend is a visitation with no casketed remains present. Instead, an urn or sometimes just a memory table with a photo of the deceased may be present.

A third change that is continuing to become more common is a more personalized setting at the visitation. If a casket is used, it may have a head panel and corners that are reflective of the deceased's life. They may represent a golfer, hunter, or fisherman. A memory table may display mementos of the person's life. This representation of the deceased's life may even be intricate, involving things such as a motorcycle or boat displayed or an entire setting, such as a garden, living room, or workshop.

The continuing trend is for the entire funeral to be more reflective of the deceased's life. Each year there is more dialogue in the professional literature about the funeral director becoming somewhat like an event planner who creates more of a celebration of life, rather than an acknowledgement of a death. This concept is receiving mixed reviews from funeral directors, but has wide support, especially by younger people. In many cases, the concept of personalized funerals has contributed to a change in the dynamics of the visitation. Photo boards and tribute videos are not enough for some families. These families wish to include objects, music, and unique ceremonies during the visitation.

There are some religious and fraternal organizations who will hold a ceremony during the visitation if the family gives approval. Usually when a firefighter or police officer dies, there is an honor guard with an officer at the head and another at the foot of the casket. There is an increasing trend to end all services at the funeral home at the end of the visitation.

For more information and ideas on personalized visitation, see Chapter 9 Personalization.

Explaining Visitation

Alan Wolfelt (2014) suggests that families should be educated about each aspect of the funeral, so that they understand its value. In regard to the visitation/wake, he suggests that to help families make choices, you must first educate them about those choices. Instead of asking, "Would you like to have a visitation?" you might say:

> *"The first part of the funeral experience is often the visitation. It's a time for friends and family to gather before the funeral itself and have a chance to greet one another and talk before the more structured ceremony begins. If the body is present at the visitation, this time also really helps everyone acknowledge the reality of the death and gives them a chance to start on the pathway to goodbye."*

Wolfelt further explains, "We can make the visitation personalized by playing favorite music in the background and by helping you put together a display of photos, a video, and/or a memorabilia table."

The more information families are given about each of the elements of the ceremony, the more their decisions become true choices. As you bring up each element of the funeral, you first educate about the purpose of that element, how the element fits into the whole funeral experience, and some way to personalize that element. Then and only then is the family equipped to make an informed choice about whether or not to include that element in the unique funeral they are planning.

Pre-Visitation

There are specific tasks that must be completed before a visitation. The deceased must be transferred to the funeral home and embalmed. A funeral director will have to make arrangements with the deceased's family. If not obtained during the transfer, clothing will need to be brought in by the family or purchased from the funeral home. Aside from these tasks involving the deceased and bereaved family, there are numerous functional details that the funeral home staff must attend to.

Upon arrival for work, a "calling hours" attendant should check:

- The appearance of the deceased. If cosmetics are needed, notify the proper person.
- Air conditioning or heat.
- Music system.
- All entrances are clean and clear of snow, during winter.
- The flowers that have been delivered and placed in the correct room.
- Register book pages are complete.
- Prayer cards are displayed.
- Restrooms are clean and have sufficient supplies.

Flowers

Permission for use of photograph granted by family.

Arrange and display any flowers that have been delivered for the deceased. There is more to displaying flowers than placing them on a stand or table. The immediate concern is to ensure that the flowers are placed in the correct room and the closest family members' arrangements are placed on or nearest the casket. A typical display of family flower pieces would include a spray from the spouse on top of the closed foot end or centered behind the open cover on a full couch casket. In addition, a basket or spray from the children would be placed at the head end, a basket or spray from siblings at the foot end, and a flower heart from grandchildren inside. Some Catholic families also have a flower rosary placed inside the casket.

The next consideration is that the flower arrangements are displayed so that the colors of the flowers and ribbons complement each other. There are short and tall flower stands available so creative displays can be designed by alternating the height of the stands.

Each arrangement will have an address card with the name of the deceased and the florist. There will also be another small card with the name of the person sending the flowers. It is a good procedure to retain the address card inconspicuously in the back of the arrangement. If there is more than one visitation going on, it is possible a flower piece could be placed in the wrong room. Having saved the address card can help locate a missing arrangement.

It is becoming more common for people to send smaller tabletop arrangements, fresh-cut flowers in a vase, or plants. People send these types in hopes the family will take the arrangements home with them.

An Embarrassing Moment

You must be careful when carrying flowers. If bumped, certain flowers can lose petals or may break. Also, be careful when placing the arrangements on a flower stand. This author was once arranging flowers and decided to raise one of the flower stands. I had already placed the flower arrangement on it. I was in a hurry and did not remove the basket of flowers from the stand. I knelt on the floor to loosen the locking mechanism and raised the stand. The basket fell off the stand right onto my head. There I was kneeling, on the floor with the basket on my head, flowers covering my face, and water running down me. Some days it does not pay to get up in the morning!

Meaning Behind Flowers

In her article, "Making the Most of Your Funeral Flowers," Jenny Goldade (2017) explains that there are meanings behind certain flowers, and that these meanings can help represent the feelings of the giver or the personality of the deceased.

- **Carnations**: Admiration, remembrance, or love
- **Chrysanthemums**: Positivity and truth
- **Gladiolus**: Strength and sincerity
- **Hydrangea**: Sincerity and understanding
- **Lilies**: Innocence
- **Orchids**: Sympathy
- **Roses**: Love or reverence
- **Tulips**: Renewal and hope.

Additionally, Goldade explains that certain colors also have specific implied meaning, including:

- **Red**: Strength and love
- **Orange**: Enthusiasm and warmth
- **Yellow**: Friendship and new beginnings
- **Green**: Nature and renewal
- **Blue**: Sadness and peace
- **Purple**: Respect and admiration
- **Pink**: Grace and innocence
- **White**: Elegance and reverence

Register Book

Source: https://cdn.funeralwise.com/wp-content/uploads/2018/01/19162655/iStock-513422131-400x250.jpg

At most visitations, people are asked to sign their names in a register book. This book will also contain information about the deceased and the services. These pages will need to be completed before the book is placed on the register stand. There are pages to list pallbearers, people attending, and those who sent flowers or memorial donations. Throughout the visitation, the book should be checked periodically to ensure there are enough empty pages for visitors to sign.

The latest entry into the Register Book market is the digital register book. These have received mixed reviews.

Prayer Cards

A prayer card is a card with the name, a picture of the deceased (sometimes), service information, a prayer or verse on one side, and a photo on the other side. Before putting the prayer cards on display, check to ensure that the information printed on the cards is correct. Place the cards on the register stand or nearby table. Cards may also be secular and non-religious.

Example of a Prayer Card

In Loving Memory of

Joan Carol Coventry

November 8, 1942 ~ December 1, 2017

In Loving Memory of

Joan Carol Coventry

Born November 8, 1942
Died December 1, 2017

Funeral Service
Amherst Chapel
December 5, 2017 at 10:00 AM
Officiating
Pastor Randy Milleville

I'd like the memory of me to be a happy one. I'd like to leave an afterglow of smiles when life is done. I'd like to leave an echo whispering softly down the ways, of happy times and laughing times and bright and sunny days. I'd like the tears of those who grieve, to dry before the sun of happy memories that I leave when day is done.

Amigone Funeral Home, Inc.

Donation Envelope

If a charity has been listed in place of sending flowers, donation envelopes must be available and displayed.

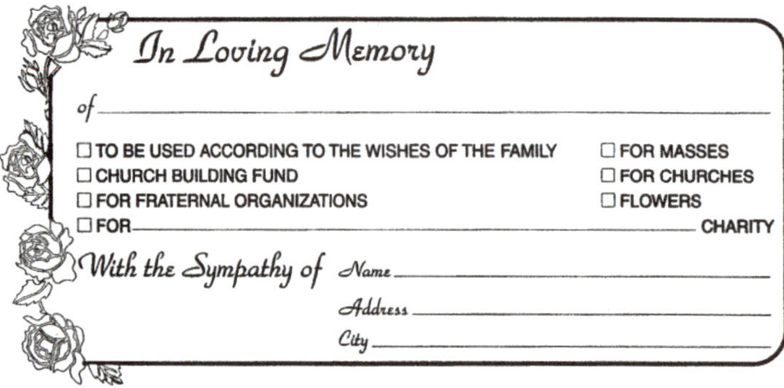
In Loving Memory

of

☐ TO BE USED ACCORDING TO THE WISHES OF THE FAMILY ☐ FOR MASSES
☐ CHURCH BUILDING FUND ☐ FOR CHURCHES
☐ FOR FRATERNAL ORGANIZATIONS ☐ FLOWERS
☐ FOR ________ CHARITY

With the Sympathy of Name
Address
City

Mass Card

The Catholic Church has Mass cards. A Mass card is a donation envelope that can be used to collect money to have a mass said for the deceased.

Newspaper Notices

The newspaper death notice and/or obituary should be checked to ensure accurate spelling of names, and that the date, time, and location of the visitation, funeral, and committal service are correct. It is a nice gesture to enlarge and laminate copies of the notice and place them on tables around the visitation room.

Sign Board

Many funeral homes use a signboard with the name of the deceased and the time and date of the service. This sign should be made up before the visitation begins and placed in a location where guests at the visitation can see it. The digital sign board is the newest type of this product. The digital sign board should be programmed correctly before the visitation.

Traditional Sign Board

Digital Sign Board

Permission for use of photographs granted by family.
Source: Buszka Funeral Home

Source: Amigone Funeral Home

Music

If the funeral home uses background music, it should be playing with the loudness adjusted to the preferred level before the visitation begins. Families may bring in their own music to be played.

Music has a way of surpassing our need for words at times. Songs say so much to us. They help us remember the person we love, using a medium of music to bring back visual memories of happier days in the past. Traditionally the music played during visitation has been pre-orchestrated and packaged for funeral homes. In order to use these recordings, the law requires that you pay a music fee. Most funeral associations have the system for you to pay the fee through them.

More families are now requesting music that was meaningful to the deceased. It may be jazz, contemporary, or even rock. This adaptation is a positive move in making a funeral more personal and memorable.

Tribute Videos

Permission for use of photograph granted by family.

Most funeral homes now offer the production of a tribute video to be played during visitation and/or at the funeral service. The family gives meaningful photos, and sometimes even video footage, to the funeral director. The director then either has the video made in house by the funeral home staff or sends them out to a company that puts them in a video format with accompanying music. If the family is using a tribute video during the visitation, it must be set up in the room prior to the family's arrival.

The author predicts that in the future, the video will be displayed on an entire wall, instead of on a television. Photos will also be displayed in this manner, instead of on picture boards.

Memory Tables

Some funeral homes have a small table available for the family to display meaningful memorabilia representative of the deceased's life, including photos, trophies, awards, or service medals. In the case of cremation, the urn containing the cremains may be on the memory table as well. Sometimes it is called a "Table of Honor."

Source: Batesville Casket Co.

Picture Boards

Almost all funeral homes offer the use of picture boards. These attractive boards display pictures selected by the family. They are placed in the visitation room in a conspicuous location. Often the family will take the board home with them after the arrangement conference. They fill it with photos and display it during visitation when it is placed on an easel. It has been suggested that the process of selecting photos can be therapeutic for the family.

Visitors before Family Arrive

Occasionally a person may enter wishing to pay respects before the family arrives. Some firms will allow this if a deceased person is casketed and in the proper viewing room. There may have been a misunderstanding about calling hours. Tell the person that the family has not yet arrived and ask that they sign the register book on the second page. Permitting them to view the remains can be a touchy subject. The family should be asked ahead of time how they want this situation to be handled.

First Viewing

The first viewing of the deceased by the family is perhaps the most emotionally charged part of the entire funeral process. In some instances, this will be the first time that members of the family see the person dead. They do not know what to expect and are often frightened and anxious. For these reasons, the first viewing should be a private affair. The family should have at least an hour to be alone with the deceased before the public arrives. The funeral director should be prepared for any type of reaction from the family. Intense crying, sobbing, and emotional outbursts can all be expected.

Permission to use photograph granted by family.

A staff member should be visible when the family arrives for their first viewing. Being immediately visible when mourners arrive can lessen the fear and anxiety some people may be experiencing.

As the family enters the funeral home, the staff member should walk up to them, introduce himself, and express sympathy if he has not already met them. If he has met the family earlier or knows them personally, he should greet them with a warm and sincere greeting and inquire as to how they are doing. Assist with the removal of any coats being worn and then hang them in the appropriate place.

If you think there are other family members that have yet to arrive, ask a question such as, "Will you be waiting for anyone else before you go in to see your mother?" You may want to make a comment such as, "Your mom looks very nice and the flowers you ordered are perfect." Some people may feel that saying that the deceased looks nice is inappropriate, because the person is dead. The author's experience, however, has found that families appreciate the gesture.

There are several ways to approach the family's entrance into the room. Two effective approaches are:

1. Lead the family into the room and proceed right up to the casket in as natural a manner as possible. Then step back and indicate that they may come forward. Though you should step back from the group, do not leave the room immediately — first, because your assistance might be needed if someone has questions or becomes emotionally overwrought; and secondly, listen for comments on the appearance of the deceased, casket, or flowers.

2. Escort the family into the room about half-way to the casket, and then stay in the background as they approach the casket. Listen for comments you may need to ask about or act on. Wait until reactions have calmed and then approach the family with a question such as, "How is everything?"

Usually the family will make positive comments such as, "She looks wonderful" or "He looks at peace and is not suffering anymore." When a family makes such statements, it means that the viewing is going to be beneficial and therapeutic for them.

There are times, however, when the family will comment about something that is just not right to them, "His hair was parted differently," or "Maybe she should have her glasses on." You should offer to make any needed adjustments. If the adjustment is minor, ask the family if they would like to stay in the room while you proceed or if they would like to go to a different room. If the adjustment is major and involves moving the deceased or reapplying cosmetics, ask the family to step out of the room until you are finished.

After the initial shock has subsided, you may want to bring a prayer card over to the family or point out a signature in the register book of someone who may have arrived to pay respects before the family arrived. The arranging director should have checked with the family during the arrangement conference to clarify how to handle early visitors. It is important to clarify if the family wants to be the first to see the deceased. If this is the case, you would explain the family's wishes to any early visitors and at least let the visitor sign the register book.

If the funeral home supplied or ordered the flowers, ask the family if they are satisfied with them. It is helpful to remind the family about the need for pallbearers, and that it will be necessary that they get together with you sometime before the funeral to write up a car list (if the funeral home uses such a list).

If the family brings in the photo boards or materials for a memory table, help them arrange the display. Restate to the family that you are there to help them during the time they are present and that you or another staff member will be nearby.

Children's First Visit

The following suggestions can be passed on to a family with children:

In the "good old olden days" when funerals were held in the home, there was no discussion whether children would attend the funeral. For a short period of time they lived the funeral. Over the years, children have become less involved with the dying process and the funeral activities. Many parents want to protect their children from the pain of losing someone.

Today, the feelings about children's participation have evolved. It is now recommended that parents should talk with their children about death, see what they already believe, and correct any misinformation. Parents should explain what a funeral is, what the child could expect if they attended the visitation or funeral, then allow the child to decide if they want to attend. Encourage, but never force a child to attend.

The parents should go into the room for their first viewing before children enter the room. This is important because children can become frightened or upset if they see their parents expressing intense, emotional outbursts. When the parents are over their initial shock, they should bring the children into the room. One of the parents should hold the children's hands and walk slowly up to the casket with them. The children should be asked if they would like to move closer or touch the deceased. If they say "no," never force them. If they say "yes," the adult should go with them and even hold their hands as they touch the deceased. Any questions should be answered in age-appropriate language or by enlisting the funeral director for help.

Experience has shown that it is best to bring a child when there are not many people visiting, such as before the scheduled visitation hours. This allows for a closer and more intimate sharing with the child. A common question that many young children have when seeing the deceased in a half open casket is, "Does he have legs?" You may open the float end of the casket to show the children the legs.

One story this author once heard involves a family explaining to a child how the "body" would be lying in a casket. The child did not want to go see the deceased at the funeral home. When asked why, the child said he did not want to see grandpa "without a head." The child had taken the parents description of "the body" literally. This story shows the importance of clearly explaining to the child what they will see and doing so in terms the child will understand.

Public Visitation

After the family has had their private viewing together, the visitation is then opened to the public. The times that the family will be present to receive friends are given in the death notice or obituary. The most common hours for families to be present are sometime between the hours of 2:00 p.m. and 8:00 p.m., one or two days before the funeral. Some families choose a shortened visitation of one or two hours just prior to the funeral service.

One of the details that must be considered during the public visitation is the location of the staff member who is working the visitation. The attendant should be in an area where he can see people entering and where visitors can easily see him.

Many funeral homes have the staff member stand at the main entrance, opening the door for those arriving. If possible, visitors should be assisted with their coats. If there is more than one visitation in the funeral home, ask the visitors which family they are visiting. If there is only one family, you can ask, "Are you here for Mrs. Jones?" Once you know who they are visiting, the ideal way of directing them is to walk them to the visitation room. If this is not possible, use a hand gesture (never finger pointing) to point the correct direction, and say something such as, "Mrs. Jones is in the Rose Room, it's first door on your right."

The person working the visitation usually has more responsibilities than just greeting visitors. If possible, the visitation attendant should be in a visible position where they can observe as many entrances as possible. This attendant should not be found sitting in an office. The attendant must be on top of what is happening in the building. They must be easily identifiable by anyone who has a question.

The attendant should not be seen talking on their cell phone or smell of smoke from smoking. A funeral home name tag gives a more professional appearance. The attendant should occasionally walk through the visitation room, walk to the casket, and give a quick check of the deceased and flowers. They do not need to speak to the family during these visits but can reassure the family by their presence. If there are no guests at a particular time during the calling hours, it is a nice gesture for the attendant to talk with those who are there.

The visitation (calling hours) attendant is an important position. In many instances they are the only funeral home staff member that the family and visitors will see during the calling hours. They must make a good, professional, caring first impression. The following suggestions can positively impact that first impression.

The attendant should:

- Be properly groomed.
- Be wearing proper professional clothing.
- Be wearing a name tag, in order to be readily recognizable.
- Be positioned to open the door for guests or to be able to see all or most of the entrances.
- Guide or direct guests to the correct room, but never point.
- Help people take off and put on their coats.
- Provide help or assistance whenever needed or requested.

Mass Cards or Memorial Donation Envelopes

You may be asked for a Mass Card, a preprinted envelope used by Catholics to request a mass to be said for the deceased, or for a memorial donation envelope, supplied by the family's charity of choice. Give the person the correct envelope and ask if he or she would like to use an empty office, room, or convenient desk to fill it out. Because the donor places money in these envelopes, suggest that the envelope be given directly to the family or put in the cardholder.

It is not uncommon to have a visitor ask a staff member to give the envelope to the family. If you accept the responsibility, do it immediately. A distraction could result in the donation envelope being put in a pocket and forgotten about. This author once forgot and had an envelope in an inside suit coat pocket for two days until the family called and said, "Mrs. Smith said she gave you an envelope for us, but we do not have it." The family should also be encouraged to either take any envelopes home with them or at least take the money out when they leave. There have been instances when these cards have been stolen.

Music

If the family brings in special music for you to play over a music system, try to fulfill their request. The music can add to the personalization of the visitation and can be comforting to them. To do this, it is necessary to have a music system with speakers that can be adjusted so a family in another visitation room won't be disturbed by the requested music. A portable sound system can also be used directly in the room.

Flowers

Throughout the visitation, you will bring any flowers that have been delivered for the deceased into the room. At the end of the evening, before the funeral, you can suggest that the family take home any table vases or arrangements of flowers they wish to keep. This will help avoid extra work or responsibility for the family to be concerned about during the funeral services.

When you talk about the flowers, it is usual for the family to ask what is going to happen to all the flowers after the funeral. They may inquire if there is some place you could take them, such as a nursing home or church. In some areas, nursing homes and churches enjoy receiving such flowers. In other areas, they do not want them. Explain the local customs and funeral home's policy about delivery of flowers to the family.

Car List

If the funeral home uses a written car list (a list stating how cars should be arranged in the cortege) on the day of the funeral, it will be necessary to ask the family to create a list. Preferably, you may want to sit down with a member of the family and create the list with them. Again, local custom and funeral home policy will determine how extensive the list will be. Some directors just list the immediate family, others list everyone who attends, and others do not use a list at all. If a car list is used, it is helpful to put the make and color of each car with the names of those riding in it. This allows the staff member arranging the cars in the parking lot on the day of the funeral to be more personal when approaching a car. Instead of asking the driver his or her name, the staff member can ask, "Mrs. Smith?" People like to be recognized.

Clergy Attendance

In many areas, it is a practice for the clergy officiating at the funeral service to visit the family at the funeral home during visitation. Some visit with the family and leave quickly. Others stay and talk with the family about issues surrounding the funeral service.

If a prayer service is scheduled, escort the clergy to a private room to prepare. If the family and clergy have not met, make introductions before the service. When the clergy is ready, either make an announcement or go around to people and inform them that the service will be starting soon. Escort the clergy to the room and introduce him to the group if needed. If the clergy needs assistance in any way, provide it.

If both the clergy card and the honorarium check are completed, they can be given to the clergy at this time.

A staff member should stand in a position outside the room during the service to notify any visitors entering that a service is in progress.

End of Evening Prayer

In some places, it is customary for Catholic families to have a short prayer said before leaving the funeral home for the night. The prayer can differ with each funeral home. An "Our Father" and "Hail Mary" are common. The funeral home staff member usually leads the prayer if there is no clergy person in the room.

About ten minutes before the closing of visitation time, ask the family if they would like the prayer said before leaving. Assure them they do not have to leave exactly at the time stated in the death notice unless that is funeral home policy. A general announcement can be made asking visitors to join with the family in a prayer before they leave.

The use of this prayer with Catholic families is a convenient way to direct the family towards leaving at the appropriate time. Funeral homes differ in their policy for leaving. Some funeral homes never mention the time to the family; they are allowed to leave whenever they want to leave. Other funeral homes may make an announcement or notify the family quietly that it is time for the visitation to end.

Before the Family Leaves

- If the casket is to be moved to another room for the funeral, advise the family that this will happen before they leave so they are not surprised the morning of the funeral.

- The night before the funeral, verify any instructions the family has regarding what is to be left in the casket and what is to be removed when the casket is closed at the funeral. Most legal advisors suggest getting these instructions in writing with a signature. It is easy to make up a special form for this. This written form will help if after the burial or cremation someone says that you were supposed to remove an item. The lead director is responsible for this. A common practice is to tape the list to the lid of the casket. This author once said to another director, "Did you do what is on the list?" He said he did but he did not. As a result, a ring was buried.

When the Family Leaves

- Assist them with their coats, if appropriate.
- Help them carry out any flower arrangements.
- If the funeral is the next day, briefly summarize the important details for them, such as when to arrive at the funeral home and what the procedures will be.
- It is a nice gesture to escort the family to their cars.
- Another sensitive gesture is not to turn off the parking lot lights until everyone has left the lot.
- Outside ashtrays need to be emptied in a fire safe container.
- Alarms should be set if used.
- The telephone answering service must be notified or the call forwarding on the phone turned on.
- Lights are turned off and doors must be locked.

Preparations for the Funeral

If the funeral is the next day, many funeral homes prepare for it after the family leaves. Funeral homes around the country differ in the construction style of their buildings. In the western and southern United States, often formal chapels are constructed in the funeral home. These chapels consist of altars, pews, and religious paraphernalia. Some funeral homes hold the visitation and funeral service in these chapels. In this case, preparations are easy, possibly just involving the removal of flower tags.

Other funeral homes hold the visitation in a separate room and move the deceased to the chapel for the funeral service. In this instance, the work involves moving the casket and flowers to the chapel.

If the funeral home does not have a formal chapel, the visitation room is usually used for the funeral service.

In this case, enough chairs have to be set up (usually in rows) to accommodate the people who attend the funeral. When in doubt about the number of chairs needed, always err on the high side. The late Daniel Amigone, Sr. said, "You can always sit 40 people on 80 chairs, but you can't sit 80 people on 40 chairs."

Source: Amigone Funeral Home

Improving the Visitation

According to Todd Van Beck (2017), there are several actions that can improve a visitation, including:

- Have soda or bottled water available.
- Encourage the use of the family's music.
- Ensure sufficient staff for large visitation.
- Have the arranging director at the first viewing.
- Display any family heirlooms or hobby items.
- Have flexibility in visitation hours for the convenience of the families, not the funeral home.
- Have a candle from the funeral home lit at visitation.
- Greet visitors at the door, offer to take their coats, take them to the visitation room, lead them to the register, and give them a memorial folder.
- See to it that one of the principal funeral directors is hosting the visitation during the most visible time. This allows more exposure to the public for key personnel.
- Have a parking attendant direct parking for large visitations.
- Play tribute video during visitation.
- Staff should always be visible and identifiable with a name tag.

Viewing without Embalming

A funeral home is occasionally confronted with a request for either a private or public viewing without embalming. Each funeral home has its own policies — some will allow it, others will not, and some restrict it to just a private viewing.

Viewing Without Embalming

Excerpt From: Melissa Johnson Williams (2005)

"How do we proceed when a family requests a viewing without embalming? It is my personal belief that prior to making any arrangements (with or without viewing), the remains should be in-house and viewed by an active embalmer, not just someone with an embalmer's license. This person understands the process of preparing remains for viewing and will be able to determine what is possible. There always needs to be communication between the funeral director making the arrangements and the embalmer. This is one of those things that just seems to be a given but is routinely forgotten or ignored in many funeral homes. If the decision is made to make the arrangements with the family without the benefit of the remains being in-house, then the family should be told that a final decision will have to be made once the remains arrive at the funeral home.

When a family makes a request for viewing without embalming the funeral director should attempt to find out what the family's reasoning is for this request. This should not be an attempt to change the family's mind. The funeral director needs to understand what the family's expectations are. The family must be told in honest and understandable language what is involved in this process and what, if any, charges they will incur. This may also mean that the funeral director has to tell the family that what they want is not possible.

A consent form should be signed by the family for whatever is going to be done (or not done). This form may have to be tailored specifically to each individual situation. Since the public, in general, doesn't know what embalming does or does not do, a disclaimer should also be given to the family about any potential problems with the viewing. These problems include seeing purging or skin slip in a body that has significant trauma.

The funeral home should also decide how to handle the charges for this service. If the funeral home is seeing an increase for this type of service, they should consider putting this specific item on the General Price List. The category of "Other Preparation of the Body" may not cover the charges that need to be made for this service. There may need to be separate categories based on the type of viewing that is going to take place.

If the family desires viewing for only a few minutes prior to burial or cremation, then seeing the facial area will be sufficient. The face and hair should be washed, the mouth and eyes closed, and the hair combed. Prior to viewing, the family should be told what they will see, that the body will be wrapped in a sheet on a dressing table or in a casket, and that the viewing will take place in the preparation or viewing room. If this viewing is for identification purposes, then a form should be signed at the conclusion of the viewing.

When the family wants a full-scale viewing for family and friends, then all the same components of the embalming process will be needed, except the injection process. Aspiration of the abdomen and thorax (without cavity treatment) will probably be necessary, and this should be explained to the family. Also, the funeral home should wash and disinfect the entire body, close the mouth and eyes, build features if necessary and desired by the family, as well as apply cosmetics and fix hair. Prior to clothing the body, a unionall (or minimally, plastic pants or coveralls) should be used. All of this should be accomplished as close to the time of viewing as possible to reduce the possibility of negative changes taking place while the remains are lying "in state."

NOTES

NOTES

Chapter 5 THE FUNERAL

Permission for use of photographs granted by family.
Source: Buszka Funeral Home

Funeral *- A general term that encompasses the ceremonies and rites held to acknowledge and honor the life of a deceased individual.*

On the day of the funeral, there are numerous details that must be coordinated. Each funeral home operates in its own way; a way that has developed because of differences from one region of the country to another. These differences can also be a result of religious requirements and the personal style of the funeral director.

It is necessary for the funeral home staff to arrive at the funeral home before the family arrives to prepare for the funeral. The average time needed will be approximately one to two hours. During this time, the funeral director should first and foremost check the appearance of the deceased and make any adjustments, such as re-cosmetization, if necessary. She should then check the building for cleanliness. The temperature should be set at a comfortable setting. The entrances should be swept clean, and during the winter, snow should be shoveled. During the winter it may be necessary to have the entire parking lot plowed. If it is raining, umbrellas should be available.

The room to be used for the service should be properly prepared if this has not already been done. If a formal chapel is being used, it will not be necessary to set up chairs. If the room for the service does not have pews, enough chairs must be set up and arranged to accommodate everyone attending the service. There should be a podium and microphone if a speaker is addressing the guests.

Car List

If the guests are going from the funeral home to a church or cemetery in a procession, the cars are usually arranged in numerical order with those closest to the deceased in the front of the cortege. The funeral director must have a plan for how the automobiles will be arranged at the funeral home to facilitate an easy and organized exit. It is common for the funeral director to create a car list in conjunction with the family's wishes. One or more staff members must be in the parking lot to arrange the cars according to the car list.

One or more staff members should have a copy of the car list. As a car arrives, this person will ask the driver if he will be part of the procession. The driver will be directed to the proper parking space. Some funeral homes have a staff member park the car for the guest. Whenever possible, car doors should be opened for the guest. On a rainy day, escort the guest under an umbrella from the car to the funeral home.

Do not mention the numerical order that the car is in the cortege. Some people get offended and belligerent if they are not closer to the family than they are.

FUNERAL CAR LIST
Funeral of

____

Date: ______________________

F/H Time: ____ **Church Time** ____

Clergy: ______________________

Cemetery: ______________________

Bearers

____
____
____
____
____
____

Special Instructions

____
____
____

	LICENSE OR MAKE	DRIVER
CAR 1		
	LICENSE OR MAKE	DRIVER
CAR 2		
	LICENSE OR MAKE	DRIVER
CAR 3		
	LICENSE OR MAKE	DRIVER
CAR 4		

Pallbearers

On the day of the funeral, the director should allow five to ten minutes to gather the pallbearers together and give them instructions. The funeral will run more smoothly if the pallbearers are familiar with what is expected of them. There are generally three locations and times that the pallbearers are used. The director may choose to use them in any or in all the locations:

1. From the funeral home into the hearse.
2. From the hearse into the church and from the church back into the hearse.
3. From the hearse to the grave.

Sample Pallbearer Instructions for Each Location:

- **At the Funeral Home**

  "You will be sitting in an area reserved for you. When everyone except the immediate family has left the room, you will file past the casket and walk into the hallway. After the family has left and the casket is closed, we will bring the casket to you. As a group, you will lift the casket and carry it into the hearse."

- **At the Church**

  "When we arrive at the church, please exit your cars and walk to the back of the hearse. We will open the door, lift the casket from the hearse, and carry it into the rear of the church. We will then place the casket onto a moveable device known as a church truck. We will roll the casket to the front of the church. I will seat you in pews that are reserved for you. When the service is over, you will come up to the casket and we will roll it to the door of the church. We will lift the casket off the church truck and carry it to the hearse."

- **At the Cemetery**

  "When you arrive at the cemetery, exit your cars and walk to the rear of the hearse. We will remove the casket and carry it to the grave. When we reach the grave, we will place the casket on a device that is located over the grave. I will then have you stand together across from the family."

Clergy or Celebrant

If a member of the clergy or a celebrant is going to be officiating the service in the funeral home, there should be a private room available where she can gather her thoughts, talk with the family, and change into vestments. A special space in the procession should be reserved for her. If possible, when the celebrant or clergy arrives, a staff member should park her car and escort her into the funeral home.

A clergy or celebrant card, which contains information about the deceased, should have been completed by the funeral home and given to the clergy person when she arrives. This would also be a proper time to give the celebrant or clergy person her honorarium if it hasn't already been given to her.

Sample Clergy Card/Record

CLERGY
RECORD

Deceased__________
Address__________
____
Family Telephone__________
Religion__________
Church Affiliation__________
Marital Status__________
Age__________
Date of Birth__________
Place of Birth__________
Date of Death__________
Place of Death__________
Date of Funeral__________
Time of Funeral__________
Place of Funeral__________
Interment__________
Clergy__________

SURVIVORS LIST AND NOTES

Funeral Home Religious Service

With many Protestant families, the religious service is held at the funeral home instead of the church. Catholic funeral mass, however, is always in the church.

The clergy or celebrant should be escorted into a private room or office to prepare for the service. He/she may wish to meet the family if that has not yet occurred. At the start of the service, the funeral director should escort the officiant into the room and introduce her to the people assembled for the funeral. Each officiant has their own method of proceeding. Some may include music, which must be coordinated with the funeral director. Others do not use music. It is a nice gesture, a few moments before the start of the service, to inform the next of kin about how things will proceed.

An example of how to do this is as follows:

> *"Mrs. Smith, we will begin the service in just a few minutes. I will escort Reverend Andrews into the room and introduce him to everyone and leave, but I will be right outside the door. After his remarks, I will re-enter the room, thank Reverend Andrews and invite other guests, starting with the last row to come up to the casket to pay their last respects to Bill, then have them proceed to their cars. After everyone else has left the room, you will have the privacy to say your goodbyes. When you have finished, I will escort you to your cars and we will proceed in procession to the cemetery. Is there anything you need or would like me to get you before we start?"*

After the service is concluded the funeral director will inform the guests that they can proceed to the casket as directed to pay their final respects and then proceed to their cars. The immediate family is usually the last to approach the casket. They should be escorted to their cars when they are ready to leave.

Music

Many funeral directors will ask the family if they would like one or more songs played at the funeral home during the service. One song is generally played before the officiant starts and one after his/her comments.

Parting Ceremony

If a member of the clergy or celebrant is not in attendance before the funeral leaves for the church, some funeral directors conduct a short service themselves. This can include music, a prayer, and the paying of final respects from those in attendance. The funeral director might play a hymn, then ask everyone to join her in saying a prayer. After the prayer, she will have the guests file past the casket and then walk to their cars. After all guests have left, the funeral director should approach the family and indicate it is time for them to go to the casket. Allow them privacy but stay in the background in case help is needed. Usually the immediate family leaves last so they can have privacy in saying their last goodbye. When the family is ready, the funeral director should escort them to their cars.

Casket Closing

Most families do not stay for the closing of the casket. This is usually done by the funeral director after the family has left the funeral home. If the family has requested to watch the closing, their request should be honored. If anything of value is to be left in the casket, it is a good idea for the funeral director to ask the family to designate someone to watch the closing and stay with the casket until it is placed into the hearse. This avoids any question by the family as to whether the object was really buried with the deceased.

The family should always be asked what should be removed or remain in the casket. Have the family sign a receipt for objects taken out, or a hold-harmless agreement for objects left in the casket. It is not unusual for families to leave photos, poems, letters, blankets, or personal mementos in the casket.

The deceased usually must be lowered somewhat in the casket before the casket is closed. This can be accomplished by using the raise/lower device included in caskets with a spring mattress. In caskets that do not have this device, usually the mattress bed is pushed lower. The material that lies over the edge of the casket during viewing (the extend-over) is arranged on the interior, and the top of the casket is lowered. If the casket has a locking mechanism, it is locked closed. Before the casket is taken to the hearse, it should be dusted off, and any fingerprints or marks left by the flowers should be removed.

Moving the Casket to the Funeral Coach

Funeral directors differ on the process of moving the casket to the funeral coach. Some directors do not use pallbearers but load the coach in a private setting. Others have the pallbearers remain in the funeral home instead of returning to their cars with the rest of the guests. The pallbearers are positioned on each side of the casket and instructed to either move the casket on the brier or to lift the casket off the brier and proceed to the coach. The cortege is then arranged.

A **typical cortege** would be arranged as follows:

1. Funeral home lead car with clergy.
2. Officiating Clergy, if she is driving her own car.
3. Pallbearers if they are driving together.
4. Hearse.
5. Closest family member's car. Often this is a limousine supplied by the funeral home.
6. Cars as designated by the family.

If honorary pallbearers or a special group is attending, they usually go between the lead car and the coach (hearse).

Church Service

The procession leaves the funeral home and proceeds to the church if a service is part of the funeral. When the cortege arrives at the church, the cars must be parked in such a way as to ensure an easy and safe departure when the service is over. Some funeral homes place "No Parking" signs in front of the church.

The funeral director leads the processional into church, followed by the pallbearers carrying the casket. The family follows the casket into church. The casket is moved into church feet first symbolizing the position of the person facing the Alter. Generally, the casket is placed parallel to the Alter with the head end to the left. When leaving the church, the casket is again positioned headfirst. In some churches, the clergy will meet the processional in the back of the church; others will wait at the Altar for the processional.

The casket is positioned at the front of the church in accordance with custom. If a pall is used to cover the casket, it is put in place if it has not already been done. Everyone is seated, and the funeral director walks to the back of the church, leaving the officiating clergy to take charge. Some funeral directors will stay in the nave of the church for the service; others will stand in the narthex; still others will go for coffee.

This author once had a surprise at a funeral service. The lead funeral director took the funeral staff for coffee once the service began. When we returned, we opened the church door to find all the attendees and the casket coming down the church aisle. The service was shorter than expected.

At the completion of the service, the funeral director walks to the front of the church and removes the pall. The casket may have to be turned into position before the recessional begins. He repositions the pallbearers and the recessional will leave the church in the same order it entered.

Author's Note: Although there is talk about the lessening of religious affiliation, it must be noted that a religious service at the funeral home, a church, or other religious facility is still an important part of the post-death activities for most families.

Committal Service

After the casket is returned to the hearse and all the guests are in their cars, the procession safely moves to the cemetery. At the cemetery, the cemetery attendant will usually indicate to the funeral director if the casket should be placed on the grave head first or feet first. The processional walks to the grave in the same order it walked into church. The officiating clergy performs prayers and rituals for committal. When he is finished, he then turns the funeral over to the director. The director may make a specific announcement to the group that the services have ended, or he will indicate that they have ended by assisting the family back to their car. The director may thank everyone for attending and make any announcements the family has directed him to make.

Some funeral directors use a short ceremony to end the funeral. Frequently used ceremonies include having pallbearers place a flower or their gloves (if used) on the casket. The family may also be given a flower or some sand to place on the casket as a parting gesture.

If the funeral home has sold the vault, the director may want to show the vault cover to the family and give a brief explanation of the procedure for sealing the vault. Someone from the funeral home should stay at the cemetery until the vault cover has been placed on the vault.

NOTES

Chapter 6 PROCESSION

Source: https://www.thestar.com/autos/2015/05/08/no-red-light-exemption-for-processions.html

> ***Procession*** *- Also called the cortege, is a symbol of mutual support and public honoring of the death. Mourners accompany one another to the final resting place of the person who died. Often, even strangers take pause and are respectful because they know someone in the family has died* (Batesville, n.d.).

All employees who participate in processions should be aware of the traffic laws regarding funeral processions.

History of Procession

Rohling (2012) outlines the history of procession. He explains that in the early history of American funeral service, the deceased would be transported to the cemetery in a horse drawn conveyance of sorts (buckboard or perhaps a hearse), while family and friends walked behind. Somewhat later, everyone rode to the cemetery in automobiles, while the traffic pulled over to the side of the road. Oftentimes, people would get out of their cars and remove their hats (males) to show respect for the deceased and those attending the service. The local law enforcement officers would generally lead the way.

Years ago, when funeral escort services were formed, processions had more visibility on the streets. The escorts would instruct the participants to turn on their headlights, follow somewhat closely to the vehicle in front, keep an eye out for inattentive drivers, and place funeral stickers or flags on every vehicle in the procession. Trained escorts would lead the way and close down intersections for a relatively safe procession. Ibid.

Procession Today

Today, immediate family members may be riding in a limousine or in their own cars. Family and close friends who will be driving their own vehicles in the procession should arrive at the funeral home or church about 45 minutes prior to the funeral to ensure that they are positioned near the front of the procession, close to the family car. All others will be parked in the order in which they arrive.

The funeral attendant typically places a magnetic flag, often bright orange in color, that reads "Funeral" on the car. The flag is placed on the top of the vehicle in the front left corner, over the driver's side. If there are many cars in the procession, the attendant may place the flag on every other vehicle or every third vehicle. Some funeral homes use stickers placed on the side and back window or a magnetic cone placed on the top of the car. They are usually orange with the word funeral on them. Drivers should be instructed to turn their headlights and flashers on for the drive to the church or cemetery. Both the funeral flags and the headlights signify to other motorists that you are part of a funeral procession.

The staff driver of the lead car should have enough money to pay tolls if they will be going through a toll booth. All lead car drivers should be aware of traffic laws pertaining to funerals.

A **typical cortege** would be arranged as follows:

1. Funeral home lead car. Clergy may ride in lead car with Director.
2. Officiating Clergy - If she is driving her own car.
3. Pallbearers if they are driving together.
4. Hearse.
5. Closest family member's car. Often this is a limousine supplied by the funeral home.
6. Cars as designated by the family.

Honorary pallbearers, or any special group attending, usually go between the lead car and the hearse.

Suggestions for Safer Funeral Processions

Instructions for Procession Drivers:

- Give instructions in both verbal and written form. Hand out instruction sheets when people arrive at the funeral home and repeat them verbally to everyone before the procession begins.
- Instruct drivers on state, city, or town laws on funeral processions.
- Instruct them on what to do if they become separated from the rest of the procession.
- Have all drivers put on their lights and flashers. Flashers are suggested because the lights on most cars go on when the vehicle is started. Flashers help to distinguish funeral processions.
- They will be driving very slowly – Usually 30-40 mph on roads, depending on the normal speed limit, and no more than 55 mph on the highway.
- They will need to stay close to the car in front of them in the procession – Do not allow room for a vehicle not in the procession to cut in.

- They need to stay in line and with the procession at all times – Even if that means going through a red light at an intersection, if local traffic ordinances give funeral processions the right-of-way.

- At the church, a funeral attendant will instruct procession drivers where to park.

- Once they arrive at the cemetery, a cemetery attendant will lead the procession to the gravesite or chapel and direct parking. The funeral attendant will collect the flags from vehicles.

Legal Considerations

The state or local traffic laws regarding the funeral procession differs quite a lot from city to city. You should check all your local and state regulations. The New Jersey State Funeral Directors Association (2012) provides an example of a clear state policy when responding to a funeral director's inquiry about whether a summons would be given to those driving in a funeral procession who go through a red light monitored by a red light camera:

> *State Motor Vehicle Code allows emergency vehicles to pass through a red traffic signal provided the vehicle is equipped with emergency lights and audible warning device and the operator has stopped to make sure safe passage is available.*
>
> *Vehicles participating in a funeral procession are not emergency vehicles. While we realize courtesy has traditionally been extended to motorists participating in a funeral procession, only a police officer may supersede a mechanical traffic control device and direct the procession through an intersection against a red traffic light. Motorists participating in an unescorted procession assume the risk of an accident and/or summons should they choose to enter an intersection against a red traffic signal. Police will issue tickets to funeral processions* (p.14).

Some cites have requirements for funeral processions. They may require that all cars have their lights on, or that a funeral flag or cone be placed on each car. Whether it is required by law or not, it is a good procedure to use both headlights and flags for every car. You want the procession as visible as possible to ensure the safety of everyone. Some cities also have regulations pertaining to funeral processions going through traffic lights. If funeral escorts are available from local police departments or through private escort services, using one can increase the level of safety for the procession as it goes through the red light.

Not Everyone Supports Funeral Processions

Bill Mayeroff (2016) argues against funeral processions. He states,

> *Anyone who's spent any time driving has been caught by one. They're hard to miss. A long line of cars with orange flags flying, their headlights on and their emergency flashers blinking. They run every red light and hold-up traffic and generally get in the way. The funeral procession is a tradition that's rich with history. It's a way friends and families pay respects as the deceased is taken to their final resting place. But this tradition could be coming to an end. I'm talking about a funeral procession, and it's time we outlawed them.*

Today the driving public views a funeral procession as an impediment, another irritating roadblock, preventing them from getting to point A to point B fast enough. Compound that with DVD players, GPS, cell phones, and texting, along with the fact that many vehicles have their headlights on whenever the car is on. Those always-on headlights make a funeral procession difficult to discern from everyday traffic. There are so many distractions for drivers on the road and funerals are just one more.

Funeral Escorts

In his article, “Are Funeral Processions Becoming Too Dangerous?” Jacob Terranova (2017), explains the role that the police have played in funeral procession, as well as the impact of the police no longer providing escort in processions. Traditionally, in many communities, police have provided their services to escort the procession to improve traffic safety. Those days appear to be coming to an end, as many police departments no longer have the resources to continue providing an escort service. The rates of accidents tend to increase without enough officers to participate in the escort.

Terranova suggests that the changes to police escorts and funeral trends seem to reflect our changing attitudes about processions around the country, as well as the growing danger involved. Each year, motorists are hurt or killed in wrecks involving funeral processions. He asserts that a lot of it has to do with a lack of understanding funeral procession laws and etiquette, as well as a lack of patience by other drivers.

Justin Nobel (2010) elaborates that “not only are people not slowing down, they are speeding up.” He suggests that the result is a growing number of funeral procession related accidents and a general breakdown in the etiquette regarding processions.

As police departments contemplate stopping funeral escorts, some funeral directors are thinking about ending funeral processions altogether. Families would be dismissed at the funeral home and meet up later at the cemetery or crematory. This could cause a backlash at the funeral home, however, because the emotional and cultural history of this custom remains strong. There are still people who believe in the cultural tradition of a procession and they would be upset if it were eliminated. It would be difficult to eliminate funeral processions altogether because they are expected in some situations, including high ranking public figures and firefighters or police officers killed in the line of duty.

In some cities when police don’t provide escorts, private escort companies provide the service for a fee. There is concern by funeral directors and the police about the training or lack of training these private escorts receive (Terranova, 2017). Some police departments do not support these companies at all and will harass or ticket the escort — and even ticket the cars in the procession for going through a red light.

Alternatives

Rohling (2012) advises bringing the funeral into the 21st century by eliminating funeral processions. He suggests the following technique. On the back of every service folder you hand out to the service attendees is a map to the cemetery you are going to (or a map handout). At the conclusion of service, tell those in attendance you will not be having a procession but will be meeting at the cemetery in a half an hour (or whatever time frame that is appropriate). Give everyone a break, time to visit the restroom, stretch their legs, and have a drink of water (make these suggestions part of your announcement). Ibid.

NOTES

NOTES

Chapter 7 AFTERCARE

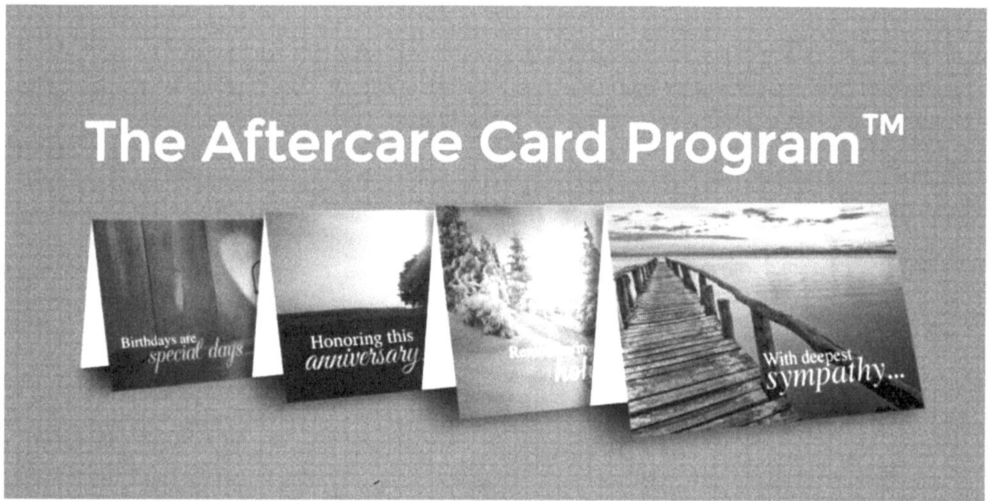

Source: https://aftercare.com/sample

<u>Aftercare</u> – *Offering services, literature, or emotional support to the bereaved after the funeral is over to help them adjust to their loss.*

Having an aftercare program can be one of your services that differentiates your funeral home from your competitors who do not offer it.

The internet should be a part of a funeral home's aftercare services. Thousands of internet users have found helpful information from a funeral home's website, or by simply typing in "grief," "death," or "widow" on an internet search engine such as Google, Ask, or Yahoo. A funeral home's website can also include a section for people to send email messages of sympathy to family, expanding their support network.

Whatever form of aftercare a funeral director chooses to provide, he or she can be assured it will be of some help to grieving families. The one exception is a funeral home that uses aftercare as a veiled cover for generating pre-need leads. Families can tell when a funeral director is sincere and when he or she is pretending for the sake of future sales.

We cannot eliminate the pain of death, but we can ease the loneliness, confusion, isolation, and despair that follows a death with an effective and sensitive aftercare program.

Kristen Dean (2017) discusses important questions about aftercare in her column, "Let's Chat," in Funeral Home and Cemetery News.

> What are you doing after the service? Do you reach out to the families you serve during their time of grieving? Are you one of the best in your profession who understands how much families need you when the service is over? Are your families and your communities able to benefit from all your expertise? Ibid.

> Thankfully more and more funeral directors are realizing how important aftercare is to the families they serve. Unfortunately, it is still a small percentage. Those embracing aftercare are making great strides in providing information and support when it is most needed, during the entire grieving process. These directors take the time to remind the people they serve that they are there for them. They know how important it can be for a family to hear "I remember." Ibid.
>
> The greatest funeral directors realize that their true gifts lie in their ability to create the moments that bring comfort. Those directors reach out to the families they serve and to all in their community. They participate in fundraisers, organize events, hold remembrance services, and much more. They are the people their communities know they can turn to in their time of grief. They are the funeral homes that families recommend. Ibid.

Aftercare is a means of supplying support to a family after a death has occurred. Funeral service aftercare usually begins after the funeral has ended and continues for about 12 months. There are two basic forms of aftercare services that a funeral home can provide:

Information Oriented Services: This can include sending family grief-oriented literature one or more times after the funeral. This can include cards, letters, brochures, books, a directory of local grief support groups or agencies, or newsletters.

Direct Care Services: Having a grief counselor on staff or retainer, sponsoring a support group(s), sponsoring grief related seminars or workshops, special ceremonies during holidays (i.e. Christmas, Mother or Father's Day, Veterans' Day, Easter), or a personal visit to the family's home by a staff member.

Canine (2011) discusses the minimum ways a funeral home can implement an aftercare program:

> A funeral home's aftercare program should include a letter to the deceased's family thanking them for the opportunity to provide service and expressing kind words for the future resolution of their grief. With the letter, or later, the funeral home should supply some type of basic information on the normal grief process. This might be a book, an assortment of brochures or literature covering various aspects of grief. Included or sent in a separate mailing should be a list of area resources, such as support groups, counselors or therapists who specialize in bereavement and educational opportunities to better understand the grief process. In special situations, the funeral home may wish to designate organizations, local or national, that may be of help to the family. For example, parents who have lost a young child might be referred to Compassionate Friends (a support group for parents who have lost a child).
>
> Funeral professionals are in the business of healing. That means creating healing experiences for your families is the biggest contribution you can make in their lives. Let's admit it, once the funeral service is over, it's hard to keep in touch with families. Offering aftercare helps you continue to make a valuable impact in their lives by helping guide them through their grief. Ibid.
>
> In addition to increasing the level of care a funeral director provides his or her clients, it also helps keep the funeral home in people's mind by keeping them connected to the community after the service ends. The days and weeks following the death of a loved one can be tumultuous, and sometimes it takes a while for the bereaved to fully understand the reality that their loved one is gone. People are afraid to ask for help or don't even know where to look for help. Aftercare can provide this help. A funeral home should always mention its aftercare offerings on its website. By doing this families know what the funeral home has to offer and can take advantage of it. Ibid.

Dan Isard (2015), founder and president of the Foresight Company in Phoenix, says that "aftercare is a form of altruism" and that regardless of how you approach aftercare, you need to get involved with it for the right reasons (p.32). He argues that due to its altruistic nature, aftercare is something that is non-commercial and philanthropic. Isard explains, however, that aftercare programs can generate (pre-need) leads if you do a good job showing families that you care and develop a dialogue with them.

Showing that you care is key because there is usually a large gap of time in between deaths of a family you've served. There is usually a 7 to 10-year gap between a parent and surviving parent dying. Isard (2015) says, "Aftercare will keep your relationship with the family and especially the surviving children current, so that they will be predisposed to use your firm at the time of the surviving parent's subsequent death" (p.33). Additionally, showing you care through aftercare programs can help the family see you as an ongoing resource as an expert on death, dying, and grief adjustment in the community.

Types of aftercare programs a funeral home can offer:

According to Todd Van Beck (2016), aftercare activities can be directed to one person (or family), they can bring a few people together, or they can be a special event that many people participate in.

A good aftercare program can include:

- Sending a support letter or grief literature a few weeks after the funeral
- Offering grief counseling
- Organizing a support group
- Sending a support newsletter
- Educational workshops/seminars
- Cooking class
- Basic home or car repair
- Offering a class on managing a budget
- Widow/widower's night out
- Senior event(s)
- Butterfly or balloon release
- Holiday program
- Veterans event
- There are also many different things that could be done on the internet, including a page of grief techniques, book recommendations, or information about places to go for help, running a chatroom grief support group, or managing a Facebook grief group

Van Beck (2016) also recommends that for an aftercare program to be sustainable it must:

1. Respect the funeral director's busy schedule and professional qualification
2. Be cost effective
3. Be effective – must have a means of evaluating the effectiveness of programs
4. Have low liability risks – using professional, licensed counselors for grief counseling
5. Be reasonable in expectations and outcomes
6. Conducted with dignity and professionalism
7. Start slow and build on successes

4 Ways Aftercare Can Help Grow Your Funeral Home Business

By: Barb Bloomquist (2015)

Successful funeral professionals recognize that the funeral service is not the end. Your relationship with families begins when you start the planning process and extends beyond the conclusion of the memorial and burial services. For some families, this relationship may only last a few weeks, while other families may benefit from aftercare for months or even years. Providing support during this critical time can endear families to your firm and help to grow your funeral home business.

Here are just a few of the ways that a strong program can benefit your firm while offering remarkable service to your families.

1. BUILDING BRAND LOYALTY.

In today's competitive market, it's important to offer services that set you apart and help build loyalty to your firm. One way to do that is to exceed your customer's expectations before, during, and after the funeral service. Offering aftercare resources and programs demonstrates your continuing commitment to their wellbeing, helps build brand loyalty, and keeps your firm top-of-mind. Naturally, people that have a positive experience with your funeral home are more likely to recommend you to their friends and family, and these third-party endorsements carry much more influence than advertising messages.

2. STAYING CONNECTED.

Offering aftercare services provides a way to stay connected with the families you've served. Whether you have an active program with staff dedicated to grief support and community outreach or simply provide information about grief support and resources on your website, it's important to reinforce that connection with your firm. Begin by simply sending a personal letter or handwritten note a few weeks after the memorial service letting family members know it was an honor to serve their loved one's needs. Provide a link to your website with information about your support programs so family and friends can access the resources when they are ready. Invite families you've served in the last year to attend memorial ceremonies throughout the year, but especially during the holidays. Finally, consider hosting grief support meetings and/or provide a grief support library at your funeral home.

3. OFFERING SUPPORT TO EVERYONE YOU SERVE.

Whether you help someone preplan a funeral or serve a family after the death of a loved one, there is an opportunity to aid everyone who has an experience with your funeral home. We believe aftercare is for everyone. One example is to provide a quarterly newsletter program. It can be filled with thoughtful, relevant information and is mailed to select family members following either a funeral preplanning experience (pre-need) or the loss of a loved one (at-need).

4. PROVIDING A CONTINUUM OF CARE.

Consider aftercare services as a continuum of the end-of-life care your firm already provides. Ideally your relationship with a family begins when you help them preplan and prefund a funeral and extends through the memorial service and internment. Providing support programs is a natural extension of the relationship you've formed with these families and helps to strengthen that bond, creating satisfied customers willing to share their experiences with others.

NOTES

NOTES

Chapter 8

MEMORIALIZATION

Source: https://www.johnsonbrownservicefh.com/make-it-personal

Memorialization *- To memorialize is to do or create something that causes people to remember. To Personalize is to mark something in a way that shows it belongs to a particular person or to change or design something for a particular person. Personalizing a funeral service adds to the memorialization factor (Merriam-Webster 2019).*

"Memorialize," by definition, means *to honor* or *commemorate*. It provides a way for us to remember or celebrate a person's life and work, to express feelings of loss and respect for the deceased and his/her grieving family, and to accept that the everyday relationship with that person has moved from physical reality into memory. Memorials are a way of saying, "this life mattered." They provide a link to the past and allow a person's memory to live on beyond death.

Memorialization

Article Excerpt From: YourTribute (2015)

There seems to be a universal human need to create memorials for departed loved ones. Some cultures honor their dead ancestors for centuries. It is a way for us to say goodbye, it helps the grieving process, and it gives us closure to our loss. It gives us comfort to be able to reflect on the joy the loved one brought to us. Memorializing a loved one also helps us with the healing process. Memorials are particularly helpful on tough dates, such as their birthday, or the anniversary of their death. But even more, it is a way for us to create a legacy that the lost beloved has left us. Memorial tributes allow us to share our memories with others and keep alive the memories of the deceased long after they have gone.

Memorialization is not simply sharing or preserving the memory of a loved one. It's a way to commemorate someone we've lost. We all want our legacy to continue after us. A memorial to someone reminds us of that legacy. A memorial can be something as elegant, elaborate, and famous as the Jefferson or Lincoln Memorial — monuments that people travel around the world to see. A memorial can also be something as humble and simple as a headstone or an urn. It can be as ethereal as singing the departed one's favorite song, writing a poem, or planting a flower or tree in their honor.

Today's consumers value individuality and uniqueness, especially when deciding how to memorialize their deceased loved one. They want the ability to choose products and ceremonies that appeal to their own sensibilities and tastes without settling. Some of the more traditional products and ceremonies that have been popular in the past may not be as appealing to families today. Products, such as jewelry and keepsakes, and ceremonies, like life celebrations, are gaining momentum. Families have many different attitudes toward memorialization. There are still a huge number of families who prefer traditional rituals and the products associated with those rituals. Other families prefer more personalization or unique approaches to sharing the story of their loved one.

Technology offers a multitude of ways to meet the desires and needs of families wanting to make a memorial to the deceased. This was difficult to do just 10-15 years ago. Now, however, because of technology, there is a huge benefit in the ability to customize services for any family. This allows families to get the most healing and comfort out of the service and allows them to move forward with their lives.

Technology is a huge deal. Webcasting or live streaming are examples of how modern technology can allow people to be part of this very important, special memorialization of a family's loved one. It is possible for anyone, anywhere, to be part of the service, to get healing and comfort. That is an immeasurable benefit. There has been some concern that webcasting could take the place of a person attending a funeral. But the benefit outweighs this fear. This is especially true for people who would not otherwise be able to attend or participate, like if one is deployed overseas.

Memorialization Story

A story shared in Funeral Service Insider (2016c) involves Justin Baxley, senior vice president of business development at Foundation Partners Group. He was at the Sanibel Harbor Marriot Resort and Spa in Fort Myers, Florida, when he stumbled across a sign advertising a celebration of life. Like any curious funeral director, he peeked inside. He was amazed when he saw that there was a video tribute, a storyteller officiating the service, and even a disc jockey and dance floor. He was so intrigued that he tracked down the hotel's event planner. He soon found out that what he had witnessed cost the family $6,000.

That cost itself might not have been that concerning, but what he heard next was. This one resort was holding 20 such events per year, and it was an uptrend. The event planner explained to him that people want a joyous experience that celebrates a life – not a morbid, sad experience. Ibid.

New Roles for Funeral Directors

"*Klicker's 150,*" 150 services most funeral homes provide to bereaved families, is listed in the introduction to this book. Along with all these traditional services, the present and future interest in memorialization and personalization in the 21st century must add new roles to the profession. **These roles include:**

Storyteller — Everyone, rich or poor, has an amazing life story to be passed on. Not just from a 10-minute eulogy, but through all aspects of the funeral or memorial event. Immersing the guests in such a way that when they leave, they feel as if they really know the deceased.

Funeral Director + Event Planner = Memorial Event Planner — Start thinking like a memorial (funeral) event planner, rather than a traditional funeral director. It looks like memorial events, such as celebrations of life, will be an important part of the future in funeral service.

Important Characteristics Memorial Directors Should Aim For

In his article "What Funeral Directors Can (and should) Learn from Wedding Planners," Joe Joachim (2013) outlines several important characteristics of wedding planners that should be utilized by funeral directors in planning memorials. **In applying these characteristics to funeral directors, memorial event planners:**

1. Aren't afraid to try new things.

Be open to trying new, creative ideas, and thinking outside the box. This is the key to stimulating a family's thinking and planning potential.

2. Help families save money.

Instead of keeping our unfortunate reputation as a profession who rips off our families, position yourself as the transparent go-to in your community. You can do that by putting together a package of services that meets both the needs and the budget of client families, rather than trying to sell them the most expensive items on your GPL. This will help you build trusted relationships with families and guarantees they will think of you again.

3. Make planning enjoyable.

Planning a funeral is not a happy event. Funeral directors or celebrants who have created personalized memorial events say this planning can be joyful. Focusing on the deceased's life story can be exciting and meaningful.

Some techniques for achieving this:

- Focus on celebration – It's an emotional time for the family, but you can make it better by helping them think of the funeral service as a celebration to be enjoyed and not endured.
- Find out what families need before you bring out the GPL – You can say, "Let's talk about some of the details of the funeral and go over the cost considerations." This keeps the pressure off pricing.
- Ask open ended questions to find out what families want and listen to the answers.
- Adopt a can-do approach to even the most unusual requests.

4. Show their value.

Funeral directors aren't great at showing the value of a funeral or how their funeral home is better than their competitors'. As funeral professionals, you have expertise in celebrating life and overcoming grief – You need to show it. Your funeral home website is a key part of making this happen. Wedding planners show images of successful weddings and testimonials from happy customers – Funeral directors can do exactly the same. This value can be underlined by showing tasteful pictures and testimonials and ensuring that your website is also a source of useful information for people preplanning their funeral.

For example, you can:

- Show photos of tasteful, personalized funeral services that are ideal for Pinterest, Instagram, Facebook, and Twitter.
- Make an ultra-short video about an aspect of your business for Snapchat, Instagram, or Facebook.

- Shoot a "case study" video that has your client families talking about the services you provided for them and post them to your funeral home's YouTube channel.
- Tweet about news of interesting funeral services from around the country.
- Set up a Facebook event for the funeral service or help families send out digital invitations.
- Share the tribute videos you create for families on your YouTube Channel, Facebook, and Twitter page.
- You can also share inspirational quotes about life and death on your social media accounts. There is no limit to what you can do. Think about the information potential client families need, then showcase it accordingly.

5. Listen.

The key to the success of memorial planners is the planner's ability to listen. Planners take the time to understand what the family wants through asking questions, then they use their knowledge to make it happen. Any funeral home that still wants to be in business in the future must do the same. Memorial planners bend over backwards to deliver new and meaningful services to their clients. Funeral homes must be **agile** in finding new ways to do business (Joachim, 2013).

Educating the Community on the Value of Memorialization & Personalization

How do you educate your community about the value of memorialization and personalization of the funeral or memorial event? The concept of memorialization and personalization should be included in your website, social media accounts (Instagram, Facebook page, YouTube, etc.), print, and media advertising, as well as any presentations or seminars you give. This education can be expressed in a simple statement such as:

> *The _____ funeral home staff are committed to helping you create a funeral or memorial event, such as a celebration of life, that will allow you to mourn your loss in a healing way and honor and celebrate the life of the deceased, regardless of financial consideration. We believe every deceased individual is deserving of respect and dignity and every bereaved family is entitled to sensitive professional care by all our staff.*

After making this statement you can give a few examples of personalized funeral or memorial events you have conducted and what product options are available to a family.

Joe Joachim (2013) asserts that successful funeral service professionals will become experts at discovering what motivates families, then matching the service and products to meet their needs, whether those preferences are traditional or extraordinary. Understanding how each family wants to uniquely remember and memorialize their loved one helps create an experience that families and guests truly value. This can be done by designing and presenting an experience, then explaining how certain products enhance that experience, raising the level of value for all involved. Do not let what you've done in the past limit your vision for what will work in today's market. The goal is to make every funeral meaningful. Meaningful funerals incorporate some degree of personalization or memorialization – in the obituary, the visitation, the guestbook, the prayer cards, the video tribute, memorial website, and the funeral or memorial service.

NOTES

NOTES

Chapter 9

PERSONALIZATION

Brayden Denton was a five-year-old boy who loved superheroes. His obituary encouraged guests to wear a superhero t-shirt or clothing at the wake and funeral. The six pallbearers donned superhero costumes (Boroff, 2014).

> ***Personalization*** - *Designing funerals that reflect and celebrate the life of the deceased. Personalized funerals tell the story of the person's life through words, activities, symbols, or all of these.*

Among the dictionary definitions for the word "personalize" is "to design or tailor to meet an individual's specifications, needs or preferences." Retailers have long understood this basic need of consumers to "have it their way." Funeral service may have been slow to the game...but that is quickly changing, especially when it comes to caskets, the funeral service, and personalization options (Martin Bartsche, 2015a).

The funeral personalization **"WOW"** movement is here. Far beyond being faddish or temporary, it is in our face, full-blown and gaining momentum. For some in funeral service, it is the cavalry bringing abundant opportunities. For others, it is their worst nightmare. Ibid.

As more and more consumers experience innovative and unusual funeral services, more and more funeral directors receive unusual funeral requests, ratcheting up our need to be more creatively responsive. If funeral directors are not responsive to this grass roots movement, some other occupational group will fill the void and provide these powerful and moving experiences for our families. Ibid.

Martin Bartsche (2015a) asserts that making personalized funeral arrangements is more of a challenge than making traditional funeral arrangements. Making personalized funeral arrangements requires good bonding skills, creativity, and risk taking. Transcending from a traditional funeral arranger to a more creatively inclined arranger adept at creating moving events is difficult, especially after years of organizing traditional-looking funerals.

A buzz phrase in the business is "creating a "WOW" experience." Creating this "wow factor" means exceeding a family's expectations. It starts by knowing the family's expectations, meeting them, but adding some surprising action, behavior, experience, or product the family was not expecting but was relevant, meaningful, and touched their heart. Ibid.

The first movement toward personalization was really started by casket companies. A memory box embedded in the half coach front panel was one of the first entries into the movement. Then came interchangeable themed casket corners, themed appliques on head panels, lid engraving, personal unique embroidering of head panel inserts, special sport team colors, military colors, and emblems. Ibid.

Today, personalized caskets can be an important aspect of some funerals, contributing to meaningfulness and healing. Ten years ago, tribute videos, picture boards, and memory tables were considered by most funeral directors to be creative, innovative, and wow-producing. Today they are same old, same old. Ibid.

Consultants and suppliers generally agree that more people would be interested in the idea of personalization if they knew more about it. Most families have limited knowledge of what options are available to them. This is not their fault but the fault of the arranging director who does not inform them, or funeral directors who do not educate their community about the subject. Ibid.

In their merchandizing or marketing, funeral directors should show and explain the many personalization options and how they can be applied to either the service or products. Ibid.

Martin Bartsche (2016c) believes that personalization can create a designer funeral. Every life has a story. Personalization allows us to create a celebration of life rather than the mourning of a life. Being able to focus on those personal pieces of a person's life also helps those who came to pay their respects. It is hard to know what to say to someone who has lost a loved one. A personalized funeral can help break the ice and get the conversation started. When you see something in the room that is familiar, it makes it easy to talk about the person, shared experiences, and the good times.

Little things can add up to a very personalized service. The funeral professional must be willing to explain what can be done and present options to a family...unless you tell them, they don't know what they can do.

Examples of WOW experiences

It took a lot of work to transform a funeral home in Bradenton, Florida, into a tropical getaway to celebrate the life of a beach-loving mother of three (Cronin, 2017).

Patti Martin Bartsche (2016c) shares a story of a young man who passed away in a car crash. He loved to drink mountain dew while fishing. When the family walked into the event room where the visitation was held, "They saw the way we set up the room and then they saw the boat with the Mountain Dew. They were overwhelmed and became very emotional, but they were also so thankful. The comment that the father said that has stuck with me the most is, 'You have captured the very spirit of our son.' They were so grateful that people cared enough about them to bring their son's personality, passions and hobbies into the visitation, and make it all about him."

The staff at Stiffler-Hamby at Parkhill Cemetery made sure to include the soda in the setting of the man's viewing due to his love of it.

Source: Striffler-Hamby

Funeral home staff set up a johnboat filled with fishing gear and soda to personalize the visitation for the 19-year-old crash victim.

Which would you rather hear? "Funerals are all the same with a different name," or "You captured the very spirit of our son."

The author believes every funeral should capture the very spirit of the deceased!!

Levels of Commitment to Personalization

Funeral directors fall into one of three levels in the personalization process. The three levels were created by the late Bill Bates, founder of the Life Appreciation Training Seminars. Bill was a pioneer in the field of personalizing funerals.

Level I: What I call a remolded traditional funeral in which one sees lots of picture boards and funeral props. At this level, funeral ceremonies are not yet what one would call "personalized," but this is a necessary beginning. Many of our colleagues get stuck at Level I, thinking it's as far as they need or can go. But others use their Level I experience to push the envelope to discover more effective possibilities. Unfortunately, the temptation to make our remolded traditional funeral the replacement for the traditional funeral is huge. One doesn't have to connect emotionally with the client or exercise any real creative ability and it can be called personalized. But it simply replaces one bad commercial idea of "one size fits all" with another.

Level II: Ceremonies are those that include picture boards and funeral props with the addition of a creative funeral site and possibly open sharing. In Level II, the emphasis is on "stuff" such as a life symbols, picture boards, hobbies, and so on. Those symbols are important to complete the context of a ceremony of appreciation, but we don't love others because they had a great career or were exceptional golfers. Personally, I stayed at Level II for an exceptionally long time. I remember feeling incomplete about the personalized ceremonies I arranged but could not visualize what the next step could be. Most of us struggle with "the next step" question as we near the time to move forward. It's not a comfortable period of time, but it's necessary and certainly "grist for the mill."

Level III: The third and final level is the "gold standard." To get to Level III takes study, effort, and a commitment to be the absolute best. Level III performers have a clear understanding that there is no top end at this level. Each ceremony creation only vaguely resembles any that came before it. This is the level at which your consistent personalization ceremonies have become significant in attracting new calls for your firm.

Level III ceremonies include all the above or none but are able to capture and demonstrate in a creative fashion what others loved about the deceased – the "wow" factor funerals. WOW factor funerals leave a lasting impression. Any funeral that fits the deceased and moves the audience can be a "wow" factor funeral, even a highly traditional funeral. The delivery of consistent "wow" factor funerals creates a competitive advantage in most communities. It takes practice and creativity to be able to express love, compassion, understanding, commitment, giving, and all that we value about being human. But it is the ability to demonstrate what others loved about the deceased that creates the all-important "wow" moment.

Consumers exposed to Level II and III ceremonies begin to consistently ask for them over and over. Some of these families may have chosen a different funeral home if it weren't for the creative funeral they experienced at the Level II or Level III firm. Funeral directors operating consistently at Level III understand that every family they serve calls for a variety of creative responses.

The Effect of Personalization

This author once performed the funeral of a man named Melvin "Scoop" Frey. This was before most funeral homes were doing pictures boards or using memorabilia. I decorated the visitation room with Melvin's bowling trophies, baseball pictures, and other items that were important to him. At the funeral, I had Melvin's friends talk about him. "God Bless America" was Scoop's favorite saying. I played "God Bless America" as we removed the flag draping the bottom half of his casket and folded it. Spontaneously, everyone stood and sang along with the song. I received the comment below from Judith Scharf, Melvin's daughter.

> *"My father's funeral was the most beautiful funeral I ever attended. Having all his treasures throughout the room made me remember so much about him. The stories his friends and family told about him and his life made me laugh and cry. When Ralph started folding his flag and "God Bless America" began to play, I knew I just had to stand and sing. When everyone else joined me, I felt so proud and touched. His best friend told me this is the kind of funeral he wanted."*
>
> Judy Scharf

These types of meaningful experiences can only be created by putting down your pen and setting aside your vital statistics form and general price list. Talk with and listen to the person or persons making the arrangement. This approach can start even before the family arrives at the funeral home. When making the removal look around the deceased's house. The things you observe can start your creative juices flowing, and personalization options can be discussed later during the arrangement conference.

Author's Note: Just to give you an example of what personalization means to different people, the same week I planned the Scharf funeral, my cousin died, and I planned his funeral. He was active as a Boy Scout when he was a boy and a scout leader as an adult. In my head I pictured Scout flags by the casket, all his Scout awards on display, and uniformed Scouts as an honor guard. All his wife wanted for personalization was to put his Scouts tie clip on his tie.

Information Gathering for Personalization

A flow of information and intimate exchange with families begins with questions one would not ordinarily ask in a 1950s funeral arrangement model. But these questions are necessary to create a personalized concept. These are questions such as:

- What would you say that the deceased believed in that was important to him and perhaps guided his life?
- In terms of day-to-day living, what was most important to him?
- How would you describe him?
- What accomplishments was he the most pleased with?
- What gave him the most enjoyment in life?
- What did he dislike the most?
- Whom did she love and what did you do together that was particularly rewarding?

- Do you know about the most difficult period of her life, and could you tell me about it?
- If she were here today, and could talk to those she loved, what do you think she would say?
- What made your mother laugh?
- What made your mother cry?
- When you reflect on the accomplishments of your father, what would you like the rest of the family and your friends to remember?
- Have you ever been to a memorial or gathering where the person's life was truly represented? What did you think?
- What do you think would make for a good funeral?
- Is there anything we could give away at the funeral that would remind people of your mom?
- Why did you say that?
- How will that decision help your family here?

Very Powerful Questions About Funerals

You can then proceed with what this author considers very powerful questions:

- Think of a wonderful memory you have of spending time with your mom. *(Pause)* Tell me about that day. What do you see, smell, and hear?
- What do you think your dad was most proud of in his life?
- What are the special things you hope friends and family will remember most about your sister?
- Who were some of your son's closest friends? What were those relationships like? How did they spend their time together?
- When your grandmother found time to relax, what would she do?
- If you had to pick one thing that you cherish most about your wife, what would that be?
- What would your grandfather want to share with those remembering him, what would he say? (Boxley, 2017)
- If you could create a ceremony that reflects the life of your dad and your family what would that be?
- What would you suggest that could create a service that honored your mom and her life?

Questions like these go to the heart of what most of us find meaningful in life. The answers to these questions provide the necessary information to create the top end of the personalization experience. None of these questions deal with the facts and figures of things like hobbies, college degrees, employment, things he/she owned, or positions held. Although determining that information is important and will provide helpful service clues, all too often when the funeral is built around those things it will not deliver the "wow" factor we are looking for.

Creating **"wow factor"** funerals is a larger challenge than the making of traditional funeral arrangements. These funerals are based more on feelings than tangibles, like hobbies and activities. They require each of us to continue to grow in our ability to use interpersonal skills, creativity, and risk taking.

Instead of obtaining this information in a question and answer period, try to obtain it through conversation. Be flexible, use some or all of the information. Add questions you feel are important.

Care Plans

The forms on the next two pages, or similar forms that you create, can enhance the services you give to a family and assist you with personalizing the visitation and funeral. I call them **Care Plans.**

The first care plan is for the family. It contains questions that can help you understand their experience with funerals, both positive and negative. By asking the last question you let the family know that you honestly care about them and want to meet their needs.

Obtaining the information in the second care plan will not only help you to learn about the deceased, but it will also give the family an opportunity to talk about their loved one. The information gained from this discussion will help both you and the family generate ideas for personalizing the visitation, funeral, or remembrance service.

How you obtain the information on the care plan is up to you. You can direct the conversation in such a way as to get it without the family even knowing it's happening. Or, you can let the family know you are going to ask a series of questions to get a better understanding of them and their loved one.

These care plans do not necessarily contain all the questions previously mentioned. You can create your own care plan containing the information that you are comfortable with.

Funeral Care Plan Example #1

Funeral Care Plan for ________________________________ and Family

Family	YES	NO
Have you had experience planning a funeral?	☐	☐

Explain: ____

Have you attended a funeral(s) before?	☐	☐

When? ____

In thinking about funeral services that you have attended, was there anything memorable that you liked? ____

____

____

In thinking about funeral services that you have attended, was there anything you disliked?

____

____

____

Is there anything you want us to definitely do?	☐	☐

____

____

____

Is there anything you want us to definitely not do?	☐	☐

____

____

____

What can we do at this point and time to help you the most? ________________________

____

____

Funeral Care Plan Example #2

Deceased

What words best describe ___________________?

____

____

What did they like most about life? ____

____

What did they believe in most; What guided his/her life? _____________________

____

What were _________________'s accomplishments in life? ___________________

____

What were _______________'s hobbies? ___________________________________

____

If he/she were here, what would they say to those attending the funeral?

____

In terms of day-to-day living, what was most important to him/her? _____________

____

How would you describe _______________? ________________________________

____

What accomplishments was __________________the most pleased with? __________

____

What gave him/her the most enjoyment in life? _____________________________

____

Whom did ______________ love and what did you do together that was particularly rewarding?

____

Do you know about the most difficult period of ____________'s life, and could you tell me about it?

____

If ____________ were here today, and could say things to those ____________ loved – what do you think that would be?

____

What made ___________ laugh?____

____

What made ___________ cry?____

____

When you reflect on the accomplishments of ____________, what would you like the rest of the family and your friends to remember?

____

____

Have you ever been to a memorial or gathering where the person's life was truly represented?______
What did you think?

____

What do you think would make for a good funeral?

____

Is there anything we could give away at the funeral that would remind people of your __________?

____

Why did you say that?____

____

How will that decision help your family heal?

____

What would you like to see done that would best reflect his/her life?

____

____

Asking the Right Questions:
Interviewing Families with an Event Planner Mindset
Excerpt From: CANA (2017)

Out of necessity, we must ask families a lot of questions. We are skilled at asking questions clearly and compassionately. However, we often focus more on the questions that meet our immediate needs, such as completing the death certificate. As event planners, or funeral service consultants, we are storytellers. We must also ask the questions that reveal memories and stories stacked with emotion and importance.

Examples of these "feeling-finding" questions are:

- Think of the most wonderful memory you have of spending time with your Mom. (Pause.) Tell me about the day. What do you see, smell, and hear?
- What do you think your dad was most proud of in his entire life?
- What are the special things you hope friends and family members will remember most about your brother?
- Who were some of your son's closest friends? What were those relationships like? How did they spend their time together?
- When your grandmother found time to relax, what did she do?

Being a good interviewer hinges upon your ability to be a good listener. Fight the tendency to tell your own stories in response to what the family is sharing — this is their time. Avoid personal distractions. With so much going on, it can be hard to listen through the answer to these types of probing questions when our mind is racing on a thousand other items — cremations to conduct, obituaries to place, flowers and merchandise to get ordered, and the list goes on and on. It is important to learn to focus only on the family at that time.

The answers to our interview questions become the ingredients to a personal and meaningful remembrance event and allows us to guide families on the choice they need to make. Think broadly, provide ideas to the family, and let their responses guide you on what they may be comfortable with. Your suggestions give them permission to be creative. Be willing to take the remembrance event outside your facility to a special venue that helps tell the story. To measure the effectiveness of your recommendations, ask yourself, "**Will this event be able to tell this person's life story effectively?"**

Remember that our recommendations flow into the event experience itself, not just the location and set-up. Following are some actual experiences arrangers have created to illustrate what is possible:

- **Ballpark** — Take the ceremony to the ballfield and sell (for the price grandpa paid back in the day) ballpark style hotdogs (great for sense of smell too).
- **Camping** — Set up a campfire on the patio, open a cooler of beer, and encourage a time of storytelling.
- **Beach** — Ask guests to draw in the sand of a beach scene created inside the funeral chapel, using a projected background and play sand.
- **Golf** — Bring in a putting green and ask the attendees to sink a ball with the decedent's favorite putter as they share a memory.

- **Cooking** — Have the result of a favorite recipe available to sample and enjoy.
- **Gardening** — Set up tables where guests can pot a seedling in memory and take it with them.
- **Non-themed** — Candle-lighting services are powerful. Don't reserve them just for the holiday season.

Our profession is not for the faint of heart — we work through long hours, changing consumer preferences, compressing profit margins, and misunderstood intentions, not to mention training, mentoring, and running a business fraught with liability. This work must be fueled by passion if it is to be a successful venture. With all that we have to do and remember to do, it is easy to forget about some of the basic building blocks that drive our success. The family consultation is certainly one of those that needs our continuous improvement and intentional focus. By focusing on asking the right questions and honing our creative event-planning skills, you can ensure that each family's experience is the best possible and that, ceremony or not, the outcome is an experience that you can be proud of having provided.

Funeral Personalization: Ideas to Try

If ramping up your personalized services is not one of your goals, it should be. Offer your families a life celebration that they will never forget. Create an uplifting ambience for your families that will help them feel comfortable and happy. It can make all the difference in how your funerals are viewed.

The following suggestions are creative ideas from Jess Fowler (2015) and Rochelle Rietow (2015).

1. **Create a memory table**

   One of the essentials of any personalized funeral service is a memory table. You can do so much with memory tables. You could even make multiple tables that are set up like "stations" to represent different chapters or passions in the deceased person's life.

A table memorial made with photos of the deceased and significant items from his life.

2. **Light candles to honor the deceased**

   It's a well-known fact that you never forget a smell. And if your family can recall a certain smell that reminds them of their loved one (think grandma's apple pie), suggest that the family light a few candles that add a healing aroma to the service.

3. Display photos in a unique way

For a lot of families, it can be incredibly cathartic to look through old albums to find photos for their relative's funeral. Most funerals today include visual elements to tell the story of the person's life with images. Directors assist families with deciding how they want to display photos of their loved ones. From enlarging photographs for display, to designing a collage by hand, to creating a photo slideshow, the many options can be overwhelming for some. Fortunately, directors can guide families through this by asking questions and showing examples of funerals handled in the past.

An artistic, clothespin-style photo board.

Sure, a memory board is a great way to display the families' photos of their loved one, but why not help them think outside the box and create something that will make the service even more beautiful? Your families could tie photos to balloons, create a wreath with them, or hang them on clothespins to add some visual appeal to the service.

An elegant and unique wreath made with framed photographs.

Framed collage photos on display at a funeral.

4. **Offer their favorite food and beverages**

   Instead of the standard coffee and water service at a funeral, why not surprise your families by offering the loved one's favorite drinks or snacks? Try to ask in a subtle way what kinds of foods or drinks the loved one enjoyed the most during the arrangement meeting and take notes. They'll be surprised and delighted by how much you pay attention to detail.

5. **Offer a memorial stone station**

   Set up a station with small stones and permanent markers. Then, create a sign that instructs every guest to write their names and a brief note on a rock to honor the loved one. The family can choose to keep the rocks in their home or garden, or to scatter them somewhere that is meaningful to the deceased

   Guests are invited to write down a memory on a stone to be placed in a vase for the family

6. **Offer a Personalized Remembrance**

   One funeral director held a remembrance tailgate party in the funeral home's parking lot instead of a traditional funeral. The funeral director worked with the family to create the experience they wanted. The funeral director helped the family move forward by helping them focus on what the deceased loved in life. A new positive and lasting memory was created and made them smile as they were grieving (American Funeral Director, 2015).

7. **Offer Keepsakes**

   Family members seek out ways to keep the memory of the deceased person alive. This is a natural part of the healing process. One idea that can provide comfort is to think of a gift that can be given to guests attending the service. Directors can remind families that this option exists and help facilitate the distribution of gifts during the wake or funeral. Some choose to give something living and others opt for a symbolic token that can be kept as a keepsake. Both options allow families to bestow a lasting reminder of their loved one's life. Handing out these small gifts that remind funeral guests of their loved one is also a great way to make your funeral home stand out. Examples you could offer include:

   - **Tree seedlings**
   - **Customized bookmarks:** Offer complimentary bookmarks.
   - **Craft individual memorial photo pins:** This is a simple yet easy way to let everyone take a little piece of the loved one home with them. Simply purchase enough artificial flowers from a local craft store for every funeral guest to take home. Then, use a safety pin to attach a photo of the loved one to the flower. You can laminate the photo or put it in a plastic holder.

A photo from the funeral service of an ice-cream truck driver.

A surfer's memorial service on the water.

Paul R Mitchell – January 14th, 2015 at 5:20 a.m.

> *"I arranged a funeral some years ago for a cowboy who owned his own ranch. The family asked to have everybody on horseback with the casket placed on a wagon pulled by a team of horses. We met that morning as the fog was just lifting. They had a big bon fire where we all gathered for coffee and sausage sandwiches. We saddled up and went on a two-hour trail ride, some 200 riders from ages 6 years old to 80. As the funeral director, I led with the lead horse they provided for me. We rode for two hours back to the small cemetery. The minister and his wife rode alongside of me with their horses. At the cemetery there was a pavilion where we had a barbecue lunch for everyone. A friend of the families drove along side of the procession and took pictures. It was a beautiful send off just the way the family wanted."*

8. Think Outside the Box

Families that want personalization appreciate funeral homes that are able to think outside of the box and come up with incredible ideas for customizing a casket.

Some of the most creative examples we have seen of funeral personalization stems from the creation of unique caskets. The examples below illustrate how funeral homes have been able to accommodate the special requests of families. While a large majority of families may opt for a traditional casket model or for cremation, directors are there to listen and to offer every option. Families that want personalization appreciate funeral homes able to think outside of the box and come up with some incredible ideas for customizing a casket.

A California funeral director worked with the Lego Corporation to design, build, and transport this incredible custom Lego casket for a 10-year-old boy

Instead of a register book for a diehard Philadelphia Phillies fan, the family had guests sign a baseball home plate.

A Texas funeral director suggested that family and friends use Band-aids to commemorate the life of a nurse who passed away.

NOTES

Chapter 10

MEMORIAL SERVICE, LIFE CELEBRATION & GATHERINGS

Source: http://www.familyfuneralcareindy.com/dm20/en_US/locations/40/4085/catering.page?

Most funerals are followed by a gathering of family and friends. This special and essential time allows your family and friends to tell stories about the person who died, to cry, to laugh, and to support one another. It is an informal time of release after the more formal elements of the funeral ceremony. The gathering is also a time of transition. In a way it is a rite of passage back to starting to live again. It demonstrates the continuity of life, even in the face of death.

"After Funeral or Cremation Gathering"

By: PlanningAFuneral.com (2008)

It is a common practice to have a gathering of friends and family after the funeral or the cremation. A gathering after either of these ceremonies is similar to a gathering following a memorial service.

If you are having a gathering, ask the funeral director or other family member/friend to make an announcement letting people know what is planned, when, and where (if there is an open invitation to all present). This can be done at the funeral home, at the end of a church service, graveside, or at the crematorium.

If you prefer to have a family-only gathering, tell the appropriate family members to pass the word among family and let them know it is a family-only event.

First you will need to decide on a location for the gathering. Here are a few suggestions:

- Home of the deceased or other family member
- Restaurant or catering hall
- A church hall
- Funeral home (if they have a facility available)

- Community center or other space available through a club or organization, such as a VFW hall, nursing home, senior citizens' activity center, park district facility
- A park
- The beach or lake
- Any other location that seems fitting

The event can be as simple or fancy as you like. You can eat out, order food in, or request that the guests contribute food dishes or other items.

You will want to estimate the number of attendees if going to a restaurant or catering hall. If going to a restaurant, it is best to make reservations and outline menu options for guests.

You can personalize the gathering by bringing favorite music of the deceased's and playing it in the background.

During this time, it would be appropriate to have someone say a few words about the deceased.

Memorial Service

A memorial service generally takes place sometime after the death and disposition has occurred. It is usually a service specifically to memorialize the life of the deceased. If a cremation has been performed, often a memorial service is conducted to inter or scatter the cremated remains at the same time as the celebration of the deceased's life. A memorial service can also be held following a private funeral service. Sometimes a family will arrange a private family funeral service, and then hold a memorial service at a later date when family who could not attend the funeral can gather. A memorial service is often held when someone had ties to a community, as a ritual to help people pay their last respects.

One benefit of a memorial service is that the family has additional time to plan and think about what they want to do and how they want to do it. In contrast, a funeral is often a three-day rush of planning, while the family is in the midst of grieving. The memorial service can be done at any time.

A memorial service can be religious or non-religious (secular). It can be elaborate or simple. The location possibilities to hold the service are endless and can include:

- At the home of the deceased or another family member
- A church service, followed by a gathering in the church hall
- Restaurant
- Catering hall
- A community center or other public space such as a Garden Club, VFW, nursing home, or senior citizen activity center
- A park
- Funeral home
- Fishing or golfing trip, trip to a ball game, beach party, concert, or any other place that has a tie to the deceased

For a more structured memorial service, consider the following:

- Make a guest list.
- Send invitations or another form of notification.
- Choose music pre-recorded or live. A performance by a friend or family member, i.e. a violin, harp, guitar, or piano can be a nice touch.
- Select pictures to put on display and/or pull together a collage of pictures on a poster board.
- Have a computer savvy family member or friend create a video slideshow on a laptop to project at the memorial service.
- Display some of the deceased's favorite things (i.e. golf club, art easel, knitting quilt, favorite hat, sports memorabilia). You want to bring the person's spirit to life as much as possible.
- Make a memorial service program so people can participate in a special song selection or prayers.
- You may use the memorial service as an opportunity to scatter ashes. **For more information on scattering options, see Chapter 18 Cremation.**

The author recently attended a memorial service that included two gatherings, one before and one after the service. The memorial service and pre-service gathering were held at a Protestant church. At the pre-service gathering we had coffee, pastries, bagels, and fruit.

The service was held in the church and was more secular than religious. There were some large photos of the deceased. Two of her grandchildren played musical numbers, while others gave the eulogies.

The best way I can describe this gathering and service was that it was uplifting and joyous.

After the service, the guests joined the family for a luncheon gathering. There were 80 people at lunch. I visited each table and asked everyone if they would prefer a "traditional" funeral at the funeral home or the type of service they just attended. 79 out of 80 preferred the memorial type event.

I have to admit that I enjoyed this memorial service. I felt like a traitor to traditional funerals.

Celebrations of Life

In the book, *Chocolat*, by Joanne Harris, you'll find this truth:
Life is what you celebrate. All of it. Even its end.

Funerals vs. Celebrations of Life

Excerpt From: Ellis Funeral Homes (n.d.)

It is interesting; funerals and celebrations-of-life have much in common, yet they often appear different. Each is a ceremony, a gathering of people who share a common loss. However, one is more rooted in tradition, while the other is the result of recent changes in social values. Both serve to do 3 things:

1. **Help the bereaved family, and their community, publicly acknowledge the death of one of their own.**
2. **Support grieving family by surrounding them with caring friends, co-workers, and neighbors.**
3. **Move the deceased from one social status to another.**

While a funeral has more to do with the orderly and is often spiritually defined, a celebration of life is more concerned with telling the story of the deceased. Celebrations of life are just that: A few people come together more to celebrate the unique personality and achievements of the deceased, rather than to merely witness or mark the change in their social status (funeral).

Celebrations of life are similar to memorial services, which can be described as a hybrid event, combining the flexibility of a celebration-of-life with many activities of a traditional funeral order-of-service.

There's more room for creativity in a **celebration of life** than a **funeral**. Since celebrations of life are commonly held after the individual's physical remains have been cared for through burial or cremation, there is much more time available to plan the event. And without doubt, this allows you to make better decisions about how you'd like to celebrate the life of someone you dearly loved. [End Excerpt]

In their resource, "Planning a Funeral or Memorial Service," SevenPonds.com (2019) make the following points about "Life Celebrations."

- "Life Celebration" is a more recent term for a certain kind of memorial service, where the emphasis is on the word "celebration," and grieving is less the event's focus.
- Life celebrations are fresh and unique. They are affairs of laughter and tears, toasts and memorials, the deceased favorites movies can be played in the background.
- Like memorial services, the body is not present at the life celebration, and the event can therefore be held days, weeks, or even months after death.

"The Difference between Funerals and Celebrations of Life"

Excerpt From: Funeral Costs Help (2019)

Funerals are traditionally held in places of worship, while celebrations of life are held in diverse locations such as homes, hotels, beaches, parks, and local pubs – usually somewhere of significance to the deceased. Generally speaking, celebrations of life are also less solemn and can make the passing of a loved one easier to cope with. The term 'celebration of life' is fairly loose. There are no formal arrangements or traditional procedures because events are specifically tailored to the deceased or the wishes of their family and friends. Fundamentally, what sets them apart from funerals is the atmosphere. Rather than focusing on grieving a loss, they place more emphasis on celebrating the life in a joyous manner.

Typical pastimes often include: Listening to the deceased's favorite music; playing their favorite movie; toasting to their achievements; viewing a slideshow; sharing personal stories; and playing their favorite games.

Funeral services tend to occur within a few days of an individual's death, which can make them difficult to arrange if they weren't pre-planned. Celebrations of life can occur at any time, sometimes months or even years later. In addition, they don't cost as much because the casket, transportation costs, and burial fees, etc., are avoided.

Some ministers argue that feeling sadness is an important step towards being at peace; therefore, bypassing the funeral and moving straight on to the celebration can be detrimental to the healing process.

NOTES

NOTES

Chapter 11 PRE-NEED

Source: Batesville Casket Company

Pre-Need - *Funeral arrangements made in advance of need.*

According to Cronin (2016a), the most effective pre-need programs incorporate a varied and assertive outreach program, often including mail, seminars, referrals, social media, and other proactive lead generation methods. These programs also include active, professional sales counselors and management structures.

Martin Bartsche (2016b) elaborates that a successful pre-need program is an integral part of any successful funeral home operation. A successful program doesn't happen by accident, though – it takes time, energy, and effort. In other words, it takes a lot of work.

History of Pre-Need

According to Glenda Stansbury (2015), pre-need planning is nothing new. Throughout history, people have planned and prepared for death. In Roman times, nearly 2,000 years ago, burial clubs held monthly meetings and collected dues to pay for members' funerals (p.25).

In the middle ages, guilds, crafts organizations, and fraternal groups collected funds in advance to pay for members' final expenses. Since ancient times, people have seen the importance of planning for the expense of a funeral honoring a dear friend's memory. Ibid

By the mid-19th century, there were over 200 burial societies/clubs in London, England that spread the cost of burial among members. With low selectivity, high rates, and weekly premiums, these clubs were the forerunners of modern industrial insurance. Ibid.

In the early 1800s, some clergy in the United States banded together for the same purpose. They founded 'death insurance,' which became today's life insurance. Ibid.

The Civil War saw some pre-planning. Families contacted embalmers who followed the major battles and paid them fees ahead of time to prepare their loved ones if they were killed. After the Civil War, pre-need existed in relative obscurity.

Stansbury explains that for many years, funeral directors did not sponsor these plans. In fact, most funeral directors felt their profession shouldn't be involved. However, after World War I, some funeral directors in parts of the United States started offering "burial insurance" (p. 25).

Many other plans followed, such as mutual benefit associations, funeral certificate plans, funeral debentures, funeral trusts, funeral savings accounts, and legal reserve funeral insurance. Benefits could be any combination of cash, credits, merchandise, and service. Ibid.

Somewhere along the way, the industry decided that it was a good business practice to get people in their doors to pre-purchase services. There was an assumption of loyalty and a belief that people would go where their pre-need funds were. Some states allowed firms to earn interest on that money. Ibid.

Types of Pre-need Arrangements

- **Pre-funded funeral arrangements** are those funeral arrangements made in advance of need, including provisions for funding or prepayment.
- **Pre-planned funeral arrangements** are funeral arrangements made in advance of need that do not include provisions for funding or prepayment.

Value of Preplanning and Prefunding Funeral for the:

Consumer

- Provides time to compare several funeral homes.
- Decisions can be made in an unhurried atmosphere.
- Provides assurance that personal wishes will be known.
- Allows for consultation with funeral director and family.
- Can plan personalization options.
- Gives peace of mind that family will not be burdened with funeral expenses and having to make difficult decisions while trying to cope with grief.
- In some instances, consumers can lock in price.
- They can be financed over longer period of time if desired.
- It can help the estate financially through Medicare spend-down.

Survivors

- Helps avoid burden of making difficult decisions while under stress and grief.
- Provides peace of mind that deceased received funeral he/she envisioned.
- All funeral related documentation is in one location: The funeral home.
- Simplifies things for family.
- Relieves financial burden.

Funeral Home

- Locks in future business.
- Assures charges are paid immediately.
- Gives satisfaction of helping consumers fulfill final wishes.
- Can be good "word-of-mouth" advertisement.
- Increases status with bank.
- Allows for continuous and positive funeral home public relations.
- Enhances funeral home branding in the community at large.
- Provides the chance to secure and/or expand market share.
- Allows for reduced accounts receivable anxieties. How many funeral homes today wait 45 days or more to get paid? If consumers pay ahead of time, receivables decrease.
- Helps create more educated consumers, which make better funeral purchasers.
- Shows that you are responsive to the public request to make the funeral planning process easier.
- Helps lay the foundation for an easier, faster, less apprehensive funeral arrangement conference at the actual time of death.

Kuhnen (2017) says, "Don't keep yourself a secret. Don't wrongly believe that consumers aren't interested in planning their final arrangements ahead of time. Consumers' interest in pre-planning is growing steadily by the day" (p.A6).

Satisfaction with Decision to Prearrange

Virtually all policy owners indicate they are completely or very satisfied with their decision to prearrange. For those who are unsure about deciding to prearrange, knowing that virtually no one regrets the decision can increase their confidence. Be sure to use this statistic in your pre-need sales presentation!

The Funeral and Memorial Information Council Study (2015) reported that 89% of people, age 40 and older, believe that discussing how they want to be remembered would be meaningful. Prearranging not only offers an opportunity for your client families to discuss their wishes, but also to put plans in place that ensure those wishes are carried out.

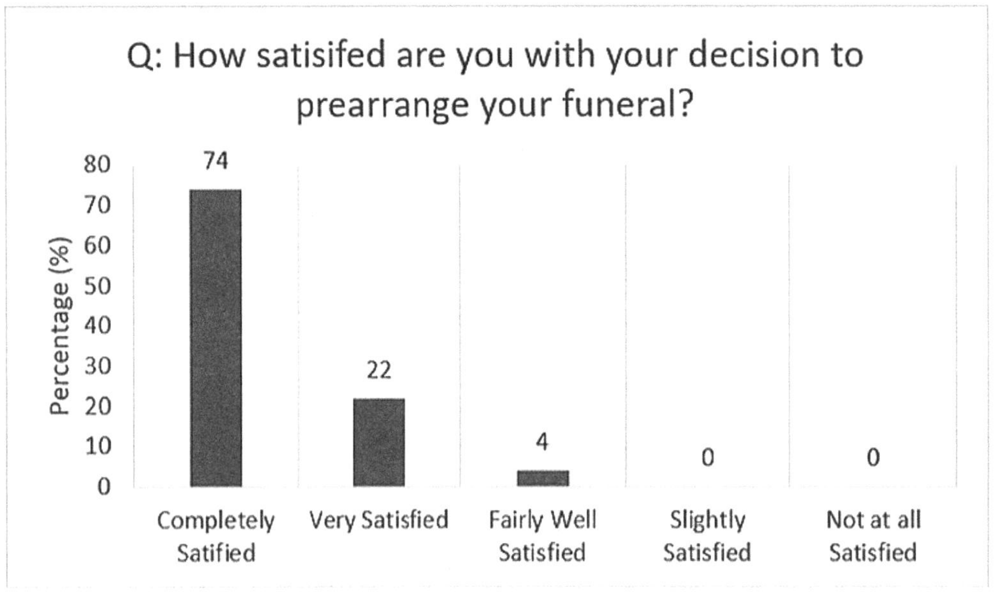

Source: Homesteaders Life Company 2017, Available at: https://www.homesteaderslife.com

Likelihood of Recommending

Homesteaders Life Company (2017) conducted a survey that revealed that 96% of policy owners would consider recommending prearranging, and more than 40% had already recommended prearrangement to someone within a few weeks of making their own arrangements.

In addition to asking for referrals, get involved in your community. This will help generate positive word-of-mouth and organic referrals. A person's friends and family members are key resources for information about prearranging. Providing a great experience for your client families is the first step in securing their recommendations. In what ways could your funeral home follow up with individuals who have prearranged to help build an ongoing relationship?

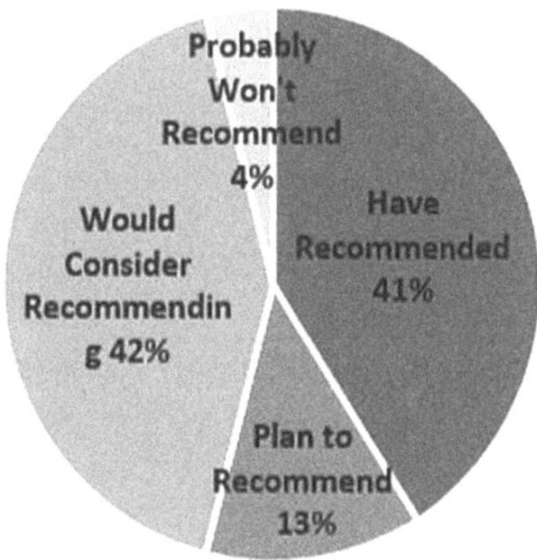

Source: Homesteader Life Company 2017, Available at: https://www.homesteaderslife.com

Negative Aspects of Prefunding for:

Consumers

- Some states do not allow prefunded contracts to be transferred to another funeral home and allow an administration fee to be taken out if a contract is cancelled or moved.
- **Scandals:** There have been scandals where the individual funeral homes, or the trust holding the funds, have stolen the money, or made bad investments and lost the funds.
- If the consumer dies before the usual excusatory timeline, only the amount paid to date will be refunded with an insurance funded contract.

Funeral Home

- The person may cancel the contract, devaluing your accumulated potential income.
- If the contract is guaranteed, the funeral home may lose money on the future funeral. Most experts are advising not to guarantee contracts anymore.
- Some consumers tell their family everything is taken care of financially with the prearrangement. It is not unusual for a family to get upset if there are items that were not paid for or if the price was not guaranteed, especially if they have to make an unplanned payment.

Types of Pre-need Contracts

- **A Revocable Contract** is one in which the contract may be terminated by the purchaser at any time prior to the death, with a refund of the monies paid as prescribed by state law.
- **An Irrevocable Contract** is one in which the contract cannot be terminated or canceled.
- **A Guaranteed Contract** is where the funeral home guarantees that the services and merchandise will be provided at the time of need for an amount not exceeding the original amount of the contract, plus any interest, regardless of the cost of providing the services and merchandise at the time of death.
- **A Non-Guaranteed Contract** is when the funeral home only agrees that the amount prepaid, plus any interest will be credited to the balance due. However, the price of the funeral will be whatever the current price is for the services and merchandise at the time the death occurs.

To Guarantee or Not to Guarantee Pre-need Cost

When considering guaranteeing or not guaranteeing the cost of pre-need contracts, funeral home owners must balance three factors that are out of their control:

1. Inflationary cost of providing merchandise and service.
2. The return on the money being held to provide for the funeral.
3. The length of time between the purchase of the contract and the date of death.

According to Dan Isard (2014), the length of time from contract date to the time of the consumer's death is a major factor in dealing with the problems associated with the pre-need cost guarantee. He explains that there are four types of funding:

1. Insurance single payment
2. Insurance installment payment
3. Trust single payment
4. Trust installment payment

While trust installment payments are extremely rare, they do exist. There is a lot of information concerning the single payment versus the installment payment. Ibid.

Single Payment		Installment Payment
78	Average Age at Issue	72
20%	Mortality in Year 1 and 2	10%
8 Years	First 50% Mortality Reached	15 Years
13 Years	Average Span for Second 50% Mortality	13 Years

More people buy single payment at an older age than installment payment. Single payment has a 20% two-year mortality rate, while installment payment has about half of that. 50% of those paying a single payment will have died within eight years, and those that do not will die within nine to twenty-one years. Contrast these statistics to the fact that installment payment has a 50% mortality rate in about fifteen years; with those that do not die within the first 15 years dying between years sixteen to twenty-eight. Ibid.

Isard (2014) asks important questions about these statistics. How are you supposed to guarantee that you can invest your money at a rate equal to the costs within and outside of your control for 21 to 28 years? Will the growth of the money being held be enough to cover the inflationary rise in cost of the merchandise and service at the time of death? For example, what if the pre-need death does not occur for 15 years?

Top Motivators for Prearranging

In his column, "Pre-need Roundtable," Steve Cronin (2017b) interviews experts on prearranging. He reports that the top factors that motivate policy owners to prearrange are:

1. Family member died recently.
2. They finally knew the arrangements they wanted.
3. They finally had the money to do it.
4. Their spouse wanted to prearrange.

Cronin (2017b) elaborates that there isn't one single consumer group that makes up those who prearrange. Three of the most prominent groups (this is not an exhaustive list) are:

1. Those going on social assistance.
2. Those who are putting their affairs in order to prepare for the inevitable.
3. Those looking to make it easy on their loved ones when the time comes. Ibid.

Each of these three groups have different motivations and require a different message to reach them.

The first group are to those going on social assistance. In most states, a funeral is an allowable use of funds that will not be considered in the five-year look back for social assistance consideration. Many people are referred by state social workers or financial planners. The value in these instances is that the beneficiary gets to use the money they earned through their lifetime to create a fitting and suitable funeral for their loved ones to say goodbye. Ibid.

The second group of people who prepay are those who have either had a recent diagnosis or suffered a personal loss of someone close to them. For these people, it is an opportunity to put things in order before, God forbid, something happens to them. The motivation for these folks is preparation and 'being ready.' Ibid.

The third group is composed of the "planners." These people like to have a bow on every package and a checkmark in every box. They are usually retired and have family, and they want to make sure the family does not need to do anything when the day comes. This group is motivated by the feeling of making it easy for loved ones left behind. Ibid.

Consumers take action to prearrange most often due to the death of a friend or family member. Reaching out to family and friends can help secure more prearrangements.

Another important reason why consumers decide to prearrange is that they know what they want for their final arrangements. You can provide a valuable service to your community by informing families of the ever-changing options available. What types of events would be effective for educating your community?

Q: What is the main reason you decided to make these plans now, instead of last year or next year?

Reason	Percentage (%)
Family member/friend died recently	23
Finally knew arrangements wanted	17
Finally had money to do it	13
Spouse wanted to prearrange	10
Have serious/terminal illness	6
Received call/mail about prearranging	5
Needed to reduce my assets	5
Recently prepared/updated will	4
Recently worked on planning estate	4
Other	14

Source: Homesteader Life Company 2017, Available at: https://www.homesteaderslife.com/

Several recent studies have shown:

23% of respondents reported they had made prearrangements for themselves. Up 4 points from 2014.
15% paid through a funeral home.
9% paid through insurance.
6% paid through a trust.

....

60% preferred to save survivors from having to pay.
44% preferred to ensure final wishes taken care of.
39% preferred to guarantee price.
51% of those who had not prearranged said they were "somewhat" to "very likely" to do so within 5 years.
17% said they were "very likely" to preplan.
30.5% said they would likely prepay.
34% of those who had not prearranged said it was not a priority.
20% said they were not interested in prearranging.
17% did not want to think about it. Up from 12.6% in 2014.

....

76% told another person.
43% chose cremation.
33% put instructions in will or letter.
23% chose a cemetery plot.
22% selected a funeral home.

Key Factors Affecting Funeral Preplanning

- Competition from corporate consolidators and insurance companies.
- Growth of 65-year-old and older population was 46.2 million. By 2030, 1 in 5 Americans will be 65 or older. In 2033, Americans 65 and older will outnumber those younger than 18 for the first time. In 2060, 24% of the population will be 65 and over, up from 10% in 1990.
- Endorsements - From groups such as the FTC, AARP, and Consumer Reports endorsement of prearranging, but not prefunding.

Design of Pre-need Programs: The Selling of Pre-need

Pre-need programs usually fit into one of two categories: Active or passive. Each category approaches the consumer in a somewhat different manner, and each requires a different style of marketing on the part of the funeral home.

Passive Pre-need Program

This is a non-assertive approach. The consumer receives pre-need information through brochures displayed in the funeral home, through the yellow pages, or newspaper advertisement. Pre-need arrangements are conducted by funeral directors who also do at-need arrangements. Most funeral directors who choose this style do not look at themselves as salespeople, and feel they are not really selling people a funeral. They see themselves as presenting the family with options in the merchandise and services they offer, and the family selects what they desire without any influence from them.

Do-It-Yourself

For many small firms (less than 100 calls), the owner himself usually does the pre-need program. This is typically a passive pre-need program. The funeral director waits for people to come to him and request a pre-need arrangement. This is not an effective way to build a successful pre-need business. In fact, you may lose future business to firms that have a dedicated pre-need employee.

Active Pre-need Program

An active pre-need approach is quite different. The funeral director usually uses more than one direct marketing approach, including direct mail, TV or radio ads, telephone solicitation, and public relations activities. The staff members who do pre-need usually do not have other functions to perform in the funeral home. They may not always be funeral directors, but rather people with sales experience. One reason for this is that in some states, you do not have to be a funeral director to sell pre-need. You only need to be a licensed insurance agent if your firm offers insurance as a means of paying for pre-need.

Hire an employee: Hiring one or more salespeople to coordinate a pre-need program is really the only way for a funeral home to create an active effective program. Research conducted by *Funeral Service Insider* shows that funeral homes doing fewer than 200 annual funerals and using a dedicated pre-need salesperson average 77% more funded pre-need sales than similar sized firms who use at-need funeral directors to do pre-need sales.

Outsourcing: Another choice a funeral home has for developing a pre-need program is to hire an outside company that specialized in pre-need selling. This is commonly known as outsourcing. The simple benefit of outsourcing is the magnitude of the results achieved. Using an outside pre-need company will usually generate the greatest number of pre-need sales in the quickest amount of time.

Common sales techniques used by active pre-need salespeople often dismay funeral directors who prefer the passive approach. Many funeral directors have more of a counseling personality than a salesperson personality. Along with using public relations and advertising methods (discussed in Chapter 21 Marketing), they may use some of the following techniques to generate leads. Many directors that run a passive program consider numbers 3 & 4 below to be sleazy and unprofessional.

1. **Referrals:** Asking a person who made a pre-need purchase for names and phone numbers of their friends and family. The pre-need salespeople will then contact the referrals saying that Mr. _____ referred them.

2. **At-need funeral files:** The pre-need salesperson will review at-need files and contact the relatives listed in the file to see if they are interested in purchasing pre-need.

3. **Funeral register book:** The pre-need salesperson will copy the names and addresses of people who signed the register book during the funeral or visitation and contact them.

4. **Neighbors of deceased:** The pre-need salesperson will contact the neighbors of the deceased.

Cronin (2017b) reports, "There is no singular way to effectively market a pre-need program. A successful pre-need marketing strategy is multifaceted. Traditional strategies such as direct marketing, offsite seminars and aftercare continue to play a significant role in any successful program. However, we find that we are spending more and more time meeting today's consumer in the digital space through email automation, Facebook, and by creating engaging digital experiences that educate the consumer about the value of a funeral" (p. 74).

Skills Needed for Pre-need Sales

Counseling

Most funeral directors possess outstanding counseling skills by virtue of personality, experience, and training. These skills come into play during pre-need counseling and in at-need situations. The emphasis in at-need counseling is helping people cope with death. With pre-need clients, however, the emphasis for counseling is on dealing with issues of personal finance and allocation of resources. For many funeral directors, this is a new area of responsibility that requires new skills and important decisions to be made. New skills must be developed to accommodate and effectively deal with this change.

A pre-need arrangement conference gives the director the time and space necessary to get to know the family and explore ways services can be customized to meet their family's unique needs without the pressure of at-need time constraints.

The pre-need salesperson will need to approach the interview in a different manner than they do for at-need. During at-need arrangements, the family has come to the funeral home to select a funeral for the deceased. The funeral director does not have to convince the family to purchase a funeral. Often in a pre-need situation, the family has agreed to only talk to the pre-need salesperson. They have not said they want to purchase anything. The pre-need salesperson must convince the family to make a purchase. To accomplish this, the salesperson's approach to the conference is both sales-oriented and educational.

Management

Since most funeral home managers have similar experiences, the problems they encounter in marketing pre-need, and their reactions, are similar. These ten steps recommended by Glenn Gould are common to most successful pre-need programs and are recommended to any funeral home intent on establishing a pre-need program.

- Develop a marketing plan detailing the program's objectives and how to accomplish them.
- Begin small first by training yourself, then others, one at a time.
- Understand the firm's attributes and liabilities from the consumer's perspective and advertise pre-need by building on strengths.
- When advertising, generate leads. Benefits from name awareness advertising are too long-term and intangible.
- Ultimately, additional staff will be necessary. Don't expect an at-need staff to accomplish two jobs successfully.
- When hiring, select people with talent and desire.
- Plan to train anyone and everyone hired. The training must be customized to the individual's work experience.
- Monitor the pre-need program to identify the most successful promotions, advertisements, and counselors. Determine why they succeeded and duplicate their success.
- Allow a program enough time to succeed.
- When a successful formula has been developed, expand on it.

Options for Locations of Pre-Need Conference

- Funeral Home
- Family Home
- Hospice
- Hospital

The setting of the pre-need conference can make a big difference in the family's overall experience. Meeting with a family at the funeral home allows you to show your firm in its best light. You will be able to take the family on a tour of your facilities, show them merchandise options, and explain the other resources your firm provides (such as a grief support library). Consider what elements make your funeral home exceptional, and how might you share those with individuals who prearrange.

Making funeral arrangements at a family's home can be comforting because they are in their comfort zone. Modern technology enables a funeral director to bring all the necessary technology to the client's home with the use of a computer, smart phone, or a hard copy catalog.

Hospice, or a hospital, may provide a location for a patient who is restricted to a bed.

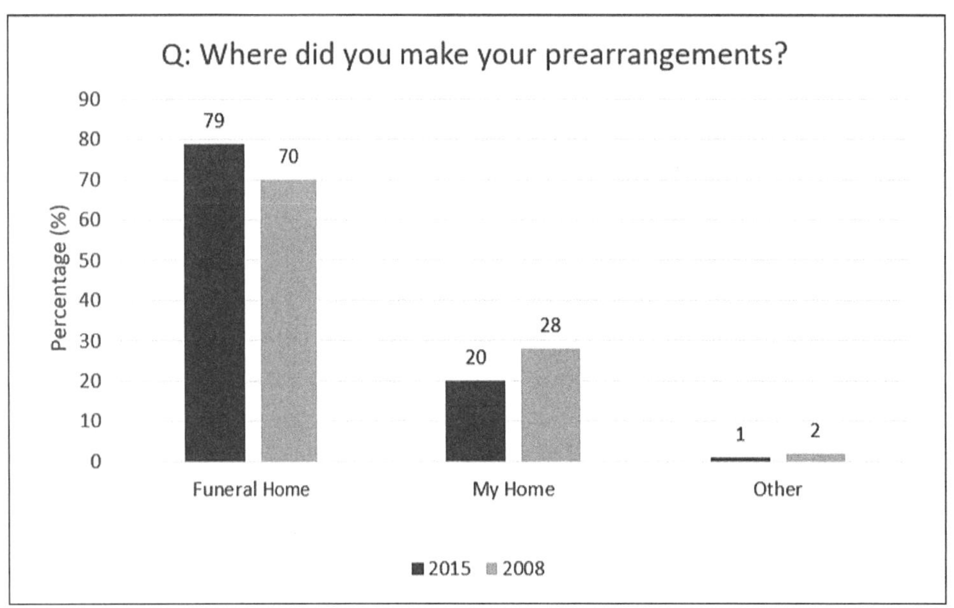

Source: Homesteaders Life Company 2017, Available at: https://www.homesteaderslife.com/

Pre-Need Staff

The people responsible for making pre-need arrangements differ from funeral home to funeral home. Some states require the person to be a licensed funeral director, while other states have no requirement unless insurance is used to fund the pre-need. If insurance is used, an insurance license may be required.

In most states that do not require a funeral director license, salespeople are responsible for making pre-need arrangements. Most have a history of selling other products before entering funeral service. This does not mean they are not caring, honest people. Most of the non-licensed pre-need salespeople that this author has met are trained professionals who really believe in the value of pre-planning and genuinely care about the people they serve.

Average Funeral Home Pre-Need Staff

A recent *Funeral Service Monitor Newsletter* reported the following staffing patterns in the area of pre-need:

Funeral Homes:	**72%** have no staff dedicated to preneed. At-need funeral directors generate preneed sales.
	15% have one preneed representative for each 200 at-need funerals.
	13% have less than one full-time person per 200 at-need funerals.

The Numbers

Dan Isard, President of the Foresight Company, says that most businesses that involve sales have a formula that gives an indication of how much prospecting (the act of generating leads) must be done to get appointments and how many appointments must be generated to achieve a number of sales. A rule of thumb in an aggressive pre-need program is:

100 = 10 = 2.5

One hundred sales letters sent and followed up by phone will generate ten appointments. The ten appointments will generate 2.5 sales. To sell 100 pre-need funerals takes 1,000 letters sent with phone follow up and 250 appointments at approximately two hours each, or 500 hours. The amount of time it takes to get these 250 appointments is 125 hours. To summarize, it takes 625 hours to sell 100 pre-need funerals using an active and aggressive approach.

125 hours to get appointments
500 hours to complete the appointments

= **625** Total hours

Methods of Funding Pre-need

Consumers have several ways to pay for their pre-need arrangements, depending on the laws of the state in which they purchase the funeral. Some states require 100% of pre-need money be put in a trust/bank account. In this case, the family can cancel the account at any time. Other states have regulations allowing a certain percentage of the total to be used by the funeral director for an administrative fee. An example would be that 90% must go into the account and 10% can be used by the funeral director.

The trust can be individual, in that each pre-need contract is in a separate account, or it can be combined into a master trust. Many state funeral director associations have developed pre-need trusts for their members to use. It is necessary to keep accurate records of all the contracts in the master trust so that none are lost or have an incorrect total.

A specialized insurance policy can also be used to pay for the pre-need funeral. The cost of this type of insurance policy can be paid in one lump sum or made in payments over a specific period of time, such as five years. Some insurance policies will not make a payment, or payment will be reduced, if the person dies within a specific time, such as one year from date of purchase.

Trust vs. Insurance

	Advantages	Disadvantages
Bank Trusts	• Simplicity and ease of sale • Local administration • Leverages funeral home's bank relationships	• Taxable requiring 1099s • Restricted in many states (i.e., 100%trusting) • Requires trust set-up at time of sale
Life Insurance/ Annuities	• Growth in non-taxable or tax-deferred • Death benefit is non-taxable for insurance or taxable annuities • Receive commission at time of placement	• Product knowledge • Licensing • Preneed statutory clarity

Honoring the Contract

When most people make a prearrangement and prepay the funeral, they expect their contract with the funeral home to be honored by their next of kin when they die. In most states, however, the next of kin have the legal right to change or cancel the contract and purchase the services and merchandise they desire instead, or even change funeral homes.

If different members of the family of the deceased disagree on honoring or not honoring the deceased's wishes, they could go to court and let a judge make the decision. In this case, the judge would consider the feelings of all parties involved and would also give much consideration to the wishes of the deceased. Often, if the judge feels that none of the survivors would be emotionally scarred by carrying out the terms of the funeral contract, he will judge in favor of the deceased's wishes. He could, however, let the arrangements be changed if he felt it was in the best interest of the survivors.

Who Make the Best Pre-Need Buyers? Women?

By: Christopher Kuhnen (2017)

Women!!

- Women control the world...at least that's what my wife always tells me.
- Women are generally less apprehensive and more practical in amenably exploring and discussing the subjects of death and dying. While most men try to avoid the subject at all costs, most women approach it in a more realistic and open manner.

- Women tend to be more thorough in their buying decisions and do more comparison investigation. While men tend to go with the first thing that “fits the bill,” women are generally selective and look for the best overall value.
- Women are usually easier to work with and very appreciative of those who take the time to work with them.
- Women represent 51% of the US population, according to the latest US Census Bureau data.
- In a study by BMO Wealth Institute, 66% of women identified themselves as primary decision-makers over household investible assets.
- Women are the primary breadwinners in more than 40% of American households, according to a report by the Center for Talent Innovation.

Given this information, here are some tips on how to best serve women:

Don’t be a salesperson! Don’t talk, act, look, or smell like a salesperson. Present yourself as an authentic, caring individual. High pressure sales will turn women away. Be relaxed, confident (but not arrogant), and easy to talk to.

Don’t talk at women, talk with them. Generally, women love to engage in free-flowing conversation that is not dominated by you. They need to be able to talk all they desire. Ask them plenty of open-ended questions to get them talking and keep them talking. The more women talk and share their ideas and feelings and fears with you, the better. They know what they need and will tell you, if you will only listen to what they say and seek to understand their priorities and what they wish to accomplish.

Seek to meet in a comfortable, relaxing environment. The arrangement office at the funeral home is not necessarily the best place to discuss funeral pre-planning with anyone, let alone women. They generally prefer to discuss the matter in the comfort of their own home or some other outside, relaxing environment.

Encourage women to invite any of their friends, associates, or relatives on your pre-need presentation appointment. Women tend to appreciate interacting with you surrounded by those they know and trust.

Women love stories. Explain the value of funeral pre-planning through stories you are personally familiar with. Allow women to share stories of their own.

Be easy-going. Don’t rush women for a decision. Women, like the rest of us, need time to process their choices and options. Provide them with the information they need and then allow them room to digest it all. Do not bombard women, or anyone, with a bunch of numbers. If they like what they see, they will find the money to pay for it. Cheapest isn’t always what women are searching for. They generally want good value and will gladly spend the price, if they feel what you present meet their needs.

Encourage women to share their positive experience with your funeral home with others. Women refer at a rate two and a half times that of men. Once they like you, get to know you, trust you, they will want all their friends to know about you as well.

Negative Views of Pre-need Planning

For years, two notable funeral service personalities have expressed negative views about pre-need. Thomas Lynch, a funeral director, award-winning poet, author, and subject of a TV special has commented:

> The pre-selling of funerals – the junk-mailed, telemarketed, bargain-in-the-briefcase, flipchart, point-and-click brand of funeral sales that has infected funeral service for the past 25 years – has not been good for the funeral, the funeral consumer or the funeral service profession. Driven by the interests of vendors, by quota and sales pitch, it has turned the funeral from a rich intergenerational, family and community event into a primarily narcissistic one. Instead of what to do with our dead when they die, it peddles, "What do you want done with you when you're dead? Have it your way at Funeral King." Funerals, which were formerly participatory and deeply meaningful events, are more often now done deals, spectator events. Family and friends need only show up. And since they didn't get to make any of the decisions that they, after all, must live with, many families are choosing not to bother even showing up.

Chris Raymond, Former editor of ***The Director***, has stated many times:

> ***We Have a Problem Here!*** Pre-need is killing your profession. Until every consumer in every state can pre-fund their service, disposition and interment choice via any investment vehicle, and sleep fully confident that their money will be there when they need it, you have a problem.
>
> You do not walk into a car dealership and say, "I'm going to have to buy a car at some point in the future. I want to put my money down now and have you guarantee that when it's time to make the purchase, I can buy it at today's prices." I don't think that would go over well. Nor have I walked into my favorite furniture store and asked the salesperson to save the couch of my dreams, so I can buy it in three years. That's layaway on steroids and not an accepted business practice in any retail or service industry that I know, except funeral service. We are the only profession that has this "buy now, use later" approach to business. We call it pre-need, prearranging, funeral insurance, advanced planning, funeral trusts — the terms are myriad, but the message is the same: Offering a chance for a person to lock in prices and make decisions months, years, or decades before the event. Ibid.

The following column from syndicated columnist "Dear Abby" appeared April 4, 2007 (Van Buren, 2007).

Funeral Director Insensitive

> ***Dear Abby,:*** *My dear 75-year-old friend, "Margery," lost her 51-year-old daughter and her 29-year-old granddaughter to cancer. (They were mother and daughter.) At the funeral home there was a table at the entrance to the viewing room with a printed card asking for your name, address, and phone number if you wanted to receive an obituary and memorial card encased in plastic. (I did.) Two days after the funeral, I received a call from the funeral home asking me what my thoughts were about the funeral. I told the man I had been to many funerals in my life but had never been called and asked my thoughts about any of them. And then, this insensitive jerk proceeded to ask me if I had any thoughts about making "prearrangements" for my OWN demise and funeral! Abby, I couldn't believe my ears! A funeral home trolling for business from grieving friends and relatives of the deceased mother and daughter two days after the granddaughter's funeral?*
>
> *Your thoughts, please. Doris L. in Florida*
>
> ***Dear Doris:*** *Just when I think I have seen it all, a letter like yours lands on my desk. Whether the person who called you was the funeral director or a salesman, that person is his own worst enemy.*

The FTC Cooling-Off Rule

Pre-need sales activities conducted away from the place of business are subject to the FTC's Cooling-Off Rule for Door-to-Door Sales.

The Cooling-Off Rule gives consumers three days to cancel purchases of $25 or more when the purchase is made at a buyer's residence. It applies even in those cases when the consumer has invited the salesperson to make a presentation at his or her residence. In a recent amendment to the Cooling-Off Rule, the FTC increased the exclusionary limit to $130 (adjusted for inflation) for purchases made from sellers in temporary locations, since sellers' practices did not appear to be as problematic when sales were made away from the consumer's home (FTC, 2015).

Online sales are not expressly addressed in the Cooling-Off Rule but would be akin to sales made entirely by mail or telephone. The Cooling-Off Rule protects consumers who are vulnerable to high pressure sales when confronted in their homes or workplaces. This exposure does not exist with online mail or phone sales since it is easy for the customer to end the communication. Ibid.

Under the Rule:

- The salesperson must orally tell a consumer his or her cancellation rights at the time of sale, without any misrepresentation, and give the consumer two copies of a cancellation form along with a copy of the contract or receipt.

- The contract or receipt must be dated, show the name and address of the seller, explain the right to cancel, and be in the same language in which the sale presentation is conducted.

The Rule states that it is an unfair or a deceptive act to:

A. Include in any door-to-door contract or receipt a confession of judgement or waiver of the consumer's right of cancellation.

B. Fail to provide the consumer with a copy of the contract or with a dated receipt containing the seller's name, address, and the following disclosure in boldface type:

> **"You, the buyer, may cancel this transaction at any time prior to midnight of the third business day after the date of this transaction. See the attached for an explanation of this right."**

- To cancel a sale, the consumer must sign and date one copy of the cancellation form and mail it to the address given for the cancellation, making certain that the envelope is postmarked before midnight of the third business day after the contract date. Saturday is considered a business day; Sundays and federal holidays are not considered business days. The FTC cautions consumers to send the cancellation form by certified mail or to hand deliver the notice. The consumer does not have to give a reason for cancelling a purchase.

- The seller has 10 days to cancel and return the contract or other signed negotiable instrument and to provide a full refund.

- The FTC Cooling-Off Rule does not preempt state laws and private contractual provisions that provide cancellation rights to consumers signing pre-need contracts and insurance policies. Some state laws provide more rights than the Rule (NFDA, 2016a).

Pre-Need Bill of Rights

Consumer Preneed Bill of Rights

Prior to purchasing any funeral goods or services or signing a preneed funeral contract, we urge you to ask us any and all questions you may have regarding your preneed purchases.

To ensure that you, as our client family, have a full understanding of the preneed funeral transaction, we guarantee the following rights and protections.

We will:

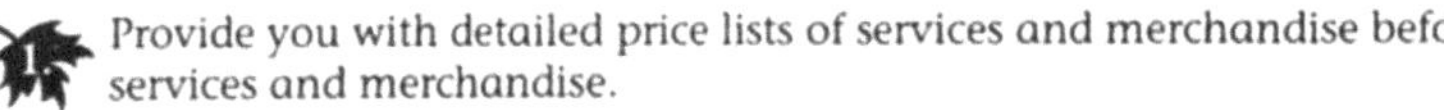

1. Provide you with detailed price lists of services and merchandise before you select services and merchandise.

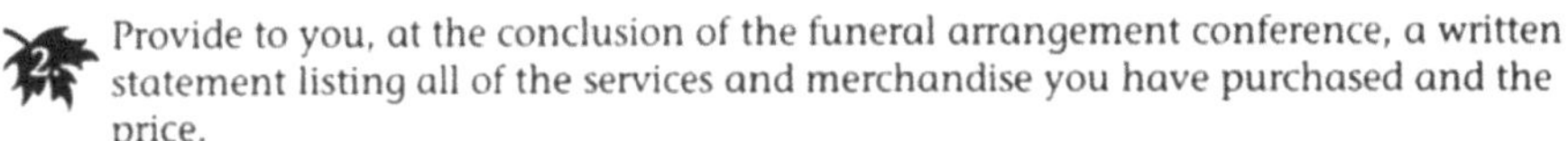

2. Provide to you, at the conclusion of the funeral arrangement conference, a written statement listing all of the services and merchandise you have purchased and the price.

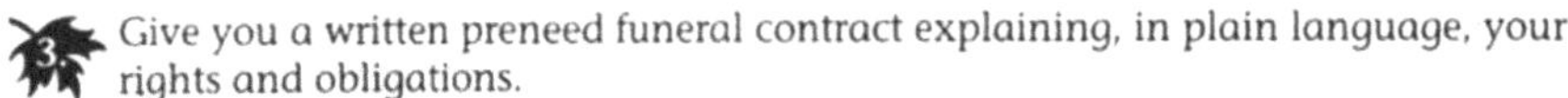

3. Give you a written preneed funeral contract explaining, in plain language, your rights and obligations.

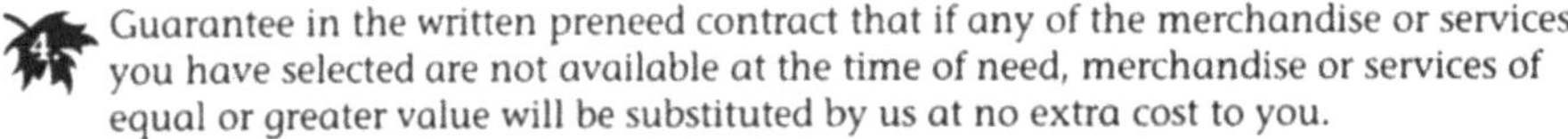

4. Guarantee in the written preneed contract that if any of the merchandise or services you have selected are not available at the time of need, merchandise or services of equal or greater value will be substituted by us at no extra cost to you.

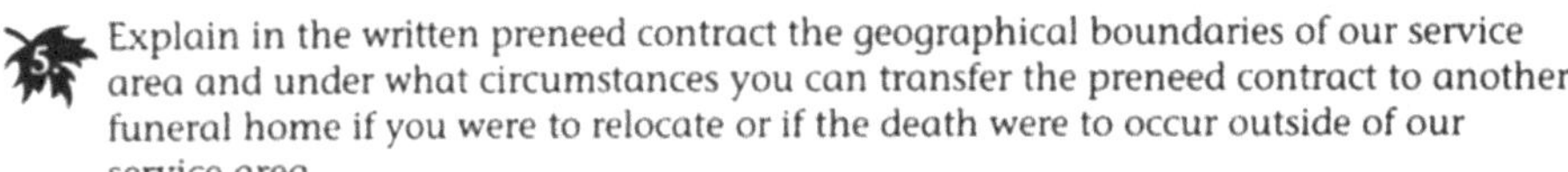

5. Explain in the written preneed contract the geographical boundaries of our service area and under what circumstances you can transfer the preneed contract to another funeral home if you were to relocate or if the death were to occur outside of our service area.
6. State in the written preneed contract where and how much of the funds you pay to us will be deposited until the funeral is provided.

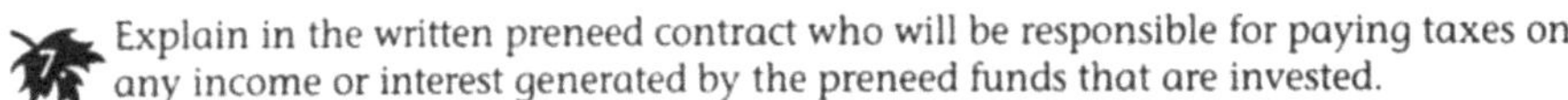

7. Explain in the written preneed contract who will be responsible for paying taxes on any income or interest generated by the preneed funds that are invested.
8. Inform you in the written contract whether and to what extent we are guaranteeing prices of the merchandise and services you are purchasing. If the prices are not guaranteed, we will explain to you in the written preneed contract who will be responsible for paying any additional amounts that may be due at the time of the funeral.
9. Explain in the written preneed contract who will receive any excess funds that may result if the income or interest generated by the invested preneed funds exceed future price increases in the funeral merchandise and services you have selected.
10. Explain in the written preneed contract whether and under what circumstances you may cancel your preneed contract and how much of the funds you paid to us will be refunded to you.

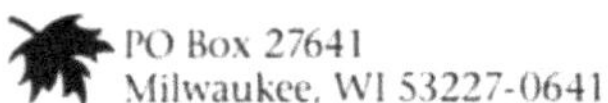

PO Box 27641
Milwaukee, WI 53227-0641

Source: National Funeral Directors Association

NOTES

NOTES

Chapter 12

CASKETS & VAULTS

Source: Batesville Casket Company

By: Gary Sokoll

Casket – A *rigid container, which is designed for the encasement of human remains, and which is usually constructed of wood, metal, or like material, and ornamented and lined with fabric* (F.T.C. Definition).

Casket – *A case or receptacle in which human remains are placed for protection, practical utility, and a suitable memory picture; any box or container of one or more parts in which a dead human body is placed prior to interment, entombment, or cremation which may or may not be permanently interred, entombed, or cremated with the dead human remains.*

Coffin – *A case or receptacle for dead human remains which is arthropodal in shape (widest at the shoulders, narrowest at the feet).*

Casket History

The forerunner of today's casket was the coffin. In the 17th century, this octagon shaped wooden container was built either by the deceased's family or by cabinet makers who produced and sold them as a part of their business. In 1848, Fisk Metallic Coffins started the metal casket industry, but wood dominated casket construction until the late 1800s.

Prior to the mid-1900s, most funeral homes utilized two types of casket selection rooms. The first offering was a room consisting of a mix of wood and metal full-sized caskets, depending on what "their families" historically preferred. Half-couch or full-couch was the variable. The second type of casket selection room lived inside a three-ring binder, aka "the book," usually utilized out of physical constraints or economic necessity (Mittenzwei, n.d.).

In the late 1900s, innovation out of necessity provided one of the biggest changes the death care industry had seen since gravity injection devices found a home on the shelf. A mortician outside of Liverpool, England, cramped for space, split three coffins lengthwise down the middle and hung them against the wall. This first system was admittedly crude, but eye-opening. Today thousands of rooms across the U.S. and Europe have evolved from this initial layout (Mittenzwei, n.d.).

The Batesville Casket Company started in 1884 as the Batesville Coffin Company. It changed to its current name in 1906. Boyertown Casket Company was started in 1917. In 1940 the Aurora Casket Company, which was founded in 1890, began producing metal caskets. By the 1950s there were over 700 casket manufacturers in the United States. Massive consolidation in the industry, however, has resulted in fewer than 175 U.S. casket manufacturers by 2007.

1890 Octagonal Draped

Both pictures Courtesy Wedekindt Funeral Home, Inc.

1922 Interior of Fine All Silk Liberty, Group Shirred and Draped

Casket Construction: Material Used in Construction

There are two basic materials most often used in casket construction – **wood and metal**. Caskets can also be made of fiberglass and plastic.

Wood Caskets

Wood is a natural material that provides a beautiful and warm appearance. Various staining and finishing techniques may enhance grain patterns. In addition, wood caskets are unique. No two caskets are the same because grain patterns may vary from tree to tree. Wood casket prices can vary depending on the species of wood selected and the amount of workmanship required to construct them.

- ***Hardwood*** - Wood that comes from trees that lose their leaves annually (deciduous trees). Close-grained resistant wood, usually more expensive than softwood casket.

- ***Softwood*** - Wood from cone bearing trees (coniferous trees). Lighter and more easily cut than hardwood.

Milled components are constructed by hand and are hand-finished. In addition, great care is taken to match grains on top panels and hold to a minimum the use of joint fillers by creating tight, crisp joints.

Raw lumber is purchased by the casket manufacturer directly from the lumber mill. Normally, this lumber is pre-dried to avoid warping and splitting of the final product. The drying process may vary from mill to mill, but generally, lumber is first air dried for an average of one to six months. This reduces the moisture content to about 35%. The lumber is pre-dried for up to 28 days in a controlled environment, further reducing the moisture content to about 20%. The lumber is then kiln dried for four to seven days, depending on the type of wood. Kiln drying reduces moisture to 5-6 %. Dried lumber is stored until it is ready for use.

Species of Wood (solid wood)

- ***Birch*** - The birch tree is characterized by its smooth, thin layered bark. The lumber harvested from this tree is a closed-grain, heavy white wood. It is a durable wood often seen in kitchen cabinetry. Birch will accept a variety of stains.

- ***Cherry*** - Cherry is another white, closed-grained wood that is often stained in a red hue. A high gloss finish complements the rich appearance of this attractive species.

- ***Mahogany*** - Considered the premier hardwood by many, mahogany is one of the more expensive species used in casket construction. This is, in part, due to the fact that mahogany is imported from Central America and sometimes Africa. Mahogany is a fine-grained hardwood that is reddish-brown in appearance. The most expensive mahogany caskets require numerous steps in the finishing process, resulting in a luxurious, handcrafted appearance.

- ***Maple*** - Maple is a light, closed-grained wood that may be finished in any stain. Consumers are familiar with maple, as it is found in furniture and bowling alley lanes.

- ***Oak*** - Known for its strength and durability, oak is a popular, light-colored hardwood. Both the red and white oak caskets have comprised approximately one-third of all hardwood caskets sold in the United States. Consumers are familiar with oak as a structural component of furniture, home interior trim, and wood flooring.

- ***Walnut*** - Like mahogany, walnut is an expensive wood found in few hardwood caskets. Walnut is a brown wood that is decreasing in popularity due to the high cost of raw lumber. In fact, it represents approximately 2% of all hardwood casket sales. Today, it is rarely used in the manufacture of furniture.

- ***Pine*** - Pine is an abundant resource in the United States. This light-colored soft wood is noted for its twig knots, which provide an attractive feature for many consumers. Pine is a soft wood that varies in grain pattern. Its relative low cost makes pine an attractive choice in wood caskets.

- ***Poplar*** - Poplar is a hardwood tree that produces soft wood when compared to other hardwood trees. Poplar's hardness is on par with that of pine or cedar, but it has a much finer grain and more pleasing appearance than the more coarsely grained softwoods.

Selected Hardwood (Salix) - A casket constructed from many different species of wood (ex: poplar, cottonwood), sometimes referred to a salix or willow; the component parts of a single casket will not necessarily be constructed of the same species of wood. Options include:

- ***Laminates*** - Gluing together sheets of different materials. Occasionally, wood caskets may be covered with a laminate. A laminate may be described as a thin covering or layer over a thick base material. Often the laminate is of finer quality than the inexpensive base.

- ***Wood Veneer*** - An example of a laminate that includes a thin wood veneer, such as oak, adhered to a thick, inexpensive material such as plywood. The purpose, of course, is to provide a rich appearance without the high cost of using the solid raw material throughout the casket shell.

- ***Artificial Veneer*** – Man-made or artificial laminates, such as vinyl, may be adhered to a wood or wood by-product base material. Artificial laminates tend to be inexpensive and provide an alternative to traditional wood and metal caskets.

- ***Wood By-Products*** - Corrugated fiberboard is a cardboard often used to construct lightweight, inexpensive caskets. Sometimes caskets made of this material are marketed as alternative containers or caskets for direct dispositions.

- ***Composition Board*** (Pressed Board, Particle Board, Flake Board) - Particles of wood bonded together with waterproof glue; the different types are distinguished by the size of the particles of wood used.

- ***Plywood*** - Thin sheets of wood glued together so that the grains are at right angles to one another; an odd number of sheets will be used so that the grain on the front and back will always run the same direction.

Some consumers do not select wood because, being a natural material, it will eventually decompose if placed directly in soil. Wood caskets also do not afford the same protection for the dead human body that gasketed metals do. Being a naturally porous material, wood may permit the entrance of water and the earth's elements over a period of time.

Metal Caskets

Metal caskets are the most popular type of casket sold in the United States today. Among the various metals used, steel carries the highest percentage of sales. Metal caskets are manufactured by assembling various component parts. These component parts, such as caps, side panels, and ends are formed from sheets of metal that are stamped from huge presses and expensive dyes. This machining process is responsible for the smooth lines and contours found in casket shells. The components are then welded together to form the body of the casket. Often, heavy gauge steel channel facing is fastened inside to provide added support by increasing rigidity and limiting flexing.

The 2 main type of metals used in casket-making are ferrous and non-ferrous.

1. **<u>Ferrous Metal</u>** - Any metal formed from iron (steel or stainless steel).

   • ***Steel*** - *A metal alloy consisting mainly or iron and carbon; used in caskets, it is low in carbon, which keeps it soft and malleable; commercial steel contains carbon in an amount up to 1.7% as an essential alloy constituent.*

   • ***Gauge*** - *A measurement of thickness of metals; the number of sheets of metal necessary to equal approximately one inch of thickness. The lower the gauge, the thicker the metal.*

   - 16-gauge = 1/16 of an inch
   - 20-gauge = 1/20 of an inch

   On average, 19-gauge is 16% thicker than 20-gauge and will last 29% longer when buried in soil. 18-gauge is 33% thicker than 20-gauge and will last 58% longer. 16-gauge is 67% thicker than 20-gauge and will last 133% longer.

   The expression of gauge is a standard measurement often referred to as United States Standard Gauge. Gauge tolerances help the manufacturer maintain uniformity and quality control of cold rolled steel. Keep in mind, however, that gauge tolerance may vary from one manufacturer to the other. It is possible to have a "heavy" 19-gauge steel casket that is thicker than a light 18-gauge steel casket. This could result in an allowable variation on thickness that is less than the advertised gauge.

   19-gauge steel is the thickest and most durable carbon steel used in the manufacturing of caskets. Stamping dies used to produce 16-gauge component parts, such as body panels, ends, caps, and corners, must be of high quality and strength. Often caskets with round corners and urn corner styles are manufactured using 16-gauge steel.

   • ***Stainless Steel*** - *A metal alloy of steel, chromium, and sometimes nickel which is used in casket construction; it is noted for its ability to resist rust. All grades of stainless steel must have at least 11% chromium to qualify as stainless steel.*

   Stainless steel represents a bridge between steel caskets and copper and bronze caskets. It offers additional corrosion protection over steel, but it lacks the longevity of copper and bronze. Stainless steel has enjoyed a steady increase in popularity among consumers recently. There are 40 types of stainless steel on the market, but casket manufacturers appear to prefer two types.

   400 series stainless steel is sometimes referred to as 409 stainless steel. It contains 11% to 12% chromium and no nickel. 409 stainless steel is what automotive mufflers are most often made of. 300 series stainless steel is a higher grade than the 400 series. Sometimes referred to as 304 stainless steel or austenitic, this series contains 18% chromium and 8% nickel. This is the highest known alloy

content in stainless steel caskets produced today. 300 series stainless steel may be found in fine tableware, sailboat cleats, shackles, and jet engines.

The quality of stainless steel may be evidenced by the fact that nickel renders steel non-magnetic. The stainless steel is of high quality if there is no magnetic attraction in the presence of a magnet. Stainless steel resists rust. Not only does the addition of chromium and nickel help protect the surface from rust, it also helps protect against oxidation caused by high temperatures.

Stainless steel caskets offer consumers more value than carbon steel. Consumers are aware of the longevity of stainless steel due to their exposure to such long lasting products as kitchen sinks, stainless steel bolts and washers, and washing machine tubs. Additionally, stainless steel caskets may be brushed to highlight the beauty of the actual material.

- ***Galvanized*** - *Steel that has been coated with zinc for increased resistance to rust.*

2. <u>**Non-Ferrous Metal**</u> - Any metal which is not formed from iron. It is measured in ounces per square foot. Copper and bronze are non-ferrous metals used in casket construction.

- ***Copper*** - A malleable, ductile, metallic element having a characteristic reddish-brown color. *S*ometimes copper and bronze are referred to as precious or semi-precious metals. Both offer natural corrosion protection and can be easily molded into graceful shapes. It is important to note that copper and bronze contain no iron and, therefore, do not rust.

The longevity of copper and bronze is evidenced by the fact that ancient artifacts made of these metals, dating back thousands of years, have been recovered in near perfect condition. Copper and bronze are virtually indestructible. Copper is a natural earth element that is relatively soft when compared to carbon steel and is easily molded/shaped. Copper takes on a reddish-to-brown hue.

- ***Copper Deposit*** - A casket made from a core of copper metal to which copper ions are deposited by an electrolytic process. This process forms a seamless unit.

- ***Wrought Copper*** - Copper metal rolled into sheets.

- ***Bronze*** - A metal alloy consisting of 90% copper and 10% tin (and sometimes zinc). This is not a natural element, but rather it is a copper alloy that is noted for its strength and ability to resist rust. The composition of bronze will vary. For example, commercial bronze contains 90% copper and 10% zinc. This is the grade of bronze that is often used in casket construction. Another grade of bronze contains 90% copper, combined with zinc and tin. Yet another grade contains only copper and tin. Regardless of the grade, to be known as a true bronze, the alloy must contain at least 90% copper.

Bronze is stronger and more durable than both copper and steel. Bronze is considered the premier metal alloy used in casket construction today because of its cost and strength. While the thickness of steel caskets is measured in gauge, copper and bronze caskets are measured in ounces per square foot. Common thickness of these semi-precious metals are 32 ounces per square foot, usually referred to as 32 oz. copper or bronze, and 48 ounces per foot, usually referred to as 48 oz. copper or bronze.

As a rule, the higher the numeric value of ounces per square foot, the thicker the metal. For example, 32-oz. copper one-foot square will weigh 32 ounces. Alternately, a thicker sample, say 48-oz. copper, will weigh 48 ounces. This standard of measurement is referred to as the *"Brown and Sharpe Gauge."*

- ***Wrought Bronze*** - Bronze metal rolled into sheets.
- ***Cast Bronze*** - Molten bronze poured into a mold and allowed to cool.

Plastic and Fiberglass

Aside from metals, some manufacturers of caskets use plastic materials. Plastics are abundant, easily formed into casket shells, and are relatively low in cost. Plastic is often limited to lower-end caskets that provide an inexpensive alternative to consumers. Fiberglass caskets are more common than plastic and can be finished in any color or pattern. Some are finished to resemble other materials, such as marble. Plastic and fiberglass both have the added feature of resisting deterioration. Both are practically indestructible when in contact with moisture or soil.

Polymer - A compound similar to plastic.

Newspaper

In England, the Borough's only independent funeral director chain is experiencing such a demand for environmentally friendly burials it has started selling coffins made entirely of old newspapers (The Guardian, n.d.). The Harold White Group, which has parlors in Old Church Road, Chingford, and in Hoe Street and Wood Street in Walthamstow, says the coffins are as robust as wood versions, but degrade quicker and produce fewer toxins if cremated. Made up of 120 tabloid-sized papers, the coffins can hold weights of up to 30 stone (420 pounds) and even the handles are made out of jute – a plant-based material which is also entirely biodegradable. They offer eight environmentally friendly colors made out of pigments which also degrade quickly. One can even choose what newspapers are used.

Casket Construction: Production Methods

- ***Cast*** *– Molten metal is poured into a mold, forming a seamless unit.*
- ***Stamped*** *- Sheets of metal are pressed by a hydraulic pump in designed forms. The component parts are then welded together.*

Production Methods

Metal

- ***Cast Hardware*** - The most expensive hardware production method, in which molten metal is poured into a mold, allowed to cool, and is then removed from the mold.
- ***Stamped Hardware*** - A hardware production method of lesser expense whereby the casket hardware sections are pressed out on a hydraulic press.

Plastic

- ***Plastic Extrusion Molding*** - A method of molding plastic by injecting molten plastic into a die.

Casket Components

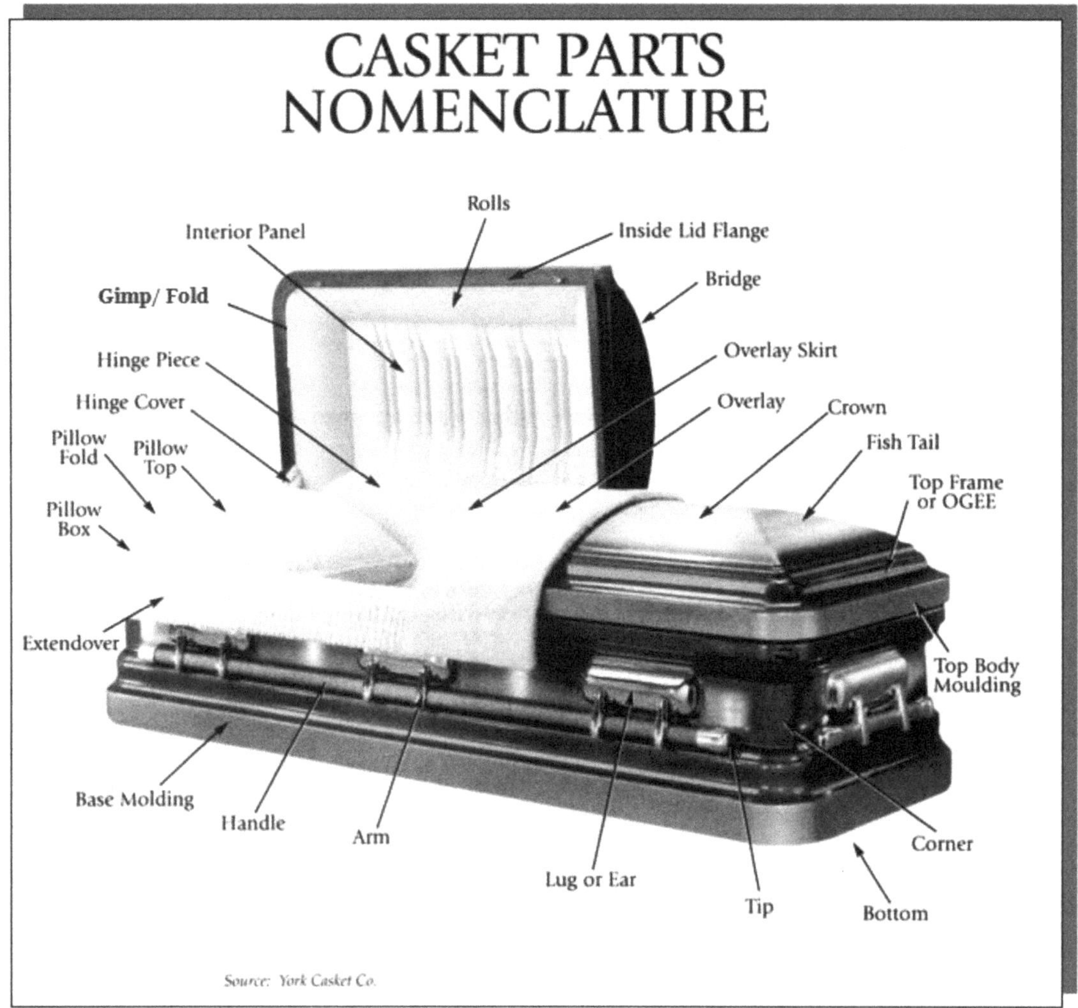

- ***Shell*** – The component parts that compose the cap (lid) and body of the casket.
- ***Cap*** – The topmost part of the casket shell, including the ogee, crown, pie, and header.
- ***Rim* (Ogee)** – An "S" shaped molding that is a component part of the casket cap.
- ***Crown*** – The uppermost part of the cap, extending from rim to rim; everything above the rim.
- ***Pie* (Fish Tail)** – The wedge-shaped portion of the cap (lid) at each end of the crown.
- ***Rim Flange*** (Ogee Flange) – The turned under edge or horizontal portion of the rim that comes into contact with the gasket or body ledge flange (top body molding flange).

- ***Gasket Channel*** – This is found on the cut top of gasketed caskets. It is an integral part of the foot panel header on gasketed caskets. Its function is to hold the transverse gasket to seal the space between the head and foot caps.

- ***Body*** – That portion of the casket shell containing the top body molding, body panel, base molding, and casket bottom.

- ***Top Body Molding*** (Body Ledge) – A molding along the uppermost edge of the body panels.

- ***Top Body Molding Flange*** (Body Ledge Flange**)** – The horizontal portion of the top body molding (body ledge) where the gasket is placed on gasketed protective caskets.

- ***Body Panels*** – These compose the sides and ends of the casket shell.

- ***Base Molding*** – The molding along the lowermost edge of the body panels.

- ***Hardware*** – The handles, ornamental fixtures, and fittings that are attached to the casket shell.

- ***Cap Panel*** – The focal part of the interior, which fills the inside of the crown or uppermost part of the cap.

- ***Full Couch*** – The casket is fully opened at the head and foot.

- ***Half Couch*** – The casket top is divided into two sections. Only the head section is open.

- ***Head Panel*** – A component part of the casket interior which is inside the head portion of the cap; no distinction is made between the head panel and foot panel in full couch caskets.

- ***Foot Panel*** – A component part of the casket interior which is inside the foot portion of the cap.

- ***Inner Panels*** – A functional or ornamental covering that usually covers the foot end of the casket in the full couch casket; may be located at both the head and foot of the full couch casket.

- ***Single Hinged Panel*** – A casket in which the cap is in two pieces; the rim (ogee) and foot panel is one piece which is hinged to the top body molding and the head panel being the second piece which is hinged to the rim (ogee).

- ***Perfection Full Couch*** – A casket in which the rim (ogee), crown, and pies are formed as one unit, and which raises as one piece.

- ***Perfection Half Couch*** – A casket in which the rim (ogee), crown, and pies are formed as one unit with a transverse cut in the cap, forming a two-piece lid for the casket.

Types of Handles:

- ***Swing bar*** – A moveable casket handle with a hinged arm. It can be full length, individual, or single.

- ***Stationary Bar*** – A non-moveable casket handle. It can be full length, individual, or single.

- ***Bail Handle*** – A single handle in which the lug, arm, and bar are combined in one unit.

Component Parts of Handles:

- ***Lug*** – The part of the casket handle that is attached to the casket body.
- ***Arm*** – The part of the casket handle that attaches the bar to the lug.
- ***Bar*** – The part of the casket handle, attached to the lug or arm, which is grasped by the casket bearer.
- ***Tip*** – The decorative or ornamental part of the casket handle that covers the exposed ends of the bar.
- ***Corner*** – An optional part of the hardware, attached to the four corners of the body panel.

Inner Parts of Casket Interiors

- ***Roll*** (Cove, Puffing) – A component part of the casket interior which lines the rim (ogee) and surrounds the cap panel.
- ***Gimp*** (Fold) – A strip of metal, plastic, or cloth that is attached to the inside of the panel, covering the area at which point the roll (cove) is anchored.
- ***Throw*** (Overlay, Overthrow) – The aesthetic covering for the foot cap or inner foot panel of the casket.
- ***Apron*** (Overlay Skirt) – The lining attached to the undersurface of the foot panel of the casket and/or a component part of the throw (overlay), which extends downward into the body of the casket.
- ***Extend-over*** – The portion of the casket interior which extends over the top body molding (body ledge) for aesthetic value.
- ***Bed*** – The portion of the casket upon which the deceased human remains are placed.
    - <u>Adjustable</u> – This type has springs that can be raised or lowered.
    - <u>Stationary</u> – This type is not able to be raised or lowered.
- ***Mattress Cover*** – Interior cloth or material which covers the mattress or bedding of the casket.
- ***Body Lining*** – Material that drapes the inside perimeter of the body of the casket.
- ***Hinge Cover*** (Skirt) – The portion of the casket interior covering the hinges that attach the casket cap to the casket body; usually extends from the roll and becomes a part of the body lining.
- ***Pillow*** – A cloth bag filled with soft material used to support the head of the deceased.
- ***Blanket*** – A piece of fabric used to cover the body of a deceased, especially the lower legs and feet when displayed in a full open casket.

Styles

- ***Crushed Interior*** – A form of casket interior created by placing the lining material on a metal form, adding weights, steaming the material, and then attaching it to a suitable upholstery (backing) material.
- ***Shirred Interior*** – A style of casket interior in which the material is drawn or gathered in parallel fashion in a specific sewing process.
- ***Tufted Interior*** – A style of casket interior created by placing a padding material between a lining material and a backing material, with subsequent stitches taken, forming small raised puffs; carriage tufting and biscuit tufting are the two most common types used in caskets.
- ***Tailored Interior*** – A tightly drawn form of casket interior style.
- ***Semi-Tailored*** – A combination of a tailored interior with one or more other styles of interior; for effect.
- ***Specialty Head Panels*** – A unique design is created in the head panel.
- ***Combination*** – More than one style used in the interior.

Materials Used in Linings

Lining Materials

- ***Crepe*** – A thin, crinkled cloth of silk, rayon, cotton, or wool.
- ***Satin*** – A fabric woven to create a smooth, lustrous face and dull back. Made from silk, nylon, or rayon.
- ***Velvet*** – A fabric of silk, cotton, and possibly rayon, with a thick, soft pile or nap.
- ***Linen*** – A fabric made from flax; noted for its strength, coolness, and luster.
- ***Linen Weave*** – A fabric woven to look like linen used as casket linen material.
- ***Twill Weave*** – A textile weave in which threads are crossed over one another to give an appearance of diagonal lines.

Backing Materials

- ***Fiberboard*** (Cardboard)
- ***Masselin*** – Pressed paper in sheet form; used in casket construction as a backing (upholstery material).
- ***Plastic*** – A synthetic or natural organic material shaped when soft and then hardened.

Padding Materials

- Cotton
- Polyethylene foam
- Shredded paper
- Spun Polyester
- Excelsior (wood wool) - wood shavings

Casket Exteriors

Wood

- ***Unfinished*** – Has no stain or protective varnish.
- ***Natural finish*** - May be stained or unstained with an outer protective coating of varnish or polyurethane.
- ***Stained*** – A color stain is applied.
- ***Unstained*** – Has no stain but may be covered with protective varnish.

Types of Finish

- ***Polished*** **(Gloss)** – A surface made smooth and glossy usually by friction and brought to a highly developed, finished, or refined state; burnished.
- ***Semi-Gloss*** – Low luster.
- ***Flat Finish (*****Matte Finish)** – A finish used on casket exteriors that is free of gloss and has a dull, lusterless surface with no shine or gloss.
- ***Satin*** – Has less luster than semi-gloss.
- ***Painted*** – The application of paint, single or multicolored.
- ***Laminates*** – Made by uniting superimposed layers of different materials.
- ***Cloth Covered*** – The wood is covered with cloth.

Cloth-Covering Materials

- ***Broadcloth*** – A twilled, napped, woolen, or worsted fabric with a smooth lustrous face and dense texture; a fabric usually made of cotton, silk, or rayon woven in a plain or rib weave with a soft semi-gloss finish.
- ***Doeskin*** **(Moleskin)** – A heavy, durable cotton fabric with a short (1/8th inch or less), thick, velvety nap on one side; woven cloth with a suede-like appearance with a nap of less than 1/8th inch.

- ***Plush*** – A woven cloth with a nap exceeding 1/8th inch (high pile).
- ***Smooth*** – A material that has no raised surfaces.
- ***Embossed*** – To ornament with a raised work; to raise relief from surface; material having designs raised above the surface.

Metal

- ***Brushed*** – A metal casket is first painted, then scratched with an abrasive material to the base metal, and then finished with a sealer and buffed until a smooth high gloss is obtained. This is found mainly in stainless steel, copper, and bronze caskets.
- ***Plated*** – The finish created when base metal is coated by another metal via an electrolytic process; it is identified when used in casket construction by the term "deposit," as in 'copper deposit.'
- ***Sprayed*** – Paint is sprayed on the casket.

Types of Sprayed Finishes:

- ***Gloss*** – High shine.
- ***Crinkled*** – An exterior casket finish in which the metal is coated with a substance that wrinkles as it dries; usually used on less expensive caskets.
- ***Hammertone*** – A sprayed finish that has the appearance of small indentations in the metal (as if struck by a ball-peen hammer); the 'indentations' are in the paint and appear as the paint dries; usually found on inexpensive caskets.
- ***Flat*** - No shine.

Fiberglass and Polymer

Fiberglass – A material consisting of extremely fine filaments of glass embedded in various resins.

Polymer – A compound, similar in appearance to plastic, that has a high molecular weight, creating an extremely durable substance.

Types of finishes:

- ***Wood Grain* -** Simulates the appearance of wood.
- ***Polished gloss* -** Shined to a high luster.
- ***Sprayed* -** Paint applied to the surface by an airbrush.

Shell Designs

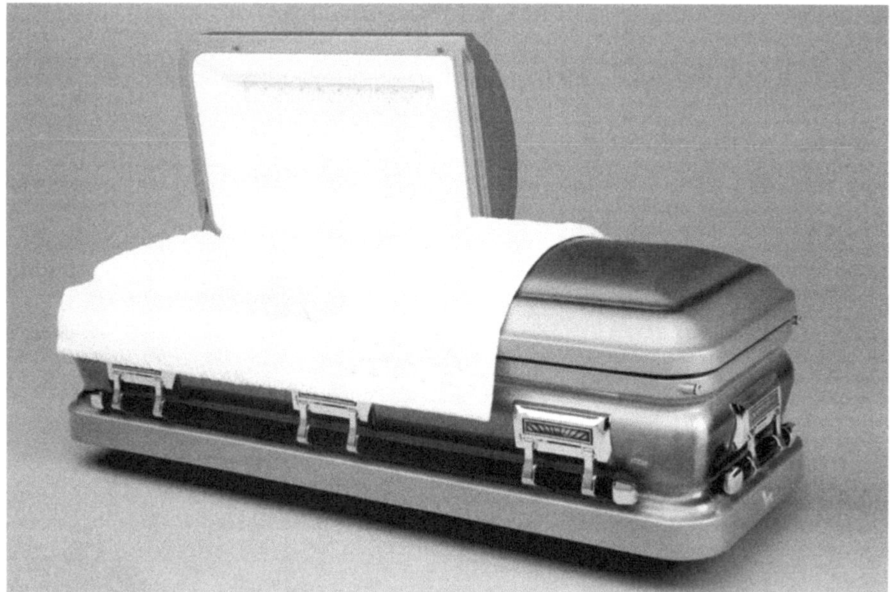

Source: https://prod12.meaningfulfunerals.net/images/products/caskets/1161.jpg

Ends and Corners

- ***Elliptic*** – A casket having ends in the shape of a half circle.
- ***Octagon*** – A casket having eight angles or corners which has eight sides or surfaces on the side of the body panel.
- ***Round Corner*** – Curved corner formed by the addition of a rounded corner piece that has been stamped or milled during the manufacturing process. The corner is welded into position.
- ***Square Corner*** – The sides and ends are joined at a 90-degree angle. Sometimes called the mitered corner, it is less expensive than the round corner because it requires fewer component pieces and fewer hours of labor.

Side (Body Panels)

- ***Flaring Square*** – A casket shell design in which the sides and ends of the casket body flare out from the bottom to the top; a casket shell design that is narrower and shorter at the bottom than at the opening of the top.
- **Vertical Side Square (State Casket)** – A casket body style with the body sides at a 90-degree angle to the bottom.
- **Urnside** – A casket design which displays a body panel with the shape of an urn.

Closure Method

To protect the deceased from water and soil, casket manufacturers employ several closure methods, including:

1. **Gasketed** – A flat rubber material is located along the top body molding flange of the casket shell. Another gasket is located between the lids in the perfection half-couch style.

   - **Components:**

     - *Gasket* - A single molded piece of rubber.
     - *Hinges* - Connect the cap to the body.
     - *Locking Mechanism* - Locks the cap to the body.

       Types of locking mechanisms:

       - End Lock
       - Side or Front Lock
       - Lever Lock

2. **Non-Gasketed**

   - ***Latch Closure*** – A simple latch secures the cap to the body after closure.
   - ***Threaded Fasteners*** – A threaded screw-type fastener used on a hinged cap-style casket.
   - ***Chemical Compounds*** – Epoxy and other cements are used. Butyl tape is used for sealing the cap and body on some infant caskets.
   - ***Hermetically Sealed*** – Airtight; impervious to external influence; completely sealed by fusion or soldering.

Ceremonial (Rental) Caskets

The term "ceremonial casket" is the preferred term rather than "rental casket." A ceremonial casket is a casket used for the visitation. It is rented rather than purchased. At the time of the funeral disposition, the deceased is transferred to a burial container. Ceremonial caskets are usually one of two styles:

1. A traditional casket that is used more than one time. It may be wood or metal. After a number of uses it is eventually sold. If sold, the purchaser must be informed of its use and status – as a used casket.

2. A casket specifically designed for rental rather than purchase. The casket consists of an outer shell similar to a traditional casket, but with no interior fabric and an end panel that opens and closes. There is a corrugated cardboard or fiberboard insert equipped with fabric and pillow that goes where the deceased is placed. Then the container containing the deceased is inserted into the casket shell for viewing.

Some directors have historically objected to the idea of renting a casket. There are some directors who still will not offer them. They feel it is undignified or would be an obstacle to selling a traditional casket. 14% of funeral homes surveyed did not offer ceremonial caskets. Years ago, this author gave a seminar on the future of funeral service. I brought up the topic of rental caskets. One attendee jumped up and said angrily that it was a stupid idea, and if it ever came to that he would leave funeral service, and I was an idiot for bringing it up. He was so angry he left the seminar.

Chris Boots (2015) asserts, however, that the rental casket is probably the best kept secret in the funeral profession. The casket/container utilized for a cremation disposition can range from a traditional solid hardwood casket to a corrugated cremation tray. Within the realm of these offerings, rental caskets resembling burial caskets are growing in popularity. Boots explains that today's consumers want to know they are receiving value for the money they spend. By renting a casket the family knows they aren't buying a product that will be used for one day and then be cremated the next.

Rental caskets are likely offered in 80% or more of the funeral homes today. Some funeral directors may occasionally cremate a hardwood casket, but there is substantial evidence that less than 2% of cremations include a hardwood casket that families buy for $2,000 or more.

According to the article "Rental Caskets: Alive and Well" (2015), rental caskets were often made available to full-service cremation families at prices between $600-$800 per use in the early 1990s. Funeral directors soon realized that a nearly retired rental casket could be sold for burial (with the right size vault) to recover the entire original cost of the casket itself. As a result, the cost-per-use of a rental casket was incredibly low. It was so low, in fact, that rental caskets could replace nearly all the cloth covered and low-end veneer hardboard caskets that hit the market in the mid to late 1990s. Ibid.

Boots (2015) reports that the most common rental casket was a button corner oak (those with more wisdom and years under their belt might call this the Spanish Oak). But, he explains, times have changed, and the casket manufacturers have really stepped up to the plate to give funeral directors much more variety in rental casket selections. It's easy to find rental caskets made of poplar, pine, oak, and cherry all in various colors and styles with options in both crepe and velvet. Other than the traditional hardwood rental casket offering, there are now painted MDF (medium density fiberboard) to look like metal caskets and lastly metal caskets converted into rentals. Funeral homes who offer 3-4 or 5 rental casket options create better value for their customer. If burial families can choose from more than one casket option, why not offer a variety to cremation families as well? Modern rental caskets have the advantage of more width as well. The new standard in rental casket width is 27 inches, allowing for the much-needed room funeral directors have longed for. Ibid.

The days of simply offering one rental casket and a couple of veneer caskets are behind us. After all, if 40% of your families are opting for cremation, shouldn't you have 40% of your selection room offerings geared to what your families are looking for (Funeral Service Insider, 2015)?

A growing trend is to offer good, better, and best rental caskets. This is helping funeral homes to move beyond the profit ceiling that a cloth-covered box has to offer (Mittenzwei, n.d.). Firms that are doing this are offering a choice of popular, oak, cherry, and maple rental units. Manufacturers also are offering wooden inserts lined with velvet interiors in the higher end rental market. Gone are the standard rose/tan crepe cardboard liners. Ibid.

Casket Sizes

When measuring a casket to ensure that a deceased will fit, you must measure inside dimensions. Although there are some differences in size among manufacturers, the average adult wood casket inside measurement is 75 x 22 inches. The average adult metal casket inside measurement is 78 x 23 inches. The height measurement is 16-22 inches for wood and 16-24 inches for metal.

When measuring a casket to determine if it will fit into a burial vault, measure the outside dimensions of the casket and the inside dimensions of the burial vault. The outside dimensions of the average adult casket are 84 x 29 inches.

Oversize Caskets

Caskets that are oversize, or larger than the average casket, increase in size by two inches in width and three inches in length. Each step increase is represented by an X after the size.

Oversize caskets may require an oversize vault, and an oversize vault may require an oversize grave.

Infant Caskets

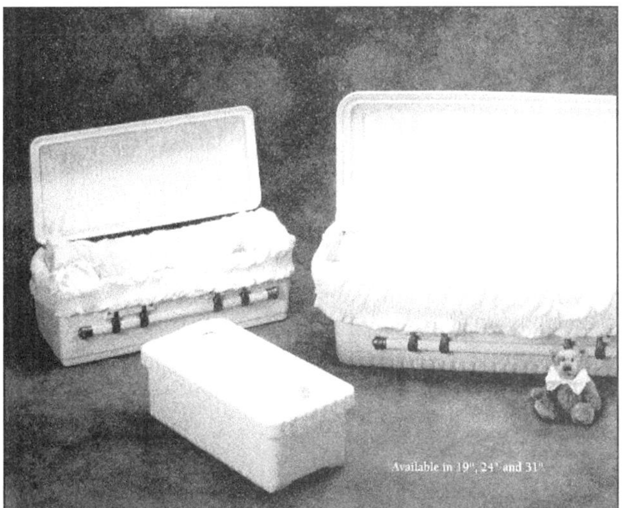

Source: Batesville Casket Company

Infant caskets are constructed of the same materials as adult caskets. Dimensions vary with the manufacturer. The increase in size of infant caskets progresses in increments of six inches in length and nine inches in height, and progress to five feet in length.

Casket Personalization: Making Your Mark

Excerpt From: Patti Martin Bartsche (2015a)

Personalization of any service, or the products that support a funeral, can help a family tell the unique story about the individual characteristics and qualities of their departed loved one. Examples could include a special emblem or image added to a casket to personalize it, like embroidering or engraving a monogram, nickname, or other personal remembrance onto the lid.

Casket personalization is achieved when a funeral professional meets the needs of a family to create a more meaningful and personal event to celebrate the deceased's life. Casket personalization can take many forms. Manufacturers offer a number of ways a funeral director can personalize a casket, including interchangeable corners, head panels, and different appliques. Many funeral directors personalize the casket beyond that by utilizing unique flower sprays, personal effects in and around the casket, and letting family members leave notes in the casket. This helps create a personal and meaningful service.

The savvy funeral director will take time to understand who the deceased was and will build a funeral service around that. The service may include memory tables, slideshow DVDs, the casket, the flowers, the food, and more. The casket is one of many vehicles to craft the stories for a family. I think personalization is important to creating a meaningful service that is valuable to the family. Creating healing moments in a service is truly important, and when the casket can be personalized it absolutely adds value. It's the little things that count. Families share memories through eulogies, videos, picture boards, and other tributes. The personalization of a casket reinforces these, adding 'color and context' to the life that is being remembered and paying homage to what made that person special.

I don't think families are aware of what is available. There has been some reluctance from funeral directors because they don't want to be perceived as pushing a sale on the family. However, there's a huge gap in consumer awareness about personalization. The statistics are startling. Three out of four consumers coming into a funeral home do not understand their personalization options. Yet, 50% of families are interested in personalizing – they just need to be educated so they can make informed decisions.

Ask the family if they would like to incorporate some of these things into the service. If the answer is yes, then it is your job now to pick and choose from your service and merchandise offerings to make the funeral personal, and to present that to the family.

In the selection room, it's important to demonstrate how caskets can be personalized and what types of personalization are available, and to let families know what features are included in the price of the casket. A recent study showed that families were confused about which elements are standard, which are extra, and even whether a personalization element is optional.

Funeral homes can approach merchandising a number of different ways, from displaying full caskets, to partial casket showrooms, to digital displays. Regardless of the merchandising method, funeral homes should ensure that they show a wide range of personalization examples and how they can be applied, to either the service or a specific product.

After deciding that a personalized funeral is what the family desires, present the options that only apply to the theme(s) that the family want to showcase. For example, if a gentleman was a marlin fisherman, offer a casket insert panel that is personalized with an embroidery of a boat like his, a marlin and also his name, date, and maybe include the name of his boat. Then also offer to display his tackle, rods, etc. around the room while playing Jimmy Buffet music, as that is what the family said he always played when he went fishing. On top of that, offer to make a memorial DVD of his pictures featuring his best catches. The family is looking for guidance, and it is up to the funeral director to craft the message and story that is going to be told during the services [End of Excerpt].

In surveys detailed in Funeral Service Insider (2018 and 2019), funeral directors were asked to share what they feel is the "largest unfilled gap" in terms of casket innovations. Their responses included:

- *We need better colors with 20-gauges.*
- *More inexpensive wood caskets.*
- *More variety in cremation caskets.*
- *Caskets that speak to younger generations.*
- *More personalization in high-end products.*
- *Color options for oversized caskets.*
- *Low-cost 20-gauge caskets that actually look good.*
- *More options for children and infants.*
- *The colors are bland and not changing enough.*
- *Create innovative ways to make caskets that lower cost. We are pricing ourselves out of business.*
- *Increased selection in extended-width caskets, although that has been improving.*
- *A simple design that doesn't look like a holdover from a bygone era.*
- *A cheap wood casket to cremate instead of a rental.*
- *Make more ethnic caskets in colors that the population prefers.*
- *Oversize caskets in a larger variety of colors and styles. People are getting larger, but the choices are very limited.*

Outer Burial Containers

Outer Burial Container – Any container which is designed for placement in the grave around the casket, including but not limited to, containers commonly known as burial vaults, grave boxes, and grave liners.

Burial Vaults – An outer enclosure which offers protection from the earth load as well as possessing sealing qualities.

The two purposes of a burial vault are:

1. Support the load of the earth
2. Limit intrusion of outside elements

Construction Materials

Concrete:

- With a steel reinforcement
- Without a steel reinforcement

Interior Lining:

- Polystyrene
- ABS Material
- Stainless Steel
- Copper
- Bronze
- Asphalt

Metal: Is measured in gauge

<u>Types</u>:

- Steel
- Stainless Steel
- Copper

Metal burial vaults are constructed so that the casket is placed on the bottom portion and the dome is secured to the bottom.

Other construction materials include **Polypropylene and Fiberglass,** which are constructed in the same style as metal vaults described above.

> ***<u>Dome</u>*** *– The top of an air seal burial vault that entraps air as it is put in position. It also supports the weight of the earth above.*

Source: Vantage Products Corporation

Source: Vantage Products Corporation

Methods of Closure

Air Seal – A method of sealing a burial vault that utilizes the air pressure created by placing the dome of the vault onto the base of the vault.

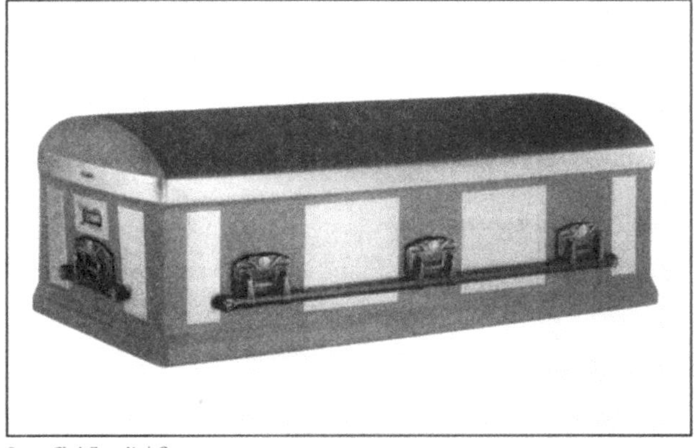

Source: Clark Grave Vault Company

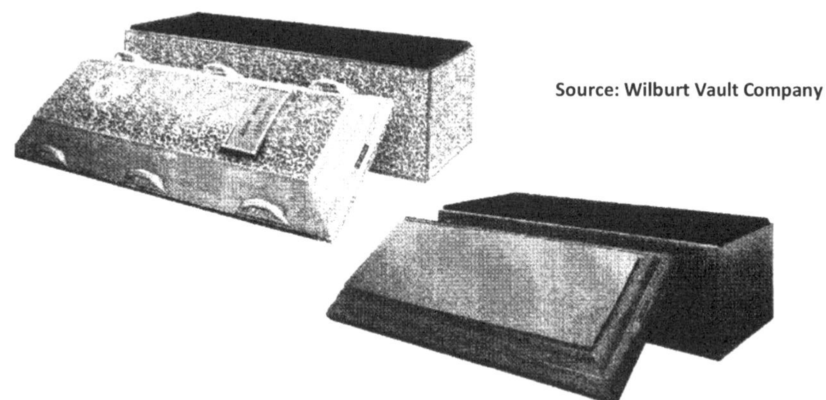

Source: Wilburt Vault Company

Top Seal – A method of sealing a burial vault that utilizes an epoxy compound in conjunction with a tongue-in-groove closure at the top of the vault.

Double Seal – A method of sealing burial vaults that utilizes the principle of the air seal in conjunction with an epoxy material at the junction of the dome and the base of the vault.

Selecting a Vault

When it comes to vault selection presentations, some firms can display full-sized concrete and metal vaults, along with a variety of miniature renditions and end-selections. For some, an outdoor setting is used to complement the overall appearance.

The following is an approach that can be helpful with the vault presentation:

"Now, basically there are two kinds of vaults: Concrete and metal. Vaults made of metal typically close on the air seal, diving bell principle. What we are saying is that the casket sits on the base of the vault and the dome comes down over top. This is much the same as when we compare an empty glass to the dome of the vault." At this point, if available, place an empty glass upside down in a bowl of water allowing a few bubbles of air to be released.

Next explain that the metal vaults consist of stainless steel or solid copper in galvanized steel and non-galvanized steel. Explain the difference between the galvanized and non-galvanized by stating that, after the vault is completely assembled, it is immersed in molten zinc, up to 800 degrees, which coats the vault inside and out. Because of this extreme heat, the zinc virtually permeates the metal to produce a galvanized vault.

Explain that concrete vaults are also available. These typically close with the top seal principle and run from those lined with copper, stainless steel, and polyurethane down to the plain concrete box, which is the minimum requirement of most cemeteries (Dawson, 2015).

Every funeral director in the industry should present the disclaimer, either in writing or print, that a vault is not required by state law. They are used only to prevent caving-in of graves, as far as cemeteries are concerned. The cemeteries make the rules, not the government!

The Standard Burial Vault Dimension is 30 x 86 inches inside dimensions

Author's Note: The top of a concrete vault can be personalized with engraving or photographs. This can be done at the manufacturer or there is equipment a funeral home can purchase to produce such products. The funeral home should have some photos of these personalization options.

Source: https://www.centurywilbert.com/pages/personalization/century_legacy_images

Grave Liner

A grave liner is an outer enclosure that offers protection for the earth load, but without sealing qualities.

Construction Materials:

- Concrete
- Wood
- Polymers and Fiberglass

Types:

- *Grave Box:* An outer enclosure consisting of a body and a one or two-piece lid.
- *Sectional* (Concrete Sectional): A grave liner consisting of six or eight slabs of unfinished concrete placed around the casket.
- *Urn Vault*: Metal or concrete vault for urns.

Other Types of Containers

- ***Transfer Container*** – An outer enclosure that protects the casketed remains during transportation.
- ***Air Tray*** – A transfer container consisting of a wooden tray with a cardboard covering for the casket.

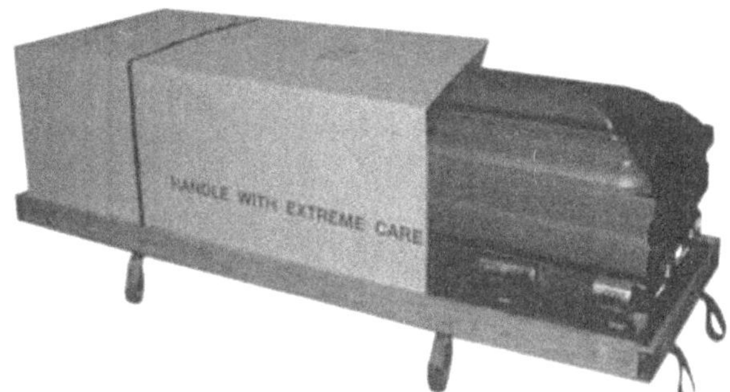

Source: https://customairtrays.com/shipping-products.php

- ***Ziegler Case*** – A metal, gasket-sealed container which can be used as an insert into a casket or a separate shipping container.

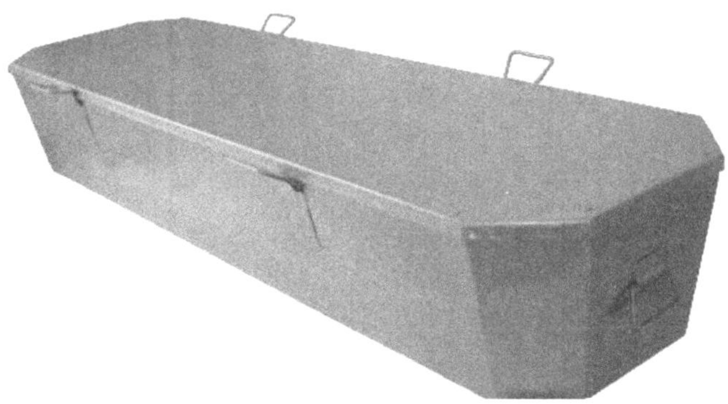

Source: https://necremation.com/product/disaster-case-ziggler/

- ***Wood Box*** – A transfer container made entirely of wood.
- ***Combination Case*** – A transfer container consisting of a particle board box with a cardboard tray and cover to satisfy air-shipping regulations.
- ***Alternative Container*** – A non-metal receptacle or enclosure, without ornamentation or a fixed interior lining, designed for the encasement of human remains and which is made of cardboard, pressed-wood, composition material, or pouches of canvas or other material (FTC Definition).
- ***Unfinished Wood Box*** – An unornamented casket made of wood which does not have a fixed interior lining.
- ***Combination Unit*** – Any product consisting of a unit or series of units which are designed or intended to be used together as both a casket and as a permanent burial receptacle.

NOTES

Chapter 13 MERCHANDISING

Source: Batesville Casket Company

Merchandise - *Goods that are bought and sold.*

Merchandising - *The purchase, display, and sales of goods.*

Typical Funeral Merchandise most funeral homes offer:

- Caskets
- Outer Burial Containers
- Urns
- Burial Garments
- Cremation Containers
- Rental Caskets
- Cremation jewelry and Keepsakes
- Register Books/Memorial and Thank You Cards
- Religious, Fraternal, and Military Symbols
- Tribute videos
- Monuments and Memorials

Merchandising

Merchandising can be an emotionally charged situation. Very few individuals lack emotion when it comes to the selection of funeral merchandise. While a family's choices will not be impulsive (very few will select the first thing they see), they will be highly susceptible to sentiment. It should not be our purpose to take advantage of this sensitivity, but rather to make a conscious effort to explain all aspects of the merchandise, answer any questions they have honestly and ethically, and support them as needed (Mittenzwei, n.d.).

Market research and focus group studies indicate that consumers typically feel intimidated by traditional full-sized casket display rooms. Some of the newer selection room styles have been compared to Hallmark stores. Have you ever met someone who was intimidated by shopping in a greeting card store? Like Hallmark's retail outlets, these rooms offer a mix of soothing colors and well-lit display areas that are professionally designed to maximize eye appeal while offering a great assortment of merchandise. "Hallmark" selection rooms are not just rooms full of caskets or casket cuts. Funeral firms utilizing this room style are reporting increased ancillary merchandise sales, along with increased casket and vault sales. Ibid.

Price is important, but it is not always the lowest price that consumers seek. Price is only one key factor. Most of the consumers you serve already know what things cost. This information is only one Google search away. Consumers today are more value driven. They form a price-to-product value in their minds during the casket selection process. Sales consultants and funeral directors report that the primary reasons a consumer selects one casket over another is due in part to what is in their wallets and what appeals to their senses.

Some funeral homes have eliminated a casket selection room in recent years, but the majority (70%) continue to use them as the primary method of showing and displaying casket merchandise. Funeral directors believe families want to see and touch the caskets before making a buying decision. The same directors also believe people will select better caskets from a show room over a computer or catalog.

The use of computerized displays is growing. Computerized displays allow families to quickly compare a large variety of caskets. You can quickly show them all options at a variety of price points. Families do not really want to be making a purchase and therefore do not really care how caskets are arranged. How a funeral home presents caskets depends more on the preference of the arrangers.

18% of funeral homes have eliminated a casket showroom in favor of a digital presentation, but more often you will see funeral homes using a digital presentation to supplement what is in their existing showroom. "No matter how you display caskets, coherent merchandising will play a vital role in creating a healthy average retail sale and profit from casket merchandise" (Funeral Service Insider, 2017).

Other presentation methods are becoming increasingly popular: Almost half of respondents use a partial-size casket selection room as well as catalogs, laminated sheets, and other paper-based materials.

Types of Casket Selection Rooms:

- **70% Traditional Selection Room** feature a selection of full-size caskets.
- **47% Fractional Display Room** feature sections of a casket, such as 1/4 or 1/8 panels or end sections, on a wall display. These may also have a limited number of full caskets displayed.
- **39% Digital Display Room** where an unlimited number of caskets can be shown.
- **47% Catalogs** paper-based item.

Differing Views of Casket Display Rooms

From: Funeral Service Insider (2017)

Pro-Computer

The casket selection room can be a significant barrier for many people. Many people are relieved to see merchandise on screen and express relief to not have to go into a casket room. Another huge benefit is that the family can immediately see personalization, and then email the possible selections to other family members. People are used to shopping on-screen. As an industry, we need to recognize this and go on-screen for families.

The computer or some version of a binder with high-quality pictures is just as good of an option for many people. Space can be limited at a funeral home these days. Ask yourself, what is the best use of that space? Oftentimes it is **not** a selection room.

Pro-Selection Room

Do not write the obituary for selection rooms just yet, however. More than 68% of the more than 400 respondents to our annual casket survey still use a full-size casket selection room when presenting caskets. 2% of funeral homes that had eliminated casket showrooms have brought them back.

Even though computers can show a wider breadth of products, it's difficult to convey the value and benefits of different features and casket choices. Giving families the opportunity to see, touch and feel the product, the texture of the fabric, the detail in the hardware, or the sparkle or shine in the finish, and choose something that represents their loved one, is something that cannot be replicated online. At the end of the day, if we don't believe the casket is worthy of presenting in person, why would we expect the family to value it? What is to prevent them from ordering it online or through some other channel?"

Pro-Combination

Different tools are effective in helping different families make informed decisions. Selecting a casket is one of the most difficult and unfulfilling aspects of planning a loved one's funeral. The lack of knowledge about caskets in general, and not having a clear idea of what their loved one would want, make this decision even more challenging. The best solution for families is one that combines consumer-friendly, digital tools that are designed to educate and inform, with physical displays and supplemental printed materials that provide much-needed context and allows families to make a personal connection.

Even though most respondents still have a full-size casket showroom, it's worth noting that some have multiple locations – and they don't necessarily have the full-sized models at every location. Moreover, 18% of respondents said that they were considering eliminating a full-size casket showroom.

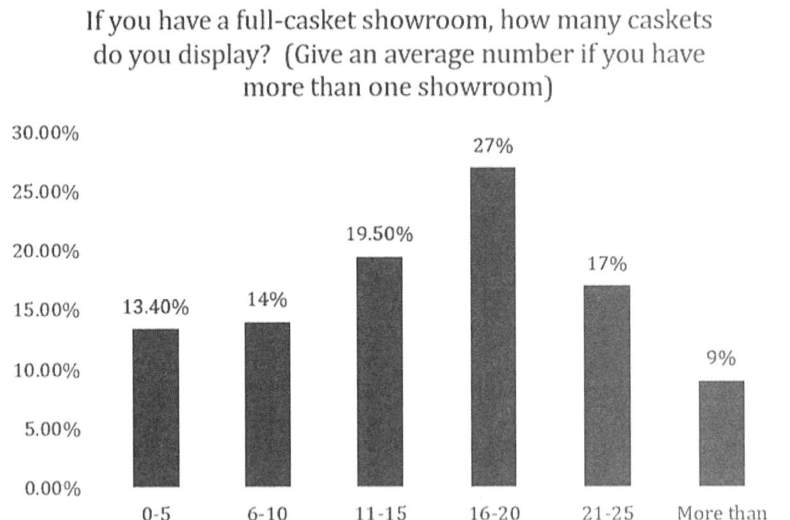

Funeral Service Insider November 6, 2017

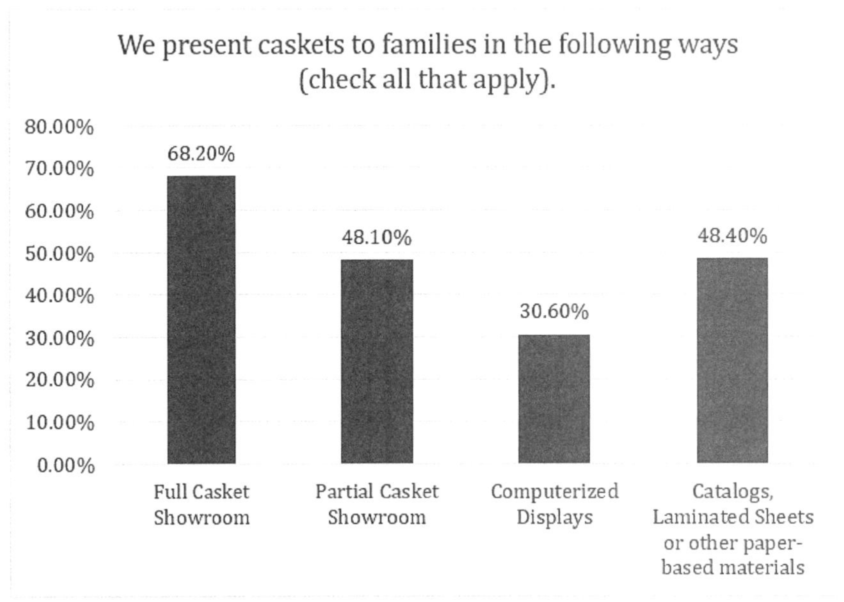

Funeral Service Insider November 6, 2017

Casket Display Room

- **Location:** Generally speaking, it is better to have a selection room located in the same building as the funeral home. All modern funeral homes are built this way. Some older funeral homes, however, do have the display room in another building, like a renovated garage.

  For ease of access, it is recommended that a display room be located on the main floor of the funeral home. If the display room cannot be located on the main level, psychologically, upstairs is preferred over downstairs. Whether it's upstairs or downstairs, an elevator should be available for those people who would find stairs difficult. The elevator should be built for the purpose of carrying people and should not be a freight elevator.

Source: Aurora Casket Company, Inc.

Source: Amigone Funeral Home

Traditional and Fractional Display Rooms

- <u>**Lighting**</u>

  It is best to use indirect, recessed, incandescent lighting. 90 to 100-foot candles of illumination measured at approximate pillow height on a displayed casket is optimum. A **foot candle** is the amount of illumination produced by a source of one candle at a distance of one foot. A "foot candle" is equal to 1 lumen of light distributed over 1 square foot. A lumen measures brightness and is the most common measure of light output. Lamps are measured in lumens and all lightbulbs have lumens listed on their packaging. Spotlights should be used to show off better caskets.

  <u>**Lighting Options**</u>

  - **Fluorescent Lighting** — The illumination produced by a tubular electric discharge lamp; the fluorescence of phosphors coating the inside of a tube.
  - **Incandescent Lighting** — The illumination resulting from the glowing of a heated filament.
  - **Direct Lighting** — Illumination directly shining on an object.
  - **Indirect Lighting** — Reflected illumination of an object.

- **Display Equipment**

Casket Rack *— A device upon which two or three caskets are placed, one on top of the other for display.*

Casket Stand (Casket Standard) *— The stand or support upon which a casket rests in the selection room. It should be:*

- Sectional cuts should be shown in an attractive display usually supplied from the supplier.
- Sturdy - Be able to support weight and movement of casket. It should give the appearance of strength.
- Attractive - Clean, dust free, with no scratches, dents, or broken parts.

Church Truck **-** *A wheeled collapsible support for the casket, used in the funeral home, church, or other location when moving a casket.*

Number of Caskets and Space per Casket

Although there is some difference of opinion on the number of caskets to have in a traditional display room, it is generally considered that **12 is the minimum and 30 is the maximum, with 40 to 60 square feet allotted per casket**. 40 square feet may not always be quite enough space and 60 square feet might be too much. **Caskets that are crowded together detract from the visual appeal of the overall display.**

Varying the amount of display space given to individual caskets enhances the value differences of those caskets. It makes it easier for the buying public to understand the value differences in the caskets that are displayed. To the unpracticed eye of the buying public, all caskets in a selection room look alike at first glance. As a result, it is necessary to do everything possible to enhance the differences in these caskets. This is done through lighting, decor, appointments, and a varying amount of display space.

Arrangements of Caskets

There are many ways caskets can be arranged in a display room. Each casket manufacturer has their own view of what arrangement is best. However, everyone agrees that there should be a furniture group in the display room, in easy view of where the family enters. A common grouping used is a table, lamp, and two chairs. The purpose of this furniture is:

- To give families something familiar to relate to, which helps to relieve tension.
- To have something available to sit on in case people feel it necessary to get off their feet.

Most agree that some form of **demonstration or educational group** of caskets be used when introducing the family to the display room. These three or four caskets are utilized to educate the selecting party regarding the elements of casket construction, differences in caskets, features that affect price, and where prices are to be found. The general layout of the display room, and how the funeral director will proceed, can also be discussed at this point.

A director must decide on how he or she will arrange caskets for the families' inspection and selection. Some funeral directors use the **consecutive method**, in which caskets are arranged in order of increasing or decreasing price. Other directors prefer to group caskets by:

- **Material** (i.e., woods, steels, coppers, bronzes)
- **Alternate Pricing** - Each group would have a low, medium, and high cost casket.
- **Appearance** - Caskets can be open or closed. If the casket is closed and the family requests to see the interior, the funeral director should open the casket or selected caskets as part of the presentation.
- **Style** - All half couch caskets may be in one area and full couch caskets in another, or they may be mixed. In many parts of the country, funeral homes will only show one style, usually half-couch caskets.
- **Traffic Flow** - The casket display is usually arranged in such a way that the family moves through the room in a manner that makes it obvious to them the differences in the quality of the caskets.

Selection Room Enhancements (Décor)

Accepting the "given" that no one really enjoys going into a casket selection room, it should be designed and decorated to be as comfortable as possible. Use light pastel paint or wall coverings that will make the room appear brighter and more open, and colors that won't clash with casket exterior or interior colors. Focal points, such as statues, flower arrangements, objects of art, and furniture groupings can be arranged throughout the room to soften the effect of the caskets. Signage should be attractive and easy to read.

Before Entering the Selection Room

Pre-selection Room Introduction

1. Before entering the casket selection room, the funeral director should give the family an introduction on what to expect when they enter the room. The introduction should include:

    - Presentation of the general price list
    - Required state and federal disclosures
    - Quantity of merchandise displayed
    - Types of merchandise displayed
    - Possible presentation of price lists
    - The amount of money they have spent before the purchase of merchandise
    - Merchandising aids

Darby (2016) notes the importance of explaining to a family what they can expect when entering the selection room. Describe the room and make it clear that they will need to select both a casket and a burial vault. Set the family's expectations before you enter the room. If you fail to do so, the burial vault can feel like an unexpected add-on. It is important to lay the groundwork for the conversations ahead of time. This can be done by spending just a few minutes with the family outside of the selection room.

Sample Introduction:

"Our casket selection room contains 15 full-size caskets made of both wood and metal. You will also see 10 partial-cut caskets that have a photo of the full casket and a sample of the interior material available. The caskets range in price from $400 to $6500. When we enter the room, I will take a few minutes to explain what makes one casket different from another and what affects the price. I will then walk with you through the room explaining individual caskets, the cut casket display, and answer any questions you may have. With your permission, I will leave you alone while you make your decision. I'll be sitting at the table outside the door. If you wish me to stay with you while you make your decision, I'll be happy to do so.

When you have selected the casket, I will then show you some scale models of burial vaults. The cemetery you have selected requires that some form of outer container be used to surround the casket to keep the ground from sinking. When we finish, we'll come back here to the conference room. You will notice that in the packet of information that I gave you, you will find a copy of our casket and outer burial container price lists. You may take those with you along with the General Price List. Do you have any questions before we go to the selection room?"

2. To reduce the initial shock of entering the room, have:

- The lights on.
- The funeral director enters the room first.
- The demonstration group near the door.
- A comfortable table and chair group the family sees as they enter. This lessens anxiety.

Author's Note: If you are using a catalog or a computer/electronic device to show merchandise, an introduction should be done. The introduction should be specific to the system you use.

Presentation Style

Every funeral director has his or her own style of presenting caskets to the family, with each method having advantages and disadvantages.

Direct Selection Room Procedure - Presenting caskets whereby the funeral director remains in the selection room throughout the entire selection process.

Advantages	Disadvantages
*Some families prefer the support given by funeral directors. *The funeral director is better able to meet the needs of the family.	*No privacy for family to discuss matters relating to their decision when the funeral director is present. *The presence of the funeral director may influence the client's selection. *Non-verbal communication which occurs can be both negative and positive. *The funeral director may misinterpret the needs of the family.

Indirect Selection Room Procedure – Presenting caskets whereby the funeral director does not stay in the selection room during the selection process, but instead leaves after his introductory presentation. This option requires that the family be given adequate pre-counseling and a clear description of the caskets, that the price be visible in each casket, and that the display easily show comparative values.

Advantages	Disadvantages
*Privacy exists for the family. *Elimination of funeral director's influence. *Nonverbal communications do not occur. *The opportunity for the funeral director to misinterpret the needs of the family does not exist. *Written information about each casket may be more carefully analyzed.	* Some families prefer the support of the funeral director. *The funeral director is not present to answer any questions which may arise. *Written information could be ignored or misinterpreted.

Author's Note: As with developing a presentation style in the selection room, you should also develop an organized approach or style when using a catalog or computer.

Merchandise Other than Caskets

Caskets are generally not the only type of merchandise a funeral home has for sale. Most funeral homes also sell burial vaults, cremation urns, clothing for the deceased, register books, memorial cards, and religious and fraternal symbols. Some funeral homes also sell flowers, monuments, grave markers, and sundry products, such as remembrance jewelry.

Burial Vaults

Cremation is impacting all segments of the funeral industry, including vault manufacturing and sales. More consolidation will begin to take place. Smaller burial vault dealers may not be able to adapt quickly enough to survive the many changes that are predicted. There will be fewer locations producing vaults and few brands to provide component parts and standards for quality production. But dealers who consistently go above and beyond for their funeral home customers and the families they serve have every reason to be optimistic (Martin-Bartsche, 2015b).

Source: https://communityfuneralservice.com/vaults

The increase in cremation rates has had a negative impact on funeral home sales of vaults. This means the burial vault manufacturers have also experienced a decrease in revenue.

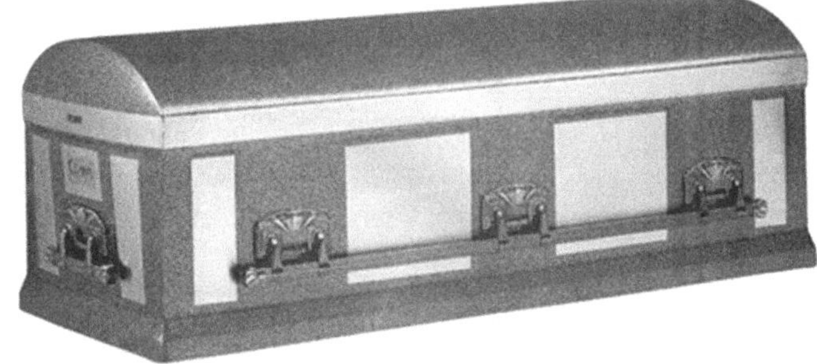

Source: http://www.clarkgravevault.com/our-vaults/vaults-casket-burial/

Outer Containers, Grave Liners, and Burial Vaults

Another major piece of merchandise sold by a funeral home are outside containers, known as grave liners or burial vaults. As with caskets, the best way to prepare families for the purchase of a liner or vault is to bring up the subject in the pre-selection room conversation. Darby (2016) gives an example of the introduction to vaults:

> ***"Along with caskets we have three examples of burial vaults. The cemetery you have selected requires a grave liner or burial vault. The purpose of these outside containers is to keep the earth from collapsing into the grave. I will show you a short video on the use of the liners and vaults"*** (p.52-53).

Scale Model Vault Display

Darby (2016) explains that technology can take the pressure off. You can play a video that uses animation to educate the family. A miniature vault sample can only demonstrate so much, but a video from your supplier can show a vault in the ground, what rising groundwater looks like, and how a concrete box can break down over time. While walking through the selection room, you can put an iPad in the family's hands and empower them to explore your vault options. Today's families are used to shopping online and navigating choices on their own. Complimenting your vault presentation with interactive technology brings the family into the process and makes them more comfortable.

Online shopping can lead to one being overwhelmed by choices. The same applies in the selection room. To increase burial vault sales, present only three vaults: Good, better, and best. This allows families to easily compare the vaults available and feel less overwhelmed. As a funeral director, you may understand the difference between a dozen different vault options, but an emotional and grieving family won't be able to decipher the differences. Ibid.

Many funeral homes have limited their number of burial vault options and watched their average vault sale rise. Most families will choose the "better" or middle option, which should be your target vault, and the one that offers the best value. Ibid.

Source: https://prod12.meaningfulfunerals.net/images/products/caskets/1161.jpg

There are many different display styles for burial vaults. Some funeral homes use full-size vaults while others use a scale model display or photographs. Vault information should be as informative as casket information, no matter which style of display is used. A complete selection of styles and price ranges should be available. Most funeral directors prefer to sell the burial vault after the casket has been selected.

Urn Vault

Source: Wilbert Vault Co.

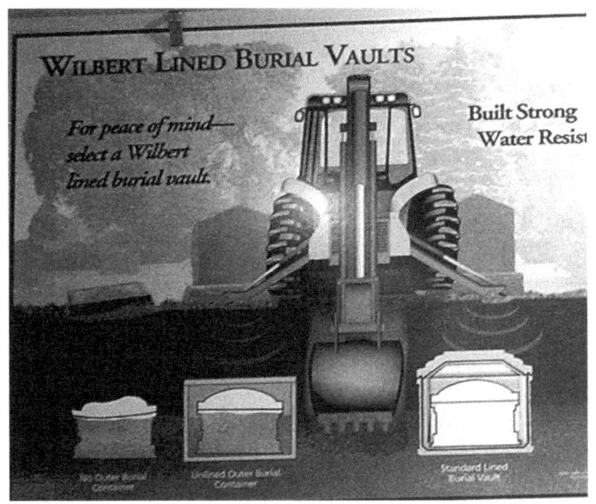

Sales Aid Picture

It can be hard to change your selection room presentation, especially if it has been working for you for many years. You do not have to replace everything you have with TVs, monitors, and iPads. Modern consumers, however, are challenging us to try new things. Do your research, push yourself out of your comfort zone, and do what is best for your funeral home. The families you serve will benefit.

Tribute Videos

Funeral service is about much more than selling a casket – even when you are dealing with a family that is opting for burial for their loved one. Personalization is key and allows for your funeral business to offer additional items, such as tribute videos and keepsakes.

Funeral Service Insider (2014) surveyed funeral directors on how they approach selling video tributes, keepsakes, and other types of personalization elements. Many firms give these things away because people will not pay for them if they are put as a line item and a price is charged for them. There is money to be made in offering these elements, but people do not have the commercial courage to charge for them.

2018 RESULTS

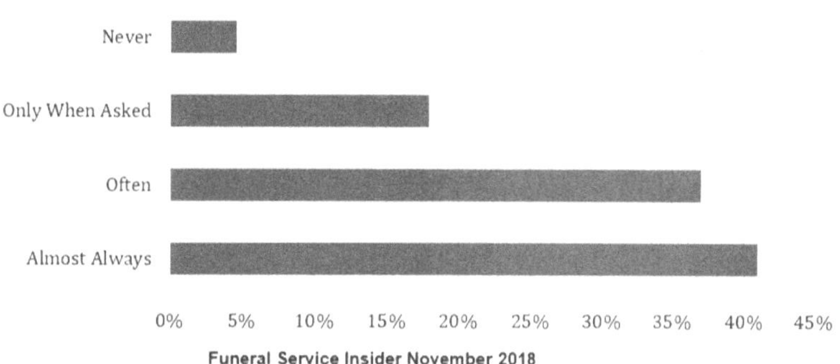

Urns

With the steady increase in cremation, the merchandising of urns has taken on new importance. Urns should be prominently and attractively displayed in either the selection room or a separate cremation room. Information about urns should be as extensive as it is for caskets and burial vaults, and a complete range of styles and prices should be available.

Urn Merchandising

Andrea Leblanc (2019) lists the following trends concerning urn selection by families.

- More families are asking for a product that is made in America.
- Families are asking for urns that can be customized with the use of photos, sketches, or any other type of image that would memorialize the life of the loved one.
- Many families are going the way of the internet and finding an urn they like at a price they can afford. They take those urns to the funeral homes and bypass the funeral home as a source for their urn purchase.
- If funeral homes want to be the urn provider to families, then they need to find better ways to get the products they want at a price they can afford.
- Displaying urns in the room where you meet with families is key. Research shows 80% of urn sales are lost if a family moves to another room to make their selection. Go one step further and position your display where a family can clearly view their urn options while they're talking to you. You may even have more than one display around the room, prompting family members to walk and browse them up close as they make other decisions.

Urn Customization

The family can choose an urn that is simple with the deceased's name and dates of birth and death. They can also include additional text if there is a favorite poem or verse that is associated with the deceased. Custom engraving, which includes exceptional adaptations of original photographs or original works of art, is as unique and personal as it gets.

Personalization such as terms of endearment, name, and life dates has become commonplace in our profession. Customization is the future of death care. When we use the phrase 'customize' with a family, it tells the family four things:

- It's just for me.
- I'm going to have to wait for it.
- I will have to pay more for it.
- Customization in our society is not only accepted, it is expected.

Cremation Language

By: Martin Bartsche (2017)

When we are standing at the casket, we do not refer to the deceased as the 'embalmed body.' We refer to them by their name or the relationship that they are to the family, such as 'mother,' 'father,' 'sister,' 'brother.' If we can show this type of respect for a family that chooses a traditional service, why can't we show this same respect for families that choose cremation?

> **Does the funeral profession need to reframe the conversation when it comes to cremation? For example, a family may be asked what type of casket they want for 'Mom' or 'Dad', but when it comes to urn selection, the deceased is often referred to in terms of 'cremated remains.' We highly encourage the Mom or Dad conversation over body/cremated remains. A combination also works – "An urn for Mom's cremated remains."**

A lot of funeral directors will ask the family if they would like to look at the urn selection or a catalog. I think we need to look at the vernacular we use. For example, let's say you are meeting with a woman named Connie, who has lost her father. You have taken the time to not only get to know Connie and her family, but also her father, and she has shared with you that her father was an accountant who loved and adored his family, but every chance he got he loved to golf. When you have come to the point in the arrangement conference that you would normally discuss the purchase of an urn, consider the following.

Instead of asking if she would like to look at urns, try something like this:

> *"Connie, the time has come to choose an urn that will become the final resting place for your father. You shared with me earlier your dad's passion for golfing. Let me show you some urns with a golf motif, and of course, if you don't see something you like, we can always have an urn customized for your father."*

You will notice that never once were the words 'cremated remains' or 'cremains' used. The urn was referred to as the final resting place for her father, treating him with the same respect that we give traditional families.

Clothing

Almost all funeral homes have selections of apparel. Clothing is a highly personalized item and the deceased should be dressed in his or her own attire if possible. As professionals, we should be willing, however, to provide a collection of both men's and women's clothing for those desiring to select from our firms. Most of these items should be marked up slightly above cost, as a convenience to those we serve. This is also an area where consumers can do an easy price comparison. "If they did this to me on the dress, how much did they mark up the casket?"

In many firms, the suits displayed in the garment area are the same as the funeral home staff wears. Burial dresses and negligees are usually handmade, hand-tailored, and double in thickness, which can be helpful when there has been a weight loss because of a prolonged illness.

A side note learned many years ago from the late Rita Barber: To avoid soiling garments, always handle the dresses by the hook on the hanger and not by the shoulder. Keep the suits in size order on the racks and do not be afraid to occasionally give away a necktie or a pair of slippers.

Register Books, Religious or Fraternal Symbols, Memorial Cards

All funeral directors do not show these items in the casket display room. Some prefer to present them in the arrangement office. No matter which method is used, a full range of styles and prices should be available.

Tips on Pricing

By: Daniel Isard

Funeral home directors do a terrible job when it comes to pricing products and services. Here are a few acronyms that describe how funeral home directors typically set prices:

AALBLY: Add a little bit to last year.

LMCPADI: Let my CPA do it.

BOHBOMC: Be one hundred bucks over my competitor.

BOHBUMC: Be one hundred bucks under my competitor.

TAWAG: Take a wild-ass guess.

Whenever you set pricing, you need to be sure to build profit in. If you don't build profit in, what are your chances of having it? None!

There are seven key steps to go through when setting prices:

1. Determine total overhead.
2. Allocate gross profit from merchandise.
3. Determine case count.
4. Set prices on services.
5. Do a hypothetical revenue test.
6. Create packages.
7. Test your consumers.

One of the most critical areas to focus on is how much you are marking up merchandise. As the casketing rate goes down, the profit you make will also go down. Due to this, you should build profit into other areas.

When setting prices, assume you are going to get fewer calls than you expect. This way, if the death rate goes down or you don't get as many calls as you thought you would, you'll still be earning the profit you want – and if you hit expectations, you'll be surprised on the upside. Assume you'll hit 90% of your projected case count and build in the profit you want based on that 90% number.

Source: Amigone Funeral Homes, Inc.

Merchandise Pricing

By: Cas Skretny

Terminology

Consumer Value Index (CVI) – The percentage derived by dividing the wholesale amount of the merchandise by the retail price of the merchandise.

$$\frac{\text{Wholesale Cost}}{\text{Retail Price}} = \textbf{CVI}$$

- Measures the value received for each dollar spent by the consumer.
- Ensures Value Progression - "If buyers spend more, they should get more!"

Gross Casket Profit (Margin)

Retail Price - Wholesale Cost = **Margin**

- Measures profit of each casket to the funeral director/firm.

Merchandise Value Ratio (MVR) – The relationship between the wholesale cost of the merchandise and the total cost of both service and merchandise to the consumer.

Wholesale Cost		Service and Merchandise		**MVR**
$200	÷	$4,000	=	**5%**

There are several methods funeral directors use to determine the selling price of caskets, vaults, and urns.

Fixed Multiple or Times Factor – A price determination method whereby the mark-up is multiplied by a constant factor. The same mark-up is applied to all caskets.

Advantages
Easy to Use Provides Quality

Disadvantages
No Improve No Incentive to Buy-Up

Example: The casket cost the funeral director $200. The funeral home's fixed multiple is 3.

$200 X 3 = $600 (the selling price)

Graduated Recovery – A pricing method where the mark-up varies. Higher priced caskets are given a higher mark-up.

Advantages	Disadvantages
Makes available lower cost	CVI decreases with higher priced funeral at low end merchandise.
	Applies negative pressure to the assortment.
	Low margin at lower end.
	Best value at lower end of assortment.

Graduated Recovery

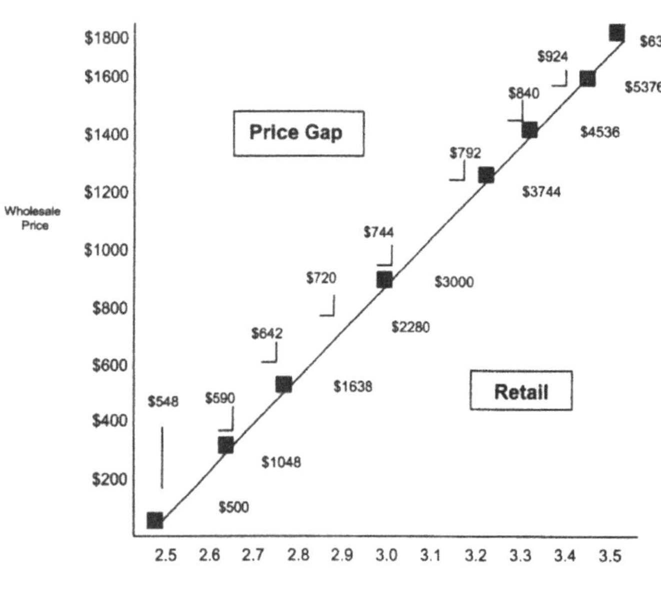

Source: Gary Sokoll

Declining Price Structure – A pricing method where there is an inverse relationship between the markup and the price of the casket. Higher priced caskets given a lower mark-up.

Advantages
CVI improves with higher priced caskets

Disadvantages
Lower-end markup may be too aggressive in some markets.
Encourages consumer to buy better merchandise.
Win-win situation

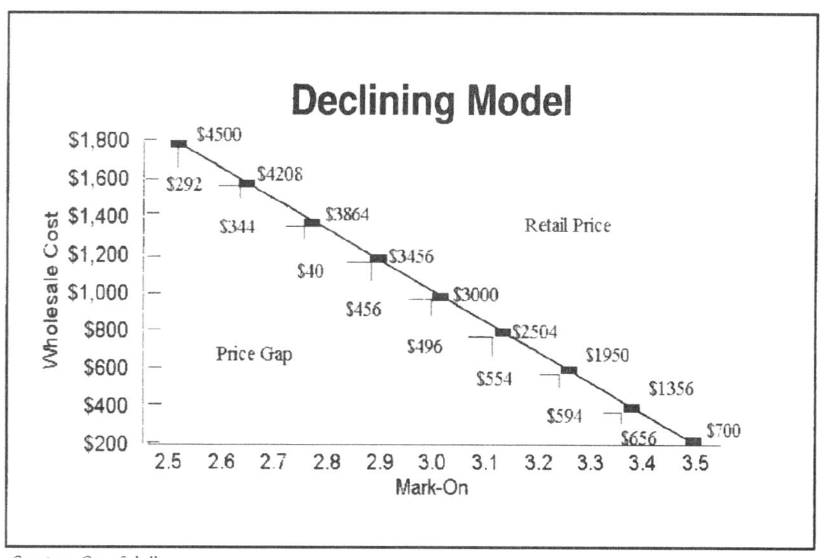

Courtesy: Gary Sokoll

Statistical Terminology

- **Average (Mean) – The sum of a group of numbers divided by the number of units.**

  Example: A director's casket sales for the week are:

$ 700.00	$4,200 ÷ 4 = $1,050
$1,500.00	
$1,200.00	$1,050 = Average Sale
$ 800.00	
$4,200.00	

- **Median – A value in an ordered set of values which represents the midpoint, whereby there are an equal number of values above and below the midpoint value.**

  Example: A director's casket sales for the week:

$ 700	
$ 800	
$ 900	Median Sale
$1,000	
$1,100	

- **Mode – The number that appears most frequently in a listing of numbers.**

  Example: A director's casket sales for a week:

$ 750	
$ 925	
$ 925	
$1,175	$925 = Mode
$1,525	
$ 925	
$ 925	

- **Quartile** – A division of the total into four intervals, each one representing one-fourth of the total.

  Example: A director has 20 caskets in the display room:

1st Quartile	5
2nd Quartile	5
3rd Quartile	5
4th Quartile	5
	Total = 20

- **Range** – The caskets sold in the 2nd and 3rd quartile.

  Example: 1st 2nd 3rd 4th

  (2nd–3rd: caskets sold in these quartiles)

Recording and Analyzing Sales

Sales Frequency – The number of times sales in a given price bracket occur over a fixed period of time.

Sales Frequency Chart – A chart showing the number of all sales in any sales bracket.

A funeral home owner or manager should have a system in place that allows keeping an accurate record of all the sales of merchandise and services that are purchased. Although this record can be kept on paper by hand, there are computer programs available that can turn this into a relatively simple task.

An analysis of sales records can show a funeral director how frequently particular caskets, vaults, or urns are being sold. With caskets, the analysis can also show the types of interior style or fabric and hardware that is being sold.

After analyzing the casket sales chart for a specific period, the director can then make knowledgeable decisions as to how to proceed in the future.

Pricing Systems for Funerals

The FTC requires that funeral directors use an itemized pricing system. This does not forbid the funeral director from offering special packages that may use the unit, bi-unit, or functional pricing systems, as long as the family receives a general price list that has everything itemized on it.

What a funeral home should charge for a casket can be tough to figure out. "There has always been a need to balance a funeral home's profitability with pricing their families can afford. Too small a margin, or too high a retail price, can hurt a funeral home in both the short and long run" (Funeral Service Insider, 2017).

Make sure from a customer's perspective that there is a progression of visual value – i.e., if I spend $200 more on one casket versus another casket, I can see a visual difference in the casket, and I feel like I am getting more for my money. Ibid.

- ***Itemization*** – A method of pricing by which each unit of service and merchandise is priced separately.
- ***Unit Pricing*** – A method of pricing which creates one total price package for both service and merchandise.
- ***Bi-Unit Pricing*** – A method of pricing that shows the price of the services and the price of the casket separately.
- ***Functional Pricing*** – A method of pricing by which the charges are broken down into several component parts. An example could be: Professional service, facilities, automobile, and merchandise.
- ***Package Pricing*** – A method of pricing where certain items of service and merchandise are grouped together and sold at a specific price.

Pricing

"How do you price funeral goods and services?" Ask several funeral directors this question, and you will probably get several different answers. Some funeral directors simply set their prices to be similar to prices charged by other funeral homes in the same geographic region. Others rely on accounting and financial service firms. Financial service firms provide funeral directors with a general idea of the costs incurred by other funeral directors in the geographic region and provide "ballpark" prices.

Pricing should be fair, allow for a profit, and be consistent. Adjust casket costs to keep up with inflation. To be fair, don't try to make all the funeral home's profit on one sale. By being fair, the firm will get more repeat calls and services from referrals that will far offset what would have been made on one unfair sale.

Profit and consistency go hand in hand. They allow for longevity in business. The profits allow the firm to operate. Being consistent in pricing allows the customers to afford the services offered by the funeral home over a long period of time, whether at-need or pre-need.

Factors that Influence Pricing

- Competition's price policies
- Legislation - fair trade laws
- Production costs
- Distribution costs
- Economic fluctuations
- Type of merchandise
- Marketing strategy
- Purchasing practices
- Selling costs

Mark Up - Difference between merchandise cost and selling price, i.e., gross margin.

Mark Down - Reduction of selling price.

Casket Mark-ups and Pricing Survey

- About 42% marked up caskets 1.5-2x – or 50 to 100% above the wholesale price.
- 11.9% marked up caskets 1 to 1.5x – or at cost to up to 50 % above wholesale
- 29.7% marked up caskets 2-2.5x – or 100 to 150%
- 12.8% marked up caskets 2.5-3x – or 150 to 200%
- 4.1% marked up caskets 3x or higher – or at least 200%

Most firms have a sliding mark-up. The mark-up will be higher on lower-priced caskets and lower on higher-priced caskets. As a result, many firms don't care which casket the family selects as the actual cash received is about the same. Smaller-volume firms in small communities or rural areas will have higher markups as they typically have less competition (Funeral Service Insider, 2017).

Inventory

Every funeral home is faced with the decision of how much inventory to keep on hand. Not having enough may cause problems in trying to meet the request of a family. Having too much may mean having money tied up that could be used for other needs.

In smaller firms, the funeral director can easily keep track of inventory with minimum record keeping. For large firms, there are computer programs that can continually update the status of all inventory items. These systems can even automatically generate reorder requests according to their programming.

- ***Inventory*** - Those goods or stock of goods which are held for resale.
- ***Inventory Turnover*** - The number of times the average inventory has been sold or used up during a period.
- ***Economic Order Quantity (EOQ)*** - The quantity to be purchased which minimizes total costs.

Sales Objectives

A sound merchandising program should start with sound sales objectives. Most sales objectives are based on evaluation of sales history, availability of products, recommendation of suppliers, and the amount of profit a director wishes the firm to generate. These sales objectives should be profit-oriented and take into consideration the normal cost of living increase and legitimate profit increase each year.

The purchase of display items, such as vaults, clothing, urns, and (especially) caskets, must be thoroughly coordinated with profit objectives. The entire line of merchandise must be coordinated so each casket, vault, or urn offers additional value above the one priced below it. This value must be readily apparent, easily explained, and easily understood by the customer.

The Human Factor - Product Knowledge

Any merchandising plan is only as good as the director's knowledge of the products being sold and his or her ability to convey this knowledge to the buyer. A family can quickly distinguish a knowledgeable director by the presentation given and the manner in which questions are answered. Instead of describing metal caskets as 16, 18, and 20 gauge, use the more easily understood thickest metal, thick, and thinnest metal.

Suppliers

An important aspect of any merchandising program is determining which suppliers to purchase merchandise from. Questions that should be considered when determining which suppliers to use are:

- **Can they provide goods** of the required quality, type, or model?
- **Do they have goods available** at desired prices, terms, and in quantities needed?
- **Are they reliable?** Do they provide reasonable and customary protection of the buyer's interests, such as quality guarantees, right to make legitimate returns, etc.?

- **Do they supply good service**, not only in making deliveries but also in handling transactions and making adjustments?

- **Do they make appropriate provisions** for managerial or merchandising aids and technical assistance when needed?

- **Do they employ representatives** with whom the business owner can work and cooperate successfully?

- **Do they provide discounts** and other incentives? For example:

  - **Cash Discount**: A reduction of the price given for payment of an account within the time limits established by the sales contract.

  - **Quantity Discount:** Reduction in the amount of a bill when a minimum quantity of merchandise has been ordered.

  - **Rebate:** A return of a portion of a payment.

  - **Consignment**: The funeral director does not have to pay for the merchandise that will be displayed until it is sold.

Merchandising Services

We have been discussing the merchandising of funeral-related products. It will be more important to put emphasis on services, as fewer families purchase products like caskets and vaults. Many funeral directors think only of products to sell, with not much thought of services as being equally important. It is predicted that in the future, services will be more important than the casket and vault as the model of funeral service becomes more funeral event planning. In this model the “EXPERIENCE” takes precedence.

Consider the following services as separate products to be merchandised:

- **Funeral Ceremony** – A service commemorating the deceased with the body present.

- **Memorial Service** – A ceremony commemorating the deceased without the body present.

- **Graveside Service** – A ceremony or ritual, religious or otherwise, conducted at the grave.

- **Visitation (calling hours, visiting hours)** – Time set aside for friends and relatives to pay respects for the deceased prior to the funeral service.

- **Direct Cremation** – A disposition of human remains by cremation without formal viewing, visitation, or ceremony with the body present.

- **Immediate Burial** – A disposition of human remains by burial without formal viewing, visitation, or ceremony with the body present, except for the graveside service.

- **Package** – More than one product or service combined into a single presentation.

- **Hospitality Service** – Offers the family a variety of products and services, including food, drink, buffets, family style meals, or a cocktail party.

- **Event Planning** – Moving beyond formal funeral planning to create a ceremony for celebrating the life of the deceased.

- **Green Offering** – Offering the disposition in an environmentally friendly method.

Pet Disposition

One of the newest funeral related services that funeral directors should consider as part of their offering is deceased companion animal disposition. In 2018, there were 89.7 million dogs and 94.2 million cats kept as pets in the United States (America Pet Products Association 2017-2018). There are an additional 7.6 million pet dogs and 8.8 million pet cats in Canada (Canadian Animal Health Institute, 2017). These pets have become loving members of their families and are oftentimes referred to as "fur babies" or as a "fur-pet." The grief at the loss of these loved animals can be intense. More families seem to be interested in having some form of post-death ceremony for their pet. This may include visitation, cremation, urn and keepsake purchases, or grave purchases and burials.

For more information on pet disposition and memorialization, see Page 468.

NOTES

Chapter 14

SHIPPING HUMAN REMAINS

Part I: Domestic Shipping

By: David R. Penepent, Ph.D.

The History of Domestic Shipping

Domestic shipping in the funeral industry can be defined as the returning of human remains to a place of origin for final ceremonies and disposition. The average funeral director will have between one and five of their case calls each year that has been domestically shipped to them for final disposition. The act is usually rooted in a person's desire to be returned to the place they "call home" as their final resting place.

The mobility of today's society is one of the reasons for the increase in domestic shipping. During earlier times, the majority of people usually stayed within close proximity of their residence. Consequently, when they died, they were usually buried in a church yard or community cemetery. During the Revolutionary War era and the War of 1812, soldiers killed in battle were usually buried in the closest local cemetery near the battlefield. With the advent of the transcontinental railroad in the early 1800s, people began to venture outside of their local community and explore the United States. Even with the railroad, when people died away from home, they were usually buried at that location because there was no means of retarding the natural decomposition of the human body. Relatives were usually notified of the death via a telegram or when people accompanying the deceased returned back home.

The development of embalming and the Civil War also influenced domestic shipping in this country. When the father of embalming, Dr. Thomas Holmes, perfected the procedures, it is doubtful he considered the tremendous implication this practice would have on funeral service in the future. This impact was realized in 1861 when the Civil War broke out and he became a commissioned officer in the Union Army. As an embalmer surgeon, he was responsible for preparing some 4,000 fallen soldiers for shipping home. Dr. Holmes found the practice of embalming and shipping so lucrative that he eventually resigned his commission. He marketed his service of body preservation and shipping to the common soldier. They would pay as much as $100.00 to ensure they would be embalmed and sent home if they died.

The third and final element that influenced domestic shipping was President Lincoln. President Lincoln was a fundamental force that promoted this new technology of modern embalming and shipping in the United States. Early in his presidency, he learned of the embalming process and he became enamored with the idea that this procedure could keep a person from decomposing for a period of time. His fascination with embalming led to his declaration to the Union Army that all Union officers killed in action were to be prepared and sent back to their hometowns for burial. The pinnacle point in domestic shipping began with this declaration. The Army developed procedures and protocol for preparing bodies for shipment back home. After being embalmed, the soldier was dressed and placed in a pine, rectangular box, delivered to the nearest train station, and was sent back to his place of origin. The person delivering the body would then send a telegram to the soldier's hometown informing the family that his remains were going to be arriving at the train station at a specific time. Keep in mind that during that period of time, the idea of receiving a loved one's remains, killed in war, from a baggage car on a train was unheard of. The family and the local undertaker, who may or may not have known about the embalming, went to the train station and received the deceased soldier, who was preserved and able to be viewed and mourned by family and friends. Embalming, at least in the northern states, became a sought-after practice that changed the way people mourned in this country, and created the concept of domestic shipping.

Two years into Lincoln's presidency, he experienced the tragic and unexpected death of his third son. William "Willie" Wallace Lincoln contracted typhoid fever shortly after his eleventh birthday. Dr. Charles Brown, an embalmer surgeon, was summoned to the White House, where he prepared and embalmed young Willie's remains. While there is conflicting evidence on whether or not Willie's body was buried or merely housed in a receiving vault at Oak Hill Cemetery in Georgetown, it is fair to say that it was never the President and the First Lady's intent to keep little Willie at this cemetery after the President's term in office had expired.

Despite sending Union soldiers home for burial becoming a common practice during the war era, it wasn't until Lincoln's assassination that the masses became aware of the importance of domestic shipping. It was at this point that people realized the value that domestic shipping had in bringing people together to mourn and pay their respects to a fallen leader. Not only was the fallen president returned home to Springfield, Illinois via the railroad, but little Willie accompanied his father on his final journey from Washington, D.C. Together, they were laid to rest in Oakridge Cemetery.

Abraham Lincoln's Funeral Train

After the Civil War and the burial of Lincoln, domestic shipping became a new avenue of service offered by American funeral directors. Rail companies developed guidelines with respect to what remains they would accept. The body needed to be embalmed and eventually the casketed remains were placed in a wooden shipping crate.

In World War I, fallen soldiers were prepared in a nearby morgue affiliated with a new branch of the service known as Graves Registration Service. They developed a way of tracking soldiers via dog tags, thus reducing greatly the amount of bodies that were unknown. Unidentified human remains were the greatest reason why 42% of all soldiers were not able to be returned back to their families during the Civil War era (*American Funeral Director,* 2007).

During WWI the military viewed returning human remains to families as a sacred obligation. However, the early process of returning soldiers' remains to their place of origin was not as rapid as one would expect. After the war ended, the War Department contacted the next of kin and asked if they wished to have their loved one's remains returned. If they indicated they did, Graves Registration Services would disinter the body and return it back to the United States via military transport. Once in the United States, the body would then be placed on a train to the appropriate place of final destination.

The next advance in modern domestic shipping can be attributed to the military as a result of World War II. The slow process of returning bodies back to their place of origin was greatly improved upon due in part to the development of aviation advances. The period of time to return human remains was greatly reduced as a result of streamlining the operations within Graves Registration Service and a commitment by the government to return as many soldiers back to their families as soon as possible. The WWII era was the first time that three forms (i.e. air, rail, sea) of shipping were used to return remains to their place of origin.

After the Korean War, transporting human remains via airlines became much more efficient and expeditious. As opposed to waiting two to three days to receive human remains from one end of the continent to the other, aviation and air cargo reduced the trek to a manageable period of time based on the airline's schedule. Gradually, transporting human remains via train became a thing of the past because of the cost factor and the amount of time required for transportation.

Service members who were killed during the Vietnam War were first transferred to in-country military mortuaries for embalming. Then they were flown to Dover Delaware Airforce base for further preparation and transfer to their homes.

Slain soldiers from the Gulf War were on American soil 48 hours after being killed in action. Once their bodies were received by a military detail in the United States, the human remains were domestically shipped to their final place of rest.

Transporting human remains via commercial airlines can best be divided into two periods of time, i.e. pre 9-11 and post 9-11. Prior to the tragedy and the terrorist attacks on the United States on September 11, 2001, funeral homes were free to send any funeral associate to the airport with human remains for domestic shipping. Post 9-11, governmental agencies in cooperation with the major airlines have restricted who is authorized to bring human remains to the airport for transport.

Shipping Today

Today in most states, a licensed funeral director or licensed trainee are the only ones who are allowed to deliver or receive human remains from an airport. The funeral professional is required to produce two forms of identification, a picture ID and their state license or registration card. Both ID's must be current and cannot be expired.

All airlines require the body to be embalmed. If the person's religious convictions do not permit embalming, most airlines will permit an unembalmed body that is packed in dry ice or with ice packs. It is important to note, however, that this could only be done shortly after death and provided the body does not show immediate signs of putrefaction or body fluid leaking. The standard practice to protect the remains of an unembalmed body, while ensuring that fluid leaking will not occur, is to place the body in a Ziegler case and then pack the dry ice or ice packs around the body. A Ziegler case is a zinc-constructed container that has a one-piece zinc top that is usually screwed to the bottom portion of the case. A Ziegler case is also commonly used in international shipping or in cases when the body is so badly decomposed that it needs to be contained in order to prevent the emission of foul odors. ***See Page 185 for photo example.***

It is important to note that both the sending funeral home and the receiving funeral home could be held responsible and liable for clean-up costs for a body that leaks outside the shipping container and creates a biohazard incident. Airlines could potentially restrict a funeral home's ability to domestically ship a body if a body causes a biohazard incident.

The process of domestic shipping today usually begins with a phone call from a family member who informs the funeral director that a death has occurred away from home. The hometown funeral director contacts a funeral director in the area where the death occurred or a company specializing in shipping remains. The family may instead contact a funeral home in the area where the death occurred first. That funeral director will then contact the hometown funeral home. In some instances, a service may be held in both locations.

Shipping Procedures for Casketed Remains

- The body should be lowered to the bottom of the casket.
- The face and hands should be covered to prevent cosmetics from accidentally rubbing on the interior of the casket.
- A box should be placed at the foot of the casket between the bottom of the deceased's feet and the end of the casket. This will prevent the body from shifting within the casket during transportation.
- If using a metal casket, the casket may be locked; however, the cap that covers the key mechanism should be placed in the information envelope on top of the shipping box. Due to the compression process that a plane experiences during flight, if this is not done, the top can collapse, thus damaging the casket. This will not happen on wooden caskets because the latching mechanism does not produce an airtight seal.
- All airlines require a casket to be placed in a wooden bottom and cardboard top shipping unit. This shipping container will prevent the casket from being damaged in flight. The shipping container can only be used once and then must be discarded.
- All flight information needs to be placed on the shipping envelope, which is attached at the head of the shipping container. In addition to the shipping information, the deceased's name as well as the funeral home of final destination should be clearly marked. Most funeral homes have preprinted envelopes for this specific purpose.
- The body transit permit should also be enclosed in the envelope. In most states, the body transit permit and the burial permit are one in the same. A body should never be shipped without the appropriate authorizing documentation.

Shipping Non-Casket Remains

Human remains that are not casketed can be shipped in a shipping unit called a "combo." The combo is smaller in size than a casket and is constructed of a wooden bottom unit and a cardboard top that usually has padding on the interior. It creates a ridged container that all airlines accept as a standard shipping unit for human remains. When shipping a body in a combo unit, the following protocol should be followed:

- Plastic undergarment (pants) should be used.
- At minimum, the body should have a hospital gown on.
- The body should be wrapped in a sheet so that the receiving funeral director will be able to remove the body more easily.
- Do not wrap the body in plastic. Moisture could accumulate and possibly cause mold.
- When shipping clothing, the clothing should be sent in a plastic garment bag.
- The body should be anchored to the bottom of the combo by the interior nylon straps provided.
- All flight information needs to be placed on the shipping envelope, which is attached at the head of the shipping container. In addition to the shipping information, the deceased's name and the funeral home of final destination should be clearly marked.
- This is a one-time use container and must be discarded after use. Airlines will not allow multiple uses of combo or shipping containers. Human remains will be rejected by airlines if a funeral director attempts to reuse one of these units.

Nearly all domestic shipping is done via airlines. Each airline company has their own department that deals specifically with human remains and can be contacted for assistance and information.

References

Abraham Lincoln's Burial Train. Retrieved on April 20, 2007 from:

http://members.aol.com/RVSNorton1/Lincoln51.html

Army Mortuary Affairs Website (2007, January 7). A short history of identification tags.

Retrieved on April 20, 2007 from:

http://www.qmfound.com/short_history_of_identification_tags.htm

Military Caskets on Transport. Retrieved on April 20, 2007 from: http://www.island-life.net/casket_016.jpg

Penepent, D., Loomis Burial.

Part II: Shipping Human Remains to Foreign Countries

By: Melissa Johnson Williams

When shipping human remains to a foreign country, it is necessary that the shipping funeral director call the embassy (or consulate of jurisdiction of the foreign country) to verify the current regulations and any fees for services rendered.

Every funeral director involved in the shipment of human remains to a foreign country must comply with the regulations of the country of destination (and any countries that the shipment will pass through) to the last detail. To an American funeral director, many of these regulations may seem either unnecessary or outmoded. Every country, no matter how small and primitive, is a sovereign power, and therefore can impose any regulations regarding international transport of the dead that it deems essential to protect the health of its citizens.

Failure to comply fully with the regulations of the country of destination may result in refusal to permit the entry of the human remains shipment and its subsequent return to the US. This would happen at the shipping funeral director's expense.

Additionally, if there is a situation where the remains are to be shipped to a neighboring country and then transported to the country of final disposition, both countries regulations must be complied with.

Special Requirements

Many countries still require the use of an all-wooden outer shipping box that may also require a zinc lining. Some countries require documents to be translated into their native language. As early on in the process as possible, try to determine what will be needed to get a start on procuring those items. Remember this is a time-consuming process and make your changes accordingly. The entire process may take 10-14 working days, many telephone calls, and additional trips to secure all the items required.

Documents and Inspections

All countries require "legalization or authentication" of the documents stating the regulations. This legalization refers to the examination by representatives of the embassy or consulate of the specifically mentioned documents. The documents will have the seal of the governmental agency impressed on them attesting to their authenticity. These documents must accompany the shipment.

All documents (certified copiers, burial and/or transit permit, non-contagious disease letter, and embalmers non-contraband affidavit) required by the individual countries must have a "dry, raised, or impressed seal." These terms refer to the use of a device to impress the insignia of a notary seal or issuing agency on a document. This requirement cannot be fulfilled by the use of a rubber stamp.

The coroner or medical examiner will need to issue a letter stating that the death is not due to a contagious disease if the death certificate is pending a cause of death.

When inquiring about the authentication process, ask if the documents can be faxed to the embassy or consulate. Many consulates permit this. If you must send the documents, send them by a service such as Federal Express and enclose a self-addressed Federal Express envelop for the return of the documents.

Many countries require an "inspection and/or sealing of casket." This requires an actual visit by a representative of the consulate or embassy to view the body, casket/contents, and outer container. The representative may require examination of the remains and/or clothing with verification of identity. The containers are sealed by cords or ribbons tied around the casket and held in place by sealing wax impressed with the seal of the embassy or consulate.

Do not send flowers with any shipment overseas, under any circumstances. This constitutes a quarantine situation and may result in returning the remains to the country of origin at the shipper's expense.

For inspections: Bear in mind that the remains may need to be transported to another city (Chicago, NYC, or Washington, DC) where the consulate or embassy is located. This will require the services of a funeral director in the city where the consulate or embassy is located, thus incurring additional expenses.

Apostille

Simply stated, an "apostille" is the verification of a notary seal or governmental agency seal and the accompanying signature. The apostille is obtained by the agency of each individual state that issues notary or governmental agency seals. This may be a Secretary of State or a country registrar. The shipping funeral director will need to contact their state authority to determine the agency responsible for the apostille.

In addition to the state apostille, some countries may require the apostille of the US Department of the State. To obtain the authentication of the United States Department of State, in Washington, D.C., the documents must be sent to: United States Department of State, Authentication Department, Columbia Plaza, 518 23rd Street, NW, Washington, D.C.

Part III: Receiving Remains from Abroad

By: Melissa Johnson Williams

The death of a US citizen who is to be returned from abroad is equally complicated as shipping human remains to a foreign country. The family will need to be in contact with the US Embassy in the country where the death has taken place. The Consular Services Representative can assist by providing information in many countries about funeral services that are available. If there is difficulty in reaching the US Embassy, the family can contact the United States Department of Overseas Services, Washington, D.C., (202-647-5225). Call this number to speak with a State Department Representative regarding the death of an American citizen abroad.

Neither the American Embassy nor the Department of State will provide funds to return a US citizen home. Decisions by the family will need to be made quickly, since in many countries the body will be buried after three days without the family's consent. After a given period of time, the family may be able to disinter the body and return it to the United States. However, in many countries this cannot occur for a minimum of two years and may be as long as 15 years.

Embalming is not uniformly available in many countries and may not equate to the process performed here. There are some countries where a generic form of embalming is available. When talking with the family about the possibility of viewing, use caution until you have the remains in your possession. Always allow at least 24 additional hours from the time the fight actually arrives in the US to schedule services. There are many delays, not under anyone's control, that could create a problem. These may include flight delays or cancellations, weather, and aircraft delays. You will also need additional time for any corrections to the body that may be necessary.

The family should select the least expensive services available in the foreign country, as they will have those charges as well as charges for services here to pay for. Inquire with the airline if the return portion of the deceased's airline ticket can be used to defray the cargo shipping charges. If the family is unable to meet the financial demands of shipping from overseas, they may have to choose cremation or local burial until such time as a disinterment is permitted.

You need to keep in mind that there are no federal agencies in foreign countries that regulate funeral services. Whatever the funeral service provider states the charges are, even if you feel it is excessive, will unfortunately have to be paid. I strongly urge any funeral home NOT to involve any US officials such as congressmen or senators. Foreign countries often do not respond well to this and if anything, this can slow down the process.

Many foreign countries either do not issue death certificates or will not issue one that has a cause of death on it. The US Embassy will issue a "Consular Report of a Death Overseas" that is accepted by insurance companies and other businesses, such as banks, that require a death certificate.

Federal Regulations on the Shipment of Human Remains to the US

When a person who has died abroad, regardless of nationality, is to be shipped to the United States, the US Embassy representative must be assured that they are properly encased and prepared for shipment. The requirements of the country where the death occurred must also be met at all times.

Part IV: Becoming a Certified Shipper

By: Joseph Shay (2019)

Our world has changed in many ways since September 11, 2001. The funeral industry has rules imposed in regard to shipping human remains aboard commercial aircraft. It wasn't until 2004 that the Transportation Security Administration (TSA) developed the "known shipper" policy. This rule was in place to provide a barrier to terrorists seeking to use air cargo to impose harm on innocent people.

The purpose of this program is to provide a chain of custody involved in preparing human remains for shipment by air. TSA agreed that the "known" status of the funeral homes that ship by air should have limited access to the preparation room and the transportation procedures.

Compliance with the 'known shipper" policy

Funeral homes are required to register as a 'known shipper' with each airline they use to ship human remains. The application process may include an inspection and payment of an inspection fee. While registering with multiple airlines can create an administrative burden on funeral homes, the TSA and airlines have told organizations such as the NFDA that the registration process must be completed.

Each airline has its own procedures for both the application and inspection process and may charge a nominal fee to cover their costs.

According to TSA and the airlines, no inspection will be necessary if the applicant is already in the TSA 'known shipper" database. If a funeral home is a "known shipper," however, owners still may be required to apply with each airline the firm uses. The "known shipper" status with one airline does not transfer to another airline.

A funeral home that is not in the TSA database may be subject to an inspection by the airline to ensure the legitimacy of the business. When a funeral home wishes to become an applicant as a "known shipper," they must contact each air cargo carrier directly to begin the application process.

This process varies from airline to airline. Each airline has its own documentation needed as well as procedures for transporting a body to another country. The NFDA has compiled a list of the major airlines around the world and their requirements. They can be found at www.nfda.org.

When a funeral home ships human remains, the following are some of the documentation that are required:

- Photo ID issued by a government agency and your state funeral director's license
- Death Certificate for the deceased
- Burial/Transit Paperwork
- Permit Letter of Non-Contagious Disease
- Embalmer's Affidavit
- Passport of the Deceased (if obtainable) for international shipping
- Letter on funeral home letterhead stating: "Only human remains are inside the casket," the flight itinerary, and the Consignee's name, address, and telephone number.

References

NFDA (2019). Frequently Asked Questions (Shipping Remains). *National Funeral Directors Association*. Retrieved from: http://www.nfda.org/resources/operations-management/shipping-remains/united-states-shipping-regulations/frequently-asked-questions.

Part V: Things to Consider When Dealing with Funeral Shipping

Excerpt From: Angela Berwald (2011)

Many times, deaths away from home are straight forward and the arrangements go smoothly. However, there is a percentage of cases that do not. It can be that the person died outside the United States, there are flight problems, the doctor is not available, or the condition of the deceased themself creates a challenge. While these issues do inevitably arise at times, there are certain things you can do to prepare yourself for cases such as these.

1. Do not set times for the service until you know when the remains will arrive. Once this information is determined, always leave enough time to allow for flight delays. You never know what might come up at the last minute.

2. Obtain all of the vital statistics from the family immediately. We do realize this can be an issue if you are helping a family that is extremely distraught. However, many states have gone to an online death registration system and all information is needed in order to obtain the permit to ship. An option may be to take the information over the phone, explaining why the information is needed so quickly.

3. Contact someone to handle the shipment who is familiar with all of the shipping regulations at the place of death.

4. Although it may sometimes be a delicate subject, talk to family about the size of the deceased. Some airlines have a weight limit of 300 pounds, and this may be the only airline that handles remains from the city of death.

5. Take into consideration the location of the deceased. Some facilities are located far away from a jetport city. Some facilities don't release in the middle of the night. And some facilities require the family's signature before they will release.

6. The day of the week the death occurred can also affect shipment. Some government offices, hospitals, and morgues are not open on weekends or holidays. This can cause a delay in both the release of the deceased as well as the acquisition of paperwork such as permits and death certificates.

7. The circumstances of the death also play a role in the shipping process. Some cases may require a Medical Examiner to be involved. This can increase a delay depending on the Medical Examiner's caseload. It is also important to give the embalmer enough time to prepare the deceased properly. Some remains may require more time than others, and additional time for observation may be requested by the embalmer.

8. Communicate with the family that every state, county, province, parish, and country have different requirements. If the person was in your care, you can easily schedule with the family the date of the service, but since the death is out of your area, you will need to explain to the family that although you understand their need to have their loved one home, there are requirements that need to be met.

9. Make sure the shipping funeral home or mortuary service is aware of final disposition so proper paperwork is obtained. This is of significant importance, especially if the final disposition is cremation. In some areas the Medical Examiner must view the remains prior to issuing a permit.

NOTES

NOTES

Chapter 15

DISASTERS

Disasters vary in size, scope, the extent of the damage, loss of life, injury, and degree of disruption to the family and the community. They can be natural, man-made, or even a combination of these events.

Natural Disasters	**Accidental**	**Man-made**
Floods	Airplane crash	Homicide
Earthquakes	Chemical	Suicide
Hurricanes	Fire	Mass Shooting
Monsoon	Train Crash	Chemical Dumping
Tornadoes	Boat Crash	Product Tampering (i.e. Tylenol)
Volcanic Eruption	Car Crash	Arson
Famine	Drowning	Cults (i.e. Branch Davidians; Jonestown)
Drought	Product Recall	Industrial Sabotage
Fires		Terrorism (i.e. 9/11 Attacks)
Pandemic/Epidemic		Kidnapping

Victims can be the next of kin, who have suffered the loss of a loved one, and whose lives will never be the same. They can be those who have lost their homes, with all the memories and mementos that no insurance policy can ever replace. Victims can be those who mourn the loss of a pet which was a child's playmate or the companion of an elderly widow or widower. Often these people are made to feel ashamed of their sorrow because others are grieving for human beings. Victims can also be the workers on disaster response teams, including funeral directors, who have been overwhelmed by the sights, sounds, and smells of a scene of unimaginable destruction.

Major Concerns

Disasters create a complex set of demands that must be met by many different paid and volunteer groups. In disasters such as the September 11th Attacks and Hurricane Katrina, there can be dozens of different groups on the scene responding.

Concerns that must be addressed include:

- Rescue of the living
- Care/medical attention for survivors
- Removal of those not involved
- Protection of disaster area
- Marking the locations of fatalities
- Removal of the dead
- Identification of remains and certification of death
- Notification of next of kin
- Final disposition
- Psychosocial and spiritual needs of bereaved

Responders

- Medical
- Police
- Fire
- Funeral Directors
- National Guard/Military
- Volunteers
- Clergy
- Public Works personnel
- Counselors
- Scientific experts
- Government representatives

The funeral director has a critical role to assume during a disaster. Participating in funeral rituals is the beginning of the grief recovery process for bereaved survivors. There is, however, another way that funeral service contributes to the needs of survivors after a disaster that involves multiple fatalities. This contribution involves the organized care and preparation of deceased disaster victims.

A disaster of any sort is unfortunate and truly takes a toll on all those involved. However, with strategic planning, it is possible to minimize the impact of the post-disaster period in a community as respectfully and quickly as humanly possible. Given the unpredictable nature of a disaster, no one person can ever be truly prepared for its catastrophic and often insurmountable consequences. However, by working in multi-disciplinary teams, disaster management personnel make every effort to ease the pain and suffering of all those whose lives are so terribly affected; this may well involve the funeral profession depending on the circumstance.

Specialized Disaster Activities

- Communication among responders and with the public
- Identification of injured and dead
- Notification of next of kin
- Distribution of care, supplies, and materials
- Consolation of sick, injured, families, and survivors

Legal Considerations

- Jurisdiction over disaster workers
- Responsibility for disaster recovery activities
- Financial – Who will pay for recovery efforts: State, Federal, local governments, or the private sector?

D-MORT (Disaster Mortuary Operational Response Team)

Some will argue that saving survivors is the one and only priority of disaster management. While this may be true, it is important to remember that very often lives are lost in a disaster and these lives demand the same respect as those who have survived. Therefore, it is only recently that mortuary service has been recognized as a key player in this multi-disciplinary approach to disaster management.

In 1990, the United States Federal Government established the Federal Disaster Response Plan to be used in any federally declared emergency. This plan encompasses 13 emergency support functions as responsibilities of the federal government. Under the Emergency Support Function Eight (ESF 8), the National Disaster Medical System (NDMS) is delegated responsibility specifically for the recovery, identification, and processing of the fatal victims of any disaster. The NDMS established one Disaster Mortuary (D-MORT) team in each of the Federal Emergency Management Agency's (FEMA) ten districts.

When activated, D-MORT teams provide all authorities with technical assistance and personnel to facilitate the difficult tasks of recovery, identification, processing, preparation, and disposition of deceased victims. The scope and severity of the emergency determines how many team members are dispatched to a disaster scene. Each regional D-MORT team is comprised of twenty-five primary responders, with an additional team base of one hundred members. Realizing the severe impact a disaster may have on a human body, teams are composed of the following licensed or certified individuals:

- Medical examiners
- Coroners
- Pathologists
- Anthropologists
- Medical records and fingerprint experts
- Forensic Odontologist
- Supply specialists
- Dental assistants
- X-ray technicians
- Funeral directors
- Mental health consultants for team members
- Security officers (police)
- Administrative assistants
- Computer analysts

This author was a member of the Region 2 D-MORT Team and was deployed to both the 9/11 attacks and Hurricane Katrina disasters. D-MORT maintains mobile mortuary container depots at Rockville, Maryland. The mobile mortuary container is a depository of equipment and supplies ready for immediate deployment to any disaster site in the continental United States, gratis to the requesting community. This mobile mortuary contains a complete morgue with fifty designated workstations for the necessary processing of fatal disaster victims. Each station is fully equipped with an inventory of prepackaged, expendable supplies to ensure the unit's self-sufficiency. After two trial operations in Beaver County, Pennsylvania and Roselawn, Indiana, the transportable morgue was installed and successfully operational in fourteen and seven hours, respectively. The team has since been pivotal in the recovery operations at several plane crash sites, at floods in the South, at a bombing tragedy, the Twin Towers in New York City, and Hurricane Katrina in Louisiana and Mississippi.

Emotional Support

The handling of the remains of deceased victims of a disaster presents psychological, emotional, and legal complications for D-MORT personnel, including funeral directors. Not only are they faced with the personal trauma of recovering human remains, but they also have obligations to the deceased's next of kin.

Emotional support, such as a critical incident stress defusing and debriefing, is available to all members of D-MORT teams and should be available to all disaster workers. These support activities allow disaster workers to discuss events they were confronted with and receive emotional intervention from trained mental health professionals.

Pandemic and the Funeral Home

In late 2019, the novel coronavirus SARS CoV-2 emerged in Wuhan City, Hubei Province, China. Most often referred to as COVID-19, or the coronavirus, it quickly became a global pandemic. The COVID-19 pandemic has been unlike anything the world has undergone since the 1918-1919 Spanish Flu. Although there have been other epidemic outbreaks, none have occurred that have had the severity or global impact of Covid-19. As of April 2021, an estimated 2.8 million people have died world-wide (New York Times, 2021a). There have been over 30.8 million known, confirmed cases in the United States, with roughly 556,000 known deaths (New York Times, 2021). There was an inability to perform widespread testing of the majority of those who were ill during the first 3 months of the pandemic in the U.S. The actual numbers of those affected by Covid-19 are estimated to be substantially higher. COVID-19 has dramatically affected all facets of life in our world. In late 2020, several vaccines were developed that help prevent serious illness and hospitalization due to COVID-19. It is hoped that the vaccines will be able to be distributed rapidly as a means to end the pandemic. At the writing of this book, COVID-19 is still on-going. Many countries, including the U.S., are battling an increase in cases while racing to vaccinate as many people as possible.

The Covid-19 Pandemic <u>MUST</u> be a wake-up-call for the funeral service industry. The following issues arose and impacted the funeral service industry. We must be better prepared if/when this happens again.

- Funeral homes may need to call on outside agencies such as D-Mort, FEMA, or the military for extra support in picking up the deceased and storing them for future interment.

- "Social distancing" (staying 6 feet apart when speaking or working with others) could be recommended for all contact with client families.

- Funeral homes should keep a larger supply of Personal Protective Equipment (PPE), disinfectants and embalming fluids on hand or have arrangements in place to purchase them on short notice.

- Funeral homes may experience a shortage of personnel due to contraction of the illness associated with the epidemic or pandemic.

- Funeral directors may have to bear the brunt of anger and abuse from client families.

- Funeral home managers should be aware of possible burnout or compassion fatigue for all staff.

- Contagion requires funeral directors to practice Universal Precautions with extra disinfection during removals, embalming and funeral ceremonies. CDC guidelines will establish protocols.

- Arrangements, visitations, and funerals could be modified according to state regulations limiting the number of days for the visitation and limiting the number of people allowed to attend.

- Cemetery/crematory regulations may be implemented limiting the number of people at grave-side services.

- The requirement of stay-at home orders and social distancing made the use of technology absolutely necessary. Zoom and other video messaging services may need to be used to enable families to grieve and morn their lost loved ones and also stay connected.

- Immediately after this epidemic/pandemic, a coalition should be formed with all funeral homes in the various geographic areas, to develop a protocol for storing large amounts of diseased bodies.

NOTES

NOTES

Chapter 16

CEMETERY / MAUSOLEUM

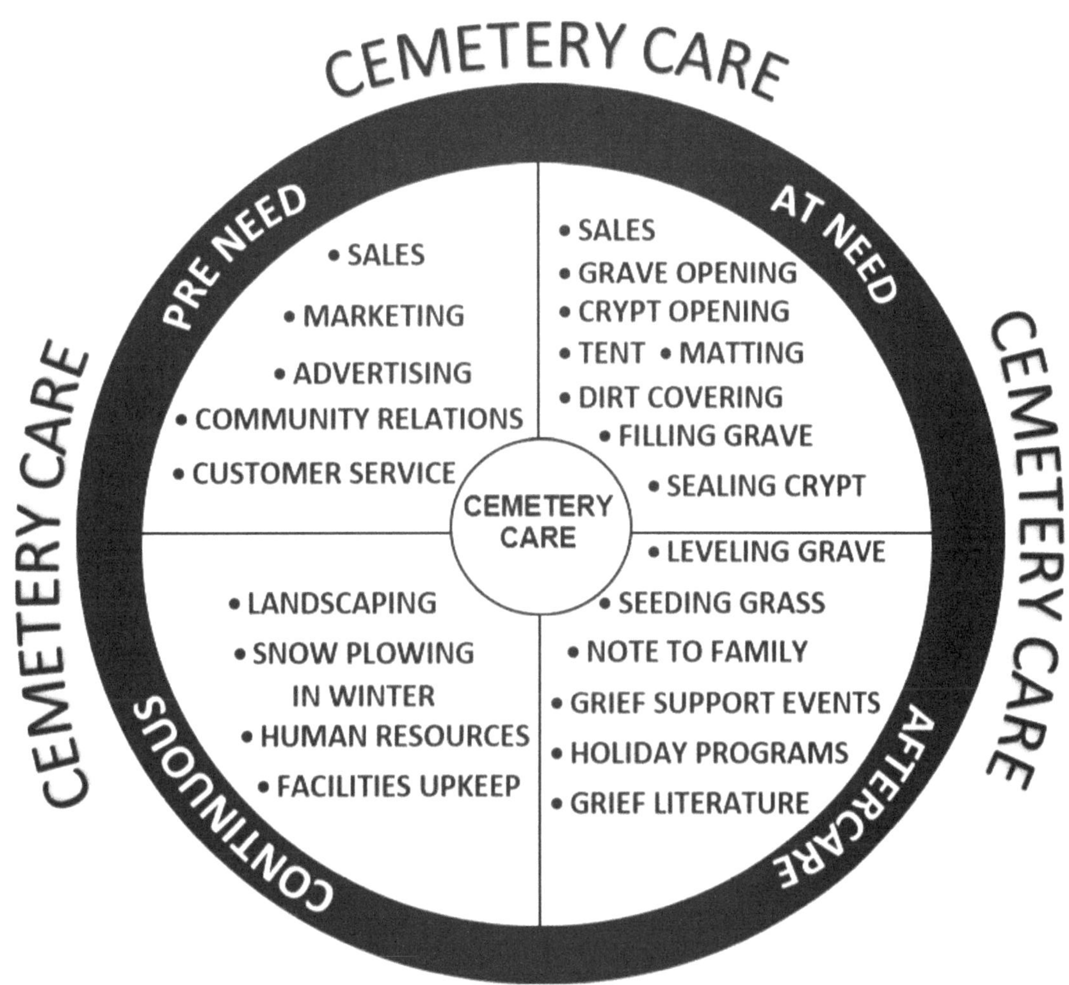

KLICKER'S CEMETERY CARE CONTINUUM

Cemeteries

"Show me your cemeteries, and I will tell you what kind of people you have."

Benjamin Franklin

A **cemetery** (from Greek – meaning "*sleeping place*") is an area of ground set aside and dedicated to the final disposition of dead human bodies or cremated remains.

The Observations of a Headstone

I am struck by how this resting place for the dead is so full of life. People caring for graves, couples walking the tree-lined roads hand-in-hand, parents with children feeding the ducks, a college student doing a headstone rubbing, and the constant flow of funeral processions coming and going.

Importance of Cemeteries

Cemeteries are important to a community because they do more than just hold the mortal remains of the deceased. They provide:

Sense of Security – Cemeteries provide a special peace of mind for people who purchase graves before the need for one arises. My own parents were examples of this. They purchased four graves with my aunt and uncle. It gave all of them a good feeling to know this task was taken care of and their families would not have to worry about it.

Long-term protection – The families you serve turn over to you their most precious possession, the body of a spouse, parent, or child. They are counting on you to care for and protect that body for the rest of their life. The need to know that the body will be protected is particularly important to grieving people. It provides them with a sense of comfort that helps them resolve their grief.

Fulfill Basic Human Right – The belief that everyone is entitled to a "decent burial" ("decent disposition" is a better term to use today) has been part of American culture since its beginning. This is evident in our society by the fact that we have social security and Veteran's death benefits, Veteran cemeteries, and local government subsidies for indigents. Being able to provide a decent disposition allows people to have and fulfill this basic human right. Survivors have a much harder time recovering from grief in cases where a body is unable to be recovered or is never found. Not being able to conduct this final disposition and provide a symbolic ending to their acute grief stage keeps some locked in grieving for years longer than normal.

Facilitate grief – Cemeteries and funeral homes are the only two places many people feel are appropriate for expressing their emotions. Crying, talking to the deceased, or just sitting or standing silently for as long as you like are acceptable behaviors at a cemetery. You do not need signs in the cemetery or anyone telling visitors that it is okay to express their emotions. People know that is what cemeteries are for. It's not embarrassing for them if other people see them. It's natural and accepted.

Immortality – Studies have shown that people want to be remembered after they die. Unfortunately, there are a limited number of ways for people to do that. One of the easiest and most common ways is with a cemetery monument of some sort. The grave, niche, or mausoleum with a person's name on it makes a statement for all to see. It says, "A person lived, was loved, and will be remembered. Remember them with us."

Aesthetic Setting – The beauty of nature springs forth during every season, and cemeteries capture this beauty and preserve it for all who want to see.

Commonalities between Funeral Homes & Cemeteries

Cemeterians and funeral home directors have more in common than either realize. Some of the similarities are in the following areas:

Serving bereaved families – Both cemeterians and funeral directors serve an important need for the bereaved. Funeral directors provide the immediate need to confront the reality of death by allowing viewing of the deceased. The ceremonies involved in the visitation, funeral, and religious service provide a sense of closure for the bereaved. The funeral is the first step in the grief-recovery process.

Cemeterians also play an important role during the initial process by being the ending ceremony for the funeral ritual. The cemeterian's primary value in the grief-recovery process is the long-term "therapy" cemeteries provide for the bereaved. Some may disagree with using the term therapy, but I am comfortable with it because visiting the grave, niche, or mausoleum does have a therapeutic effect on many people.

Many people obtain a sense of comfort in visiting the cemetery for years after a death. Bringing wreaths, trimming grass, and planting flowers lets mourners do something tangible at a time when most feel it is too late to do anything. I saw a good example of this recently when I visited my parent's grave on the Fourth of July.

Across the road, two men pulled up to the grass. One went up to a grave and placed a single red rose and then stood there for quite a while, silent. The other man cut the grass on the grave with a gas-powered lawn mower and had two large flowering plants that he replanted in urns on either side of the headstone. For some, the beauty and serenity of the cemetery gives them a sense that the deceased is resting in a peaceful and comforting place.

Pre-need and at-need sales – Both cemeterians and funeral directors have merchandise and services that are needed by the same limited market. Both sell products and services on a pre-need or at-need basis. The amount the consumer spends with one group may affect either positively or negatively the amount purchased from the other. Cemeterians have more history with selling pre-need than funeral directors. However, in the last ten years, funeral directors have made great leaps in catching up.

Personnel – Cemeteries and funeral homes need various levels of personnel to operate effectively. Both need owners, managers, mid-level executives, maintenance people, and secretarial support. Both must be able to motivate staff to function at the highest level. Good employees must be rewarded with adequate salaries, health insurance, retirement benefits, and a career ladder.

Cemeteries and funeral homes must build a sense of loyalty and commitment to their organization, and help employees understand the unique needs of customers. A disinterested evening attendant in a funeral home or a rude groundskeeper at a cemetery can have negative impressions on potential customers. You must develop in-service training programs that teach your staff what you want them to value and know.

Government regulations – OSHA, EPA, disability access, and nondiscrimination are issues cemeteries and funeral homes must deal with. An inspector can show up at either of our doors unannounced. If you are not in compliance, they may levy fines against you. Both funeral homes and cemeteries face a future with increasing government regulations.

Advertising and public relations – Cemeteries and funeral homes need to attract new business. There are similarities in some of the activities they do to make the public aware of your services. Besides media advertising, some funeral homes and cemeteries sponsor holiday programs, offer seminars on death education, and give tours to schools and community groups.

General business activities – Funeral homes and cemeteries struggle with business issues, including how to make an honest profit, maintaining the facility's equipment, cars, and trucks, getting better service from suppliers, and computerization. In the last ten years, both groups have seen an explosion of mergers and acquisitions.

There are certainly enough similarities between cemeterians and funeral directors to warrant a closer relationship than I see in most areas. If you do not meet as colleagues in the death-care profession, you will never be able to work out any issues that arise.

What is a Cemetery?

By: Patrick McGowan

The evolution of the cemetery can be traced by three occurrences:

1. The Churchyard cemetery
2. The Garden cemetery
3. The Memorial Park

The Churchyard / Urban Cemetery

According to Dr. Oliver McRae (2004), one of the most significant influences on American cemeteries was the transition from a rural, agrarian society to a more urban, "community" based society. Rural folk along with immigrants from Europe were flooding into urban areas. One of the first structures built in a new town was a church. The church grew to serve as the focal point of worship and community affairs in the town.

McRae further explains that it was at this time that the people decided that the most appropriate place to bury the dead was in the church. They believed this would enable the deceased to be close to God. Immigrants from Europe were familiar with the practice of burying the dead inside the church. The wooden floor of the church would be lifted, and the body would be buried in a hole. As in life, the deceased's station in life would determine their place of burial in the church. More prominent and prosperous individuals were buried as close to the altar as possible. As the church congregation grew and the space inside the church became limited, burials moved outside to the churchyard. Ibid.

McRae also suggests that the churchyard cemetery established memorialization norms that are still used today. The churchyard burial utilized the first single slab "tomb stone" memorial similar to those used today. The inscription on the memorial included the name of the deceased, the date of birth and death, and a favorite passage of scripture. Ibid.

The Garden Cemetery

In his book, *Purified by Fire - A History of Cremation in America*, Stephen Prothero (2001) describes a rapid growth of urban areas in the early 1800s. This caused concern over sanitation conditions that were deteriorating in Northeastern towns and cities. Cholera, yellow fever, typhoid, diphtheria, smallpox, and other infectious diseases plagued the US. Some blamed the immigrants from Ireland, Germany, and Italy. Other officials believed that these contagious diseases were caused by *miasma*. Miasma was an invisible noxious vapor that was the result of decomposing organic matter. Sewage, garbage collecting, street cleaning, and the decomposing underground corpses were among the environmental concerns of the time. Public health officials in New York City recommended "that the interment of dead bodies within the city ought to be prohibited" (p. 47-50).

Unfortunately, all the warnings were ignored, and urban cemeteries continued to be overcrowded. In 1822, sixteen thousand citizens died from yellow fever in New York (Van Beck, 1994). Boston and Philadelphia were also affected by the epidemics. The Boston City Council required that inter-city burials cease immediately. They also ordered the exhumation of all crammed or shallow-buried corpses. Ibid.

McRae reports that the first American suburban cemetery, Mount Auburn Cemetery, was established in 1831 in Cambridge, Massachusetts. Mount Auburn Cemetery was designed not only to "quarantine" the dead from the living, but also as a place to celebrate life and eternal life. The garden cemetery was designed to resemble the rambling gardens of an English estate. It was "picturesque" and peaceful, "where man walks in tranquility and harmony with God." Ibid.

Not only was the garden cemetery the answer to America's burial problems, it was also the answer to America's death care problems. For the first time in its history, the death care industry was accepted and seen as a meaningful and beautiful part of social life, instead of being viewed as morbid and unpleasant. Ibid.

The Memorial Park

The next phase following the garden cemetery movement was the Memorial Park. A *Memorial Park* is a cemetery or section of a cemetery with only flush to the ground type makers. The first memorial park was Forest Lawn Memorial Park in Glendale, CA. It was founded by Dr. Hubert Eaton in 1917. Dr. Eaton's "memorial park plan" eliminated upright monuments. He envisioned Forest Lawn to be "a great park devoid of misshapen monuments and other signs of earthly death, but filled with towering trees, sweeping lawns, splashing fountains, beautiful statuary, and memorial architecture." This new cemetery would be a place "where happiness is recalled, and sorrow forgotten. (Van Beck, 1994). Dr. Eaton's vision and Forest Lawn had a profound impact on the cemetery industry in this country. The memorial park eliminated the upright memorial and the aesthetic garden setting found with the garden cemetery. As a result of these changes, the time and labor associated with ground maintenance was greatly reduced. In 1942, Dr. Eaton combined the funeral home with the memorial park, creating Forest Lawn Memorial Park and Mortuary.

Green Cemeteries

One of the most dramatic changes in cemetery design is the growing trend of "green burial." A green, or natural, cemetery ensures that the burial site remains as natural and simple as possible in all respects. Interment of the bodies is done in a biodegradable casket, shroud, or a favorite blanket. A green cemetery is designed to let nature takes it course.

A green burial is a viable alternative to "traditional" burial practices in the United States. It is an earth friendly option when considering burial vs. cremation. Many families choose cremation because it's seen as more environmentally friendly than traditional burial. With a green cemetery, or memorial nature preserve, there are no embalming fluids and no expensive caskets or outer burial containers. The simplicity of a green burial is in tune with nature and need not be expensive.

Green burial was common among U.S. pioneers, who were often buried directly into the ground when caskets weren't available. Green burial, however, is not common in the U.S. today.

The new, ecologically motivated practice of green burial is more popular in Britain than the United States. Currently there are approximately 215 green burial sites in Britain, and more are planned.

Cemetery Terms

- **Section** – A subdivision of a cemetery containing several blocks.
- **Block** – A subdivision of a cemetery containing several lots; blocks make up sections.
- **Lot** – A subdivision of a cemetery containing several graves or interment spaces; lots make up blocks.
- **Grave** – An excavation in the earth as a place for interment.

Monuments & Markers

Memorializing the dead is one of mankind's oldest traditions. It is a powerful and meaningful way of expressing our love and honor for those who have touched our lives. Just as there are many ways to personalize a funeral, there are also many creative and unique ways of memorializing a loved one. As funeral directors, it is important that we understand and appreciate the plethora of ways to memorialize someone.

As part of their merchandise mix, both funeral homes and cemeteries now offer monuments and markers. It's imperative that we have a basic understanding of the design, craftsmanship, and artistry that goes into a memorial. This understanding and appreciation will not only help us, but also the families we serve. It enables us to ensure that the families are comfortable with the memorial they select.

- A ***monument*** is a structure, usually of stone or metal, erected to commemorate the life, deeds, or career of a deceased person; from the Latin word "monumentum" meaning "to remind."

- A ***marker*** is a small headstone, usually one piece, used to identify individual graves.

- A ***memorial*** is a physical object that is designed for the purpose of remembering.

Types of Markers (Monuments)

- ***Upright Marker/Monument:*** This is the most common form of memorialization used today. It consists of 2 pieces. The top piece is much larger and is called a "tablet" or die. The bottom piece is known as a "base."

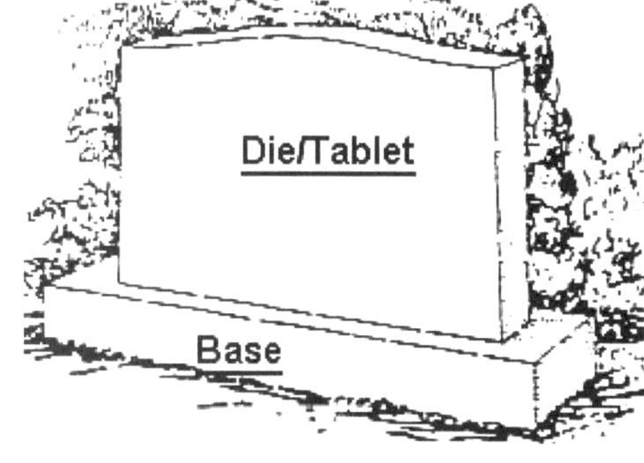

  - **Die (Tablet)**. The main part of a monument, the upright portion above the base where the inscription is located.

  - **Base**. The lower or supporting part of the monument.

- ***Slant Marker:*** This typically stands 16" to 18" in height with the front slanting or sloping back at a 45-degree angle.

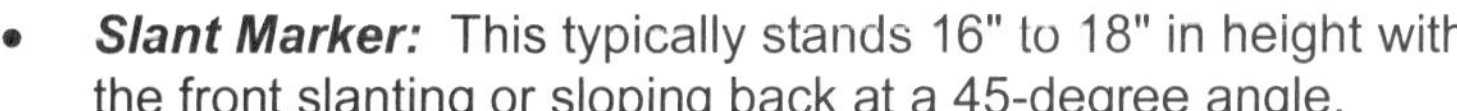

- ***Flat Marker:*** These lay flush with the ground. They are generally 24" x 14" but can be larger or smaller depending upon cemetery requirements.

- ***Bench Memorial:*** A bench made of granite. They typically consist of a top piece supported by two standards. These can serve as enduring memorials dedicating a park or other suitable location. They can also be used as cemetery memorials. Granite benches are growing in popularity as landscape furniture in private residences. Permission is needed by the cemetery before a bench memorial may be installed.

- ***Bronze Marker:*** A flat marker cast out of bronze. These are either mounted to a granite or a cement base that serves as a foundation.

Bronze Marker, Dept. of Veteran Affairs

Memorial Finishes

There are several different types of finishes associated with memorials. Many hours of design and labor go into finishing the granite used to produce various monuments and mausoleums around the world. The two basic finishes are **polished** and **pitched**.

- **Polished -** A *polished* finish creates a smooth surface of the stone. Abrasives are used similar to sanding wood to make the stone smooth and then the surface of the stone is buffed to a glass like polish. Polished finishes are available in several options. The most common are:
    - Polished 2 - Front and back of the memorial are smooth.
    - Polished 3 - Front, back, and top of memorial are smooth.
    - Polished 5 - Front, back, top, and sides of the memorial are smooth.

- **Pitched**

  Another type of finish available on memorials is *pitched*. A pitched finish gives the stone a natural rough finish. Many of the upright memorials and bases have a pitched finish. Although it may appear that this type of finish is simple to create, it is not. A pitched finish requires great skill to create a "natural" pitch versus an artificial appearance. The artisan uses a hammer and a set of chisels to create the desired product.

Memorial Design

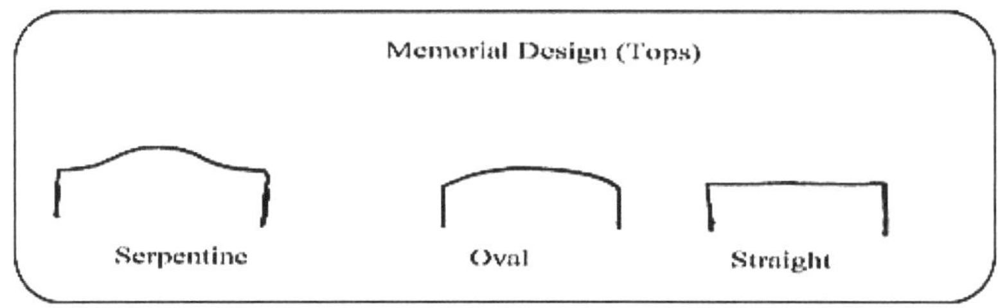

Lettering & Ornamentation

- An **Epitaph** is an inscription on a monument to commemorate the deeds or qualities of the departed.

- ***Sand-carving – A process used in creating a memorial***. Sand-carving is most often used in lettering and creating the ornamentation that is present on the memorial. Skilled craftsmen prepare the memorial by first placing a rubber stencil on the memorial. A direct stream of abrasive is blown under high pressure (approx. 100 psi) against the memorial. When the stream strikes the rubber, it bounces off, but where the rubber has been cut away, the stream etches the pattern into the stone. This type of sand-carving produces two-dimensional designs, such as lettering.

- **Etching**: Another type of memorial design utilizes an etching process. Etching is normally done on dark granite for more contrast. Skilled workers use a diamond tip-engraving tool to remove some of the polished areas of the granite. As the polished areas are removed, the lighter etched areas remain to create beautiful works of art. Families are able to etch pictures, favorite religious verses, or interests into the memorial.

Cenotaph

A cenotaph is a monument erected to the memory of the dead, with the dead human body not present.

World War II Memorial, Washington, DC.

Mausoleums

Definition – *A building containing crypts or vaults for entombment; an above-ground structure for burial.*

The first known above-ground tombs can be credited to the Egyptian Pharaohs. In 353 BC, the first mausoleum was constructed by the Persian Queen Artemisia for her husband Mausolus. Mausolus was a satrap (governor) of the Persian Empire and virtual ruler of Caria in southwestern Anatolia, from 377/376 to 353 BC. After he died at a relatively young age, Artemisia honored him with a tomb that was so spectacular that his name has become synonymous with all above-ground tombs; we call such tombs *Mausoleums*.

There are four types of mausoleums: Private/family mausolea, community mausolea, chapel community mausolea, and garden mausolea.

- A ***Private/Family Mausoleum*** is a very premium form of above-ground entombment. The private mausoleum is constructed to provide above-ground entombment to an individual or family at a pre-selected site at the cemetery. There are several factors to consider with private mausolea. These factors are:
  - The expense associated with the construction of the mausoleum.
  - Cemetery restrictions and regulations.
  - The number of individuals to be entombed in the mausoleum.
  - The style of mausoleum to be constructed.

- A ***Community Mausoleum*** differs from a private mausoleum in that it is designed to accommodate a large number of people. The community mausoleum is more affordable than the private mausoleum because the cost of construction and care is spread out among a larger group of people. The community mausoleum has provided cemeteries with opportunities to efficiently make use of land in the cemetery. Above ground entombment has been increasing in use because of the availability of developable burial space in cemeteries is at a premium (Secking, 2005).
- A ***Chapel Community Mausoleum*** is a building with indoor crypt spaces. These are climate-controlled for year-round comfort. They can offer a quiet setting with natural lighting, carpet, stained-glass windows, features, seating areas, and a comfortable atmosphere for services or for all who visit their loved ones.
- A ***Garden Mausoleum*** is a building with all exterior, outdoor crypt spaces. There can be features and benches around the Mausoleum.

Terms

- A ***Crypt*** is a chamber in a mausoleum, of sufficient size, generally used to contain the casketed remains of a deceased person.

- ***Lawn Crypt*** – A grave space where two or more persons may be buried in a grave liner, which have been stacked one on top of the other. The first person who dies is buried in the deepest grave liner with subsequent burials on top.

- ***Columbarium*** – A structure, room, or space in a mausoleum or other building containing niches or recesses used to hold cremated remains.

- A ***Niche*** is a recess or space in a columbarium used for the permanent placing of cremated remains.

Reasons Why Families Select Above-ground Entombment

1. Some want clean, dry, above-ground entombment.
2. Some individuals do not want to be put in the ground.
3. Some want to make it more convenient for their loved ones to visit during inclement weather.

Mausoleum-Related Concerns

The following information was provided by David Yearsley, the Founder and CEO of Ensure-A-Seal. The four major concerns that exist concerning mausoleums are **bodily fluid leakage**, **decomposition odors**, **infestation**, and **casket deterioration.** These concerns have continued to exist regardless of the following:

1. Geographical location - North, south, east, or west.
2. Type of mausoleum - Chapel, garden, and private family mausoleum.
3. Type of construction - Poured-in-place or pre-cast concrete crypts.
4. Type of caskets entombed - Gasketed-metal, non-gasketed metal, or wood caskets.
5. Quality of the entombment procedures.
6. Age of the mausoleum.
7. Extent of an Integrated Pest-Management Program.

The 4 Major Concerns as described by Yearsley are:

1. **Body Fluid Leakage**. Most of the time fluids flow into the adjacent crypts and the crypt chambers beneath the problem crypt. The fluids can exit a crypt even when the plastic shutter is perfectly caulked in place because concrete is porous. Once the fluids reach the marble or granite fronts, severe staining occurs. New crypt fronts need to be used and the old crypt fronts are removed from the mausoleum.

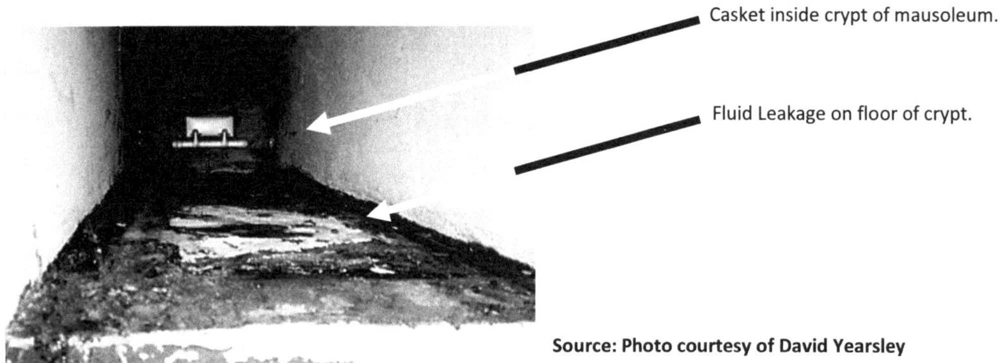

Source: Photo courtesy of David Yearsley

2. **Decomposition Odor.** The vent in the crypt chamber is designed to evacuate the odor from the chamber. When the flow of air is limited or non-existent, the decomposition odor is absorbed into the concrete and can become recognizable in the mausoleum.

3. **Infestation.** The Phorid Fly, Megaselia scalaris, has become a persistent pest of the mausoleum industry. Enormous numbers of these flies can scurry over marble and granite surfaces and fly into people's faces throughout the year. The nuisance flies can become so intolerable that visitors are forced to leave the building. Many families and visitors find the insect electrocution lights loaded with dead flies to be equally disgusting. The male flies are mostly attracted to these lights. The "bug lights" detract from the beauty of the building and interrupt prayer and meditation.

   Conventional pest-control methods are not effective on mausoleum Phorid flies because the source of the problem is within the occupied crypt chamber. As mausoleum structures age and become more occupied, the infestation levels increase. Even with operational improvements, ventilation, crypt sealing, etc., this insect has proved much too difficult to control.

Infestation on the outside of a casket following removal from an above ground crypt.

Photo courtesy of David Yearsley

There are two ways to reduce infestation in the mausoleum. The first is to control the casket using a Casket Protector, followed by a pesticide program that will reduce the population by killing female flies.

4. **Casket Deterioration…Over time.** Recognizable problems have occurred with caskets entombed only nine days from the date of entombment. Caskets have become active for fluid leakage, odors, and infestation after being entombed for thirty-plus years.

In addition to the four major concerns facing mausoleum managers, they must be prepared for ground removals to the mausoleum, transfer cases from other cemeteries, temporary entombment's communicable disease cases, poorly embalmed cases, unembalmed cases, and problem cases that become recognizable years after entombment.

Casket Protector

A **casket protector** is a sealed unit that is designed to provide a controlled environment for the casket. A casket protector will cover both metal and wood caskets. The casket protector is engineered to allow gases to escape, to contain liquids, and to control infestation.

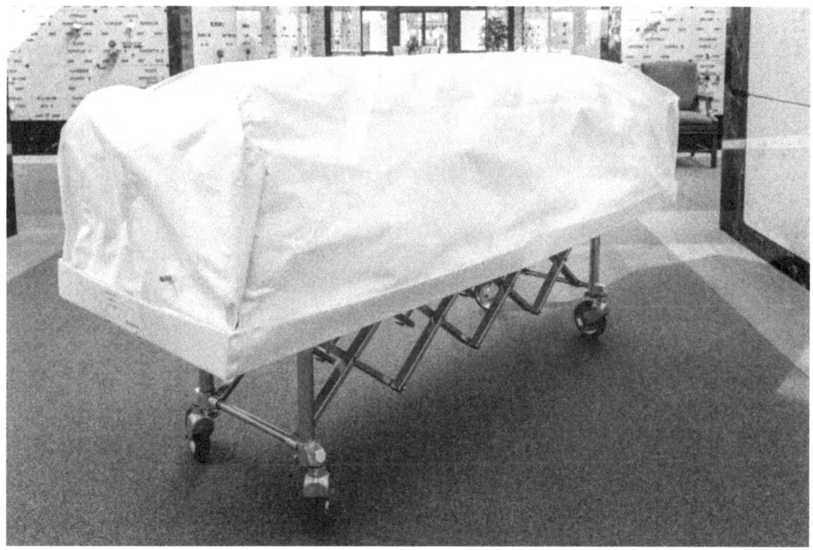

Source: http://hollandsupplyinc.com/product/ensure-seal-casket-protector/

<u>The use of a casket protector has a three-fold purpose:</u>

1. To maintain the overall quality of the cemetery/mausoleum;
2. To contribute to the general well-being of the environment; and
3. To provide additional peace of mind and comfort to the families of the deceased.

NOTES

Chapter 17

CLERGY/CELEBRANT-FUNERAL DIRECTOR RELATIONS

Source: https://people.com/politics/michael-curry-bishop-meghan-markle-prince-harry-royal-wedding-bush-funeral/

Clergy

By: David Tackett, M., Div., CFSP

Most funeral services in the United States are religious in nature. Most Americans consider themselves to be "spiritual" people and prefer a clergy person present at a funeral. Surveys show that about 50% of Americans formally belong to a church, synagogue, or mosque. Around one third of those people regularly attend worship services. As pastors know quite well, even many "unchurched" families seem to want some "religious" presence at the time of death. There are exceptions to these generalizations. There are some regions within the U.S. where secular services are becoming more prevalent. The funeral celebrant movement of recent years has sought to respond to this trend by training people from different backgrounds to conduct meaningful, personalized services. Many celebrants are clergy. In most cases, funeral directors will share the responsibilities for the funeral or memorial service with a clergy person.

Clergy-funeral director relations are important for all funeral service practitioners to understand and appreciate to be successful. The funeral director must cultivate good working relationships with the local clergy to be successful in funeral service. It has been said, fairly or unfairly, the clergy can live without the funeral director; the funeral director cannot survive without the support of the clergy (and their congregations). The responsibility is on the funeral director to cultivate, develop, and nurture these vital relationships. The funeral service professional must be willing to make the necessary overtures and accommodations to build bridges of understanding with the clergy. As I was told as a young associate pastor, "It is your job to do 99% of the getting along with the senior pastor." The same is true of funeral directors and the clergy.

It is important for funeral directors to understand that many clergy have had little training or exposure to funerals during their theological education. "How to do a funeral" is usually included in a liturgy course, but often not covered in depth. Many newly ordained clergy do not really know how to perform a funeral service. They may know the theological issues related to death and funeralization, but not how to officiate at a service. It is often the local funeral director who walks them through the actual mechanics of a funeral (particularly if the service is held at a funeral home). When this lack of education is combined with the fact that the clergy view the funeral as a worship service first and foremost, one can readily understand how misunderstandings can sometimes develop between clergy and funeral directors.

Most clergy are unaware of what the funeral home staff must do for a service (and some don't care)! The numerous logistical concerns of the funeral director are generally not shared by the clergy. This accounts for some disagreements that can arise regarding casket placement, flowers in the sanctuary, procession order, etc. The clergy are generally not concerned with these things and may consider them irrelevant to their goal of conducting a meaningful worship service. The funeral home staff, on the other hand, is vitally concerned with these "nuts and bolts" issues. It is crucial to understand this difference in perspectives. Stated simply, what funeral directors think is important (a well-embalmed body, properly displayed casket, memorial folders, register book, casket spray, vehicle line-up) likely is not on the clergy person's list of priorities.

The fundamental difference in perspective between the funeral director and the clergy is often the source of tension and, sometimes, conflict between the two vocations.

Some potential "Hot Button" issues include:

1. Notification of Clergy

Because clergy identify so closely with their parishioners, they rightly expect to be immediately notified when a member of their congregation has died. The wise funeral director will tend to this notification as quickly as possible. For families without formal religious affiliation, discussion should still be held early in the arrangement conference regarding who will officiate, and contact made immediately. Any discussions of the actual content or details of the religious ceremony should be left to the clergy and family. Usurping the pastoral role (or even the appearance of doing so) is an invitation for trouble.

2. Place of the Service

Many religious traditions recommend that the funeral of a member be held at the local house of worship. Many families and funeral directors prefer that the service be held at the funeral home, due to convenience. It will be in the funeral director's best interest to defer to the desires of the clergy on this point. Any indication that a family was persuaded by the funeral director to hold the service at the funeral home, rather than at the house of worship, will almost certainly result in a major conflict with the officiating clergy. If a "churched" family has a strong desire to stay at the funeral home, the funeral director should stand aside and let the family address this thorny issue with their pastor. This will not likely be an issue with unchurched or unaffiliated families for whom funeral home services are already the norm.

3. Public Viewing of the Body (To open or close the casket?)

This question tends to be emotionally laden for all involved. The difference in perspectives mentioned earlier is keenly evident with this issue. Embalmers spend much time and effort preserving and restoring human remains to an acceptable appearance. A great deal of professional pride is invested in presenting a body to a family for final viewing. Many funeral directors consider this the most important service they render. Some clergy agree, but many do not. Depending upon their theological convictions (and personal opinion), a number of clergy simply do not see much value in viewing dead human remains. They believe the focus should be on God during this time, not the physical body. This explains the insistence of some clergy for a closed casket service. Some may not permit a casket inside their building.

This can also explain the tendency of some clergy to discourage certain casket selections and the presence of flowers in the house of worship. The mandated use of a pall in some churches is likewise designed to keep the congregation focused on the worship service, rather than the casket. Issues of financial stewardship are also raised by some clergy. I heard one pastor complain about "spending money on fancy caskets and showy flowers." This attitude is not uncommon among many clergy.

The family, in consultation with the clergy person, should make decisions on the delicate issue of viewing the body in an open casket. Inside the house of worship, the clergy's preferences will likely prevail. In the funeral home setting, it may come down to a compromise solution between an officiant who wants the casket closed and the family who wants it open. The funeral director does have a legal obligation to obey the instructions of the person who has authorized the funeral contract. If necessary, this fact can be made known to the clergy person, who may fail to understand the unique relationship funeral directors have with their client families. Usually the issue can be mutually resolved to everyone's satisfaction. Funeral directors may also be able to educate the clergy on the positive effects of viewing. Sharing position observations and comments from families that were helped by viewing their loved one's body may cause some "anti-viewing" clergy to reconsider their position.

4. Honoraria

An honorarium is a payment for professional services upon which custom forbids a price to be set. An honorarium is almost always made to the presiding clergy at a funeral service. The presentation of this gift should be made discreetly and in private. A sincere word of appreciation for the clergy's time and availability should accompany the presentation. If the clergy person wants to return this gift to the family later or donate it to charity, they may do so. Clergy are busy people, and it is often a major time commitment for them to officiate a funeral service. In those rare cases where a family elects not to give any honorarium, the funeral director should present one out of the funeral home's petty cash fund. This is simple courtesy. The amount should be consistent with the norms in the community. Funeral directors should never refer to the honorarium as "pay" or a "fee." Most clergy do not appreciate the suggestion that they are somehow employees of the funeral home. Tact and sensitivity should always govern this transaction.

5. Funeral Costs

Critics of contemporary funeral service have influenced many clergy. Some are quite critical of the funeral profession. Almost inevitably, the concerns focus on the costs of a funeral. Funeral directors must be able to courteously discuss this issue without becoming defensive or hostile. Imparting information, supported by personal stories of satisfied families, will prove more helpful than an argument. Clergy desiring to be present at the arrangement conference and in the selection room should be openly welcomed. Many clergy have no idea of what really goes into a funeral, or the numerous details and manual labor that make up the funeral director's daily routine. Funeral service is a business they often have no knowledge of, other than what they have read or have heard in the media. Educating the local clergy on why and how things are done at the funeral home can be an effective response to unfounded criticisms about prices. The prices must be sensible and defensible as well. The free market role of the family can also be discussed. People choose what they want to purchase. Some of the business realties of the contemporary funeral industry can also be tactfully discussed when appropriate. Many clergy do not realize the intense competitive pressures faced by funeral homes in today's changing market. Some critical clergy have reconsidered their opinions about funeral service upon hearing the facts, rather than only relying on media reports.

Forging positive relations with the clergy takes time, effort, and a willingness to openly discuss issues. Nobody likes to be challenged or have their vocation questioned. Maturity, tact, and information are the funeral professional's best response to difficult clergy they may encounter. The strategy of "killing them with kindness" is a good one. Being courteous and even-tempered goes a long way to winning over difficult people eventually. Likewise, the many friendly and supportive clergy we work with can help funeral directors build relationships to treasure as we serve bereaved families together.

Funeral Celebrants

According to Howard-Fusco (2015), the civil celebrant movement started in Australia in 1973. The Anglican and Roman Catholic Church liturgy was not working for the general population, especially those who were divorced. The government started licensing celebrants – non-clerics who could perform weddings and funerals outside of a religious ceremony. The movement recognized that non-believers and secular people have a place of equal respect in society.

The term "celebrant" is a general term that describes a person who acts as an officiant at some type of service or celebration. A celebrant may officiate at a wedding, or at a religious or non-religious rite of passage. A specially trained funeral celebrant is someone who works with a grieving family to organize and conduct a funeral service according to their wishes, beliefs, values, and the lifestyle of the deceased.

Celebrants are becoming popular. A growing number of people define themselves as spiritual but not religious and do not wish to include religious aspects in the funeral service. Many, but not all, celebrants' services are secular. A family may request some religious aspects in the celebrant ceremony.

The use of celebrants by funeral homes has not been universally accepted by funeral home owners or managers. Some funeral directors reject using celebrants, even though the author has never heard a funeral director say that the goal of celebrants in creating a meaningful service is not a good goal. This is usually more for the benefit of the funeral home than for the family. When I have talked to funeral directors about not using a celebrant, they have said that it is because they are afraid the clergy members in their community will get miffed at them for using one. It is not unusual for some clergy to get out of sorts when a funeral home uses one clergy more than another. Some directors also have clergy who are adaptable to conducting a secular service, so they do not want to "rock the boat."

A celebrant's primary purpose and intention is to provide personalized, unique, and specialized services for any person, but usually for those who do not wish to have a denominational or religious-based experience. Does that mean that celebrants only serve families who are atheists? Not at all. Many families who utilize celebrants request prayers or readings from Scripture or familiar hymns from their past. The difference is that celebrants approach each funeral service as a new and individualized service that is written and designed for one person, for one family. There is no template, no outline, and no Funeral Sermon #3. The service grows out of the stories, memories, words, and ceremonies meant to honor that individual life. Celebrants usually spend eight to ten hours working on a service. There is no such thing as "insert name here" in a celebrant's world.

The Family Meeting

The most important element of a celebrant's work is the family meeting. This is not just a time to gather the stories and hear how the family wishes the service to be designed. Some amazing things can happen in a family meeting, where stories are shared, perhaps for the first time. In this meeting, emotions are expressed, and memories begin to take shape into lasting pieces that will be there long after the flowers have faded and the music has ended. A celebrant does not rely on the obituary, the clergy record, or a few emails from friends and family. A celebrant's best work happens when he or she makes a concerted effort to set a time and place for a family meeting, so each person has a chance to be part of the experience.

The Celebrant Service

The service itself is at once normal and amazingly different. The family, funeral director, attendees, casket or urn, and flowers are all there. The video tribute may be viewed, and the music is played. What sets a celebrant service apart is that from the very first words uttered, the service is about the deceased – about the life, the memories, the grief of those left behind, the acknowledgment or the special place on earth that the life occupied. The celebrant or family members may light candles, a memory token might be handed out to remind the participants of the person, a friend could share a poem or story, the celebrant may incorporate a special ceremony of remembrance. Through it all, family and the audience will be engaged in a tribute to the life by hearing the stories and sharing the laughter and tears. If a celebrant has done his or her job well, each person who leaves the service will feel as if they know the deceased a little better, feel more connected to the family, and understand ways they can be of assistance during the grief journey. They will also understand how important and meaningful funeral services can be. Celebrants hope to move people in a way that is wonderful, memorable, and life changing.

Clergy/Celebrant Relations Ideas

Todd Van Beck (2017) lists ways that funeral directors can maintain excellent relationships with the clergy/celebrants in their community, including:

- Mail grief counseling newsletter to all clergy
- Invite several local clergy to grief seminars
- Host clergy appreciation breakfasts/lunches/dinners
- Attend as many church dinners, lunches, festivals, anniversaries, and activities as possible by posting events on the office calendar and assigning staff to attend
- Solicit clergy recommendations on how to improve services
- Complete Clergy Preference Form for all clergy
- Laminate articles on clergy and churches
- Donate staff services for church events
- Make donations to church building or other projects
- Have clergy on mailing list to invite to all funeral home special events
- Offer transportation for clergy for all funerals
- Take clergy golfing or other events
- Sponsor grief seminars at churches
- Specifically meet with every clergy to make sure of their desires for funerals
- Send thank you notes to clergy following each service they conduct
- Provide the full obituary to clergy
- Provide a private room for clergy prior to the service
- Contact clergy for a family following a death
- Advertise in church bulletin or newsletter
- Provide calendars
- Invite the clergy to the arrangement conference.

NOTES

Section II

CREMATION

- Cremation

Chapter 18

CREMATION

Source: https://lashibifuneralhomes.com/media-center/news/58-ghanaians-opt-for-cremation

Cremation – *The process of reducing a dead human body to bone fragments using flames and extreme heat.*

Cremated human remains – *Commonly called cremains by funeral personnel or ashes by the public. These are the end-product after the bone fragments have been pulverized.*

Cremator – *The unit designed for the cremation process. Also known as a retort.*

Liquid Cremation – *This is a new technology used to describe the process of* ***alkaline hydrolysis****, which is a water-based dissolution process for human remains that uses alkaline chemicals, heat, and sometimes agitation and/or pressure to accelerate natural decomposition. Bone residue that remains using this process is similar to the volume customarily obtained after cremation; after being pulverized, the remains are made available to the family to retain in an urn or for disposition by other means.*

Cremulator – *The machine that is used to pulverize bone fragments into a finer consistency.*

Witnessing Room – *A designated room in a crematory or funeral home that allows a family to gather together and observe the deceased being placed in the cremation unit. The family does not watch the actual cremation process.*

How Is Cremation Done?

Cremation **prepares the body for final disposition**. It can be performed at a cemetery, crematory, a funeral home offering cremation services, or a stand-alone crematorium.

Cremation Resource (2019) explains the cremation process. In this process, the dead body, encased in a casket or container, is placed in a cremation chamber, and subjected to extreme heat and direct flame to convert it into bone fragments known as cremains. It usually **takes about two to three hours**, depending on factors like weight of the body, the type of casket or container in which the body is placed, and temperature in the retort, etc. After the container is burned away, the heat dries the body, burns the skin and hair, contracts and chars the muscles, vaporizes the soft tissues, and calcifies the bones so that they eventually crumble. The gases released during the process are discharged through an exhaust system. The cremation technician may have to crush the partially cremated remains with the help of a long hoe-like rod.

After the cremation is completed, the bone fragments are then collected in a tray or pan and allowed to cool for some time. These remains, however, also contain non-consumed metal objects such as screws, nails, hinges, and other parts of the casket or container. Tiny amounts of residue may remain in the chamber and mix with the particles from subsequent cremations. Ibid.

In addition, the mixture may contain dental work, dental gold, surgical screws, prosthesis, implants, etc. These objects are removed with the help of strong magnets and/or forceps after manual inspection. All these metals are later disposed of as per the local laws. Ibid.

Mechanical devices, especially pacemakers, must be removed beforehand because they may explode due to the intense heat. This could damage the cremation equipment and staff. It is also suggested to remove jewelry items like rings, wrist watches, and other similar objects, as these items are likely to break down during the process. Moreover, the metal pieces are removed before the use of a cremulator in the next process because they may damage the equipment used for pulverization. Ibid.

A final part of the process, as detailed by Cremation Resource (2019), involves the dried bone fragments being further ground into a finer, sand-like consistency using a machine called a cremulator.

The Past, Present and Future of Cremation

Excerpt From: D.M. Isard (2017)

Source: https://en.wikipedia.org/wiki/Cremation

Most do not know the history of cremation. We are ill-equipped to deal with the results of the past if we don't understand history. While the roots of cremation go back more than 5,000 years, we began the modern age of cremation in the 1870s. Before the modern world of cremation, bodies were cremated in outdoor pyres or within outdoor cremation pits. Cremation became "modern" in the 1870s, when an Italian professor named Ludovico Brunetti invented the first commercial cremation chamber. Brunetti demonstrated his cremation "furnace" at the Vienna Exposition in 1873. An improved commercial retort was demonstrated at the World's Fair in 1876 in Philadelphia. With the World's Fair of 1876, the modern crematory became an option for a new civilized society.

The man credited with being the first official person cremated in the United States was Joseph Henry Louis Charles, Baron de Palm. Baron de Palm was an Austrian-born immigrant living in the United States. Prior to his Dec. 6, 1876 death, Baron de Palm had arranged for his body to be cremated. This cremation was a public event, and, by all indications, it was not a pretty sight. For one thing, it was difficult to find a crematory to use. After months of searching, Baron de Palm's friends located a crematory built by Dr. Francis J. LeMoyne based roughly upon Brunetti's concept. LeMoyne was an eccentric physician, inventor, radical politician, and abolitionist. His home was a stop on the Underground Railroad, a safe haven for escaping slaves during the 1850s.

Finding a crematory and arranging for disposition in the 19th century was not as easy as going online. It took Baron de Palm's associates more than six months to set up the cremation event. Baron de Palm died in May in New York City. His body had to be preserved while the details of the cremation were worked out, and then had to be shipped hundreds of miles to LeMoyne's estate.

Early embalming techniques were just being accepted at the time of Baron de Palm's death. His body was injected several different times with arsenic and later with a sterner treatment of potter's clay and crystalized carbolic acid. The effect of this preservation effort met with mixed results. When the coffin containing Baron de Palm's body was opened for inspection Dec. 5, 1876, the results were poor. The body was badly shrunken and discolored. Some marveled that Baron de Palm was recognizable at all. "No spectacle more horrible was ever shown to mortal eyes," gasped one newspaper report.

Baron de Palm's cremation generated a media circus that would make our modern-day paparazzi cringe. Just before his death, Baron de Palm had joined the newly formed Theosophical Society and, true to its vision, he left instructions to conduct his funeral "in a fashion that would illustrate the Eastern notions of death and immortality" and then to cremate his body. This was precisely the public relations opportunity the Theosophists needed to attract attention to their cause. They set about making public ceremonies of both the funeral and the cremation. This was the first record of commercial equipment being used for a cremation in the United States.

The actual cremation was relatively uneventful: As the Baron's body slid into the furnace, there was reportedly a brief sizzle and a puff of smoke, and then the predictable golden and rosy hues of the body as it burned. Most reviews of the day, however, were not kind. Words like "folly," "farce," "weird," "objectionable," "repulsive," "revolting," and "a desecration" were used by reporters writing up their stories. "For all the ceremony that was observed," one reporter noted, "one might have supposed that the company had been assembled to have a good time over roast pig."

This was the first of what would become the choice of more than 50% of all deaths in the United States. Almost immediately after the LeMoyne crematory was used, a second crematory was constructed a few miles away in Lancaster, Pennsylvania. [End of Excerpt]

Phases of Cremation Growth

The Cremation Association of North America's (CANA, 2018) Statistics Report identifies six phases typical of cremation growth:

- **Starting point**: Trending begins when cremation rate reaches 5%.
- **Lighthouse period**: 5 to 20%, which can take anywhere from 10 to 25 years.
- **Acceleration period**: 20 to 60%.
- **Deceleration period**: After 60%, the growth rate starts to slow. It can take anywhere from 10 to 20 years to reach 80%.
- **Plateau period**: Once an 80% cremation rate is attained, the growth rate almost evens to a flat line. It could take many decades to reach the upper limit. What exactly that limit is, we don't know. According to CANA, it is unlikely that our society would reach 100% cremation rate.

History of the Growth of Crematories & The Cremation Rate in the U.S.

The need for crematories grew as cremation became an increasingly useful and popular option. The following timeline shows the growth of both the opening of crematories as well as the growth of the cremation rate in the U.S.

1900- There are 20 crematories in the U.S.

1913- There are 52 crematories in the U.S.

1967- Cremation rate is 4% in the U.S.

1975- There are 425 crematories in the U.S. and 150,000 cremations.

1999- There are 1468 crematories in the U.S. and 595,617 cremations. 25% of all deaths.

2005- Cremation rate is 32.4%

2010- Cremation rate is 40.8%.

2016- Cremation rate is approximately 50%.

2018- Cremation rate is approximately 53%.

2025- Projected rate to be 58.8%

According to the NFDA (2017), cremation rates will continue to rise over the next 8 years, so that 44 states will have cremation rates over 50%, compared to only 16 states having that rate in 2010. It is further estimated that by 2035, the nationwide cremation rate will reach 78.8% (Katz, 2017). Many other countries already have high rates of cremation. Japan, for instance, has a cremation rate of 99%.

The growth of cremation in the U.S. has resulted in an increased need for crematories. Nearly 30% of funeral homes now operate crematories, with an additional 9.4% planning to open a crematory in the next 5 years (NFDA, 2017).

Regional Differences in Cremation Rates

The rate of cremation varies in the U.S. by region. Katz (2017) reports that these differences can be attributed to religious observance, as well as education. People who are non-religious are more likely to choose cremation. Additionally, the impact of a more transient society can affect the rates of cremation, as people often do not want to be buried where they die, if living far from home. Ibid.

The 2018 Annual Statistics Report by the Cremation Association of North America shows the regional variation in cremation rates by looking at states with the highest and lowest rates of cremation.

Top 10 States with Highest Cremation Rates	
STATE	**% of Cremations**
Washington	77.3%
Nevada	76.9%
Oregon	75.8%
Maine	74.4%
Montana	73.6%
Hawaii	72.5%
New Hampshire	71.6%
Wyoming	71.3%
Colorado	70.2%
Vermont	69.7%
Bottom 5 States with Lowest Cremation Rates	
STATE	**% of Cremations**
Mississippi	22.5%
Alabama	27.7%
Kentucky	29.5%
Louisiana	31.6%
Tennessee	33.1%

Source: NFDA 2017

States that Allow Alkaline Hydrolysis

Alkaline hydrolysis is a newer technology in cremation. It is a water-based dissolution process for human remains that uses alkaline chemicals, heat, and sometimes agitation and/or pressure to accelerate natural decomposition. Bone residue that remains after using this process is similar to the volume customarily obtained after cremation. Alkaline hydrolysis is also known as liquid cremation.

As of 2018, 15 states allow funeral homes to offer alkaline hydrolysis to the general public. According to the Cremation Association of North America, these states include:

- Oregon
- Wyoming
- Minnesota
- Illinois
- Vermont
- Idaho
- Colorado
- Missouri
- Georgia
- Maine
- Nevada
- Kansas
- Maryland
- Florida
- California

Community Demographics and Cremation

According to the Cremation Association of North America (2018), there are 2 main types of communities that affect the cremation rate. They include roaming and rooted.

Roaming Communities — Communities with a large portion of the population that is mobile and has less connection to their geographic origins. These communities have a higher cremation rate and can include:

- Areas with a high concentration of small businesses and businesses owned by women.
- Areas with less religious affiliation or affiliation with religions other than Christianity.
- Areas with higher incomes.
- Areas with lower home ownership but higher home values.
- Areas with higher education levels achieved on average.
- Areas with more immigrants and populations that speak a language other than English in the home.

Rooted Communities — Communities with a large portion of the population that does not move to other states. These individuals are deeply rooted to their community and deeply connected to their employers and the traditions they grew up with. They have lower cremation rates and can include:

- Areas with high active affiliation with Christianity.
- Areas with lower income.
- Areas with higher home ownership rates but lower home values.
- Areas with lower education rates achieved on average.

The Average Cremation Consumer

- Higher education levels
- Higher income levels
- Less religious
- Fewer ties to tradition
- More Protestant than Catholic
- Many live alone - 60% of those over 70 live alone, while 80% of those over 80 live alone
- Both male and female
- More mobile
- More blue-collar people are choosing cremation
- Many do not trust funeral directors, as earlier generations did

Three Types of Consumers

Price Driven – This is the consumer who will select the lowest price provided.

Value Driven – These consumers compare cost and value.

Experience Driven – These consumers are willing to pay for an experience they feel is meaningful.

Trends Affecting Cremation Consumers

- People are dying older and choosing cremation for themselves.
- Migration to retirement locations is increasing.
- Cremation has become acceptable.
- Environmental considerations are becoming more important.
- Level of education is rising.
- Ties to tradition are becoming weaker.
- Regional differences are diminishing.

People Who Chose the Least Expensive Cremation Option

A recent Starmich Funeral Products survey showed:

- 92% of this group wanted body cremation as fast as possible.
- 2% expected embalming.

- 6% expected refrigeration.
- 25% expected the body to be dressed.
- 38% would use a local funeral home.
- 28% would call the cremation society.
- 37% would seek out the lowest cost.
- 44% did not think a container was needed.
- 18% would choose a cardboard box.
- 38% thought an urn was included with casket.

Cremation Market

Research conducted by Jim Rudolph showed the cremation market is mainly segmented into three groups: **Baby boomers**, **men over 55**, and **women over 55**.

Baby Boomers:

- Fail to see the value in a funeral service.
- Do not have the same religious beliefs as their parents.
- Are attracted to personalized and flexible services.
- See a funeral as a religious event, not a social event.
- Think of church when they hear the word "funeral."
- Price shop.

To be successful with baby boomers, we must communicate the social value of coming together, sharing, and grieving.

Men Over 55

The "throw-me-in-a-pine box" segment of the cremation market, men over 55, do not want a fuss. These cremation consumers also are non-traditional thinkers, non-conformists, tend not to belong to a church, and are Sunday golfers, tennis players, hikers, and fishermen.

Women Over 55

Women over 55 tend to be socially active mothers who want to protect their children from the stress of making funeral arrangements. They almost always are the spouses who want to prearrange.

Why People Choose Cremation for Family Members

- **Wishes of deceased** when they were alive.
- **Cost**: They want the less expensive option. We must respect this opinion.
- **Simplicity:** Easier than a funeral, if the cremation is immediate, because:
    - Fewer decisions
    - Less planning ahead
    - Less time involved
- **Decline in loyalty to one funeral home.**
- **Desire to have choices:** Cremation allows more choices in types and locations of services and disposition.
- **Family mobility:** Extended family is no longer in same area as the deceased.
- **Increased longevity:** Friends and family members have died or are too infirmed to attend a funeral.
- **Luxury of time:** There is no time pressure for final disposition with cremation.
- **Peer pressure:** Influence of family and friends may affect the disposition option.
- **Wish to remember deceased as healthy, happy, and peaceful, not emaciated, jaundiced, traumatized, in pain, and stripped of dignity at the time of death**.
- **Previous poor experience:** At another funeral with the embalming or services.
- **Green alternatives:** Less negative ecological footprint and saves land.
- **Avoid grief:** Many believe there will be less pain by avoiding a funeral.
- **Portability:** Cremated remains can be taken anywhere for a final disposition.
- **Weakening ties:** People today are less loyal to traditions, religion, and any one funeral home.
- **Religious acceptance:** Most religions accept cremation.
- **Body not in earth:** Some people have an aversion to the idea of being buried in the ground. In a discussion in 2019 before his death, Allan Kick stated, “I don’t want bugs or worms crawling over me.”

Looking Ahead: Projected Funeral Costs vs. Cremation Costs in 2030

The Heart in Diamond Company (2018) asks some important questions concerning price of funeral costs and issues surrounding it. One of these questions is: Have you ever thought about what the price for your funeral or cremation might be? The answer to this question is probably "no" if you are not facing end-of-life circumstances. You should think about this issue, however. The cost of a typical funeral is quite significant, and the process is a major expense to families. Cremation is a more affordable option, but it still carries a hefty price tag.

Heart in Diamond (2018) further poses this thought problem: Let's say you die in 2030. What is the cost estimation for a funeral or cremation in 2030? How would the funeral and burial cost combined compare to the cost of cremation? You might be surprised when we compare these figures in terms of what the cost of death care for yourself or a loved one might be.

The annual inflation rate has stayed consistent at 3.43% since 1913. We can calculate the cost of a funeral and a cremation from 2017 to 2030 using this rate.

TYPE	COST 2017	COST 2030
Funeral	$8,000	$15,000
Cremation	$3,330	$6,500

Source: Inflationdata.com

Treatment of Families Selecting Cremation

They are no less important.

According to Darby (2015), it is important to recognize that a family who chooses cremation is no less important than a family who chooses a traditional burial. No matter what form of disposition they choose, the family has still lost a loved one and is grieving their loss. Their loved one was important, and their life mattered. Remember, when families come to you, they may not know their options. Just like we educate families about the reason for a burial vault and the different casket options, we need to educate them about the importance of a ceremony when cremation is chosen. We should also educate them of the many unique memorialization options that cremation allows.

No matter what form of disposition a family choose, they need to have peace of mind in knowing that their loved one's life mattered. As long as the families we serve walk out of our doors with an understanding that cremation is no less important than traditional burial and the importance of leaving their legacy in a permanent way, we can help them focus on what really matters – helping them begin to heal. Ibid.

Preparation for Unembalmed Viewing

Prior to cremation, the body may be identified by a family member or next-of-kin. The level of care given to the body before identification varies with each funeral home and sometimes depends on whether the funeral home has a refrigeration unit. The charge for identification also differs with each funeral home and may be determined by the amount of preparation required.

A recommended procedure for preparing remains for identification is:

- Aspirate cavities, but do not add cavity fluid
- Clean the body
- Close the eyes and lips
- Remove pacemakers, IV's, catheters
- Wash and comb hair
- Position body in natural repose
- Cover with clean sheet

It should be noted that most funeral homes do not require identification. The reasons range from not wanting to take the time to prepare the body to not wanting to put stress on the family. One funeral director contacted the author and reported that he followed all the recommendations, but the family still became angry with him because of the way the body looked.

This author handled one case where the family had agreed to 30 minutes of identification and saying good-bye for just two family members. The body was placed in a small viewing room on the cot. The family came and was satisfied. The author went out to receive a casket that was delivered and when he came back ten minutes later, 12 additional friends were in the room with the original two people. The family had invited them and never notified the funeral home that they were coming. Some of the friends made comments about how the body was presented because they were expecting a regular wake.

Verifying Deceased

A verification process should be in place to ensure that the deceased to be cremated is the correct body, and that the cremated human remains returned to the authorized agent are the correct person.

Identification upon Transfer/Removal

When a death occurs, the removal staff needs to verify the deceased they are taking into their care is the one they have been requested to remove. In his article, “Properly Managing Cremated Human Remains: Identification Verification Procedures,” Jim Starks (2015) outlines the following procedures that should be implemented during the removal to reduce misidentification:

- Use waterproof identification bands made of tear resistant material. It should be impossible to remove the band by any method other than cutting.

- Keep identification bands in each removal vehicle. If an outside removal service is used, furnish the service with a supply of identification bands for their removal vehicles.

- Clearly print the information on the identification band using a pen with indelible ink (i.e., a Sharpie). At a minimum, include the full name of the deceased and date of death.

- Under no circumstances should the deceased's name or other information be written on the arms, legs, or any other part of the body.

- Before attaching the funeral home identification band, the deceased must be identified. This can be accomplished by a pre-existing identification band, a relative or a person who knew the deceased, an employee of the hospital or nursing home, etc. It is important that the name of the deceased corresponds with all existing paperwork.

- Attach the identification band on the deceased at the place of death. Even if there is other identification on the deceased, the band should still be attached.

- Place the identification band around the deceased's ankle or around the wrist if an ankle cannot be used. If the deceased is in a disaster pouch, securely attach the identification band to the pouch.

- Never remove the identification band once it has been attached.

Cremation Arrangements

The cremation arrangement is like a burial arrangement with a few exceptions. The 21st century arranging director should be able to walk into the arrangement conference without having any idea of what type of final disposition the family will be requesting and function in a perfectly normal and efficient manner. Once discovering what the final disposition will be, she will modify her approach to best serve the family.

A true professional arranging director can accomplish this without skipping a beat if he/she has:

- Knowledge
- Experience
- Training
- An open mind
- Flexibility
- The ability to really listen
- A desire to do whatever they can to help the family

Cremation Arrangement Approach

The way in which a funeral director approaches any arrangement conference is important, especially with families who chose cremation. The following is a suggested approach:

- Start by meeting people at the door.
- Suggest to the family that you take a tour of the funeral home together.
- Instead of saying the overused sympathetic phrase, "I am sorry for your loss," say something such as **"This must be very hard for you."**
- Offering some sort of refreshment, even if it is just water.

Make the arrangement conference an opportunity to serve:

Do not start the conference by being a vital statistics collector. Learn as much as you can about the family and their loved one. It is difficult to make suggestions or offer valuable assistance in planning a customized, 21st century service experience when you do not know anything about the deceased or their family (Devaney, 2016).

Even if you are meeting with a family that has expressed a strong desire for cremation without viewing services, it is important to collect their story. Take time to listen to what they feel is important about the life of their loved one. Use phrases like, "I did not have the privilege of knowing your mother, so I would like to spend a little bit of time getting to know her better through you, this will help me make suggestions as we proceed. Please tell me about your mom." Ibid.

Once you learn that the family is seeking cremation, educate yourself more about the family:

> ***"Do you have any funeral experience with a cremation?"***
>
> Then, try stating something such as,
>
> ***"There will be no problem providing you with a cremation. Would it be ok if I explained the cremation options that we have available? Rest assured, whatever option you choose we will provide the service in a professional, dignified manner, as we do with all our funeral services."***

Or

> ***Has anyone ever explained what options are available with cremation?***

Your cremation options should include (Have these options printed on a sheet that you go over with the family and that they take with them):

- An open casket viewing, visitation period, religious or secular service, and the cremation. The casket can be purchased, or it can be a ceremonial casket that is rented for the time of the visitation and service. Before cremation, the deceased is transferred to a cremation container.
- A closed casket visitation and service with the purchase or rental of a casket.
- A cremation completed before a visitation or gathering of family and friends, with the deceased's cremated remains present in an urn or not present. The gathering can include a secular or religious service and can be held in the funeral home or a location of your choice.
- A cremation, completed first, and then the urn containing the cremated remains will be taken to the cemetery for a committal service.
- The deceased will be taken to the crematory for cremation, and then his cremated remains will be returned to you in an urn or functional container.
- You may have what we call a short goodbye visit with your loved one. They will be embalmed or prepared for viewing. He will be covered with a blanket with his head and arms exposed. This is a restrictive viewing limited to __ people for a period of __ minutes.

With any of the options above, you can plan a **gathering** of friends and family for a celebration of life event. Instead of focusing on your loved one's death, it would focus on their life. This can be as simple or as creative and involved as you wish. If you were to plan such an event, how would you make it reflective of your loved one's life?

If they wish to have a gathering, consider asking the following questions:

- What days do you want your family and friends to be with you?
- Do you want this gathering at our facility or another site?
- Do you want your loved one's cremated remains to be present at this gathering?
- Who can work with us to create a video memorial to be shown at the gathering?
- Do you want the gathering to have religious leadership or a specialized celebrant to lead the event?
- You will have to consider what food or refreshments you will want to offer at the gathering.

For more information, see Chapter 10: Memorial Service, Life Celebration & Gatherings.

Cremation Procedure

Family identification at the funeral home:

All firms should require positive identification before cremation. This policy needs to be standard on all cremation cases that are not having a private or public viewing. This identification must always take place at the funeral home and not at the residence or other place of death. Before the family identification takes place, it is critical that staff verify the identification band on the deceased.

The most appropriate and efficient way to have the identification take place is in the container/casket selected by the authorizing agent(s). There are two reasons to do it this way. First, the family will know that the container/casket they selected is the receptacle that their loved one will be cremated in. The second reason is that by doing it this way there is one less move of the human remains by the funeral home. When the human remains are identified on a dressing table, then wheeled back to the embalming room or refrigeration unit, the human remains could be mistaken with another.

Identification before leaving the funeral home to the crematory

There needs to be verification that all the paperwork has been completed before the deceased is transferred to the crematory. Once the paperwork has been verified, two staff members should further verify that the name on the paperwork matches the identification band placed on the deceased at the time of the removal.

The name of the deceased should also be on the head end of the container going to the crematory. If a casket was selected, the name can be written on masking tape and placed on the head end of the casket. Again, the name on the container should be the same as on all the paperwork.

Identification upon delivery to the crematory by crematory officials

Specific permits are required before a cremation may occur. The funeral director must verify all required permits accompanying the deceased are fully completed with the same name on all paperwork. If any of the required paperwork is not fully completed, the crematory operator should hold further processing of the deceased until the paperwork is complete.

Verify that the "Authorization for Cremation" Form is completed and has not been altered. Never use correction fluid on any paperwork. If a correction or change is needed, either start a new form or draw a line through the mistake and write the correction next to the mistake with the initials of the authorizing agent.

Verify that the name on the Authorization for Cremation form corresponds to the name on the container and the ID on the deceased. After the identification has been completed, a pre-numbered stainless-steel disk needs to be assigned to the deceased. This number should be recorded on all accompanying paperwork and written on the container. Once the cremation process starts, this disk is the only identification that can track and verify who the cremated human remains are.

Authorization to Cremate

The undersigned hereby authorizes, ____
Name of Funeral Home

And or its agents, to arrange for the cremation of the body of ________________________
Deceased

I (We) hereby represent that I am (we are) the nearest in relationship to the deceased and/or are legally authorized or charged with the responsibility for disposition of his/her body. I (We) agree to hold harmless the above-named funeral home, its officers, agents, and employees from any and all claims, suits or causes of action arising out of the cremation and final disposition of the cremated remains. Unless arrangements are made directly with a funeral home/cemetery/crematory for the final disposition of the cremated remains, I (we) shall call for the cremated remains from _________________ within in 60 days. After that time, ________________ __will have no responsibility for the cremated remains and may dispose of any said cremated remains in any lawful manner.

________________________ ________________________
Name Relationship

________________________ ________________________
Name Relationship

________________________ ________________________
Name Relationship

Witness ________________________ Date ________________________
Signature

Funeral Director ________________________ Date ________________________
Signature

When an urn/container is given to the funeral home by the crematory

First, verify the name on the urn compared to the funeral home's paperwork at the crematorium. The name on the urn must be the same name on the authorization accompanying the deceased to the crematory.

The other critical area to verify is that the name on the "Certificate of Cremation" Form also corresponds to the name on the authorization. If a tracking number is used and listed on the paperwork, it must be the same number on all identification documentation.

Before an urn/container is given to the family:

Before the cremated human remains are released to an authorized representative, it is critical that the name on the temporary container, or urn, and the Certificate of Cremation match the name on all the other paperwork. If the crematory uses an identification number on the temporary container, or urn, and Certificate of Cremation, then these numbers must also correspond. It is important to verify that the cremated remains are in the correct urn and that the cremated remains were placed in the urn. It is not unheard of for a funeral director to give a family member an empty urn.

When the authorized representative takes custody of the cremated human remains, complete a signed and dated receipt stating control was transferred. Make a copy of the representative's identification and attach it to the receipt. This documentation can protect the funeral home from future claims by the family of releasing the cremated human remains to the wrong person.

Important Issues Concerning Cremation & Cremated Human Remains

Having a clear understanding of the issues unique to cremation and the process of cremation is critical during the arrangement conference. Below are several important issues to be aware of.

1. **Verification of correct body**

2. **Cremation Authorization**

   The authorization for cremation must be fully completed and signed by all individuals that have the right to control the disposition of the remains. Some states require a "majority," and some require "all" of the signatures of the people who have the right to control the disposition. It is recommended to obtain **all** signatures to err on the side of caution.

3. **Contents of Cremation Container**

   It must be clearly communicated that non-combustible items may **not** be placed with the deceased for cremation. There should only be cremated human remains present when they are returned.

Holding Cremated Remains

It is not unusual to find an area of a funeral home designated for storing cremated remains that the deceased's family failed to retrieve after the cremation. Some funeral homes have cremated remains that they have stored for decades. Funeral Director and Funeral Service Educator David Penepent Ph.D. gives several reasons why families abandon remains by not picking them up from the funeral home, including:

1. **Cost** – If they have not paid the bill, they do not want to contact the funeral home. They would rather leave the remains then incur a cost.

2. **Family Conflict** – When a family cannot come to agreement about what to do with the remains, it is easiest just to leave them at the funeral home.

3. **Final disposition in the future** – The surviving spouse will ask the funeral director to hold the cremated remains until he/she dies, and then bury them together.

4. **Avoid reality** – It can be a way to avoid a confrontation with the reality and pain of death.

Holding remains for an extended length of time should be avoided as much as possible because of the potential liability it presents. Like a human body, cremated remains are considered quasi-property. The emotional response they evoke is like that of a deceased body.

Inform the family of your policy for holding cremated remains. The following is an example:

> *"Our policy is that we will hold Bill's cremated remains for (amount of time). After that time, his remains will be placed in a cremation vault at the cemetery. You will be billed $_____. The reason behind our policy is that we believe that all deceased persons must be treated with respect and dignity. We do not believe that placing an urn of cremated human remains on a shelf at our funeral home for an indefinite period-of-time is dignified respect.*

Liability Example:

A common example of liability involves a story such as this. Twenty-five years ago, a family failed to pick up the cremated remains of their father. You stored them in the basement of the funeral home along with other urns. Ten years ago, you experienced a fire at the funeral home. Some of the plastic containers holding cremains melted and you have no idea what happened to the cremated remains they contained. It is now present day and you receive a call from the family stating they would finally like to collect the remains of their father. You do not have the cremains, due to the fire 10 years ago. You inform the family what happened. It would be nice if they understood and even shouldered some of the responsibility because of their long delay in retrieving the remains. Instead you receive notification from the family's lawyer that you are being sued because you did not take all necessary precautions to ensure the safety of the cremated remains. You have a good chance of losing this lawsuit.

In the past, funeral homes were willing to hold cremated remains as a courtesy to families until they made up their minds as to what to do with the remains. The result was often continued procrastination on the part of the families. All families have good intentions, but not all follow through for varying reasons. Sometimes they are planning some type of event in the future, a party at the house in the summer, a family memorial over the holiday season, or waiting for someone to come home from military service. The farther away these good intentions get from the date of death, the less likely they are to be planned at all. How practical is it to have an organized family reunion nine months later? Most relatives have moved past the death, and don't want to revisit it. This can result in unclaimed cremated remains. Before litigation was a factor, funeral homes were also slow to follow up in this situation.

According to Albrecht (2017), the most common allegation in cremation lawsuits is the wrongful cremation of a deceased due to misidentification. This may seem ridiculous, but it happens more often than one would think. It can even happen to the most experienced, well-trained funeral professionals. The second most common mistake that can give rise to cremation liability is an ineffective cremation authorization, specifically a lack of permission from next of kin.

Next to misidentification and lack of proper permission, the mishandling of cremated remains can have a devastating emotional impact on family members. Handling cremated remains is the same as handling remains in any other form. The seriousness of this must be reflected in how everyone involved acts toward the cremated remains. Not only is cremation irreversible, but cremated remains cannot be replaced if lost. They also cannot be distinguished once commingled. The importance of proper handling of the cremated remains should take place during the processing, storage, and delivery of cremated remains. Ibid.

To prevent errors at each of these stages, funeral homes must store cremated remains in a safe, secure location. They must maintain thorough records to document the chain of custody until the moment the remains are picked up by the recipient designated in the cremation authorization form. This should not happen without a proper signature obtained upon receipt or dropped off with a courier for delivery, in accordance with written instructions signed by the authorizing agent. Ibid.

Streamlining the Release of Cremated Human Remains

Asking the authorizing agent specific questions can reduce the likelihood of the funeral home storing unclaimed cremated human remains, which will reduce the risk of long-term liability. Jim Starks (2017) advocates incorporating the following four "W's" into the final stages of the conference.

The Four W's:

- **What** will be done with the cremated remains?
- **Who** will be authorized to pick up the cremated remains from the funeral home?
- **When** will they be picked up?
- **We will ask** for identification of the person picking up the remains.

1. What will be done with the cremated human remains?

By asking the family what will be done with the cremated remains, the arranger can identify any red flags. If a family does not know what they will do with the cremated remains, it is possible and probably likely that the cremated remains could be left at the funeral home for a long period of time. The funeral home should have a policy of only retaining cremated remains for a clearly communicated, specific period of time. This policy must be explained to the authorizing agent. The arranger should also know what options are available in the area for a permanent memorialization and be ready to inform the consumers of such options.

2. Who will be authorized to receive the cremated remains?

The arranger should ask who will be authorized to receive the cremated remains, or exactly whom the funeral home may release them to. That person(s) must be documented on a form, which must not change unless the authorizing individual visits the funeral home and changes the authorized person. This process can prevent confusion and the possibility of legal action if the remains are released to the wrong person.

3. **Appointment to Retrieve Cremated Remains**

   Tell the authorized agent that an appointment must be scheduled for them to receive the remains when the remains are returned to the funeral home. This will help both parties be prepared. The funeral home should prepare the necessary paperwork and a room to present the cremated human remains to the authorized agent in a professional and dignified manner.

4. **Identification Request**

   Inform the authorized agent that the funeral home will require identification in order to release the cremated remains. Identification from the authorized agent is a critical part of documentation for the release of cremains. Setting up an appointment and notifying the authorized agent that they will need their identification at the time they receive the cremated remains ensures a smooth process. The authorized agent may not realize that identification is required, since they have already met with the arranger.

   Following the four W's can reduce the amount of unclaimed cremated human remains stored at the funeral home and can help ensure that these remains are released to the correctly identified individual. Streamlining the process through these steps increases the likelihood of satisfied clients, which can reduce the likelihood of bad press and/or litigation.

Disposition of Cremated Remains

Common Options for Final Disposition of Cremated Remains

- Deciding to keep the cremated remains in an urn on display in the family's home or office. While the typical urn is either a wooden box or a vase, personalized urns that look like the deceased can be made using 3D technology and facial recognition software.

- Choosing to bury the cremains and have a headstone. This can be like a traditional gravesite but can be in the garden or yard of a family member or in a cemetery.

- Having the cremains stored in a columbarium, which is basically a mausoleum, or a building with niches in the walls that hold the urns.

- Having a deceased family member live on by having the cremains planted with a tree. This option is increasingly growing in popularity.

- Scattering cremated remains in a place that the deceased visited or cherished, such as in a certain garden, in the mountains, in a river, or other destination indicated by their loved one before they died.

Scattering of Cremated Remains

Families do not need a funeral director to scatter cremated remains. The funeral director can give the consumer guidance as to scattering options and any legal restrictions they may need to follow. The funeral home can offer scattering ceremonies as a value-added service to families. These ceremonies or services can be private or public, simple, or elaborate. The offering of these services can strengthen customer loyalty and the building of relationships.

There are several options for scattering:

- **Casting** – Tossing cremated remains to the wind. Most cremains will quickly fall to the ground, but some lighter dust will become airborne. Knowing wind direction with this option is important.

- **Trenching** – A shallow trench is dug in the soil and filled with cremains. The soil is then placed over the cremains. This could be done on a beach, garden, or forest. The design of the trench can be simple or creative.

- **Raking** – The cremated human remains are poured onto the ground and raked into the soil/ garden.

- **Water Scattering** – The cremated remains are scattered over a body of water. One option is to place the cremains in a water-soluble urn that will slowly degrade and disperse the cremains.

Sea-Scattering of Cremated Remains

Scattering cremated remains in the ocean is a straightforward process that is regulated by the United States Environmental Protection Agency (EPA) under the Marine Protection, Research and Sanctuaries Act (MPRSA) (EPA, 2018). According to EPA regulations, sea scatterings must be performed from vessels or aircraft that are at least 3 miles offshore. The required distance prohibits casting cremated remains over the ocean while standing on a beach, dock, or pier. Additionally, a MPRSA general permit is required to dispose of any remains in any ocean.

The EPA does not have a depth requirement for cremation scatterings. Flowers and wreaths made of readily decomposable materials may be placed to mark the scattering spot. The EPA must be notified in writing within 30 days of a scattering. Ibid.

EPA regulations require that this notice include:

- Decedent's name
- Type of remains (cremated or non-cremated)
- Date of cremation
- Date and location of the scattering/burial site (latitude, longitude, distance from shore)
- Vessel's name and contact information (the owner or captain's name and phone number)
- Port of departure
- Name and phone number of funeral director in charge of the decedent's final disposition

You can visit the EPA website (https://www.epa.gov/ocean-dumping/burial-sea) for exact details on the proper process for sea-scattering or disposal of any remains into the ocean.

Scattering in Lakes, Rivers, and Streams

A family should check with the funeral director about any local restrictions for scattering cremated remains in lakes, rivers, and streams. The EPA and MPRSA only cover "ocean waters" (EPA, 2018). States have their own regulations regarding rivers, inland lakes, and streams. A funeral director should have a basic knowledge of the environmental laws and state and local health regulations on the scattering of human cremains in the state they operate in so that they can give families proper advice. This will allow families to avoid any issues with their scattering ceremony, as well as any liability issues for the funeral home.

Less Common Disposition Options

- **Memorialized in Art** - Turning a loved one into a literal work of art by mixing the cremains with paint, which is then used to paint a portrait of the deceased; or having them created into glass sculptures. A new form of art seems to be available each year.

- Having cremated remains processed into **diamonds**.

- Transforming the cremated remains into music on a **vinyl record**. Family members can choose the music to be put onto the record and the photo or images to be used on the album cover.

- Having cremated remains **turned into an hourglass**, although these can't be guaranteed to keep perfect time. They can be passed down as a symbol of the passing of time.

- **Keepsakes** – Small amounts of cremains can be placed inside pendants for families to wear, or there are specialized small containers that are used to divide cremains among family members.

- **Launched into Space** – Families can launch a small portion (1-7 grams) of the cremains into space to either orbit the earth or be sent into deep space.

- **Submerged Underwater as a Reef** – Specialized companies will mix the cremated remains with concrete. The concrete is fashioned into a reef that is eventually submerged onto the ocean floor. The cremains can be commingled with other cremains for larger reefs, or a smaller reef can be constructed of one individual.

Urn Merchandising

Families select urns for the same reason they select caskets:

- They perceive its value.
- They like the way it looks.
- There is an association between the product and the deceased.

Urn Display Location

- **Separate Room**
  - This communicates to the family that this is a special place just for cremation customers.
  - There is no distraction from other merchandise.

- **In Casket Selection Room**
  - Customers see full range of products, including caskets and urns.
  - Seeds may be planted for future funerals.

- **Either display option is only a tool. The success of that tool is only as good as the:**
    - Perception of need
    - Merchandise mix
    - Knowledge of the funeral director
    - The information the customer has been given and perceived value
    - If the family likes how it looks
    - Is there an association between urn and deceased?

Number of Urns to Display

Three amounts have been suggested:

- 20
- Show same number as caskets you are showing.
- Show the same number of urns as your percent of calls that are for cremation.

Price

- Have a complete range of prices but focus on mid-price range.
- Have a card with each urn listing name, description, and price.

Urn Name

- Use regional references
- Reflect interest of your community
- Use themes:
    - Military
    - Sports
    - Hobbies: Gardening, music, cars, etc.

Show Urn Construction

- Wood
- Metal
- Stone

Caskets and Alternative Cremation Containers

Any casket made of wood is suitable for cremation. Alternative containers can be made of any combustible material and can be stand-alone units or as an insert in a specialized cremation unit.

When it comes to the cremation container, you may explain it this way:

> *"Mr. Jones, we now need to select a container for your wife to be placed in for cremation. This is a similar concept to selecting a casket for burial, and I understand as well as you that it will be cremated with her."*

Other Cremation Merchandise

- Cremation jewelry
- Cremation keepsakes
- Miniature memorial urns (small containers used when dividing the cremated remains)

Cremation Pricing for Direct Cremation

Pricing for direct cremation should include:

1. A proportional share of the overhead cost
2. Removal/transfer of deceased
3. Transport to funeral home and crematory
4. Refrigeration for a specific number of days, if necessary and available
5. Arrangement conference
6. Filing of death certificate and obtaining cremation permit
7. Cremation casket or container

NOTE: Do not let your competitors' prices dictate your pricing. Your price structure should reflect an analysis of your expenses, overhead, and profit.

Cremation Ark

A cremation ark is a decorative platform with handles for four pallbearers and a glass receptacle in which the urn is placed.

- When handles are removed it can be used as a cremation display or vestibule.
- It allows dignity and care in the urn presentation.
- Do not charge for ceremonial casket, use it as a service level enhancement.

Source: https://www.porterloring.com/services/types-services/

Witnessing Rooms: Giving Cremation Families Options

According to Cronin (2017a), some important aspects on providing a witnessing room include:

- Whether for religious, cultural, or other reasons, a witnessing room is a wonderful opportunity to provide a space for ceremony for grieving families.

- The family witnesses the body, in the container, placed in the retort. The door closes and the family may wait until it is finished. They do not actually watch the flames and heat consume the body.

- Only a small portion of the families who choose cremation take advantage of the witnessing room, but the number of witnessed cremations has been rising each year.

- Some people appreciate the finality of witnessing the cremation from a witnessing room. For them, it is like watching a graveside service.

- Families who have chosen to witness a cremation have reported that it felt important to accompany their family member's body through to the start of the cremation process. They also report that witnessing gave them assurance that the cremation was carried out as requested.

Third Party Crematories

By: Albrecht (2017a)

It is incumbent upon the funeral home to ensure that the third-party crematory you use is ethical, legal, and compliant. There are two reasons for this:

- The family deserves dignified, respectful service.
- You must protect your funeral home from legal liability

Albrecht explains that it is important to keep in mind that any third-party crematory that you work with is ultimately going to be an extension of your own establishment in the eyes of the families that you serve. It is important to take the same steps to protect yourself externally that you practice in your daily operations. Approach this situation as if you were operating a crematory internally. This begins with a process of significant vetting in your selection of a third-party crematory.

- Do not work with any third-party crematory whose representatives you would not be comfortable hiring to work in your own funeral home.

- Do not work with any third-party crematory whose policies and procedures do not align, at the very least, with the minimal requirements for your state.

- Recognize that any third-party crematory's lack of transparency of these standards is a red flag.

Selecting a third-party crematory is no different than interviewing a job candidate. After all, that is precisely what you are doing – but on a larger scale. Ask to meet with their management, as well as personnel. As with everything else in this industry, documentation of this process is key – so prepare a list of specific questions to ask each interviewee and take notes of their responses. Gather information about the crematory staff, facilities, and operations.

- Ask about the facility's history – when it was constructed.
- Find out how many employees it has and what its hiring process looks like. What type of training and/or certification does it require for its crematory operators? Are background checks a part of the hiring process? What is the staff turnover rate?
- Ask about facilities and equipment – The make, model, and year of retort(s) being used and what type of processing station is used. Find out whether they have refrigeration and, if so, how many bodies the business is equipped to store properly at any given time. Does the facility have an alarm or security system?
- Ask about day-to-day operations. Focus on the procedures being used to identify remains awaiting cremation, remains in the cremation chamber, cremated remains in the processing station, and the urn or container holding cremated remains.
- Find out where and how remains are stored when awaiting cremation.
- How long is a body typically held before cremation?
- How are cremations scheduled?
- Does the business sell or offer cremation services directly to the public?
- Does it allow witnesses? If so, what type of facility is set up to accommodate witnesses?
- Ask how the business deals with commingled cremated remains dust. Is there a policy in place for handling excess cremated remains?
- What are the requirements for cremation containers?
- What are the procedures for the recovery, handling, and disposition of jewelry, dental gold, prostheses, medical devices, and casket hardware?
- Does the business allow metal caskets and, if so, what does it do with the charred shells afterward?
- How does it identify and label cremated remains in urns or temporary containers?
- What are its policies for packaging, shipping, and delivering cremated remains?
- How does it handle unclaimed cremated remains?
- Does the firm offer a scattering service, and if so, how does it work?

Ask if it has ever been involved in previous litigation, funeral board complaints, etc., and, if so, when was the last time it had such an issue?

After the interview, ask to tour the facility on the spot. Take note of the environment as you walk through – Are the crematory operators and employees dressed appropriately and conducting business in a professional manner? Are the overall crematory facilities maintained in a neat and orderly fashion? Are human remains that are awaiting cremation in the holding area or present elsewhere in the crematory covered, being handled in a respectful and dignified manner? Is the facility sufficiently staffed with crematory operators to monitor the number of cremations taking place at the time?

Confirm that a satisfactory identification system is in place by which human remains awaiting cremation, remains in the retort, cremated remains being processed, and cremated remains in storage are being properly identified at all times. Ask to see the storage area for cremated remains, and verify that it is maintained in a clean, sanitary, and secure condition. Confirm that there are no visibly detectable cremated remains, fragments, or dust anywhere in the crematory.

Make sure that any and all equipment is clean, maintained, and operational. Refrigeration equipment should preserve a 38 degrees Fahrenheit holding temperature. Verify that all deceased are stored in proper containers, one per shelf, without evident leakage of bodily fluids. Take a close look at the retort(s) to ensure things are working properly, that the primary chamber is clean and allows for complete retrieval of cremated remains. Check between the loading door and frame or rear/side clean-out for residual cremated remains. Observe the use of processing equipment to ensure that remains are being reduced to powder with no identifiable fragments, that processing stations are clean and free of dust, and that there is no outside venting. Ask to see the equipment maintenance schedule, verify annual inspections and calibrations, note repairs, and confirm that everything is up to date. Ask to look at the crematory log, verify that it is up to date with current operations, and take note of how diligent the staff is about record-keeping.

Current licenses and permits should be posted in plain sight. Check the expiration date for the crematory license, environmental permit(s), and operator certifications to make sure they are all still valid and in effect. Confirm that their insurance policy is still in effect and note the date of expiration or renewal. Request a copy of the employee handbook, along with any other written policies or procedures, so that you can review them to verify that they comply with industry standards. Similarly, ask for a copy of the facility's authorization form to ensure that it complies with all state and federal requirements, fully explains the entire process, discloses what is and is not returned, clearly states disposition of nonreturnable items, clearly states that there will be some incidental commingling, explains what happens when cremated remains are not picked up within 30 days, covers all implants (radioactive, mechanical, prosthesis), and outlines the policy on removal and disposal of casket hardware. Consult with an attorney, as necessary.

Management should be cooperative and forthright in allowing such an inspection to take place, without exception. If you have any concerns, raise them with crematory management at the conclusion of your inspection. Pay close attention to their responses. Ask for a time frame to follow up and find out whether any such issues have been addressed and resolved to your satisfaction.

As a final matter, before working with any third-party crematory, make sure that it is willing to list your funeral home as an additional insured on its professional liability insurance policy and request policy documentation to the same effect. As an added layer of protection, if your professional liability insurance policy does not cover errors and omissions by third-party crematories, the best practice is to invest in an umbrella policy as backup coverage in the event that litigation is pursued against your establishment for a mistake made by the third-party crematory. And last, but certainly not least, always, always, *always* confirm that any third-party crematory you are considering working with permits unannounced inspections by funeral home personnel. Then take the time to conduct an inspection, at the very least, once a year.

Shipping Cremated Human Remains by U.S. Mail: Recommendations from the U.S. Postal Service

The United States Postal Service (2014) offers the only legal method of shipping cremated remains domestically or internationally. When a family member assumes the responsibility of shipping a loved one's cremated remains, they can trust the USPS Priority Mail Express® Service.

The USPS has specific requirements for preparing, packaging, and shipping human or animal cremated remains. These requirements are detailed in their publication called *How to Ship & Package Cremated Remains*. By following these requirements, you can be confident that you have done everything you can so that your loved one's remains can arrive at the intended destination safely.

How to Ship & Package Cremated Remains

Excerpt From: The United State Postal Service (2014) Publication 139

Packaging

Choose a Container

There are many options available to store cremated remains — From simple wooden boxes to decorative urns. However, if you plan to ship the cremated remains, you will need to have padding and two containers: An inner container and an outer container:

Inner Container

- Consult with a licensed funeral director to help you select the best container. This will be helpful especially if you have plans to divide the remains among family members.
- The inner container must be strong, durable, and constructed so that it protects and securely contains the contents inside. It must be properly sealed so that it is sift-proof. A sift-proof container is any vessel that does not allow loose powder to leak or sift out during transit. While not a requirement, the Postal Service recommends that you PUT THE SIFT-PROOF CONTAINER IN A SEALED PLASTIC BAG.
- For international shipments, the inner container must be a funeral urn.

Use Padding to Protect Your Container

If you are shipping cremated remains in a decorative vessel or urn, use proper padding to keep the container stable and prevent breakage due to processing and transportation.

For example, wrap or cushion the container with:

- Foam peanuts
- Air bubble wrap

Outer Container

The outer container must be strong, durable, and sift-proof. We recommend that you line the shipping box with plastic or other material that will prevent leakage in case of damage. Insert your inner container into the shipping box and add padding to the bottom, sides, and top to prevent movement. Make sure there is no movement of contents within the shipping box. Before closing and sealing the shipping box, add a slip of paper with both the sender's and addressee's address and contact information inside the box. If, for any reason, the address label on the box is obscured or lost, postal employees will still be able to identify the sender and receiver of the package. We recommend you use a Priority Mail Express box. The Postal Service offers these boxes free to customers who use Priority Mail Express service.

Clearly Identify and Mark the Contents

To make sure the Postal Service can identify your loved one's cremated remains during processing and transportation:

- Mark the identity of the contents on the address side next to the shipping label.
- Use the Postal Service Cremated Remains label (Label 139), which is available at your local Post Office™.

Verify Address, Legibly Write or Type It, and Recheck It

To help ensure delivery to the correct address, make sure you have the correct address and telephone number on the following:

Service	Label or Form	Title
Domestic Items		
Priority Mail Express	Label 11-B	Priority Mail Express
International Items		
Priority Mail Express International	PS Form 2976-B	Priority Mail Express International Shipping Label and Customs Form

Source: The above text, pictures, and charts were from USPS (2014).

Code of Ethical Cremation Practices

By: Jamie Watts (2009)

We believe that cremation should be considered as preparation for memorialization; that the dead of our society should be memorialized through a commemorative means suitable to the survivors. It is because of these beliefs that we adhere to a strict Code of Ethical Cremation Conduct.

In the practice of cremation, we believe in:

1. **DIGNITY and RESPECT** in the care of the deceased, in compassion for the living who survive them, and in the memorialization of life.
2. **ETHICAL, QUALIFIED, AND COMPETENT STAFF**: We believe that the greatest care should be taken in the appointment of crematory staff members, any of whom must not, by conduct or demeanor, bring the crematory or cremation into disrepute. All staff involved shall adhere to the Code of Ethics, be competent in the tasks that they perform, and must hold suitable qualifications.
3. **OUR HIGHEST PRIORITY**: The care of the deceased person and their family is the highest priority in what we do. The deceased family member will be treated with the same care and respect that we would show to a member of our own family.
4. **RESPECTFUL AND DIGNIFIED CREMATION** – At all times, the process of cremation shall be carried out in a dignified and respectful manner.
5. **PROTECTION OF THE DECEASED** – The deceased shall always be properly attired and protected in accordance with local tradition and recognized practices.
6. **SEPARATE CREMATION – NO MIXING OF CREMAINS** – All cremations shall be carried out separately to ensure that there is no mixing of cremains.
7. **CREMATION OF HUMAN REMAINS** – Only human remains shall be cremated in our crematorium.
8. **RIGHT OF AN INDIVIDUAL TO DECIDE DISPOSAL OF CREMAINS** – Ultimately it should be an individual's right to determine the final method of the disposal of their cremains.
9. **CREMATION TO BE THE ONLY OFFICIAL TERM** – The word "cremation" shall be the official word used to describe the disposal method practiced by our funeral home.
10. **IDENTIFICATION OF THE DECEASED UNTIL THE FINAL CREMATION PROCESS** – Appropriate steps shall be taken to ensure adequate identification of the deceased on arrival at the crematorium, through the cremation process, and until the final disposition of the cremains.
11. **BAN ON THE COMMERCIALIZATION OF PRODUCTS OR RESIDUE OF CREMATION** – The products or residue of a cremation shall not be used for any commercial purpose.
12. **ALL MATERIALS USED IN CREMATION TO BE ENVIRONMENTALLY SOUND**
13. **ALL PERSONS HAVE THE RIGHT TO CHOOSE CREMATION** – An individual shall have the right to choose cremation and due regard shall be given to such desire.
14. **RESPONSIBLE EDUCATORS** – We believe as cremation experts and responsible educators that we have an obligation to educate those choosing cremation on the cremation process and all options available to them.

NOTES

Section III

MANAGEMENT

- Management
- Human Resources
  - Hiring, Terminating, Resigning
  - Personnel Management

Chapter 19 MANAGEMENT

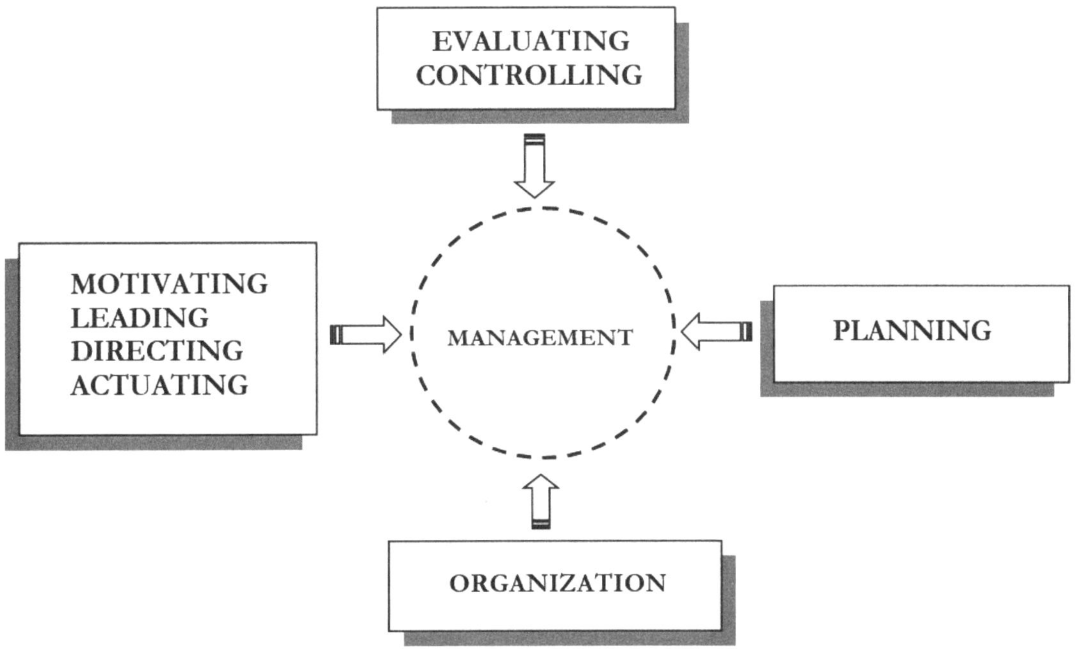

Funeral home management – *If a general definition of management is "the act of motivating people towards the achievement of a goal or goals," then a simple definition of funeral home management is "achieving the goals of a funeral home through the use of people and resources."*

A Manager's Real Job

The book, *Managing for Dummies*, by Nelson & Economy (2010), explains that a manager's job is twofold. They should both inspire employees to do their best and establish a working environment that enables employees to reach their goals. The best managers make every possible effort to remove the organizational obstacles that prevent employees from doing their jobs. They also obtain the resources and training that employees need to do their jobs effectively. All other goals, no matter how lofty or pressing, must take back seat.

Like other businesses, funeral service has both primary and secondary objectives. The primary objective is to meet the death-related needs of grieving families that select the funeral home to serve them. The secondary objective, which many financial managers feel is really the primary objective, is to ensure that funerals generate enough money to meet expenses, make capital improvements, and generate a reasonable return on investment (ROI) or profit.

Most funeral home managers must supervise employees and keep the business operating efficiently and profitably, while also ensuring that it is adhering to all state and federal laws and maintaining quality control in all matters dealing with customers.

The manager accomplishes this through the four functions of management:

1. Planning
2. Leading
3. Directing
4. Actuating

Planning

The planning phase is an exciting aspect of management. In making plans, the manager must be able to envision the end result at the start of the process. A successful manager must develop the ability to think through every project and task, and then develop a thorough, complete plan to carry the project to completion. The key to the success of a funeral home is not only good operational planning, but also the ability to think strategically.

Developing a Mission Statement

Management in any organization, including funeral homes, begins long before any employees are needed. It starts by determining why the company is in existence. This means more than saying, "the purpose of this business is to make money." It can best be accomplished by creating a Mission Statement. An organization's mission statement (usually no more than one or two sentences) describes the purpose of the organization. It is aimed at enabling all members of the organization to share the same view of the company's goals and philosophy. The mission statement describes the business and typically speaks to the:

- Reason the organization exists.
- Products and services offered.
- Clientele served.
- Nature and geographic marketing territory of the business.
- Areas of specialization.

Setting Goals and Objectives

Goals – These are broad statements about what an organization wants to achieve. Goals are developed in the planning process. They form the basic plan or direction toward which decisions and activities are focused. Goals are motivational in nature and are usually stated in broad, general terms without reference to a time period.

Objectives – These are specific action statements, the achievement of which are contemplated within a specific time period. Objectives are used in the management control process and provide a quantitative and time framework for the organization's goals. Objectives are accomplished by a specific date and are stated in specific terms, preferably in such a way that there is some measurable basis for determining the extent to which they have been achieved.

Example:

- **Goal** – Improve the outside appearance of the funeral home.
- **Objectives** – (1) Contact Frank's Painting Service by April 1. (2) Have building painted by May 1.

Organization

To master organization, the manager must integrate the firm's employees, work processes, and material resources towards achieving the funeral home's goals. The work that needs to be completed should be divided into manageable units. Specific people or groups of people should be given the responsibility for each unit. The manager should remember that when people work closely together as a team, there is a synergistic effect that increases productivity and raises morale.

Directing (Actuating)

Managers must manage people. A successful manager must not just be a good analyst and developer of systems and plans, but also must be part psychologist and part social worker. The manager must have the ability to deal with people and their problems. This function involves getting the members of the organization to perform in ways that will achieve the company's objectives. A good manager can inspire employees to do their best. The manager does this by removing organizational obstacles hindering employees, establishing an enjoyable work environment, and obtaining sufficient resources.

The manager must:

- Focus on systems and structure, as well as people.
- Understand the dynamics of effective human relations.
- Inspire trust and loyalty.
- Develop employee participation.
- Be tolerant of diversity in people.
- Create a dynamic working environment.
- Look at the present bottom line, have a vision of the future, and be able to communicate and articulate this vision.
- Constantly improve service to client families and the community.
- Share the spotlight with employees.
- Be fair, but firm.
- Demonstrate the work ethic.
- Set and live by high ethical standards.
- Challenge the status quo.
- Treat other funeral directors as colleagues rather than competitors.
- Encourage creative thinking and problem solving.
- Demonstrate effective leadership.
- Communicate effectively.

Evaluating or Controlling

In addition to having people skills and being a skillful developer of plans and systems, the manager must be responsible for results — both good and bad. This is accomplished by establishing standards of performance, measuring the performance, and comparing it to the company's expectations. The manager must take actions to correct problems if performance is not at the expected level.

It is critical that these managerial skills are used, so that the manager can control the results and thus know when the firm's goals have been achieved. The word "control" should not mean "power" to a manager, and employees should not see the manager's control in a negative way. Objectives should be changed, as necessary. Modern managers continually develop new concepts and revise old ones. The manager will need to project plans into the future while also being flexible.

Funeral service requires managers with exceptional skills in numerous areas. There is usually only one person in a management and leadership position as a result of the structure of a funeral home. This person must be the proverbial "Jack of All Trades." He must be both a manager and a leader.

Being an effective funeral service manager (leader) is not an easy task. Successfully managing a funeral home requires a broad-based knowledge of many different specialties, including the following key areas.

Finances:

Accounting systems
Budgeting
Management of capital
Management of assets & liabilities
- *a. cash flow*
- *b. receivables*
- *c. inventory*
- *d. fixed assets*

Marketing:

Product
Price
Distribution
Promotion
Advertising
Public relations
Customer relations

Resources:

Hiring
Firing
Motivation
Communications
Staffing
Compensation
Evaluations

Monitoring

Cost analysis
Price structure reevaluation
Financial ratios

Facilities:

Construction
Maintenance
Government compliance
OSHA
ADA
EPA
Real estate
Groundskeeping
Motor vehicles
Telephone systems

Communications:

Funeral options
Religious rites
Types of disposition
Product knowledge
Merchandising
Funeral ceremonies
Cultural differences
Care of deceased
Legal documents

Technical:

Bereaved
Dying
Staff
General Public
Clergy
Competition
Government Agencies
By Telephone
Person to person
Groups
Media

Office:

Equipment
Banking
Computers
Internet
Government
Pre-need
Arrangements
Correspondence
Answering Systems
Software
FAX
Record Keeping
At-need
Personnel

Good Management Practices

Important Skills for a Manager include:

1. People skills
2. Strategic thinking (planning ahead and predicting what is going to happen)
3. Vision-Oriented/Growth-Oriented
4. Flexible/adaptable to change
5. Self-management
6. Team Player
7. Solve complex problems and make decisions
8. High ethical/personal standards

Sugars (2014) shares important words that forge a positive relationship between a leader and his staff:

- The six most important words: ***"I admit I made a mistake."***
- The five most important words: ***"You did a good job."***
- The four most important words: ***"What is your opinion?"***
- The three most important words: ***"If you please."***
- The two most important words: **"Thank you."**
- The one most important word: ***"We."***

Examples of other important skills/characteristics

1. Be Consistent

- Exercising authority, with integrity, so that people can trust you and know you mean what you say.
- Being fair, honest, and direct with everyone.
- Holding everyone to the same standards.
- No favoritism.
- Treat everyone equally.

2. Learn to Listen to Your Employees

- Smile and lean forward. You'll be amazed at the effect a simple smile can have. You send the message that you're fully engaged in what the person is saying by smiling and leaning forward.

- Always ask questions. Questions tell the employee that you've been listening and are committed to resolving whatever issue is being discussed.

- Start your own comments by paraphrasing the employee. This tells the employee that you've been listening; it also helps you get the issues clear in your own head before you speak your thoughts.

3. Make No-Decisions-When-Angry

If you are angry, it's probably not a good idea to decide until you are past the initial stages of emotion. This is a great way to avoid making decisions you could end up regretting, as well as garnering respect from your workers for your position of no reaction while you are processing your feelings.

4. Motivate Your Staff

Keeping staff motivated is an important responsibility of managers. This does not happen with a one-time display of appreciation. The following suggestions practiced consistently help keep staff motivated.

- You cannot expect to have an inspired staff if you yourself are not inspired and positive about the company and your job.
- Morale is not improved just by a one-time dramatic display of appreciation. This can only be part of an approach. Consistent appreciation and the development of a culture of respect is key for morale.
- Every time you interact with an employee it makes an impression, and either a positive or negative difference.
- Communicate with respect and interest. Praise in public, reprimand in private.
- Show an interest in your employees' lives outside of work. Ask about their families, be happy when something good happens, and empathize with their hardships. You can do this and still be their boss.
- Involve employees in decision-making wherever possible. Ask for suggestions and input.
- Share your company's vision.
- Create a growth mindset.
- Show employees specifically how their individual and group efforts positively contribute to the departments and company success.
- Have clear goals for employees. This lets them get a feeling of accomplishment when they achieve them. Develop these goals together.
- Encourage social interaction. A department or company social event can create camaraderie.
- Be honest and truthful with your staff.
- Lighten up a little – have some fun, celebrate your successes. Help make the work environment enjoyable.
- Express your appreciation.
- Show pride in your staff.
- Nothing else can quite substitute for a few well-chosen, well-timed, and sincere words of praise. They are free and worth a fortune.

NOTES

NOTES

Chapter 20

HUMAN RESOURCES

Source: http://trophyclub.org/213/Human-Resources

HIRING **TERMINATING** **RESIGNING**

There is an impending employment crisis in funeral service. The field will need more funeral directors and embalmers than there are available. The reasons for this shortfall are:

1. A large number of baby boomer licensed directors are now or in the near future approaching retirement.
2. There are not enough graduates from funeral educational institutes to fill the void.
3. Too many directors will leave the profession within five years.

Finding and retaining good funeral directors, embalmers, and managers will be a major concern for many individual funeral homes and large funeral corporations. Funeral home owners and managers will need to be assertive and creative in their search for sought after candidates. They must be clear in the job description and analysis for prospective and current employees.

Job Description – A document that lists the major responsibilities and tasks of a job.

Job Analysis – The process of determining the critical components of a job for the purpose of selecting, training, and rewarding personnel.

Job Description

The hiring process starts before the first ad is placed or any interviews are conducted. It starts with creating an accurate job description. It cannot be overemphasized that a written job description, available to prospective employees, is an important employment condition. Job descriptions help to avoid any misunderstandings between new employees and employers as to what is expected. The written description should give the job title, the supervisory person to whom the employee reports, qualifications, specific details about the position, and it should answer any questions about the job that might arise.

The job description should go into specific details about the responsibilities of the position in order to avoid any "surprises" later. It is the foundation on which every good employee-employer relationship develops. It forces the employer to thoroughly describe every aspect of the position and provides the prospective employee with a complete picture of the job. Once in existence, the job description can be added to or subtracted from when necessary and when mutually understood. It is never a static document.

Recruiting

After an accurate job description is created, it is necessary to start looking for the right person to fill the vacancy. Some ways to procure a pool of candidates can include:

- **Funeral service colleges/programs**. All schools maintain a list of graduates or soon-to-be graduates who are looking for employment. Schools are interested in helping their graduates obtain employment. Job placement statistics is an area of interest to potential students and accrediting agencies. The more students that obtain employment, the better the school looks. Most schools will be honest with job seekers. If a student or graduate inquires of a school what they know about the funeral home as an employer, it will tell them the truth. If a funeral home has a positive reputation, it will encourage students to apply. If the funeral home has a negative reputation, it will inform the student of that as well.

- **Ads in professional publications.**

- **State and private employment agencies.**

- **Contact colleagues.**

- **Ask supplier representatives.**

- **Newspaper ads in the help wanted section of your local paper or funeral publication**. Local ads will generate responses from people living in your local area. Many funeral homes look for local candidates because they may have a circle of friends, family, or connections that can be potential customers. Ads in funeral publications will usually reach a more diverse audience.

- **2 Examples of Advertisements**

The Services that members of the funeral profession provide for their communities and the difficulties they encounter were dramatically presented by Dawson (2015a) in the form of a help-wanted newspaper advertisement.

A Unique Newspaper Ad

"If you are willing to work at all times in an atmosphere of grief; if you are willing to be 'on duty' 24 hours a day, 7 days a week, all year round; if you are willing to be called by police and fire fighters to care for disfigured victims of an accident or violence – at any time of the day or night; if you are willing to work always under pressure of split-second timing; if you want to do a job that even your friends look upon with some discomfort; if you don't object to being singled out for national criticism in press, radio, and television; if you want to be investigated by governmental committees because private individuals level criticism at you for their own gain; if you have the ability to control hundreds of details that must be attended to immediately, if not sooner; if you want the expense of maintaining a large business establishment with specialized equipment, custom-built vehicles, official records, and if you are willing to accept a modest return for your labors while everyone thinks you are getting rich –

then funeral service is for you!"

(Dawson, 2015a)

Licensed Funeral Director Outstanding Career Opportunity

Funeral Home and Crematory, located in downtown Mechanicsburg, PA, is searching for a dedicated, licensed funeral director to join our growing firm. Our Compassionate team of professionals is committed to providing exceptional care for each and every family.

We offer:

- Reasonable work schedules that ensure work/life balance.
- Attractive on-call schedule that will not change. When you're off, you're off!
- Generous paid time off.
- Medical, dental, vision, and prescription coverage.
- In addition to regular wages, the employee will receive overtime, bonuses, and on-call pay.
- 401(k) plan with generous 6% match.
- Company-sponsored social and community events.
- Clothing and dry-cleaning allowance.
- A great place to work, live and play!
- Company cell phone provided.

Funeral Home and Crematory is committed to the highest levels of service and professionalism. If you would find fulfillment in being a part of a team that makes a real and meaningful difference in people's lives, you might find a home at Funeral Home and Crematory.

Ad found on Funeral Home and Cemetery News (2017).

The Employment Application Process

In addition to name, address, phone number, Social Security Number, and employment history, the employment application should only contain information that will aid in deciding if the applicant is qualified to perform the job. Recent legislation and court rulings requiring equal employment opportunity and affirmative action (social justice) effectively prohibit inquiries concerning an applicant's race, sex, religion, age, color, ancestry, or arrest and court record.

Information required for records, such as age, sex, and number of dependents, may be requested AFTER the applicant is hired, providing such information is not used for subsequent discrimination, in promotion or layoff. Management must be aware of and abide by the anti-discrimination laws that regulate them throughout every step of the hiring or firing process, and while a funeral director is employed at a firm.

The Employment Interview

The employment interview is the primary way of judging the applicants' appearance, poise, speech, attitude, knowledge, abilities and/or experience. It can be a formal, structured interview with a predetermined set of questions or an informal/unstructured interview with questions being developed as the interview progresses.

The person conducting the interview is responsible for the creation of a calm and respectful atmosphere in which the applicant never feels threatened. There is a direct relationship between how comfortable and secure a candidate feels and how much truthful and sensitive information he is willing to reveal.

The more applicants feel threatened, the more likely it is they will say only those things they think will put them in a good light, whether they are true or not. If candidates do not feel threatened, they are more likely to be talkative, thereby dramatically increasing the chances of showing a fuller, less edited version of themselves and their experience.

<u>There are certain types of questions that cannot be asked during an interview:</u>

- Maiden name
- Arrest or conviction records
- Citizenship or country of origin
- Age
- If lawsuits were filed about previous employers
- Marital status
- Whether the person has children or plans to have children
- If the person is HIV positive
- Disabilities
- Birthplace
- Credit rating
- Salary
- Type of military discharge
- Requiring a photo
- Race
- Religion
- Gender & gender identity
- Sexual orientation

Avoid questions that can be answered "yes" or "no."

Ask open-ended questions, such as:

- "What did you like best about your last job?"
- "What did you find most stressful about your last job?
- "How did you handle it?"

If the person is giving very brief answers and you're having difficulty in drawing them out, keep silent for a few moments while looking at them — they're likely to "fill the silence" by talking more.

The key to effective interviewing is to get past the applicant's programmed information and into the total picture of the person. Silence is extremely valuable in drawing out information. Many interviewers interfere in their own information gathering process by rushing in themselves to fill a gap in the conversation.

Some firms may use an employment agency or consultant to assist and advise them. Standardized I.Q. and personality tests can also be used.

Reference Checks

Personal references (ministers, friends, and relatives) are often subjective and cannot be depended upon for critical evaluation. As a rule, the most objective references will be from former supervisors, work associates, and customers. When contacting references, project a professional but congenial image through your conversation. Remember, the person contacted has no obligation to cooperate. Use a "telephone reference form" as a guide. Ask questions concerning any incidents in the applicant's history or to clear up contradictions raised by the interview or application.

<u>If the individuals contacted are reluctant to cooperate:</u>

1. Advise the person contacted that the applicant is aware of the employment check and provided his/her name in advance.

2. Assure the strictest of confidence of all information received.

Social Media Checks

60% of respondents surveyed check to see if a candidate has a Facebook account, 56% of respondents conduct an Internet search on a candidate's name, and 31% of respondents check to see if a candidate has a LinkedIn account. At minimum, it is recommended to search Facebook, Twitter, and Instagram to get insights on someone's personal life and LinkedIn to get a sense of their professional profile. In addition, a basic internet search of the candidate's name can yield interesting results. Websites such as Intelius, ZabaSearch, and Peoplefinders provide a myriad of details about a specific person, including their employment, family members, and criminal records. For a small fee, this information can be relevant and useful as you investigate a candidate. Taking the time to examine someone's online footprints can lead to eye-opening revelations (Funeral Service Insider, 2016).

Orientation

All new employees should go through an orientation program designed to assist them in adjusting to their new job and work environment. The program should also instill a positive work attitude and motivation.

You have selected the job candidate you feel is the best fit to be a valuable asset to the future of the firm. The next step a funeral home must take in order to be proactive in fulfilling the above expectations is to have an excellent orientation program.

Brown (2002) explains that good orientation programs can:

- **Reduce startup costs**. Proper orientation can help new employees get "up to speed" much more quickly, reducing the costs associated with learning on the job.
- **Reduce anxiety**. Any employee will experience anxiety that can impede his ability to learn the job, when put in a strange new situation. Proper orientation helps reduce that anxiety.
- **Reduce turnover.** Employee turnover increases when employees feel they are not valued or are put in positions where they can't possibly do their jobs. Orientation shows that the organization values the employee. It also provides necessary tools to succeed in the job.
- **Save employees' time.** Simply put, the better the initial orientation, the less likely it is that supervisors and coworkers will have to spend time teaching the new employee.
- **Develop realistic job expectations, positive attitude, and job satisfaction**. It is important that employees learn as soon as possible what is expected of them, what to expect from others, and the values and attitudes of the funeral service business. People can learn from experience, but along the way they'll make many unnecessary and potentially damaging mistakes.

Three main reasons that orientation programs fail:

1. The program was not planned.
2. The employee was not made aware of the job requirements.
3. The employee did not feel welcome.

Evaluation Period

Use a legal employment agreement and employee handbook to explain that the *orientation/evaluation period* consists of the first 90 days on the job, during which a decision about full-time status will be made. During this 90-day period, avoid saying "full-time employment," which could endow the new employee with certain contractual rights. If an employee is found to be unsuitable for the position, it is legally acceptable for you to terminate him within the first 90 days if an "orientation/evaluation period" was designated.

Termination Process

Termination is never pleasant for the employer or the employee. An employer's right to terminate an employee has been limited by federal and state laws (see the "Federal Legislation Affecting Employment" section on page 301). Courts have also determined that a discharge is wrongful whenever a company fails to follow its own policies and procedures – written or implied. This does not mean that a funeral homeowner/manager cannot terminate an employee for such reasons as poor job performance, unsatisfactory embalming, failure to follow dress codes, inappropriate behavior with client families, etc.

Stephanie Ramsey (2017) suggests keeping the conversation brief and to the point when terminating an employee. She elaborates,

> "No detailed explanation is needed. Make sure to follow the state requirements in your area for the final paycheck, as well as any and all accrued benefits that must be paid. You are not required to provide a reference for the terminated employee. If the employee asks for one, simply inform them that you will only provide information required by law. Make sure the terminated employee leaves the property quietly, as there is no reason that the other employees or any families on site should be disturbed."

Joan Klicker, a management consultant with the Thanos Institute, suggests the following procedures to ensure a fair process for terminating an employee:

- **Required Documentation**

    1. Are there written policies and/or procedures that were used to provide education and orientation to the employee? Can it be shown in writing that the employee was observed performing the required tasks in the job description and he/she knows how to perform the tasks in question?

    2. Is there a written policy and procedure on discipline, i.e. progressive, starting with oral, then written, then suspension and termination? Does your policy list an example of what constitutes an immediate suspension or termination?

    3. Have all employees been given a copy of this policy and procedure at the start of hire? Is it part of their Employment Handbook? Have they signed that they have received the Handbook?

    4. Is there a form specific to disciplinary action that includes the following sections:

        - The company policy that was violated.
        - The specific details of the violation, witnesses, location, date, time.
        - The discipline to be given. Make sure every written disciplinary action includes the phrase "a continuation of this violation will result in ... (add each of the remaining steps to come up to/including termination)."
        - The corrective action the employee should take to prevent this from occurring again.
        - A comment section, where the employee can state her thoughts on the discipline involved.
        - A signature line for both employee and immediate supervisor and date for each.

- If the company is unionized, make sure to ask the employee if he wants a union representative. If he refuses, have that statement written on the form and have the person initial it. If the union representative is present, make sure that he or she also signs and adds the title of union representative to any written memorandum the employee may receive.

- Should anything be added to the form at the time of counseling with the employee, and it falls below the signature lines, make sure all parties present sign that sentence.
- Whenever possible, ask the employee to write his version of the incident and sign it, regardless of what he includes.
- If the firm is unionized and a union representative is present, always have another management person taking notes of the meeting or simply sitting there as a management witness.

Resigning

There are right and wrong ways of resigning from your job. Adhering to appropriate resignation protocol goes a long way towards leaving a lasting, positive influence and "squeaky-clean" employment record. This is important because you don't want to leave any bad feelings between you and your employer. You never know when you'll need favorable references or a recommendation. You never know when you'll have to make your way back across the same bridge. The adage, "What goes around comes around!" holds especially true in the funeral profession. Whatever you do, resist the temptation to walk out without the appropriate notice. This act will unquestionably come back to trouble you in your professional career. Make sure that you handle your resignation with self-assuredness, class, and dignity.

Thoroughly read and study your employee instruction manual and/or company handbook to see exactly how much notice you are required to give. This varies with each employer and oftentimes depends on your position, tenure, and/or duration of service. Follow the guidelines your employer provides about giving proper notice. Where no time period of notice is specified, you should properly allow between two and four weeks for any transition.

Whatever you do, stay quiet about your decision to leave your employer. Don't mention it and/or spread it around to anyone on the staff or even vaguely associated with the staff. This includes vendor and supplier representative, delivery personnel, part-time personnel, or anyone else. People love first-rate gossip and will spread the news faster than a raging wildfire. The "first individual" you want to learn about your decision to leave is your immediate manager. He should be told as soon as you make your "final" decision, in a personal meeting. By telling others, you stand the very real possibility of your news reaching your manager before you do. This is not a situation either of you wants to be placed in.

Place your formal resignation in writing and have it ready to personally present to your manager at your meeting. Date the letter the same day as your meeting. Type the letter and print it on high quality stationary with a proper heading that includes your full name, address, telephone, and e-mail address. In its simplest form, a resignation letter should include your name, date, the person it is addressed to (your manager), notice of termination of employment, when this is effective from, and your signature. Use simple, straight to the point sentences that plainly outline your intentions. Here is an example.

> *"I'm resigning my position as a Funeral Director from the Klicker Funeral Home effective January 1, 2020. It is time to move forward in my career and I have accepted a position elsewhere. I wish you all the best and would like to sincerely thank you for having me as a valued member of your staff."*

The resignation letter is not the place to criticize, complain, offer unsolicited advice, or seek revenge. This letter of resignation will become a permanent part of your employment record. Keep it simple and upbeat!

Federal Legislation Affecting Employment

- **Title VII of the Civil Rights Act of 1964** as amended in 1972 and amended again in 1978 by the Pregnancy Discrimination Act.
  - Primary prohibitions: Bans discrimination in employment based on race, color, religion, sex, pregnancy, or national origin.
  - According to the American Bar Association (2012), there have been numerous unsuccessful attempts over the past 30 years to amend the Civil Rights Act of 1964 to include sexual orientation and gender identity (LGBT). Federal Courts across the United States, however, have started to hold that LGBT individuals are entitled to some protection from discrimination under Title VII of the Civil Rights Act of 1964 (American Bar Association, 2012).
  - Jurisdiction: Employers with 15 or more employees; unions with 15 or more members; employment agencies; union hiring halls; institutions of higher education; federal, state, and local governments.
- **Age Discrimination in Employment Act of 1967**
  - Primary prohibitions: Bans discrimination in employment against those over 40 years old.
  - Jurisdiction: Employers with 20 or more employees; unions with 25 or more members; employment agencies; federal, state, and local governments.
- **Equal Pay Act of 1963**
  - Primary prohibitions: Bans pay discrimination based on the sex of the worker.
  - Jurisdiction: Employers engaged in interstate commerce and most employees of federal, state, and local governments.
- **Rehabilitation Act of 1973**
  - Primary prohibitions: Bans discrimination in employment based on handicaps of workers who, with reasonable employer accommodation, could do the job.
  - Jurisdiction: Section 503 covers Federal Government contractors with contracts of $2,500 or more.
- **Vietnam Era Veterans Readjustment Act of 1974**
  - Primary prohibitions: Bans discrimination in employment against Vietnam era Veterans.
  - Jurisdiction: Covers Federal Government contractors with contracts of $10,000 or more.

- **Americans with Disabilities Act of 1990**

  The ADA became law in 1990 and was amended in 2008. At its heart, the ADA is a law that prohibits discrimination against individuals with disabilities. The ADA consists of five separate sections, the most relevant in the employment setting being Title 1 (which addresses employment practices of private employers with 15 or more employees). Title 1 requires an employer to provide reasonable accommodation to qualified individuals with disabilities who are employees or applicants for employment, except when such accommodations would cause an undue hardship on the employer.

  - Primary prohibitions: Prohibits discrimination against any qualified individual with a disability.

  - Jurisdiction: Covers firms with 20 or more employees for the first two (2) years after the law is in effect; after that, firms with 15 or more employees will be covered.

- **Fair Labor Standard Act (Wage and Hour Law)**

  - Primary prohibitions: Bans discriminatory practices in pay; requires employers to pay a minimum wage to employees and to pay a minimum of one and one-half of the regular wage rate for any hours beyond 40 worked in a week; amended by the Equal Pay Act (1963).

  - Jurisdiction: All businesses are covered under federal and/or state legislation. Determination of rate (yearly, monthly, weekly, hourly).

- **Immigration Reform Act of 1987**

  - Primary prohibitions: Prohibits non-documented persons from being employed in the U.S.

  - Jurisdiction: Covers all employers.

- **Family Medical Leave Act**

  The intent of FMLA is to provide employees a method to take reasonable unpaid leave for certain family and medical reasons. This law applies to certain employers and affects employees who are eligible for the protections of the law. Specifically, FMLA applies to all:

  - Public agencies, including state, local, and federal employees.
  - Private sector employers who employ 50 or more employees for at least 20 workweeks in the current or preceding calendar year.

- **Bona Fide Occupational Qualification (BFOQ)**

  - ***Definition*** – *A qualification that is absolutely necessary for the job. It is an allowed and approved reason for discrimination. Approvals are to be sought and granted on a case-by-case basis (American Board of Funeral Service Education).*

- **Workers' Compensation**

  Workers' compensation is a type of insurance that helps replace lost wages and provides medical benefits to employees who are injured while performing their job. Each state has its own specific workers' compensation laws. Federal workers' compensation applies to federal employees and other specific classifications of employees only.

Personnel Management

Employee Manual

The funeral home employee manual is one of the most important communication tools between your company and your employees. It sets forth the expectations for your employees and describes what they can expect from the company. It is essential that your company has one that is as clear and unambiguous as possible. It must be written in understandable language that makes the company's policies accessible.

The company employee handbook and related personnel policies are usually the first formal communication that you will have with an employee after he or she joins your team. Make sure it is a good first impression. In the event of a dispute or poor performance review, this will be the first place that the employee turns.

Content

An employee manual should include but not be limited to the following information:

- **History of business.**
- **Business Philosophy or Mission Statement** - This statement summarizes why a funeral home is in business, how it operates, and how it deals with families.
- **Probationary Period** – Explain the length and responsibilities of both the funeral home and the employee during this time and when benefits will begin.
- **Work Hours** – Explain the work week and the amount of time allotted for lunch and breaks. Allow the opportunity for rescheduling work hours for a given period. Also, indicate the length of the pay period and the day on which employees will be paid.
- **Time Off** – Indicate how the schedule of days off will work. Make sure each employee understands the rotation if there is one. Explain that the employee may be called in if the firm because busy. Explain, however, that should this occur compensatory time will be given at a later date.
- **Vacation** – When does an employee qualify for vacation time and how much is given? Can it be split up or must it be taken all at once? May an individual work during his or her vacation and be paid double — Once for vacation and once for working?
- **Sick Days** – Do you give sick days as paid days? Do you allow employees to take time off when they are sick? If a sick employee comes on site, can you send them home?
- **Holidays** – What are recognized holidays? How many holidays do employees have to work? What is the rate at which they will be paid if different from straight time? What else changes for employees who work on these holidays?

- **Salary** – Detail regular wages, plus the following:
    - Overtime Pay - Indicate when overtime pay will be allowed and how much will be paid.
    - Performance and Salary Reviews - Annual performance reviews are generally held around the anniversary of the date of hire or at the end of the calendar year. Explain when a review will be held and the factors determining salary increases, including performance and responsibilities.
- **Fringe Benefits** – Detail all benefits and include the following if appropriate:
    - Bonus
    - Insurance - Health, Life, Accident, Long Term Care, etc. Refer to the separate book provided by the insurance company. Include any employee co-pays, who is eligible, and any waiting periods involved.
    - Company car
- **Physical Examinations**
    - Maintaining employee's health
- **Operational Practices**
- **Staff Communications**
    - Organization of the firm including Organizational Chart that shows flow of authority and the lines of communication.
    - Assignment of duties
    - Maintain harmonious relationships
- **Staff Development**
    - Professional growth
    - Continuing education - Indicate when an employee will be allowed to attend conferences or seminars to obtain continuing education credits, and whether management will pay for any of the cost incurred.
- **Responsibilities of Personnel in Professional Practice:**
    - What are they allowed to do?
    - Who do they report to?
    - What happens if they need to make a decision?
    - Personal conduct

- **Personal appearance and attire**
    - Indicate whether a certain form of dress is required for visitations and funerals.
    - Inform the employee if allowances will be given and what they are.
    - If a clothing allowance is provided, employees should have a clear understanding of the type of clothing covered.
- **Sexual Harassment Policy**
    - Define what is unacceptable behavior.
    - If employees feel they are being harassed, what is their recourse to find a safe haven?
    - What happens if it is management that is being accused of sexual harassment in a small business? Is there an intermediary that can investigate this for the potential victim's protection?
    - Most funeral home owners do not fully understand the necessity for developing an anti-harassment policy and providing training to their employees and management team. Failure to provide sexual harassment policies and training of staff could leave the funeral home owner vulnerable if he or she were ever charged with wrongdoing.
- **Smoking Policy** – If you allow smoking, where do you allow it? Remember, secondhand smoke is a health issue. Also, OSHA could be involved if an employee is smoking in an area where there are commonly found "blood borne pathogens."
- **Occupational and Safety Health Administration (OSHA)** – Assert all common OSHA notifications, as well as other Federal work-related matters. Provide access to your OSHA Policy and Procedure Book as well as any required OSHA training.
    - Grievance Procedures - If employees feel that they are working in an unsafe or hostile work environment, what should they do? Whom do they report to?
- **EPA** – You have many areas where the environment can be threatened. Assert your commitment to the environment and know what to do if there are environmental incidents.
- **Confidentiality** – Inform employees of the importance of confidentiality within funeral service. It should be made extremely clear they are not to discuss matters that occur within the funeral home with anyone.
- Address the policies surrounding **computer, cell phone, and social media use**.

Employee Turnover

In her article, "How Much Employee Turnover Really Costs You," Suzanne Lucas (2013) identifies employee turnover as an important issue in funeral service. Despite talking about the high cost of turnover, most people do not really know the actual costs. The costs are largely hidden. Turnover does not show up on the profit and loss statement. It's not in the budget. There are some hard costs, like the cost to post a position on a job board, for specialized positions, or the cost of a headhunter. There are costs to losing an employee, even if you recruit strictly through word of mouth and employee referrals for a replacement.

So, what do all these costs add up to? Estimates run as high as 150% of annual salary. Much less for lower level positions, but still significant enough to make retention a high priority for your business. Ibid.

Some of the impacts of employee turnover include:

- **Lowered Productivity.** The person who left was doing something. Who is doing the job now that the position is vacant? No one? That is lost productivity right there.

- **Overworked Remaining Staff.** Until a new employee is hired, reassigned staff must do the work the fired employee was doing. The longer the position stays vacant, the more discontent the remaining employees become.

- **Interviewing Costs.** These costs can also include advertising costs, which can be local or material. If a professional recruiter is used, they can be expensive. There can be possible travel costs for a prospective candidate. Non-monetary costs involve time needed to review resumes and interview meetings. Ibid.

NOTES

NOTES

Section IV

MARKETING

- Marketing
    - Introduction
    - Advertising
    - Public Relations
    - Publicity
    - Customer Service

Chapter 21

MARKETING

Introduction

Marketing *– Any activity a funeral home engages in to create public awareness, generate new business or retain present business.*

Consumer buying motives usually fit into one of six categories:

- **Comfort**
- **Prestige**
- **Convenience**
- **Health**
- **Security**
- **Economy**

No business, including a funeral home, can succeed without being involved in some form(s) of marketing. An effective marketing plan generally does not include just one venue to accomplish its goal. It includes **branding, advertising, public relations**, and **publicity**. The Marketing Funnel below illustrates this.

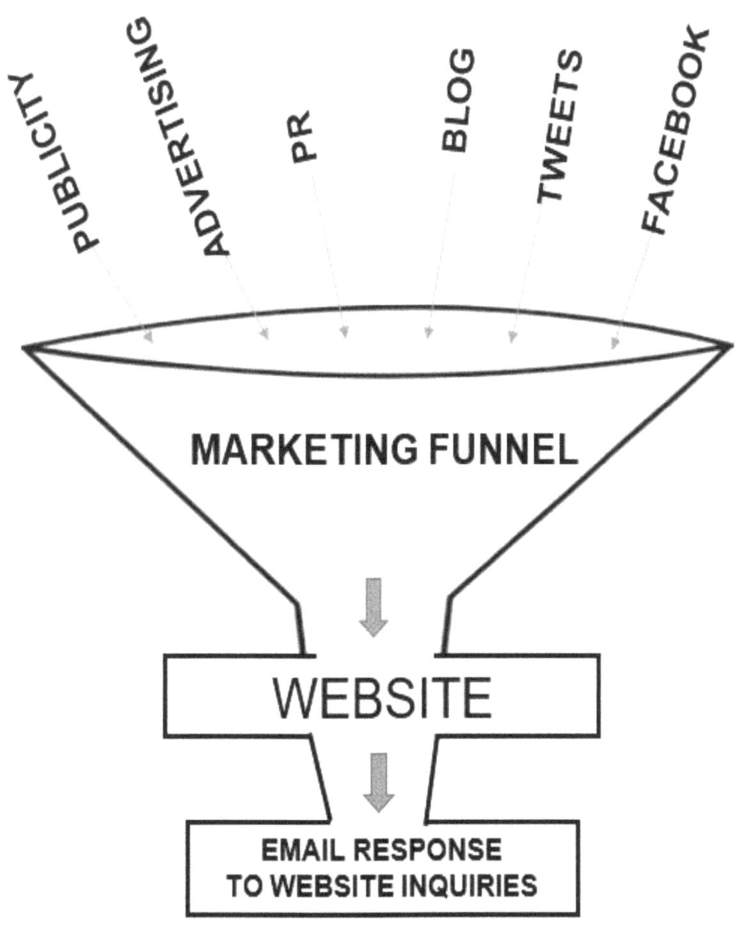

Funeral home marketing must get the funeral consumer to take two important steps:

Step 1: To use your funeral home instead of your competitor's funeral home.

Step 2: To purchase services other than a direct disposition.

A survey by Funeral Service Insider (2016) revealed the following reasons that funeral homes use marketing:

PRIORITY	% INTERESTED
Increase at-need sales	79.9%
Increase pre-need sales	76.4%
Respond to changes in local demographics	33.9%
Fight low-cost competitors	29.3%
Respond to competitive pressures	25.9%
Push cremation options	21.8%
Respond to decline in sales	13.8%
Other	4%

*Funeral Service Insider April 4, 2016

The first and most essential component of a marketing plan is deciding what you have to say about your business that sets you apart from your competitors. This is referred to as the unique selling proposition (USP) or brand message. This is the hardest part of creating a marketing plan because, in many cases, you do the same things as your competitors. Ferreting out a unique point of view requires introspection, creativity, and genuine objectivity. How many funeral homes market on the basis that their people are "caring?" Being "caring" is only the opening ante that all funeral homes must provide to be in business. Instead, this vital question must be answered:

What message can you fulfill every day that makes your funeral home truly unique?

According to John Callaghan (2015):

> Traditional marketing involves using various advertising media to put your message in front of prospective families and hoping that they will call you when they need you. For most funeral homes, their traditional marketing involves putting a large ad in the Yellow Pages book, an ad in a few church bulletins, an ad in the obituary section of the newspaper, maybe a radio or TV ad, and maybe a few online ads as well.
>
> The problem is that in today's world no one sees your ads anymore. Seriously, when is the last time you looked in a phone book? The circulation of newspapers has dropped dramatically. Families record TV and skip over the commercials or watch Netflix or Amazon commercial free, they listen to music from iTunes on their iPhone and they are extremely annoyed when you try to interrupt them with advertising.
>
> By the way, this problem is not unique to the funeral home industry. All businesses are finding that traditional marketing and advertising has become less and less effective.
>
> Leading businesses of all kinds (including funeral homes) have begun to make the shift to Inbound Marketing.

50% of respondents are still spending money on Yellow Pages advertising. This is not something for which you get a solid return on investment (Funeral Service Insider, 2016). It is worth asking yourself, when was the last time you looked something up in the Yellow Pages? Is there even a Yellow Page directory in the funeral home? Martin-Bartsche (2014) explains that media, such as Yellow Pages and newspapers, that served the industry well for decades are no longer productive and are extremely expensive.

There are only four productive media:

- Internet
- Television
- Billboards
- Some direct response media, some of the time

Opposing View

In a recent marketing survey, 176 respondents agreed that the two most important priorities when it comes to marketing are increasing at-need sales and pre-need sales (Funeral Service Insider, 2016). The survey presents a case for the value of traditional forms of advertising. It's important to realize that baby boomers – usually prime prospects for funeral home marketing – grew up with traditional media such as radio, television, newspapers, and magazines. They still rely on these types of media. Even though these traditional types of media are more expensive than social and online media, they are where you'll find this crucial audience. This fact makes it money well spent. Ibid.

Direct mail, email, television, billboards, or even church bulletins can all be effective. It does not matter what type of media you use, but rather what you do with it.

What forms of marketing do you engage in?	
Printed advertising	77.8%
Community events	69.3%
Free social media (Facebook, Twitter, Pinterest, LinkedIn, YouTube, etc.)	65.9%
Church bulletins/calendars	64.8%
Chamber of commerce/service club memberships	64.2%
Yellow Page advertising	50%
Direct mail	46%
Google AdWords/other search engine advertising	33%
Sports team sponsorship	31.3%
Radio	31.3%
Paid campaigns on Facebook, other social media	28.4%
Press releases	23.3%
Television	21.6%
Outdoor advertising (billboards, benches, etc.)	18.2%
Funeral home newsletter (printed or electronic)	11.9%
Other	11.4%
Blogging	9.1%

Source: Funeral Service Insider, 2016

The marketing survey in Funeral Service Insider (2016) also asked respondents to share some of their marketing successes, so that others might learn from them. What works in one market might not work in another, but these successful suggestions from the survey might provide you with some ideas:

- *Present a holiday service.*
- *We send out a quarterly newsletter via direct mail.*
- *I, the owner, am very involved in the community.*
- *We ran Facebook ads pushing interested people who were local to our firm to a webinar registration. We present a webinar where we provided information on preplanning and offered a small discount for individuals who filled out a form at the end and paid for their arrangements.*
- *Publishing our price list on our website for both at-need and pre-need. Other funeral homes refuse to make their prices clearly known.*
- *Community events that gain coverage from the media.*
- *The only marketing efforts that have shown consistent return is direct mail for pre-need purposes.*
- *What works best is walking inside nursing homes and just introducing myself.*
- *Face-to-face contact in the community is the best asset I have. Attending chicken barbecues, ham dinners, and social events.*

Pre-need tools **vs.** **At-need tools**

What is your top performing marketing tool for families that pre-arrange?	
Direct mail	28.9%
Other	20.2%
Community events	16.2%
Printed advertising	12.1%
Google Ads	5.8%
Social media	4.6%
Television	4.1%
Church bulletins/calendars	3.5%
Radio	2.3%
Yellow Page advertising	1.7%
Blogging	0.6%

Source: Funeral Service Insider, 2016

What is your top performing marketing tool for at-need families?	
Other	25.7%
Community events	18.7%
Printed advertising	18.7%
Television	8.2%
Direct mail	6.4%
Social media	6.4%
Google Ads	5.9%
Radio	4.1%
Church bulletins/calendars	2.9%
Yellow Page advertising	1.2%
Outdoor advertising	1.2%
Blogging	0.6%

Marketing Frustrations

Gould (2015) explains that one of the frustrating features of managing a funeral business is the time delay between promotional cause-and-effect. The results of a strategic action will not manifest themselves in terms of at-need or pre-need volume for a long time – in some cases it may take as long as five years, regardless of whether the ramifications are positive or negative. The truth of this is evident in nearly every market:

- A desperate operator with declining volume drops prices well below the local standard but doesn't realize an increase in volume.
- A firm known for low prices can raise prices, oftentimes even higher than its competitors, and consumers continue to perceive it as the low-price leader.
- A family firm is acquired by a consolidator that raises prices, changes operating procedures, and releases longtime staff. Volume declines by as much as 50%, but not until the fifth year.
- An owner makes a significant investment in new facilities, creating a clear difference between his or her firm and local competitors, only to realize little or no increase in volume.

The point is that the funeral home business is at the extreme end of the cause-and-effect continuum in terms of being able to impact "sales" in the short term. Many other businesses can initiate marketing efforts that pay dividends in the short term. For example, with Twitter blasts, a restaurant or bar/lounge can increase business the same day! In contrast, a funeral home invests in advertising but sees no direct results. Does that mean that the advertising failed? Or did it need more time to work? Ibid.

Branding

A brand as defined by the American Marketing Association is:

> *"A name term, design, symbol, or any other feature that identifies one seller's goods or services as distinct from those of other sellers. The legal term for brand is trademark. A brand may identify one item, a family of items, or all items of that seller. If used for the firm the preferred term is trade name"* (Cohen, 2011).

What is a Brand Image?

Brand perception is something that sticks in a person's mind. The brand image is a mirror reflection (though perhaps inaccurate) of the brand personality or product. Brand image is what people believe about a brand – their thoughts, feelings, expectations.

Nike provides a good example of brand image. The Nike "swoosh" is immediately recognized as a symbol/logo for the Nike brand. The thoughts, feelings, and expectations you form about Nike when you see the "swoosh" are the "brand image." The thoughts, feelings, and expectations that Nike marketing executives *want you to have* when you see their "swoosh" or hear their name is the "brand personality."

An important first step in your marketing plan is to **identify your brand**. Without a brand you are just another name among many other funeral home names. A brand gives you an immediate identification in the consumer's mind.

Branding is inherently related to what was said earlier in this chapter. You must determine what is distinctive in how you serve your families. Do not fall back on old standards that everyone else uses. Statements such as "We are the best, the most caring" is an example of this. **You must be about something your competition is not for your brand to be effective.** It must be true and easily experienced by your customers. Once you have your brand, promote it in every way possible.

The goal of branding is to produce a unique definition of your business that appeals to both the logical and emotional needs of your customers in a way that your competition cannot equal. Branding is not just a logo or a tagline. Logos and taglines are both are considered "brand assets." The brand must be a statement or promise of who you are, what you do, and what you can do for your customers (Reid 2005).

Funeral directors in today's market must be proactive with marketing and public relations because our consumers are more educated. Today's consumers know what they want and will keep looking until they find it. They ask questions, price shop, and compare services. They are not willing to accept things at face value. Their purchase decisions must make sense to them and meet their needs. They know what they want and are willing to do what it takes to get it. Ibid.

Reid (2005) suggests that in order to overcome consumer hurdles and create a business that is labeled "remarkable" by those you serve; the following should be considered:

- **You must cast your vision**. Determine what your long-term ideas are and what you want your business to look like. Define your principles and standards of care. Don't ever compromise them. Know what you want people to think of when they think of your funeral home.

- **You must have a formal marketing plan** in which your goals and objectives have been defined and shared with your employees.

- **Put your goals and objectives in writing** because it makes them real and allows for accountability for both you and your employees.

- **Be flexible and willing to adapt**. Stay on top of market trends and be willing to adapt your goals to move with the trends.

- **Look for ways to capitalize** on your strengths and shore up your weaknesses.

- **Look at how to capitalize** on the weaknesses of your competitors, while maintaining integrity and intention to meet the needs of the consumer. Remember that unless your service and commitment are at least as great as your product, the public will begin to find substitutes.

- **Raise the bar on customer service**. Failing to make customer service a priority will allow your competitors to show your customers what good service really means.

- **Know what your consumers want,** capitalize on your competitive edge, and work on building your reputation so consumers know you are willing and prepared to give them what they need.

- **Plan advertising campaigns** that demonstrate quality of service, standards of care, philosophy and principles, and communicate confidence and competence.

- **Focus not only on attracting new customers** but also on keeping the ones you already have.

Branding Loyalty
Excerpt From: Glen Gould (2015)

Logos are not your brand – consumers perceive your business as your brand. Your logo naturally impacts how the public perceives your business. For example, if your logo is the same as Cadillac motor cars, a religious symbol, such as doves, or contains reference to 100 years of service with a horse-drawn carriage, your business will be viewed a certain way. Most funeral home logos were developed in a different era, when nearly every death resulted in a full funeral and the only question was how much would be spent on the casket and vault.

A modern logo should reflect contemporary styles – fresh colors, with designs that relate to community or a fresh perspective on your funeral facility. The firm's name, which is an integral part of the logo, should include the words cremation or crematory. Combinations include both funeral home and crematory services, as it is an important part of contemporary funeral service and should be how consumers think of your business.

A logo speaks to the public through symbolism without the use of many words. Consult a logo expert to help design your logo. They understand the effect certain symbolism (AKA glyph) has on people's perception. Once your logo is completed, don't hide it; use it in every conceivable way you can. Stationery is a given, but also make sure your logo finds its way onto everything else that gets printed, including bulletin ads, listings, and even signage and door mats, if you use them. Before long, your firm will be recognized at a single glance.

Advertising

Advertising — *Making the public aware of services or a commodity that a business has for sale.*

Advertising, public relations, and community service activities make up the bulk of a funeral home's marketing strategy. Advertising is important to any business because it increases the name recognition of a firm, attracts people to the firm, helps in building a good reputation, and helps to create a preference for a firm before the services are needed.

Advertising can include newspapers, radio, television, mail, billboards, Internet, yellow pages, church bulletins, business cards, and word of mouth. Advertising is more important now than in the past because society is more mobile today. People often leave one area to move to another. As a result, they do not have the loyalty to their "family funeral home," as they did in their hometown. We are also in competition with more than just other area funeral homes because in some cities, casket stores and retailers are also selling merchandise. Some cemeteries also sell burial vaults and urns. People can purchase merchandise over the Internet. Memorial and Cremation Societies also vie for people's business.

Every day, the average American is bombarded with over 600 advertising messages. Your advertisements must be focused and clear in order to break through this barrage of messages. The advertisements must focus on real differences, including the advantages and benefits you offer. *To be most effective, your advertising must be focused on the mindset of the families you wish to serve.*

Advertising Plan

To be effective to the consumer, advertising must be **relevant, entertaining, informative**, and include a **call to action**. It must be well planned. As important as it is to have a general marketing plan, you should also have a plan for each advertising strategy that you use. The plan should include:

- **Objectives**. What is the purpose of the advertising? What do you hope to achieve from the ads? Is it to raise awareness, move products, or bring people through your door?

- **Audience**. Who are they? What do they feel? What do they need? Try to define the audience as clearly as possible. A clear, specific definition is more effective than a broad one. For example, targeting "women ages 50 to 79" is too broad and therefore less effective. A much more specific and effective audience definition would be "married women, ages 50 to 79, who are college-educated, employed full-time, and have career aspirations."

- **Promise**. Do not waste your money telling your target audience the history of your firm, that you are the best, or that you have the newest fleet. Don't talk about yourself with words like "we," "us," or "our." Instead, tell them how you can fulfill their needs, what you can do for them, and how they will benefit.

Repetition

The foundation of advertising is repetition. Experts estimate that 21st century consumers must see an advertisement between 9 to 15 times, in a relatively short period of time, before learning the message. Putting an ad in or on some form of media only once or twice is not effective.

To reach consumers, Dale Filhaber (n.d.) says you need to constantly send them messages about why they need to do business with your firm. Thomas Smith's 1885 guide "Successful Advertising" provides advice that could be said to still hold true today:

> *The first time people look at any given ad, they don't even see it.*
> *The second time, they don't notice it.*
> *The third time, they are aware that it is there.*
> *The fourth time, they have a fleeting sense that they've seen it somewhere before.*
> *The fifth time, they actually read the ad.*
> *The sixth time, they thumb their nose at it.*
> *The seventh time, they start to get a little irritated with it.*
> *The eighth time, they start to think, "Here's that confounded ad again."*
> *The ninth time, they start to wonder if they're missing out on something.*
> *The tenth time, they ask their friends and neighbors if they've tried it.*
> *The eleventh time, they wonder how the company is paying for all these ads.*
> *The twelfth time, they start to think that it must be a good product.*
> *The thirteenth time, they start to feel the product has value.*
> *The fourteenth time, they start to remember wanting a product exactly like this for a long time.*
> *The fifteenth time, they start to yearn for it because they can't afford to buy it.*
> *The sixteenth time, they accept the fact that they will buy it sometime in the future.*
> *The seventeenth time, they make a note to buy the product.*
> *The eighteenth time, they curse their poverty for not allowing them to buy this terrific product.*
> *The nineteenth time, they count their money very carefully.*
> *The twentieth time prospects see the ad, they buy what is being offered.* Ibid.

Filhaber (2016) applies this to today's context in her book, Lead Generation Made Easier. She reports that you need to always be promoting your firm – and in different mediums too. Repetition is important as it often takes people up to 20 times to see a message before they respond. It is important to be able to use a variety of marketing channels to avoid putting all your eggs in one basket. You need to do a variety of marketing media to make sure your message gets across, rather than just direct mail. Not everyone responds to the same forms of marketing in the same way.

It is important to use both inbound and outbound efforts in marketing. Inbound efforts create situations that make it easy for prospects to find you. An example of inbound marketing is a great website that ranks well on Google. Outbound efforts entail actively reaching out to your prospects. Direct mail is an example. Ibid.

Types of Advertising

Direct Mail

A funeral home can send an advertising piece, such as a brochure or letter, directly to individuals in a direct mail approach. An advantage of using direct mail is that the funeral director decides who will receive his message. A disadvantage is that there is no guarantee that the people selected will read it. It is best to hire a professional graphic designer or marketing agency to design your direct mail piece rather than to create something that may look unprofessional. Before you mass produce the copy, have your partners and employees look it over to ensure that it conveys the message you want to send.

> **Tip:** Don't schedule anything to arrive in mailboxes the first two weeks in November. Due to elections, it is challenging to cut through all the political ads and clutter.

Source: Permission of Joseph Lombardo

Radio

Radio is effective, especially in areas where automobiles are the primary mode of commuting. People are captive listeners in a car, truck, or RV. Shorter ads played more often are more effective than one long ad. Again, **repetition** is the name of the game.

Television

In most markets, television used to be the best advertising option, if played on local stations rather than nationally. You reach a greater local audience and spend less money than advertising on a national station. Use a professional company to produce your commercials. Television is no longer as effective as it once was, however, because viewers can now record shows and bypass commercials, or watch on Hulu, Netflix, or other streaming alternatives.

Yellow Pages

Using the Yellow Pages is a standard for most funeral homes. To be effective, you do not need a full-page ad. A smaller ad done right can be highly effective. The funeral home's name, address, and phone number need to be easily found by someone who is looking for it. According to marketing consultants, Yellow Page ads are not as important as they once were because of the internet and mobile technology.

Church Bulletins

Most funeral directors feel they must advertise in local church bulletins in order to keep up good relations with clergy and keep their name in front of members. Advertising consultants in funeral service suggest this is not as effective as funeral directors believe. Most funeral homes will continue this practice, however, because it is also a way of supporting the church.

Business Cards

Business cards, as a form of advertisement, may seem out of place here with the more sophisticated methods already mentioned, but don't underrate the power of a quality-printed card. They are inexpensive, multifunctional, can be personalized, and are easy for people to store and refer to. This is a form of advertising you can carry in your pocket or purse.

Billboards

This form of advertising has several advantages, including communication of quick and simple ideas, repetition, and the ability to promote nearby locations. Outdoor advertising is particularly effective in metropolitan and other high-traffic areas.

Newspaper Advertising

Most studies show that a smaller ad placed more frequently is more effective than a large one-time ad. The obituary page offers the best opportunity for an ad to be seen by those interested in funerals. This is the most common form of advertising used by funeral homes, besides the phone book.

Jingle

There are few funeral home jingles, mainly because conservative funeral directors do not believe they are appropriate. Jingles have been effective for other types of businesses.

The Internet

An effective website is as necessary to a funeral home as a telephone.

Why would a funeral home want to advertise on the Internet?

Internet use can:

- Increase profitability and efficiency by accessing products and services online.
- Increase market reach and name recognition.
- In 2018, 89% of the U.S. population was using the internet. This means access to 275 million U.S. internet users (Statista, 2019).
- Interest a person in obtaining funeral information through the internet when they may not want to talk to a funeral director.
- Reach new customers.

Digital marketing through Facebook and email provide the best Return on Investment (ROI) today, due to their incredible reach, targeting, and ability to automate. With Facebook, you can reach nearly 70% of the adults in your community and further target your message to increase engagement and conversations. By converting your Facebook audience into an email list, you can automatically follow up with them over time and nurture your leads directly in their inbox.

Offline marketing should no longer be your primary marketing channel, although it still plays a valuable role within a digital marketing funnel. To be most effective, your offline marketing should integrate with your digital assets so that every piece of offline content should drive visitors to targeted landing pages on your website, which offer the ability to collect information for the visitor. That way you can continually nurture the leads and convert them into customers.

While digital marketing is important, firms should still maintain offline marketing efforts. Allocate a growing portion of the marketing budget toward digital marketing. Use the remaining budget to integrate offline marketing with the digital plan.

There is no question that baby boomers have rapidly adopted digital mobile media. They, however, are still statistically strong consumers of offline media as well. Further, they consume digital medial differently than younger generations. To reach this audience, it would be perilous to abandon the media choices they still hold as valuable. In fact, at a recently held special event at a client's cemetery, more than 70% of attendees said they learned about the event from the newspaper, even though it was advertised through Facebook posts, Facebook ads, online banner ads, and other digital media. No one medium is the silver bullet (Martin Bartsche, 2017a).

Advertising and Media Types

According to Anita Campbell (2018), **paid**, **owned**, and **earned media** are three types of media that have become popular in the modern marketing world. These types of media can be used to communicate your brand and should be included in a good marketing campaign.

Media Type	Definition	Examples	Role	Benefits	Challen-ges
Owned Media	Company creates the message and controls its placement	Website Facebook/ Twitter Pages Fliers & Brochures	Build a longer-term relationship with existing customers	Longevity of message Cost-effective Targetable to niches	Niche audiences Perceived propaganda Takes time to scale
Paid Media	Company pays a third-party channel to leverage its message	TV Commercial Newspaper Ads Online Banner Ads	Reach out to prospects to inform them of your key attributes	Immediate Controll-able message Persuasive	Cluttered environment Poor credibility Declining response rate
Earned Media	What others, including customers, say about you and your business	News Articles Retweets & Shares Word of Mouth	Comple-ment the message delivered by owned and paid media	Most credible Cost effective Transparent and lives on	No control Can be negative Hard to measure

Source: Campbell, 2018

Advertising Budget

Most experts in the field recommend that a funeral home spend between 2-5% of its yearly gross income on advertising.

Evaluate Effectiveness

Each funeral home should develop some method to measure the success of each type of advertising used. This could include:

- A return coupon to send in on a pre-need ad.
- An evaluation of overall sales or items sold (for instance, urns).
- An evaluation of the increase in the number of families served.

It is only after the results have been analyzed that the success of any type of advertising can be determined.

Market Research

Before starting an advertising campaign, a funeral home would be wise to invest in some market research. The decision on how and what you are going to advertise should not be based on price or what the owner thinks the public wants to see. Rather, it should be based on a careful analysis of a funeral home's needs and the demographic and psychographics of the target market.

Market - A group of potential customers having purchasing power and unsatisfied needs.

Demographics - The statistical study of human populations with respect to their size and density, distribution, composition, and income.

Economic base - Wealth produced in or near a community that provides employment and income to the local population.

Ask the following questions: What are the demographics of your target market? Who are your customers? Where do they come from? What are their ages, religions, incomes, education, and occupations? What are their **psychographics - reasons for making buying choices**? What do they think about funerals and your funeral home? Why do they feel that way? What would make them call you?

Sources of Published Market Data

Census of Business - A source of market data that explains where certain businesses are located.

Census of Housing - A source of market data that keeps track of new home sales by region and/or the construction of new houses by region and specific area.

Census of Manufacture - A source of market data that explains where manufacturers are located.

Census of Population - A source of market data that compiles population statistics and distribution of population by region, area, etc.

Funeral Home Surveys

An increasing number of funeral homes across America are coming to rely on survey research to gather much-needed market intelligence. A well-conceived, developed, and implemented survey can help funeral home owners and staff better understand consumer preferences, attitudes, concerns, characteristics, behaviors, or opinions about our industry, services, and merchandise. A survey can also help identify market opportunities for growth and expansion.

Survey research can:

- Help your funeral home gain much-needed consumer intelligence from any population segment.
- Create more value for your funeral home in the minds of the consumer.
- Help you face increased competition from a basis of factual knowledge, rather than weak speculation and inference.
- Combat shrinking or changing market territories and/or demographics.
- Increase profitability.

The best ad evaluation method that this author has ever seen is outlined in the following article. This ad evaluation method should be used by every funeral home in the creation of their ads.

Funeral Home Ad Checklist

By: Robin Heppell (2015)

Create the Best Funeral Ads

This checklist has been adapted from marketing expert Dean Jackson, and I have made it relevant for Funeral Service. Looking at the Funeral Home Ad Creation Checklist, in the top area we have the Ad Creation Canvas where you can sketch out things on or make notes on, and the bottom is the checklist.

Funeral Home Ad Creation Checklist		
Ad Creation Canvas		
1.	**Have you selected a single target market?** Are you speaking to a specific group? Have you identified a specific connection?	
2.	**Have you offered something of value?** After reading your ad, will they be compelled to take the next step? Is there something in the ad that could get them excited?	
3.	**Is the headline engaging? Is it client family-focused?** Remember that the headline is the ad for the ad. It should be about them, not about the funeral home.	
4.	**Does the ad look like valuable information and not just an ad?** Is there something that brings the reader in and gets them to read it? Is it more than just name, rank, and serial number? Is it more than just a business card saying that you provide great service?	
5.	**Is the copy conversational or talking to one person?** We want to connect directly and specifically to one person or to one group. We don't want to say we "serve all faiths," because no one is all faiths. Remember that the person seeing the ad is receiving it individually, even though you are creating it for mass consumption. It is important to revert to #1 and select the single target market.	
6.	**Is there a specific call to action?** Have you told the reader to do something next? It is important to do so rather than saying "for more information, call us" or "for more information, visit our website."	
7.	**Is there an invitation to more, non-threatening information?** Instead of just making them phone you, send them a free online video or a free recorded message. These will build rapport in a non-threatening way.	

Now let's apply these steps to an actual ad and perform an ad makeover.

This was an ad created specifically for a funeral home. I don't like to rip apart previous work because I think it is always a process. Ads I currently create can always be improved upon. Now we will use the checklist as a process of how we can make this ad better.

Going through our list:

- ✓ ***Have we selected a single target market?*** It doesn't look like it. This ad went into a newspaper that has an annual edition about estate planning and planning ahead. But there's nothing identifying that single target market.

- ✓ **Next, *have you offered something of value?*** Not really. After they read the ad, they might know a little bit more about the funeral home, but not much about how it will help the consumer. In the center section is a listing of the various features, but they're not really client family benefits. The easiest way to turn a feature into a benefit is to add the words "*and what this means to you is.*" This could be done for all the features listed.

- ✓ **Third, *is the headline engaging, is it family-focused?*** In this case it's not. This happens with many funeral home ads – The company logo and information go at the top. It takes a while before the ad has anything that relates to the person reading the ad.

- ✓ **Next, *does the ad look like valuable information and now an ad?*** No, I think this looks like an ad – it just has the basic features and some contact information.

✓ **Fifth, *is the text conversational?*** It's not. It's just blurting out these different features; there's no real engagement and the words are more "commanding" like "visit" or "contact" or "learn more" instead of speaking in a conversational tone.

✓ **Next, *is there a specific "call to action?"*** While there is a *call to action* – one of them being "contact or visit one of our locations" – there's no *reason why.* The other call to action would be "learn more @ the funeral home website" and then a link. This part is good as they have put a tracking link so that they could maybe see the effectiveness of the ad. However, it doesn't tell the reader why they should learn more or that they will get anything extra out of visiting that web page.

Now let's see how we can improve this ad.

What we've done with the new ad is taken basically the same information and applied the guidelines from the checklist.

✓ **Back to #1, *have we selected a single target market?*** The newspaper is Lake County. At the top of the ad we're trying to identify them and let them know this is a free planning resource for Lake County residents. Doing this means we have made this more special for them.

✓ **For the headline, we move down to #3, *is the headline engaging?*** "Claim your copy" – we want to use words like "your" and "you" instead of just having it third person (just like this article). The headline continues: "Your copy of the Funeral Planning Checklist with the special Celebration of Life section." If we break this headline down, we are giving them something of value: Pre-planning Checklist. People like checklists. Then we say they can claim their copy, which is better than just saying "get" your copy.

- ✓ **The reason we use "Celebration of Life" is that more and more people are saying, "I don't want to have a funeral, but I want to have a celebration of life."** For the funeral-minded people, we still have "funeral planning" in the ad, but also include the special Celebration of Life section.

- ✓ **Next, we engage the reader by asking, "Does your family know the answers to these questions?"** followed by "Burial or Cremation?" "Celebration of Life or Funeral Service?" "Roses or Carnations?" and "Hymns or Contemporary Music?" These questions plant seeds for someone to say, "Oh! You know what – my family, they may not know that I hate carnations!" or "They may be wanting me to have some old hymn, but I want to have some contemporary music at my service."

- ✓ **Moving to #5, *is the copy conversational/talking to one person?*** In this ad we are talking to one person. We say "your," "your family," "claim your free funeral planning checklist."

- ✓ **Next, *is there a specific call to action?*** Yes, there is a very specific call to action: "To claim your Free Funeral Planning Checklist visit: www.DeJohnCares.com/Checklist." This is a tracking link, and that will track the number of people that go to that page. Plus, "/Checklist" is the specific item they want, so they will type that URL in specifically.

- ✓ **Lastly, *is there an invitation to more non-threatening information such as online videos or free recorded messages?*** The non-threatening information is the free download. We could also add a video or audio recording or a free recorded message on the landing page. In this case though, we created just the checklist to download.

- ✓ A few final points – We added a few items to draw their attention. The arrow pointing to the "Celebration of Life or Funeral Service?" and the hand-drawn underline are there to grab their attention and will hopefully get them to act.

We are giving the reader value they can use versus information that they have to extrapolate out of the ad to see if it applies to them or not. We are trying to get them to feel the emotion in the ad and compel them to want to have that discussion with their family.

Please use this checklist so that you can take ads you have used in the past – perhaps a Yellow Page ad or a newspaper ad – and see how you can do an "Ad Makeover" yourself.

I hope you found it beneficial going through this exercise. Some people think that when an ad doesn't get any results, they blame other things. They may be quick to blame the media channel when they don't get the results that they want, but more often than not, it's usually the message that is at fault.

[End of Excerpt]

Public Relations

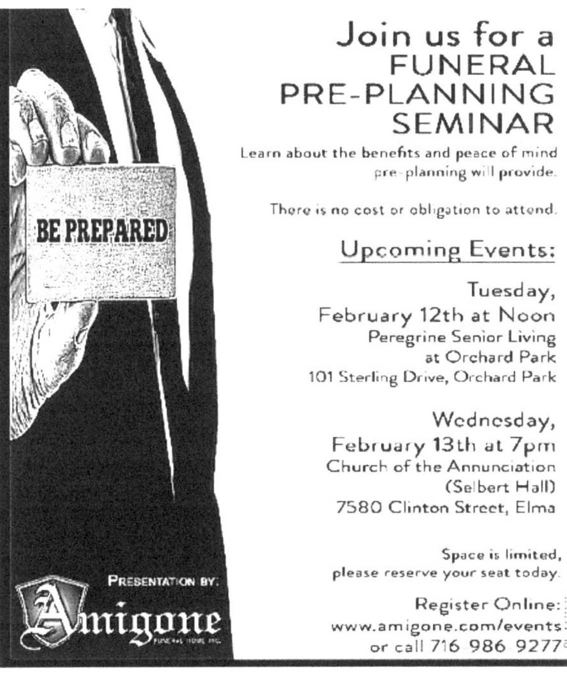

Source: https://shopping.buffalonews.com/places/view/22376/amigone_funeral_home_inc_.html

Public Relations *— Inducing the public to have a positive feeling about a business. A well-organized public relations program can reinforce a funeral home's advertising, increase the credibility of the firm in the eyes of the public, and position the funeral home in the community as a leader in the field.*

Public relations can be considered a part of the marketing strategy, as long as it complements the other aspects of the marketing plan.

Many funeral directors mistakenly believe that the only public relations work they need to do is to volunteer with business and community service groups. However, I suggest expanding from a role of community leader to that of someone who educates the community on the value of the funeral and the reasons to select them as their funeral director. At every opportunity, funeral directors must try to get the message out: "Although grief can break a person's heart, funerals can help mend that broken heart. Our funeral home can help in this process better than anyone else can."

The number of people selecting immediate dispositions and funerals with limited services has increased, despite funeral directors having been so active in their communities. Public relations are immensely important for this reason.

Developing a Public Relations Campaign

The following are examples of public relations activities that the average funeral home can participate in without a large financial investment. These activities should support your general marketing-PR plan in building your reputation as a leader in the field.

- Public presentations
- Tours of the funeral home
- Open houses
- Newsletters
- Company brochures
- Seminars
- Grief literature

Public Presentations

Most funeral directors wait to be asked to give a talk on funerals or their funeral home. I suggest being pro-active. Contact groups and offer to give a talk about topics relevant to them. I have found that most funeral directors underestimate the number of topics about which they could talk. What funeral directors fail to realize is that their education and experience have given them a unique foundation on which to build. With a little studying and research, a director can give a number of interesting talks.

The following are examples of just some of the topics that with a little reading and brushing up, most funeral directors could speak on with confidence:

- The value of the funeral
- Embalming — how and why
- Grief and funerals
- Children — death and funerals
- History of funeral customs
- Funeral service as a career
- Senior citizens and funerals
- Death in today's society
- Preplanning
- Medical Spend-down

If you open your mind to the range of topics to speak on, you'll find there are many groups to which you can speak.

- Senior Citizens' groups
- Service clubs
- Employee Assistance organizations
- Nursing Associations
- Social Workers' Associations
- Police Officers and Firefighters
- Business Associations
- Teachers
- Clergy
- Support groups

A summary of topics that can be presented to different groups.

Embalming Chemistry	General Grief	Natural Disaster & Grief	Cremation	Flowers & the Funeral	Aftercare	Funeral Service Career	Embalming & Public Health	Death of a Pet	Death of a Parent	Sibling Grief	Parental Grief	Death in a School	Grief & the Family	Death in Workplace	Accidental Death & Grief	Homicide & grief	Suicide & grief	Elderly & grief	Children & death	Funeral customs	History of Funeral Service	Preneed	Value of the Funeral	
	*		*		*			*		*	*		*					*				*	*	Senior Citizen
	*		*		*			*	*	*			*									*	*	Service Clubs
	*							*	*	*			*	*								*	*	Business Clubs
	*	*	*		*	*		*	*	*	*	*	*	*	*	*	*	*	*	*			*	Educators
	*	*			*			*	*	*	*	*	*	*	*	*	*	*					*	Mental Health Counselors
	*							*		*	*		*	*	*			*					*	Nursing Home Staff
	*	*	*		*			*	*	*	*	*	*	*	*	*	*	*	*	*			*	Clergy
	*	*						*		*			*	*	*	*	*						*	Police & Fire
	*	*	*					*	*	*	*		*	*	*	*	*	*	*				*	Hospital Staff
	*	*			*			*	*	*	*	*	*	*	*	*	*	*	*				*	Social Service Workers
*	*	*	*		*	*	*	*	*	*	*	*	*	*	*	*	*	*	*	*	*		*	College Classes
*	*	*	*		*	*	*	*	*	*	*	*	*		*	*	*	*	*	*	*		*	High School Classes
	*	*				*	*	*	*	*	*	*	*		*	*		*	*	*	*		*	Elementary/Middle School Classes
	*			*																			*	Garden Clubs
	*																			*	*		*	History Clubs
	*			*																			*	Florists
	*	*	*		*			*	*	*	*	*	*	*	*	*	*	*	*	*			*	Hospice Staff
	*				*				*	*	*		*	*	*	*	*	*					*	Support Groups
	*							*					*					*	*				*	Veterinarians
	*							*					*					*	*				*	Pet Groups

Baby boomers, born in the late 1940s and early 1950s, are the dominant age group of this era. They have an insatiable appetite for information. They want to know the "who, when, why, and how" of products and services they purchase. When they believe in these products or services and the "image" is one that fits in with their lifestyle, then cost is not a major factor in their purchasing decisions. Although studies have shown this group is not interested in pre-purchasing funerals for themselves, they are influential in arranging funerals for their parents.

Funeral directors across the country have found that sponsoring public education seminars have proven to be an effective way to educate communities and gain valuable recognition. The types of seminars sponsored have ranged from single topic programs, such as making pre-need arrangements, to multi-topic programs, including: Understanding grief, the value of the funeral, financial assistance, and pre-need and at-need arrangements. It can be effective to have professionals from allied fields, such as cemeteries, crematories, grief centers, organ donation agencies, and estate planners be a part of the program.

Open House

One way to introduce the funeral home to the public is by sponsoring an open house. This can be done as a means of recognizing the opening of a new building, the completion of remodeling, a change in ownership, or a celebration of a special event. People who attend are interested in seeing the funeral home and come with an open mind. This type of event gives the funeral home staff the opportunity to talk directly to interested individuals and answer questions they may have.

An open house can provide an opportunity for the funeral home to put its best foot forward. Visitors can be impressed with who you are, what the funeral home is like, and what they can expect when they call for help.

Newsletters (either by email or U.S. Mail)

Newsletters are being used successfully by funeral homes to develop a continuous method of keeping in contact with families, businesses, social groups, and the clergy. A newsletter sent on a regular basis allows a funeral home to maintain communications with families they have already served and people who have made pre-need arrangements. It also initiates communications with new families and individuals. Newsletters can also provide helpful information on grief after the funeral is over and friends and family have returned to life as usual.

A funeral home newsletter can be produced in-house, on a computer, or can be purchased from a professional company. To be of help to the public, as well as effective for the funeral home, it should at least contain the following:

- Information on grief.
- Suggestions for coping.
- An uplifting personal story.
- Interesting news from the funeral home.

Holiday Programs

Each year more funeral homes are offering holiday support programs. Most of these programs are presented during the Thanksgiving-Christmas season, but they are appropriate for other special occasions such as Mother's Day, Memorial Day, Father's Day, Veterans Day, or Easter. These programs usually include information about the dynamics of grieving during the holidays, suggestions for coping during this trying time, meditation or prayer, and some type of ceremony such as candle lighting.

Holiday programs have proven to be a huge success. Funeral directors can take pride and satisfaction in knowing they touch the hearts of those who attend. Starting such a program not only helps the community, but also results in highly positive public relations.

The late Sandra Graves, Ph.D., gave the following suggestions during her seminar for holiday activities:

(1) Purchase and distribute a good booklet or brochure about grief and the holidays. Have yourself or your aftercare worker at the funeral home available at specific times to answer questions or give support to the people coming in for the booklet.

(2) Sponsor a seminar or community workshop to help grievers cope with the holidays.

(3) Sponsor a special support group for the holidays.

(4) Put a memorial candle in a special area of your funeral home with the names of all who have died since the previous New Year's Eve displayed near the candle. Invite the public into your funeral home to add a candle, sign a register, or in some form commemorate their friends and loved ones.

(5) Sponsor a special radio program of Christmas carols in honor of those who have died this year.

(6) Use your advertising space during the season to either give helpful suggestions on coping during the holidays or memorialize those who have died.

Tips for Creating an Effective Community Outreach Program

Excerpt By: Beverly Brown (2015)

1. Community Outreach is a Form of Advertising.

Hosting an outreach program will give you a bigger presence in your community. An effective program can allow you to decrease your advertising expenses and increase your volume of both pre-need and at-need sales.

2. Build Community Relationships.

It is what makes you different from your competitor. In fact, to many community members, your company's outreach program is the only tangible manifestation of your organization that they have seen, which is why it can play such a critical role in encouraging the community to be loyal to your firm.

3. A True Altruistic Focus has to be at the Heart of How You Run Your Program

Outreach is designed to build good will rather than to sell your firm's services. Focus on compassion and generosity in such a way that anyone who looks on you from the outside can say, 'that is the most compassionate, generous, competent group of people I have ever heard about or been around. I am so glad that they are in our community.'

4. Loyalty is a Matter of Emotion.

Find ways to create memories for program participants that will motivate them to attend your events and come back often. Part of that involves striving for at least one creative element with each new event. Be more than your guests expect. Wow them beyond what they expected. In return, word of mouth flows from the mouths of your guests.

5. Put on Your Detective Hat and Do Some Research.

Find out what you can do about each target group that you would like to touch in your community. What are their most challenging struggles? What are their needs? This will enable you to develop an effective outreach strategy.

Publicity

The firm's name, and that of the staff, consistently reported in the local press, on radio or television establishes the firm as a professional, reputable authority. Good press eventually leads to increased business because it brings in clients who want to deal with a name they know or someone they have read about. Unlike advertising, a positive editorial mention carries a unique benefit: It appears to be a third-party endorsement by the medium in which the activity is reported.

How to Get Free Publicity

One of the basic tools that should be used by any company to earn media coverage is the News Release, also called a Press Release.

The News Release

A news release is information about an event, activity of staff, awards received, training completed, or any information that can be of interest to the public. Newspapers will often print information from your news release in their paper. However, newspapers differ in their policies on printing news releases.

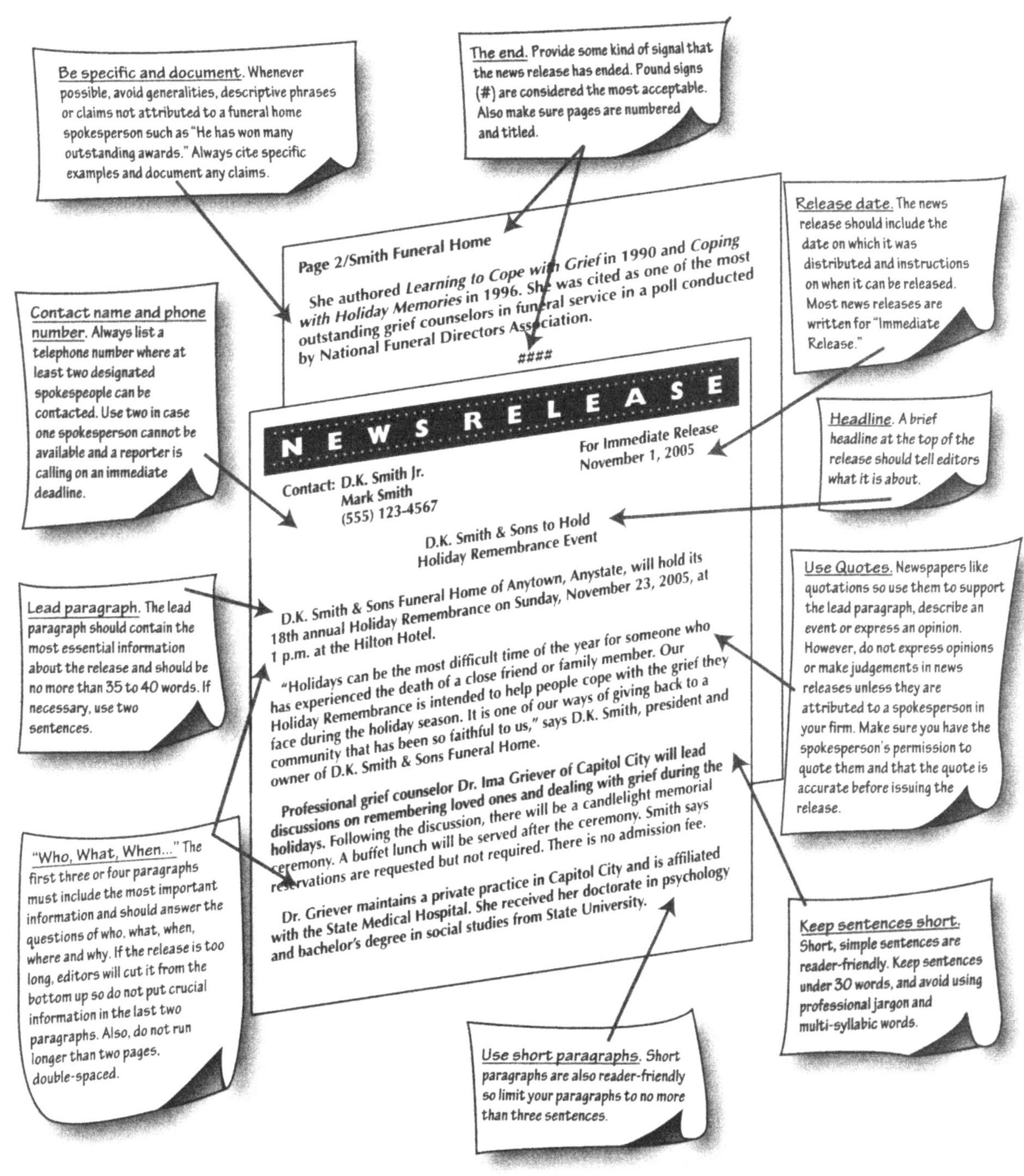

Source: The Director (February 2006)

10 Tips to Create Press Releases that Get Published
By: Joe Weigel (2015)

1. CREATE A STRONG HEADLINE.

The opening of a press release – just as with a magazine article or any piece of communication – is the most important. A strong headline (and the email subject line when you send out and pitch the release) will pull in editors and reporters seeking good stories for readers and viewers in your community. Your headline should be as engaging as it is accurate.

2. GET STRAIGHT TO THE POINT.

Since journalists are busy people, you must assume that they will only read the first sentence and then scan the rest – and even that's a generous assumption. Get the message of your press release out quickly. Every important point should be addressed in the first few sentences. The subsequent paragraphs should be for supporting information for what you communicate in the first paragraph.

3. KEEP THE RELEASE TO ONE PAGE (TWO PAGES MAXIMUM).

As with most good writing, shorter is better. Limit yourself to one page, though two pages are acceptable. This will also force you to condense your most significant information into a more readable document.

4. OFFER ACCESS TO MORE INFORMATION.

While you should limit your press release to one page (or two, if you must), that doesn't mean you can't show the reporter how to learn more. Providing links to your funeral home's website where prospective writers can learn more about your firm is a crucial element to the release. Don't make writers search for more information – guide then as quickly as possible to your website and keep their interest piqued.

5. WRITE YOUR RELEASE SO IT CAN EASILY BE CUT DOWN IN LENGTH.

Make sure to keep your word count to about 400 words. This is vital to getting your release published, since most newspapers and magazines have limited space for feature stories and news (the remainder is devoted to ad space). The same goes for radio stations with their limited newscasts.

6. AVOID JARGON AND ACRONYMS.

Certain terms and phrases may be well known by those in funeral service but won't mean anything to journalists or their readers. The same goes for acronyms. Be sure to spell out phrases the first time you reference them in your release. After that, it's acceptable to use the acronym.

7. ENSURE IT IS GRAMMATICALLY PERFECT.

Proofread your press release – and let a few others proofread it as well – before sending it out. Read it for clarity, spelling, and grammar. Even a single mistake can discourage a reporter from taking you seriously.

8. INCLUDE QUOTES WHENEVER POSSIBLE.

Including a good quote from someone in the funeral home can give a human element to the press release and be a source of information in its own right. In addition, quotes are the one place in the press release where you can deliver a promotional message about your firm.

9. PUT IN YOUR CONTACT INFORMATION.

A common oversight that can render a press release useless is a lack of contact information for reporters with which to follow up. Whether you or someone else at the funeral home is the point of contact, don't forget to include an email address and phone number on the release (preferably at the top of the page).

10. MAKE IT A CONVERSATION, NOT A ONE-WAY COMMUNIQUE.

Starting off a pitch with a fake personalized greeting like "Hi editor! How was your weekend? Ugh, don't you hate Mondays!" is not acceptable. Rather, use something like, "I have a press release that I think your readers will find interesting. Email me if you want to chat or need more information beyond the enclosed release." Remember that you're positioning yourself as a media resource.

Developing Media Relationships

No publicity campaign can even begin until you develop a relationship with the media in your area. This includes radio and television personalities, print reporters, and editors. Glawe (2006) and Clark (2006) recommend pursuing the following activities in developing these relationships:

- **Identify and make a list of potential contacts**. Do not limit yourself too much. Don't just stick to the business section or morning talk shows. The work you do is wider-ranging and can be of interest to any number of journalists.
- **Carefully craft what you want to say to these people.** In other words, what is your story? Why will it be of interest to them? Put this in written form for a news release and in a script for you to use in a follow-up phone call. Think about questions that the reporter might ask you and write down your answers. Explain the "who, what, when, and why" it is important to consumers.
- **Send the news release addressed to a specific person,** not just editor or producer.
- **Place a follow-up phone call**. Persistence pays off. Tell them you are calling to ensure they received the release and ask if there are any questions you can answer or additional information you can supply.
- **If they spend any time talking to you, send a note thanking them for their time**. Include your business card. If nothing else, the card may end up in the reporter's Rolodex.
- **If the news release generates a mention or a story,** write the reporter a note telling him or her how well you thought it went.

Press Kit

Press Kits are folders containing relevant information distributed to the media. They should include:

- The company's history
- Staff information
- A photo of the building and owners
- Industry statistics
- Information pertinent to the event you are referring to
- Phone, Fax, Cell Phone number, Website, and social media business page names/handles.

Customer Service

<u>Good Customer Service</u> *means to exceed the customer's expectations.*

When someone experiences "WOW" customer service, you are giving them a pleasant surprise. You are exceeding their expectations. You are addressing their needs thoughtfully and in unexpected ways. It is an expression of your authentic interest in the person who seeks your services, not just in the transaction. It is about making enduring personal emotional connections with empathy, generosity, and gratitude. It is about awareness of common human concerns that make a difference to each customer. It is about truth, it is about meaning, it is about details that cannot be measured by metrics and charts (Hsieh, 2010).

A customer wants to feel that they're at the center of the funeral home's world. All that matters to the customer is the customer and the people whom the customer cares about, a category that only tangentially includes you, the service provider. It's important to absorb this reality – because it is reality.

Bartsche (2016) recommends 3 rules of customer service that a business should never break:

1. The customer may not always be right, but it makes sense to make them feel that they're right.
2. Try to start from a position of 'The answer is yes. Now what is the question?'
3. The customer is the center of the customer's universe. Make sure they feel that they're also at the center of yours.

In 1919, Frank Campbell, a New York funeral director, made this relevant statement:

> *"To me, the most successful service to a family is only achieved when we put ourselves in their shoes. If we can learn to stand mentally alongside the family – seeing through their eyes and sensing their attitude toward ourselves and what we are doing and selling – we more rapidly fall into step with their thoughts and hence, the funeral becomes an experience of value."*

Satisfied families, who feel they have received value from the services and merchandise provided by the funeral home, should be the central driving force of any organization. All staff members of a funeral home must always be fully committed to excellence in customer service. Nothing less should be acceptable.

Why Customers Leave

CX Solutions reports that customers leave, on average, because:

- 1% of them die.
- 3% of them move to an area where you do not provide products and services.
- 5% develop relationships with other service providers – They are talked into moving their business.
- 91% of customers leave for reasons that you have direct control over such as:

  - These customers are actively shopping for value, which is defined as: Value = Price + Product + Caring Service. Customers can always find someone with comparable prices and products. Caring service the only piece of the equation that will set you apart from competitors (FSI, 2017).

  - **They are not satisfied with a product or service they purchased**. This is often the result of overpromising and under-delivering. This can often be the result of small broken promises. For example, if you tell a customer that you will call at 1 p.m., but you don't call until 1:15 p.m., you have broken a promise. It seems like a small thing, but customers keep a scoreboard in their head, and anytime you break a small promise, a check mark goes on that scorecard. Ibid.

The following two sets of information are as relevant today as when they were published, in 2006 and 2004. They will continue to be relevant in the future.

SESCO (2006) reports that customers' top ten requirements are:

- **Treat me with respect**. I am a customer, not an account number.
- **Follow through** on your commitments.
- **Communicate** with me about both the good and the bad.
- **Talk to me** without interruption.
- **Answer** the phone quickly…and get back to me when you say you will.
- **Provide** alternatives when we have a problem.
- **Allow me** to talk to someone in authority when there is a problem.
- **Clearly state** what I should expect from you.
- **Know** everything about your products and services.
- **Be a customer advocate**.

Baklarz (2004) lists the benefits an organization can receive by providing great service:

- Increased market share
- Increased sales and profit
- New customers
- Increased market share
- Repeat business
- Fewer complaints
- Lower employee turnover
- Enhanced reputation

Handling a Customer Complaint

What do most consumers do at the first sign of an issue with service or product? No matter how big or small the issue, they pull out their smartphone and, right then and there, vent on social media. They may even do this before trying to resolve the issue with a salesperson or manager of the business (Koth, 2015).

What if you find a complaint or negative post on social media? First, try to determine whether it's a legitimate complaint from a family you have served. If it's absolutely clear that you've never served the family and it's an unfounded personal attack, ignore it. While that may sound counterintuitive, getting into a battle with someone you don't know or with whom you have no business relationship is an exercise in futility. Ibid.

If the complaint is from a family you have served, all hope is not lost. Post a reply such as:

> *"This is May from Smith Funeral Home. We want to ensure that your family is cared for and completely satisfied. A member of our staff will reach out to you today to discuss your concerns. If we miss you, please call us at 555-5555."* Ibid.

The funeral director who served the family, or a manager of the firm, should reach out by phone to determine the exact nature of the family's concern and what might be done to resolve it in accordance with your firm's customer service protocols. Oftentimes, when you successfully resolve the issue, you'll likely wind up being the subject of a positive social media post or an amended review that highlights the lengths you went to in order to ensure the family's satisfaction. Ibid.

Additionally, Koth (2015) suggests that you should:

1. **Take notes as the complainant talks**. You enhance resolution when you are perfectly clear on the nature of the complainant's issue, so read your notes back to the complainant to ensure you are both on the "same page."

2. **Assess the complaint** – The "who, what, why, when, and where." You might need to discuss the complaint with any staff members involved before you can present an explanation to the family. Do not tarry. A complainant expects timely resolution, so ensure that you meet that expectation.

3. **As you gather information from employees and others**, document what you have been told and by whom. Do not trust your memory to keep the facts straight.

4. **Review any documentation you might have about the event**, as well as any documentation you create when talking with others. Keep all of it together for presentation to the complainant.

5. **Prepare a written explanation**, listing the sequence of events, and incorporate all your documentation. Admit an error if that is the case. Attempting to cover up a mistake you know occurred will only make the situation worse.

6. **Meet again with the complainant**. This is your time to talk. Present your explanation verbally, using your written explanation as a guide. Again, admit an error if one occurred. Present your written explanation to the complainant and keep a copy for yourself.

7. **Re-discuss the issue at this point**, now that you have heard the complainant's concerns, and the complainant has heard your explanation. Sometimes the explanation alone will resolve the issue. If you were in error, sincerely apologize. Do not say, "We were wrong, but..." Simply apologize. If your funeral home was in error, follow up your verbal apology with a written apology. After this meeting, document the discussion in detail.

8. **If your funeral home erred** and an apology alone does not bring closure to the incident, ask the complainant what he or she would like you to do to resolve the matter. At this point, negotiation and compromise on your part might be in order. Sometimes, even if you are in the right, the complainant will continue to assert that he or she was wronged. Remember, however, that your future business depends upon your ability to remain calm and proceed with utter professionalism; anything less might exacerbate the situation.

9. **If you and the complainant are unable to agree** on a resolution after you have made every attempt to resolve the issue, a third-party mediator might be necessary.

Suggestions for Improving Customer Service

By: Mary Ann Schueble

- Answer your phone by the third ring. State the name of the funeral home, your name, and ask, "How may I help you?"
- If you must put a person on hold ask, "May I put you on hold?" and wait for their response. If it will take longer than a minute or two to get back to the person, ask if he/she would prefer to be called back. Call them back promptly!
- If you must transfer a call, explain why you are doing it, and give him/her the person's name and extension in case a disconnection occurs.
- You should use the person's name if you know it. People like to be recognized.
- Be punctual for appointments.
- Treat emails as business letters. Always include a greeting.
- Create a newsletter of helpful information and send it to your families. Never sell your mailing list.
- Keep your funeral home neat, clean, in good repair, and updated in furnishings and style.
- Ensure that all staff are knowledgeable, friendly, courteous, and helpful.
- Be dependable; don't make promises you can't keep.
- Be proficient in what you do; take pride in your work.
- Dress and act professionally always. Convey the image you want your business to be known by.
- Don't "nickel and dime" your families by charging for every little thing. A person recently reported to the author that he had spent $13,000 for a funeral and when he went back for 50 more thank you cards, he was charged extra.
- Make your website easy to navigate and user friendly; don't make visitors register before they can browse; do not use pop-up or banner ads; do not use excessive graphics.
- Provide aftercare services that have nothing to do with pre-need sales pitches.
- Provide families with a survey to complete regarding the services they received.

NOTES

Section V

STARTING OR BUYING A BUSINESS

Chapter 22

STARTING A BUSINESS

Source: https://articles.bplans.com/business-startup-checklist/

What is a Small Business?

Small Business – *A business that is independently owned and operated and is not dominant in its field of operation.*

Entrepreneur – One who organizes, manages, and assumes the risk of a business firm.

Quantitative Criteria to be a Small Business

Number of Employees

- Mining/manufacturing - 500 to 1,500 employees
- Wholesale trade - Up to 500 employees
- Retail trade - 20 to 100 employees (except a limit of 500 employees in department or variety stores)
- Services - 25 to 300 employees

Qualitative Sales Criteria to be a Small Business

- Actively managed by its owner(s)
- Highly personalized
- Largely local in its area of operations
- Largely dependent on internal sources of capital to finance its growth
- Business is not a major force in its industry (not dominant)

Types of Activity

- ***Manufacturing*** - A business that makes finished goods from raw materials by hand or machine.
- ***Merchandising*** - A business that purchases finished goods for resale.
- ***Services*** - A business that provides a service as opposed to a product.

Economic Contributions of Small Business in the United States

- Interdependence of business
- Stimulating economic competition
- Innovation

Steps for Start-Up

Before purchasing an existing funeral home or building a new one, you should decide on the legal form of operation that will be the most advantageous to you. You can incorporate, be a sole proprietor, a partnership, or a limited liability partnership. You should not make this decision alone. Your financial advisor and lawyer should help you make the decision. Each category has both positive and negative aspects that are listed below.

Sole Proprietorship

A **sole proprietorship** is an individual conducting a business as an individual and sole owner. A funeral director operating a funeral home as a **sole proprietorship** will be held personally liable for all his or her acts and those of his or her staff. If someone falls at the funeral home or is hurt during a funeral service, the director will probably be sued, and if there is negligence, be held personally responsible.

Advantages	Disadvantages
Ease of starting	Unlimited risk
Low cost or organization	Limited size
Freedom to manage	Limited life
Profit Incentive	Limited management ability

Partnership

Partnerships can be either General or Limited.

- A **General Partnership** is an association of two or more persons who conduct business as co-owners. **General partners** are personally liable for the obligations of the business.
- A **Limited Partnership** is where there are general partners and partners who have a limited interest. **Limited partners** are usually investors who put up capital, have a limited interest in the profits, and their liability is limited to the amount of their capital.

- If the funeral home is operated as a **General or Limited Partnership** and you are one of the **General Partners**, you could have personal liability if the funeral home is sued.

Advantages	Disadvantages
Combined management, talent, capital	Lack of continuity
Easy to form	Decisions binding
Efficiency of labor	Frozen investments

Corporations

Corporations are legal entities established under state law. **Profit corporations** have shareholders and are usually established under the State's Business Corporation Act. Shareholders would rarely be personally liable for the actions of a funeral home corporation. In addition, directors and officers of a funeral home corporation would probably not be personally liable for their actions if they were acting within the scope of their employment. It is for this reason that the corporate form is usually the preferred manner for owning and operating a funeral home.

Advantages	Disadvantages
Continuity in existence	Legal restrictions on activities
Ease of ownership	Separation of ownership/control
Limited liability	Lack of personal interest
Large financial capability	Double taxation of earnings

Limited Liability Company

A legal entity that has the option of being taxed, like a partnership, but shields assets from business debt, like a corporation.

Advantages	Disadvantages
Corporate-like limited liability and asset protection	If not properly structured, can be taxed as a "C" corporation
Flexibility of partnership	Must have limited life, usually 30 years
No significant requirements	
Tax status of partnership	

Before You Start Your Business

1. **Obtain the following:**

- **Sales Tax I.D. Number** - Contact your State Department of Taxation and Finance to obtain a sales tax kit.

- **State Required Permits and Licenses** - Contact the office of Business Permits and Regulatory Assistance (OBPRA) to obtain a permit assistance kit.

- **Local Licenses and Permits** - Contact the city/town hall and the county office for local requirements.

- **Federal Taxes and Federal Employer Identification Number – EIN** - If you are forming a corporation or a partnership, or if you plan to hire employees, you must file for an EIN (IRS Form SS-4). If you are a sole proprietorship with no employees, you may use your own Social Security number on federal tax forms. Contact your local IRS office to obtain the appropriate paperwork.

- **If You Plan to Hire Employees** - Obtain an Employee Identification Number (EIN) by contacting the IRS. Once you return the completed form, you will receive the forms that you will be required to submit to the federal government.

    - Contact your state Department of Labor to determine your obligation to state unemployment.

    - Contact your state Department of Taxation and Finance regarding forms for state withholdings, if relevant.

    - Check on obtaining Workers Compensation and disability insurance coverage for your employees.

2. **Build a Team of Advisors to Help You**

- ***Certified Public Accountants*** - To advise on tax strategies and record keeping.

- ***Lawyer*** - To review and produce legal documents and general advice.

- ***Commercial Insurance Person*** - For liability coverage and any other forms of insurance your business may require.

3. **Open a Business Checking Account** – Maintain this account separate from your personal account! The bank will require a stamped and certified DBA certificate and a copy of your incorporation papers with your corporate seal affixed.

4. **Arrange for a business phone line to be installed** – By doing this, you will be entitled to a business listing. Consider an answering service for calls that come in during your absence.

Create a Business Plan

Business Plan *– A summary of how a business owner, manager, or entrepreneur intends to organize the business endeavor and implement activities necessary for the venture to succeed. This plan will encourage loans, promote growth, and provide a road map to follow.*

What is in a Business Plan?

1. **Executive Summary** – A concise overview of the plan, together with a history if an existing company.
2. **Market Analysis** – Illustrates your knowledge of the business you are in. It should include target market information, market test results, evaluation of competition, and regulatory restrictions.
3. **Company Description** – Include information about the nature of your business and a list of primary factors you believe will make your business successful.
4. **Organization and Management** – Includes your company's organizational structure, details about the ownership, profiles of the management team.
5. **Advisors** – Include a list of any successful people in the business who are acting as advisors to you.
6. **Marketing Strategies** – How do you plan to market your business? Include information in your goals for advertising, public relations, and communications.
7. **Service Product Line** – Describes your services and products. This is not just a description, but also a "how you are better than your competition" and why people will want to come to you for these services and merchandise instead of your competitor.
8. **Funding Request** – You request the amount of money you will need to start or expand your business.
9. **Financial Data** – Most creditors will want to see historical data for an existing business for the last three to five years, including income statements, balance sheets, and cash flow statements. For start-ups, or growing businesses, creditors will want financial projections including forecasting income and expenditures for at least the first year and usually from three to five years.
10. **Appendix** – This may not have to be included in the plan but should be available on request and should include your credit history, letters of reference, details of market studies, licenses and permit copies, legal documents, leases, contracts, and the names of your attorneys and accountants.

Other Factors to Consider:

- **Keep a cash cushion on hand for emergencies** – Three-to-six months' worth of expenses.
- **Announcements** – Send to the media, potential customers, and friends.
- **Contact the U.S. Small Business Administration for information.**
- **Utilize FREE counseling services with:**
    - SCORE - (Service Corps of Retired Executives)
    - SBDC (Small Business Development Centers)

Types of Capital Needed

- **Working Capital, Circulating Capital** - Difference between current assets and current liabilities.
- **Fixed Capital** - Long-term capital invested in the business.

Sources of Funds

- **Personal, Equity Capital** - Capital invested in the business by the owner(s).
- **Debt Equity** - Borrowed or loaned capital invested in the business that must be repaid to creditors. This may include:
    - Loans from friends
    - Mortgage loans
    - Commercial loans
    - Small Business Administration (SBA)
    - State and regional development companies
    - Taking in partner(s)
    - Issue capital stock
- **Trade Credit** - Credit extended by one business to another to help finance distribution of a producer's goods.
- **Venture Capitalist** - Private individuals or groups who loan money for business.

Ways to make financing more affordable

- Leasing vs. buying
- Selling off excess inventory
- Factoring

Buying a Funeral Home

This section will only touch on some of the points that must be considered when buying a funeral home. The plethora of information on this topic could be a book all to itself.

Factors to Consider - What is/are the:

- Reason(s) the owner is selling.
- Profit potential.
- Tangible Assets - The physical asset that possesses genuine value.
- Intangible Asset - A type of asset that is not able to be physically touched but is retained by a small business because of its genuine value appeal.

- Competition - The practice of trying to obtain something that is being sought by others under similar circumstances at the same time.
- Human Resource Forecast - Determining personnel needs in terms of numbers of individuals and their required skills.
- Number and type of funerals the firm does each year.

Paul Kuper, a consultant and broker of funeral homes, suggests that a person looking to purchase a funeral home consider the following questions:

- ***Who are the potential buyers for the funeral home?*** *Are they funeral homeowners, non-owners, or national consolidation companies?* The presence of other potential purchasers will drive the price up because the competition to purchase a good funeral home is intense in today's market.
- ***Are there growth opportunities in the market?*** If the death rate in an area is not increasing, the only way to increase business is by taking it away from other funeral homes. This is not an easy task and can be expensive. *Will you be satisfied personally and financially if the business will not grow in market share?*
- ***Have you considered what your quality of life will be like?*** *If you cannot afford to hire employees, are you willing to put in the time and effort for years to come – possibly forever?*
- ***Is your decision a sound financial one or is it based on emotion?***
- ***Do you have experienced advisors to assist you?***

Steve Cronin (2017) shares the following advice from an interview with Jake Johnson – A leader in the acquisition field:

1. Are most funeral professionals who want to own a business prepared for the task?

Most funeral directors who work for someone are not prepared financially to either open a business or purchase a business from their current employer. In fact, 90-95% will *not* have the financial capability. Most of them did not get into this profession for a financial windfall; most entered funeral service to have a secure future and assist families in their time of need. Those that want to take the next step to ownership can oftentimes be ill prepared for the multifaceted responsibilities that ownership represents.

2. What is the biggest financial issue facing funeral directors in this position?

First, they will have quite a bit of debt, something that they are not used to. This, in and of itself, can create quite a bit of stress. Secondly, with the headwinds that are facing funeral service today, including the rise in cremation and clients opting for lesser service and caskets, future revenues will be impacted in a negative way. This could cause more stress for the new owner. This stress appears to be felt most by current funeral homeowners in the United States.

3. When should someone who wants to become an owner start planning for the challenge?

They should start planning today. You can try to accumulate money in your current position, but the likelihood of that amassing to a significant number is difficult. What can they do? They could talk to the owner and let them know what their dream would be. If the current owner will participate in some owner financing, it would assist tremendously in crossing the finish line. One problem is that there have been countless owners who have told their key employees, 'Stick in here with me, and someday you will own this firm.' That reality often never takes place, as most owners opt for a secure financial transition upon a sale whereas selling to an employee can be risky.

4. **What are some pitfalls aspiring owners need to avoid?**

The biggest pitfall is the lack of planning when opening a new firm or purchasing from the current owner. Aspiring owners need to put together a business plan that speaks to the financial and nonfinancial pieces of the business ownership. In that plan, they will need to project what the future looks like through a business pro forma. They need to find out what their breakeven point is and how long it will take them to get there. They also need to be conservative, because there are many along the path of ownership that had great aspirations but set their financial goals way to high.

5. What can aspiring owners do to improve their chances of success?

Aspiring owners must talk to the owner and see if there is any chance of purchasing the firm down the road. If so, try to get some timelines and concerns on their part. They may talk to leaders in the community to see if there is anyone who would like to be an investor in the ownership plan. That does not necessarily mean they will get ownership. However, if they do not, they will want a nice return on their investment over time. Be sure to create a business plan. This is essential. They need to do this to secure outside investors and banks to obtain the financing that one would need to do the transaction.

[End of Cronin, 2017]

In Determining the price, what is the:

- **Value** of tangible assets.
- **Book Value** - The cost of a fixed asset less accumulated depreciation.
- **Replacement Value Approach** - The fair market price to purchase similar assets.
- **Liquidation Value (Market Value) Approach** - The anticipated value of an asset that would be realized in case of liquidation of the business.

Value of the Intangible Assets:

- **Name**
- **Goodwill** – An intangible asset such as the name of a funeral home; also, an intangible asset which enables a business to earn a profit in excess of the normal rate of profit earned by other businesses of the same kind.
- **Copyrights** – The registered right of a creator to reproduce, publish, and sell the work that is the product of the intelligence and skill of that person.
- **Patents** – The registered right of an inventor to make, use, and sell an invention.
- **Trademark** – A name, symbol, or characteristic identifying a product officially registered and legally restricted to the use of the owner or manufacturer.

The Terms of Sale

- Cash
- Owner financing
- Third party financing

Sources of New Venture Ideas

- Prior work experience
- Personal experience
- Hobbies
- Accidental discoveries

For more information, See page 471 "Funeral Home Buyers Guide."

Applying for a Loan

Whether applying for a loan from a bank, private lender, or through the Small Business Association, the following requirements will be similar.

General Credit Requirements - SBA uses much the same criteria as any private lender. The three primary tests of credit worthiness are:

1. **Cash flow** - Applicants must show that they can meet business expenses, owner's draw, and all payments from the earnings of the business. This is usually demonstrated with a cash flow projection.
2. **Management** - Applicants must show ability to operate the business successfully. For a new business, applicants must have significant management experience as well as experience in the type of business they propose to enter.

3. **Equity** - Applicants must have enough of their own capital at stake in the business.

    - For a **NEW BUSINESS** (or when buying a business), applicants should have approximately one dollar of cash or business assets for each two dollars of the loan.

    - For an **ESTABLISHED FIRM**, the proforma (after the loan) ratio of total debt to net worth should be approximately 4:1 or better.

The Problems and Risks of Business Ownership

Causes of Failure

External Problems:

- Human resource planning
- Capital shortages - Lack of available money
    - Securing funds, good rates
    - Maintaining reserves
    - Securing equity capital
- Tax burdens
- Government regulations
- Consumerism

Internal Problems:

- Lack of expertise (mismanagement)
- Financial shortages
- Human resource management

Business Building Location and Design

Building Requirements and Design Factors:

- **Suitability** – If you are building "from the ground up," you can design the type of facility exactly as you want it. If you are buying an existing building, you may have to consider remodeling to meet your needs and government regulations.

- **Customer Accessibility** – Factors to consider can include: Stairs both inside and outside the building, ramps, and restrooms adapted for individuals with disabilities. Are you ADA compliant?

- **Internal/external flow** – Every funeral director has his/her own requirement for how people should enter and leave during visiting hours and during the funeral. In designing a new build, this will be a major consideration in the design. In purchasing an existing building, remodeling may have to be completed to meet the director's needs, or the funeral director will have to change in order to accommodate the design of the funeral home.

- **Room for Expansion and Visual Spaciousness** – Most funeral directors hope to increase their business in future years. In buying a building, future expansion should be a consideration. The right design can give the appearance of more space than there really is.

- **Internal and External Appearance** (physical appearance) – In general, people want to go to an attractive, modern, and clean funeral home. It should be in good repair, painted with furniture, rugs, window treatments which are also in good repair, clean and modern.

- **Parking facilities** – Off-street parking should be a definite consideration in building or buying. People do not like parking on the street, and in some instances that is not allowed. To be competitive in today's market, a funeral home should have adequate off-street parking.

- **Equipment/fixtures Requirements** – Just as visitors do not want to visit a dirty, broken down funeral home, most funeral directors do not want to have to deal with worn out equipment like a church truck, cots, embalming machine, instruments, and auto equipment. A wise funeral director will invest in body lifts and an elevator to prevent injuries that are so common to the funeral directors of past generations who did not consider these necessary.

- **Customer Service and Merchandise Organization** – One design factor to consider is the casket display room in your funeral home. Most funeral homes offer this. However, there are a growing number of funeral directors that feel this is a waste of space and feel just as comfortable merchandising caskets and vaults from a catalog or computer program.

Design Factors and Guidelines

- Physical Surroundings
- Visual spaciousness
- Customer image
- Space utilization
- Government regulations

In some states, the non-smoking rules have eliminated the need for a smoking room. It is also common in some areas for a funeral home to have a reception room where funeral breakfast can be served. Other funeral homes have a coffee room where families can have refreshments and just relax. States, such as New York, have laws that prohibit food or beverages in a funeral home.

Zoning – You must check the zoning regulations for the area you want to build in or purchase. A real estate agent and lawyer should be consulted.

ADA – You must be in compliance with the Federal ADA (Americans with Disabilities Act) ensuring your funeral home is accessible to people with disabilities.

Cost Analysis

When determining the cost of doing business, the following information should be taken into consideration:

Fixed Expenses

Definition – *A cost that, for a given period of time and range of activity called the "relevant range," does not change in total but becomes progressively smaller on the per-unit basis as volume increases. These expenses do not increase with increased business, nor do they decrease with declining business activity.*

Examples:	Rent	Depreciation
	Supervisory	Insurance
	Salaries	Debt

Variable Expenses

Definition – *A cost which is uniform per unit but fluctuates in total in direct proportion to change in the related activity or volume.*

Examples:	Supplies	Hourly wage expenses
	Repairs	Utilities
	Taxes	

Overhead – Any cost not specifically associated with production of identifiable products and services and can include all of the above.

The Break-Even Point (break-even analysis) – The point at which total sales revenue equals total costs.

Cost Control

Expense Classification – Based on the industry

Ratio Examples – Comparison to industry standard.

Definition – *Profit and each item of expense in the income statement is expressed as a percentage of sales income.*

Examples:	Total operating expense ratio	Employee wage ratio
	Net profit	Proprietor's wage
	Rent expense ratio	Advertising expense

Extending Credit

All funeral homes are faced with the issue of offering credit to their funeral purchasers. Like most aspects of the profession, credit policies have changed over the years. Thirty years ago, most funeral directors agreed to wait until the deceased's estate was settled before being paid. Many funeral directors even advanced third-party costs, such as church and cemetery fees, and waited for that money. In other words, the funeral director not only offered credit, he loaned the purchaser money.

As the saying goes, "Times have changed." The tight financial situation and economics of recent times have changed most funeral directors' policies for extending credit. Today, almost all funeral homes require families to pay up front for expenses, such as church, cemetery, newspaper, and flowers. Each year, more funeral directors are requiring the purchasers to pay the entire funeral bill before the funeral is over. Others will extend credit for 30, 60, or 90 days, but they do charge interest. There are both advantages and disadvantages to extending credit.

Advantages of Extending Credit

1. Sales are increased. Experience shows that, in retailing, credit-granting stores are more profitable and do a larger volume of business than do strictly cash stores.
2. A more personal relationship can be maintained with credit customers who feel a bond with the firm.
3. Credit customers are likely to be more regular than cash customers, who tend to go where bargains are greatest.
4. Credit customers are more likely to be interested in quality and service than in price.
5. Goodwill is built up and maintained more easily.
6. Goods can be exchanged, and adjustments made with greater ease. If necessary, goods can also be sent out on approval.
7. Credit applications and charge files contain customer information that is useful in planning inventories and special sales promotions.

Disadvantages of Extending Credit

1. Capital is tied up in merchandise bought by charge customers.
2. If the firm has borrowed the extra money required when credit is granted, the interest must be added to the cost of goods sold.
3. Some losses from bad debts, and customers with fraudulent intentions are bound to occur.
4. Some credit customers pay slowly because they overestimate their ability to pay in the future.
5. Credit customers are more likely to abuse the returning of goods and sending goods out on approval.
6. Credit increases operating and overhead costs by adding the expenses of investigation and bookkeeping entailed in keeping accounts, sending out statements, and collecting payments.

Types of Consumer Credit

- Charge accounts
- Installment credit
- Open-end credit - revolving accounts
- Credit card services - VISA, MasterCard, AMEX

Common Business Credit/Sales Terms

- 2/10, n/30 (a 2% discount if paid in 10 days; net bill is due in 30 days)
- MOM (Middle of Month)
- EOM (End of Month)
- CWO (Cash with Order)
- CBD (Cash before Delivery)
- COD (Cash on Delivery)

Collection Policy - Problems with Collection

- The older an account becomes, the harder it is to collect.
- Attempting to collect money due takes time away from other duties.
- Former customers avoid the firm because it is embarrassing to meet when they owe you money.
- Collection ties up funds needed to operate other aspects of the business.

Funeral directors who practice lax credit arrangements usually do so for fear of offending their clientele or losing business. However, our society is accustomed to more formal credit arrangements; therefore, this fear is usually a misconception.

Credit Collections

A general procedure for collecting outstanding bills is:

- 1st - A friendly reminder
- 2nd - 2nd Request/Reminder Letter
- 3rd - Personal contact
- 4th - Collection agency
- 5th – Lawsuit. This should be a last resort.

Factoring - Obtaining cash before payments are received from customers by selling off one's accounts receivable to a third party.

Risk Management - All efforts designed to preserve assets and earning power associated with a business.

- Eliminate risks - Remove the cause
- Minimize risks - Good management
- Shift risks - Purchase outside insurance
- Absorb risks - Self-insure

Insurance

Definition – *Protection for the small business or small business owner with regard to monetary compensation in the event that a business and/or personal peril is experienced. Insurance evolved over the years to produce a practical solution to economic uncertainties and losses. Life insurance, which is based on actuarial or mathematical principles, guarantees a specified sum of money upon the death of the person who is insured (Dearborn Financial Publication, 1996).*

In planning the types of insurance a funeral home may need, the funeral director should consider the following types of losses that could occur:

- Loss or damage of property, including supplies, fixtures, and buildings
- Loss of income resulting from interruption of business due to fire, natural disaster, etc.
- Liability to employees
- Liability to the public
- Death of key employees
- Extensive loss from bad debts
- Faulty title to real estate
- Riots or civil disobedience
- Shoplifting
- Loss through dishonest employees
- Financial hardships
- Vehicles
- Burglary/robbery

Types of Insurance

The following types of insurance can cover a funeral for unexpected losses. The purpose of insurance is to reduce a risk.

Accident and Health Insurance – Insurance against loss through accident or sickness.

Automobile Insurance – Insurance covering motor vehicles.

Buy-Sell Life Insurance – Insurance on an owner of a business that will supply enough money for a partner to buy his share of the business upon death.

Business Interruption Insurance – An insurance that protects companies during the period necessary to restore property damaged by an insured peril. Coverage pays for lost income and other expenses related to recovery.

Casualty Insurance – Insurance that provides monetary benefits to a business that has experienced an unforeseen peril such as flood, fire, etc.

Credit Insurance – Insurance that protects non-retailing businesses from abnormal bad-debt losses.

General Liability Insurance – Insurance covering business liability to customers who might be injured on or off premises or from the product sold to them.

Endowment Life Insurance – Life insurance that allows the insured, rather than the beneficiary, to collect the face value of the policy upon maturity or to collect that value in annual payments.

Key-Person Life Insurance – Life insurance that protects a firm against losses due to the death of a key employee.

Life Insurance – Insurance that provides death benefits to the survivors of the insured.

Product Liability Insurance – Insurance that protects a firm against claims that its product caused bodily injury or property damage to the user.

Self-Insurance – A form of risk management whereby a part of the firm's earnings is earmarked as a contingency fund for possible future losses, specifically for individual loss categories such as property, medical, or worker's compensation.

Term Life Insurance – Life insurance that has no cash value whenever the policy expires.

Universal Life Insurance – A combination of whole life insurance and term life insurance.

Whole Life Insurance – Life insurance that gives lifetime protection to the insured person.

Coinsurance Clause – A clause in an insurance policy under which the insured agrees to maintain insurance equal to some specified percentage of the property value or otherwise to assume a portion of any loss.

Deductible Clause – Insurance policy provision that makes the insurer liable only for losses in excess of the stated deductible.

Malpractice Insurance – The type of insurance to purchase for protection against litigation is commonly referred to as Professional Liability Insurance. It often is additional coverage under a General Liability policy, but sometimes it can be purchased on a separate basis. Some of the associations in the industry have group policies available to their members, so this is an important area to check. A funeral homeowner should arrange to purchase as much coverage as can reasonably be afforded because both the cost of defending litigation and paying a claim could put a funeral home or crematory out of business.

As with any aspect of your business, read your contract carefully. Go over the contract section-by-section with the insurance agent, asking for clarification of any item you do not fully understand. Insurance documents are not the easiest forms to understand because of the way they are written. You do not want to think that you have coverage only to find out that you don't when a tragic event occurs.

For more information on funeral insurance, see Page 477 in Supportive Readings.

Inventory Requirements

As with most businesses, funeral homes must maintain an inventory of merchandise and supplies.

Merchandise includes items such as:

- Caskets
- Vaults
- Urns
- Prayer cards
- Register books
- Religious items such as crosses, rosaries
- Thank-you cards
- Memorial jewelry
- Clothing for deceased

Supplies include such items as:

- Embalming chemicals
- Coveralls; PPE (personal protective equipment)
- Funeral flags and stickers for cars
- Office supplies
- Cleaning supplies

Selecting suppliers:

The decision of which casket, vault, or urn company(s) to purchase from can be based on several factors, including:

- Do you want to purchase from the actual manufacturer or from the wholesalers?
- Do you want to purchase from a cooperative buying group?
- Do you want to consider imported products from countries such as China?

Consideration Concerning Suppliers

- How fast can you receive the item?
- How adaptable is the company to customizing the product?
- Can you receive discounts or rebates?
- Do you like and trust the sales representative?
- Is the quality of the product good, better, or best?
- Is their customer service fair, good, great?
- Do they honor warranties or guarantees?

- Do they provide training and technical assistance?
- Do they provide sales aids?
- Are prices competitive?
- Can you buy on consignment?
- Are you comfortable in selling their merchandise?

Inventory Control Considerations

- Economic order quantity
- Inventory turnover
- Accurate records

Pricing Policies and Strategies

Pricing refers to how much you are going to charge for your services and products (merchandise). The price you charge must be competitive, but still allow you to make a reasonable profit. The keyword here is **reasonable**. You can charge any price you want to, but there's a limit to how much a consumer is willing to pay. Your pricing strategy needs to take this consumer threshold into account.

Determining Price

Funeral homes, like all businesses, professions, and industries, are in business to make a profit. Making a profit is essential for a funeral home, whether it is owned by a major corporation like SCI, or by an individual. The first step in determining what you should charge is to understand what it costs you to operate your funeral home. Factors to consider:

- Cost of products, including any shipping and handling costs
- Operating expenses including overhead, payroll, and marketing

Other Factors Related to Determining Price:

- What your competitor charges
- What your customers are willing to pay
- Amount of profit you desire
- Supply and demand
- Economic fluctuations
- Business conditions
- Marketing strategy
- Value of the merchandise

Methods of Pricing

Many pricing strategies exist. Some strategies are more suited for funeral homes than others. The most recent trend in funeral planning is to decrease the amount charged for merchandise and increase service charges. Funeral directors who use this method feel that an increased price for service is justifiable because most of what a funeral home provides is service. They also believe this method keeps them from pressuring customers to select more expensive caskets, because they make the same profit on all caskets.

This strategy is being recommended by funeral consultants because it reduces the loss if families purchase a casket from a casket store or online.

- **Competition Based Pricing** – Setting the price based upon the similar products and services charged by the competition.

- **Cost Plus Mark-up Pricing** – This is achieved by adding a pre-determined percentage or amount to the cost of the product. This is done in different ways in different funeral homes. Most funeral homes mark up the cost of the caskets two to three times the purchasing cost. Some use the same percentage as the cost of the casket increases. Some funeral homes charge more for services and add the same dollar amount to every casket no matter what it cost to purchase.

- **Loss Leader Pricing** – This occurs when you advertise a lower price in hopes that people will find something more expensive that they like. This is illegal if you don't sell the inexpensive merchandise or service and it was just a trick to get people to come in. If, however, you do offer a lower price alternative and you do not pressure people to buy something more expensive, then it is legally and morally acceptable.

- **Penetration Pricing** – Setting an initial low price at the beginning of your business in hopes of attracting customers. The price will rise later as you gain more market share.

- **Economy Pricing** – This is a no-frills, low price. It is used by funeral homes that decide this will be the philosophy of their business. These types of funeral homes are often called discounters.

- **Package Pricing** – Many consultants are advising funeral homes to create one or more offerings that include a set service and merchandise package at a set price. This price is usually slightly lower than if everything was purchased separately. This is legal according to the F.T.C. if it can still be itemized for purposes of the General Price List. Consultants advise that consumers like the ease of purchasing packages.

- **Psychological Pricing** – This is a strategy where the merchandise price ends in an odd number such as 5, 7, or 9 (example $1,997.00 instead of $2000) because it is believed that consumers perceive it to be a fairer price. They tend to round down rather than up. They perceive the price to be $1900.00 rather than $2000.

Other Factors Affecting Pricing

- **Legislation** – Funeral directors must conform to federal and state rules regarding every aspect of doing business, including pricing.

- **Types of Merchandise** – The director must determine the quality of the merchandise he or she will be selling. Will it be high-end products, low-end, or a mixture of both? Funeral homes do differ; most have some type of mixture but may display more of one category than another.

- **Purchasing Practices** – Most casket companies have special deals for funeral directors who purchase a certain number of their products per year or sell their products exclusively. These deals result in discounts for each item or a rebate one or more times per year on the dollar value of the items. How a funeral director utilizes these rebates or discounts is also an individual choice. He or she can keep the money and consider it a type of bonus, put it back into the business, or pass the discounts on to the consumer in the form of lower prices.

- **Desired Clients** – Some funeral directors have a desire to serve more of a certain type of customer. Directors that market inexpensive funerals will probably get customers who want to spend less money. Directors who want what was once called "the carriage trade," or more affluent people, can't always be guaranteed that this type of customer will spend more on the funeral. The statistics on cremation show that a large percentage of cremation customers are more affluent.

  Do not pre-judge a family. You never know who will spend what until they actually buy. Most directors will tell stories of customers who wanted the least expensive funeral possible, then they spent thousands of dollars on the monument, flowers, or even a reception. Then there are those clients who thought they would spend a certain amount only to find they spent a completely different amount.

  No matter what you charge for the cost of your funerals, you should have a good reason why a family should select your funeral home over a competitor. What makes you better than the funeral home down the street? It must be more involved than "We care more," or "We provide better service." What exactly do you mean? Times are changing and the old family loyalty (I will go to funeral X because my parents went there) is not as strong in all areas as it used to be. In some areas, price and price-advertising are important factors. Those funeral homes that are providing very personalized, creative, and different funeral services are affecting a family's decision to switch funeral homes.

NOTES

NOTES

Chapter 23 THE NEW GRADUATE

8 TIPS to Succeed at a Job Interview

Excerpt From: American Funeral Director (2016)

Whether you're just out of college or looking for a better deal with another company, landing an interview takes work. Once you've earned that interview, you don't want to mess it up. Lisa Quast, author of the book, *Secrets of a Hiring Manager Turned Career Coach: A Foolproof Guide to Getting the Job You Want Every Time*, offers ways to make an interview a success.

1. **Ensure all documents are ready for the interview**
   Preparedness says so much in an interview. It's better to have any and all documents that could be needed and not need them, than vice versa. Have multiple copies of your resume and reference list. Recommendation letters may not be required, but they're good to leave behind. Other items that will either be necessary or useful include the job description, portfolio of your work, paper, and pen.

2. **Dress for positive impact**
   The dot-com era ushered in a more casual approach, but the recession brought back a more dress-for-success style. Dress appropriately for the position and also the geography. For example, a jet-black pantsuit in Florida during August will make you uncomfortable and make you look out of place. Match your attire with the image of the company.

3. **Anticipate interview questions and prepare answers**
   There are five groups of questions you should consider for the interview: Your background; familiarity with the field/industry; your functionality and competency for key aspects of the job; your style and personality; and how you see your future. It's helpful to think about questions the hiring manager might ask and prepare how you could respond.

4. **Prepare questions for the employer**
   Good questions indicate to hiring managers and owners that you know what you are talking about. Consider questions about the character of the company, the history, nature, and future prospect of the open position, and the department.

5. **Conduct practice interviews**
   The more you do something, the easier it gets. Practice helps your interview performance and helps you further develop content for the discussion. Conduct mock interviews with someone you trust. When you get to the interview, remember to be yourself and don't be afraid to show your personality.

6. **Prepare to answer the toughest interview questions**
   One of the hardest questions to answer in an interview is "What's your biggest weakness?" How you answer this question offers insight into your level of self-awareness, how you handle obstacles, and how much you know about the position.

7. **Practice watching the hiring manager's non-verbal cues for important clues**
   People say plenty while not verbally saying anything. Facial expressions, eye contact, posture, and gestures tend to work together to create an overall impression. What are these cures telling you? The answer could help you overcome challenging moments in the interview.

8. **Learn to close the interview with class**
   Don't forget to ask the hiring manager about the next step in the interview process. How would you know if you got the job if an interviewer doesn't tell you what's next and you never ask?

Job Candidate Concerns

A Funeral Service Insider survey revealed common complaints funeral directors had with job candidates:

- Making too many demands.
- Overconfidence.
- Lying or misrepresenting themselves.
- Blast-mailing their resume and not stopping by the funeral home to ask for an interview or to introduce themselves.
- Asking about salary before there is a fit.
- Complaining about having too many hours at a former job.
- Dictating their schedule and salary.
- Thinking this is an eight hour per day job or easy money.
- Assuming that they will get hired because it is a large firm and therefore "always hiring."
- Saying what they want in a job to further their career, rather than saying how they can improve the firm and serve the families.
- Asking about money right away instead of learning about the schedule and job responsibilities.
- Being more concerned about what's in it for them, instead of showing concern for helping families.
- Overstating their qualifications.
- Not being prepared to answer behavioral-based questions.
- Being late or not showing up.
- Walking in off the street during a visitation or funeral.
- Talking negatively about previous employers.

Frustrations for Management in Hiring

According to Funeral Service Insider (2016b), there are several common frustrations in hiring young, new funeral directors. These include:

- Younger funeral directors often lack a dedication for serving others. Most are interested in salaries and benefits. There is also a lack of ethics.
- There is an expectation of higher salaries, more benefits, and more days off in funeral service from interns or newly licensed hires with little-to-no experience.
- The new hires right out of school expect to receive a large salary.
- Finding someone who wants to work weekends and nights is difficult.
- Funeral directors are becoming prima donnas, wanting to work less and be paid more. The word “entitled” is coming up more and more. Previous generations were raised with the “earn it” mentality. Many in the younger generation do not have this same work ethic. Yet, with declining revenues, they will not be retained if they don’t soon get it.
- It is hard to find reasonably priced benefits for employees.

What Do Employers Want from Their Employees?

Excerpt From: SESCO (2014)

This SESCO (2014) Management Report outlines the following traits that employers are looking for in potential employees:

- **Go the Extra Mile**. Employers value an employee who is willing to go above and beyond what is typically required of them on the job. Employees who take on projects that fall outside their normal responsibilities and can expand their skill set and explore new venues for professional growth are highly valued.
- **Wear Multiple Hats.** Employees who simply show up just to do their job as assigned are not increasing their value. Employees who ultimately succeed are those who show an eager willingness to do whatever needs to get done, not just what’s in the job description.
- **Positive Attitude.** Managers expect a positive attitude from all employees. Negative employees and naysayers are a drag on the culture and the organization.
- **Decision-Makers.** Experts agree that all employees must have the ability to think critically and make appropriate decisions on a daily basis.
- **Passion.** Managers are passionate about their “cause.” Thus, it is critical for employers to find employees who are just as passionate about their profession as is their manager. When an employee believes strongly in the organization’s mission and purpose, their job is no longer a job. It is a calling.

- **Organized.** Most businesses are doing more with less because of ever tightening profit margins as well as a shrinking qualified applicant pool. Thus, it is critical that employees be organized.

- **Communication**. Communication is a skill of utmost importance. Employees must have excellent communication skills to include oral, written, telephone, and email.

- **Conscientious.** Employees must be conscientious, and this proves to be a top indicator of good job performance within the business.

- **Positive Representation.** Managers seek individuals who will enhance their organization and their reputation. Managers want employees who are trustworthy, have solid reputations – inside and outside work – and have excellent work ethic.

Professional Habits: Tips for a New Funeral Director

Excerpt From: SESCO (2014)

When you show professionalism in your work, you are presenting an image of yourself that says, **"I am proud of who I am, and I care about what I do."**

- **Always be on time.** Showing up late for work or meetings immediately gives the impression that you don't care about your job or those you are serving.

- **Don't be a grump.** All of us have good and bad days. However, the professional leaves bad moods at the door when they come to work.

- **Dress professionally.** For many positions in the organization, suits and ties are required. However, all employees should always be neat and clean and wear appropriate attire.

- **Watch your mouth.** There is absolutely no place for any swearing, cursing or inappropriate language in any workplace. If you wouldn't say it to your grandmother, refrain from saying it at work, even if you think it is in private and with a close colleague.

- **Offer to help colleagues.** A true professional is always willing to help his or her co-workers when they need help or are overburdened.

- **Don't gossip.** While you may be tempted to tell your colleagues what you heard about someone in the workplace or about a customer, gossiping makes you look like a juvenile or a middle school student. Also, you must always expect that if you tell a close co-worker, "Don't tell anyone but did you hear about…?" it will be spread further.

- **Always remain positive.** Negativity at work brings everyone down and your superiors certainly will not appreciate a resulting drop in the morale among staff.

- **Listen.** A professional demonstrates good communication skills, especially the ability to listen actively and accurately. Listening includes showing interest in what is being said to you.

- **Telephone etiquette.** A professional has good **telephone etiquette.** They:
    - Speak slowly and clearly
    - Listen attentively and do not interrupt
    - Introduce themself AND introduce the organization
    - Always thank the person for their time
    - Follow up with voice messages as soon as possible and no later than the same day.

- **Email etiquette.** Be formal and not sloppy. Keep messages brief and to the point. Use sentence case. Using all capital letters looks as if you are shouting and using all lowercase letters looks lazy. Don't use email as an excuse to avoid personal contact. Remember that email is not private. You must assume whatever you put in an email will be read by someone for whom it was not intended. Don't participate in chain letters and don't email anything that is not work related. Finally, always remember that your tone can either be obvious or misunderstood in an email. Emails should always contain a signature that includes contact information.

- Think of yourself and others as professionals.

- Treat people the way you wish to be treated.

- Be friendly and helpful.

- Smile.

- Consider the opinions and feelings of others.

- Be generous with praise, cautious with criticism.

- Take time to make others feel comfortable.

- Always conduct yourself expertly in the performance of your job.

- Always look the part.

For the New Funeral Director – Tips from the Field

Caleb Wilde (2013) offers tips and advices from first generation funeral directors who are new to the field and who are successful through having them answer the following questions:

1. "Do you have any tips for funeral students trying to get an apprenticeship at a funeral home?"

- From Boyd C. - Be willing to relocate (especially for an apprenticeship).

- From Ada O. - Write up a solid resume and cover letter. Mail it to as many places as you can and follow up in two weeks if you don't hear from anybody. I did this for 15 funeral homes and finally got an apprenticeship.

- From Courtney N. - There are internships out there! You just have to be proactive. I am not from a family of funeral directors, so I am a first generation. You will most likely have to relocate, there are headhunters out there as well who do assist in finding inters/internships.

- From Matthew S. - Personal Presentation is HUGE. Dress nice, but don't look like a hooker or pimp. Hide all crazy tattoos and piercings! (And you should probably shave your beard and cut your hair.)

- From Boyd C. - Follow up. Call funeral homes and ask to just meet with a director to ask questions about the industry.

- From Anna K. - Yes, you will work a ton of hours your first year. But at what professional job would you not? Besides, if you love the job you won't mind spending the time developing your skills and know that it won't be a waste of time. Those hours will pay off in the long run. There are good firms out there. Just be proactive and stay positive.

- From Hannah K. - As an apprentice or new guy/gal everyone is your boss. You do not have a job description. Do your best to do whatever (within legal and moral boundaries) you are asked to do. Ibid.

2. "I just got my license. How do I land a job at a funeral home?"

- From Tony G. - Interview, interview, interview. Don't be desperate to find a funeral home. You will end up quitting and jumping from one frying pan to another. Don't rush it. You will know when you find the right place.

- From Kristin J. - I had no connections when I started. Talk to teachers, they are huge assets and can help put in words of recommendation. Post resumes on state board websites and NFDA. Be open minded and it helps to be willing to relocate. Make sure it's something you feel passionate about because it's hard day in and day out. Supportive family is a must since hours are all over the place and you don't get holidays or weekends.

- From Leslie S. - It's easier in a bigger city that has corporately owned funeral homes. They tend to hire more workers.

- From Ron M. - SCI (Dignity Funeral Homes) are always looking for new hires. I'm a former Location Manager (No License). I started as a General Duties and learned as much as I could. Eventually that led to several promotions.

- From Rosa A. - Learn proper composure. Walk and talk in such a way as to lend dignity to your profession. Sharpen your listening skills. React with compassion, but do not speak in platitudes. Don't say, "Good morning" or "good evening" when answering the door. Instead, say "welcome." Have tissues handy in your pocket. Don't chew gum.

- From Rachel M. - Don't get discouraged. It may seem difficult to find a job, but it is worth the wait. This is a very rewarding profession and you can't stop before you start.

Social Superstar:
How to Show off Your Best Self to a Potential Employer on Social Media
Excerpts From: Darci Swisher (2018)

Looking for a job? Consider being less social and more savvy on your social media accounts. Do some light housekeeping before interviewing. A smart job seeker is aware that they're going to be looked at by potential employers and they are strategic about it.

According to the CareerBuilder Survey, 44% of employers have found content on social media that led them to hire a candidate. For this reason, clean up a Facebook page rather than making it private or deleting the account altogether.

Twitter users are especially vulnerable since most have their accounts open for all to see. The immediacy of Twitter often leads people to tweet and retweet – perhaps with comments – without first considering the consequences. Clean your account before you start looking for a job.

One social media platform to beef up, instead of trim down, is LinkedIn. Your LinkedIn account can paint a picture of you as a professional in your career, as opposed to Twitter and Facebook. Most recruiters use LinkedIn. The more complete your LinkedIn profile, the better. Always include both the months and years for work experiences, associations and degrees, GPA, and volunteer and extra-curricular activities.

Be sure to update your contact information. Many people still have their college email address listed. When potential recruiters or employers try to contact them about some great opportunities, it goes to these old email addresses and is never seen.

Behave Yourself on LinkedIn
By: Carolyn Hyams & Joe Troxler (2012)

Many funeral directors are on LinkedIn these days. And if you're not, you should be. It's a brilliant professional, online business networking site and a place where you're expected to promote yourself through your own profile and other areas of the site. Whether you are new or a Veteran of the site, make sure to avoid making these annoying missteps:

Don't Lie – You will be found out, and it will be embarrassing.

Don't Fake Friendship – Never send an invitation to connect stating that you're a "friend" if you don't know the person. People hate it and won't accept it.

Don't be Lazy – People can get really irritated when others send generic, blanket emails asking to connect. It makes us think they're just trying to connect to as many people as possible, rather than looking to nurture a professional relationship. Unfortunately, on some LinkedIn pages like on some "people you may know" (and on iPad and smartphone) LinkedIn sends invitations to connect without giving people the opportunity to customize their message and without warning. Cringe! LinkedIn should fix this.

Read the Profiles – Don't send the same message to everyone. True story: I received an invite to connect with a message asking to meet for coffee to explore a potential partnership. When I asked what he meant by "potential partnership," the person apologized and admitted that he hadn't read my profile properly.

Post a Profile Image – No exceptions. LinkedIn is a professional networking site, people-to-people, not people-to-logos. There is a different and better place to post your logo, on "Company Pages."

Use Your Full Name – Ignore the option to use your first name only with an initial for your family name. Doing that only looks suspicious and unprofessional (spammers often do this). And while we're on the subject, don't change your privacy settings to "anonymous" when you're looking for other people's profiles. It makes them feel like someone is stalking them.

Don't Boast Too Much – Although LinkedIn was primarily built as a business networking tool, no one likes to see you constantly talking about yourself or your company. Every now and then is okay. Like other "social" sites, sharing interesting information you've found is appreciated – even if you didn't originally find it or write it yourself. And don't forget to credit your sources.

Be Low Key – Don't overdo your status updates. These updates appear in the newsfeed of all of your connections, so if you constantly add updates through the day, it's going to annoy the regulars. Stick to a maximum of three per day – spread out over time.

Be Selective – Don't post links or updates to every single group you belong to. Think about what you are posting and decide which groups would be interested in what you have to say. Warning: Many groups don't like members posting links to other blogs/websites. It comes across as a promotion masquerading as a discussion. Some prefer pure discussions/questions. So read the group rules before you post.

Watch Spelling and Grammar – Think of Twitter as a "cocktail party" and LinkedIn as a "business conference." Customize your message accordingly. On LinkedIn, you are expected to be articulate. Using "u," "r," or "gr8" doesn't cut it. You can get away with this a little on Twitter because of the character limit but, trust me, you will be "professional" judged on LinkedIn.

Ask Before You Email – Never add a connection's email address to your email database without asking permission. Just because they agree to connect with you doesn't mean they want your email marketing. They will report you and your company as a spammer. Likewise, don't treat LinkedIn as an email database and email your connections every bit of news you can think of. This is how people get "unliked" as a connection.

Author's Note

1. There is a saying that "poop rolls downhill." You should remember you are at the bottom of the hill, so expect to get the menial tasks, like washing the cars, that the licensed directors do not want to do. It is called paying your dues.

2. Before final printing of this book, I personally interviewed many funeral home owners and managers to ensure the recommendations and comments in this chapter were still relevant. After they received the information, they agreed that it is still relevant and important in 2020 and will continue to be so in the future.

NOTES

NOTES

Section VI

GOVERNMENT AGENCIES

- Veterans Benefits, Burial at Sea & Social Security
- Federal Trade Commission/OSHA

Chapter 24

VETERAN BENEFITS, BURIAL AT SEA, & SOCIAL SECURITY

Source: https://va.org/military-funeral-honors/

NOTE: *The death benefit allowances for service-related deaths and non-service-related deaths have been changing through the years. Below are the most recent updates. The author recommends that the reader go online to:* http://www.cem.va.gov for the most recent numbers.

Burial and Plot-Internment Allowances

By: U.S. Department of Veterans Affairs (2018)

What are VA Burial Allowances?

The Department of Veterans Affairs, hereinafter referred to as "VA," burial allowances are flat-rate monetary benefits. They help cover eligible Veterans' burial and funeral costs. Generally, they are paid at the maximum amount allowed by law. A 2014 VA regulation change helped simplify the program. Eligible surviving spouses are now paid automatically. This happens upon notification of the Veteran's death. There is no need to submit a claim. However, VA may grant additional benefits after receiving a claim. These include plot or internment allowance and transportation allowance.

Who is eligible?

If the surviving spouse has not been automatically paid, the VA will pay whoever files a claim first out of the following:

- The Veteran's surviving spouse.
- The Veteran's children, regardless of age.
- The Veteran's parents.
- The executor or administer of the estate.

- The survivor of a legal union with the Veteran. This applies to formal relationships that continue up until the Veteran's death. The couple needs to have formalized the relationship under the law of the state. There should be state-issued documentation of the relationship.

The Veteran must have a discharge other than dishonorable. The Veteran must also have met one of the following conditions:

- Death as a result of a service-connected disability.
- Receiving VA pension or compensation at the time of death.
- Entitled to receive VA pension or compensation at time of death, but instead received full military retirement or disability pay.
- Died while hospitalized by VA or while receiving care under VA contract.
- Died while traveling under the following circumstances:
  - Under proper authorization and at VA expense.
  - To or from a place for the purpose of examination, treatment, or care.
- Had an original or reopened claim for VA compensation or pension pending at the time of death.
  - Only if the Veteran would have been entitled to benefits from a date prior to the death date.
- Died on or after October 9, 1996, while a patient at a VA-approved state nursing home.

How much does the VA pay?

For Service-Connected Deaths:

- If the Veteran died on or after September 11, 2001: Maximum $2,000.
- If the Veteran died before September 11, 2001: A maximum of $1,500.
- If the Veteran is buried in a VA national cemetery: Some or all of the costs of transporting remains.

For Non-service-connected Deaths:

- If the Veteran died on or after October 1, 2017: $300 burial allowance; $762 for a plot.
- If the Veteran died on or after October 1, 2016, but before October 1, 2017: $300 burial allowance; $749 for a plot.
- If the Veteran died on or after October 1, 2015, but before October 1, 2016: $300 burial allowance; $747 for a plot.

Effective Oct. 1, 2011, non-service-connected death rates have changed. Payable rates are higher if the Veteran was hospitalized by VA at time of death.

- If the Veteran died on or after October 1, 2017: $762 burial allowance; $762 for a plot.
- If the Veteran died on or after October 1, 2016: $749 burial allowance; $749 for a plot.
- If the Veteran died on or after October 1, 2015, but before October 1, 2016: $747 burial allowance; $747 for a plot.
- If death occurred while the Veteran was hospitalized by the VA; some or all costs of transporting remains.
  - This also applies to VA-contracted nursing home care.

NOTE: If the Veteran dies while traveling at VA expense, VA will pay burial, funeral, plot, or internment allowances. VA will also pay transportation expenses. The traveling must have been for the purpose of an exam, treatment, or care.

For unclaimed remains:

- If Veteran remains are unclaimed, the entity responsible for burial can receive a $300 burial allowance.
- If buried in a VA national cemetery, VA may reimburse:
  - The cost of transporting remains.
  - The cost for a plot.

How can you apply?

Apply by filling out VA Form 21P-530, "Application for Burial Benefits (**See next 2 pages for example**)." You can find the form at: http://www.vba.va.gov/pubs/forms/VBA-21p-530-ARE.pdf. Attach a copy of the deceased's discharge document and a death certificate. Attach a receipt if you are claiming transportation expenses.

Mail your application to the VA regional benefit office in your state. You can find your office location by visiting: http://www.benefits.va.gov/benefits/offices.asp.

For more information, call 800-827-1000, or contact your local VA regional benefit office.

OMB Approved No. 2900-0003
Respondent Burden: 15 Minutes
Expiration Date: 04/30/2020

Department of Veterans Affairs

APPLICATION FOR BURIAL BENEFITS (Under 38 U.S.C. Chapter 23)

IMPORTANT - Read instructions carefully before completing form. YOUR COMPLIANCE WITH ALL INSTRUCTIONS WILL AVOID DELAY. Type or print all information.

(DO NOT WRITE IN THIS SPACE)
(VA DATE STAMP)

NOTE: You can ***either*** complete the form online or by hand. Please print information using blue or black ink, neatly, and legibly to help process the form.

PART I - PERSONAL INFORMATION

1. FIRST, MIDDLE, LAST NAME OF DECEASED VETERAN'S NAME

2. VETERAN'S SOCIAL SECURITY NUMBER

3. VA FILE NUMBER

C/CSS -

CLAIMANT'S PERSONAL INFORMATION

4. CLAIMANT'S NAME *(First, middle initial, last)*

5. CURRENT MAILING ADDRESS *(Number and street or rural route, P.O. Box, City, State, ZIP Code and Country)*

No. & Street

Apt./Unit Number

City

State/Province

Country

ZIP Code/Postal Code

6. PREFERRED TELEPHONE NUMBER *(Include Area Code)*

7. PREFERRED E-MAIL ADDRESS

8. RELATIONSHIP OF CLAIMANT TO DECEASED VETERAN *(Check one)*

- ☐ SPOUSE
- ☐ CHILD
- ☐ PARENT
- ☐ EXECUTOR/ADMINISTRATOR OF ESTATE OR PERSON ACTING FOR THE ESTATE
- ☐ OTHER *(Specify)*

PART II - INFORMATION REGARDING VETERAN

9A. DATE OF BIRTH	9B. PLACE OF BIRTH	
10A. DATE OF DEATH	10B. PLACE OF DEATH	10C. DATE OF BURIAL

SERVICE INFORMATION *(The following information should be furnished for the periods of the VETERAN'S ACTIVE SERVICE)*

11A. ENTERED SERVICE		11B. SERVICE NUMBER	11C. SEPARATED FROM SERVICE		11D. GRADE, RANK OR RATING, ORGANIZATION AND BRANCH OF SERVICE
DATE	PLACE		DATE	PLACE	

12. IF VETERAN SERVED UNDER NAME OTHER THAN THAT SHOWN IN ITEM 1, GIVE FULL NAME AND SERVICE RENDERED UNDER THAT NAME

VA FORM APR 2017 **21P-530**

SUPERSEDES VA FORM 21P-530, JUN 2015, WHICH WILL NOT BE USED

Page 3

Source: https://www.vba.va.gov/pubs/forms/VBA-21P-530-ARE.pdf

VETERAN'S SSN [ ][ ][ ] – [ ][ ] – [ ][ ][ ][ ]

PART III - CLAIM FOR BURIAL ALLOWANCE

13A. TYPE OF BURIAL ALLOWANCE REQUESTED *(Check one)*

- ☐ NON-SERVICE-CONNECTED DEATH
- ☐ SERVICE-CONNECTED DEATH
- ☐ VA MEDICAL CENTER DEATH *(See instructions for definition.)*

(If VA Medical Center Death is checked, provide actual burial cost.)

$

13B. WHERE DID THE VETERAN'S DEATH OCCUR? *(Check one)*

- ☐ VA MEDICAL CENTER
- ☐ NURSING HOME UNDER VA CONTRACT
- ☐ STATE VETERANS HOME
- ☐ OTHER *(Specify)*

14. IF YOU ARE THE DECEASED VETERAN'S SPOUSE, DID YOU PREVIOUSLY RECEIVE A VA BURIAL ALLOWANCE?

☐ YES ☐ NO

15A. DID YOU INCUR EXPENSES FOR THE VETERAN'S BURIAL?

☐ YES ☐ NO

15B. ARE YOU SEEKING BURIAL BENEFITS FOR THE UNCLAIMED REMAINS OF A VETERAN?

☐ YES ☐ NO

PART IV - CLAIM FOR PLOT OR INTERMENT ALLOWANCE

16. PLACE OF BURIAL OR LOCATION OF DECEASED VETERAN'S REMAINS *(Specify)*

17A. DID YOU INCUR EXPENSES FOR THE VETERAN'S PLOT OR INTERMENT?

☐ YES ☐ NO

17B. WAS VETERAN BURIED IN A NATIONAL CEMETERY, OR ONE OWNED BY THE FEDERAL GOVERNMENT?

☐ YES ☐ NO

17C. WAS THE VETERAN BURIED IN A STATE VETERANS CEMETERY?

☐ YES ☐ NO

18A. DID A FEDERAL/STATE GOVERNMENT OR THE VETERAN'S EMPLOYER CONTRIBUTE TO THE BURIAL?

☐ YES ☐ NO *(If "Yes," complete Item 18B)*

18B. AMOUNT OF GOVERNMENT OR EMPLOYER CONTRIBUTION

$

PART V - CLAIM FOR TRANSPORTATION REIMBURSEMENT

19. EXPENSES INCURED FOR THE TRANSPORTATION OF THE VETERAN'S REMAINS FROM THE PLACE OF DEATH TO THE FINAL RESTING PLACE *(Attach itemized receipts)*

$

PART VI - CERTIFICATION AND SIGNATURE

I CERTIFY THAT the foregoing statements made in connection with this application on account of the named veteran are true and correct to the best of my knowledge and belief.

20A. SIGNATURE OF CLAIMANT *(Sign in ink) (If signed using an "X", complete Items 22A thru 23B) (If signing for firm, corporation, or State agency, complete Items 20B thru 21)*

20B. OFFICIAL POSITION OF PERSON SIGNING ON BEHALF OF FIRM, CORPORATION OR STATE AGENCY *(Please sign in ink.)*

21. FULL NAME AND ADDRESS OF THE FIRM, CORPORATION, OR STATE AGENCY FILING AS CLAIMANT

WITNESS TO SIGNATURE IF MADE BY "X"

NOTE - If claimant signed above using an "X", signature must be witnessed by two persons to whom the person making the statement is personally known, and the signatures and addresses of such witnesses must be shown below.

22A. SIGNATURE OF WITNESS *(Sign in ink.)*

22B. ADDRESS OF WITNESS

23A. SIGNATURE OF WITNESS *(Sign in ink.)*

23B. ADDRESS OF WITNESS

PENALTY - The law provides severe penalties which include fine or imprisonment, or both, for the willful submission of any statement or evidence of a material fact knowing it to be false.

DEPARTMENT OF VETERANS AFFAIRS HEADSTONES AND MARKERS

The Department of Veterans Affairs will furnish, upon request, a Government headstone or marker at the expense of the United States for the unmarked graves of certain individuals eligible for burial in a national cemetery, but not buried there. These individuals may include any veterans with an other than dishonorable discharge who dies after service or any servicemember who dies on active duty. Certain other individuals may also be eligible for the headstone or marker. Headstones or markers for all individuals in a national or post cemetery are furnished automatically without request from the family.

For additional information on burial benefits go to the web site, www.cem.va.gov/hbene_burial.asp. To obtain VA Form 40-1330, Application for Standard Government Headstone or Marker go to www.va.gov/vaforms or contact your local VA regional office. The address of that office can be found at to www.va.gov/directory.

VA FORM 21P-530, APR 2017 Page 4

Source: https://www.vba.va.gov/pubs/forms/VBA-21P-530-ARE.pdf

Burial Benefits

Excerpts From: National Cemetery Administration (2019)

Burial benefits available include a gravesite in any of our 138 national cemeteries with available space, opening and closing of the grave, perpetual care, a Government headstone or marker, a burial flag, and a Presidential Memorial Certificate, at no cost to the family. Some Veterans may also be eligible for Burial Allowances. Cremated remains are buried or inurned in national cemeteries in the same manner and with the same honors as casketed remains.

Burial benefits available for spouses and dependents buried in a national cemetery include burial with the Veteran, perpetual care, and the spouse or dependent's name and date of birth and death will be inscribed on the Veteran's headstone, at no cost to the family. Eligible spouses and dependents may be buried, even if they predecease the Veteran.

The Veteran's family should make funeral or cremation arrangements with a funeral provider or cremation office. Any item or service obtained from a funeral home or cremation office will be at the family's expense. The VA created Planning Your Legacy: VA Survivors and Burial Benefits Kit to assist Veterans and their family members in pre-need planning and record storage.

Burial Flag

A United States flag is provided, at no cost, to drape the casket or accompany the urn of a deceased Veteran who served honorably in the U.S. Armed Forces. It is furnished to honor the memory of a Veteran's military service to his or her country. VA will furnish a burial flag for memorialization for any other than dishonorably discharged:

1. Veteran who served during wartime.
2. Veteran who died on active duty after May 27, 1941.
3. Veteran who served after January 31, 1955.
4. Peacetime Veteran who was discharged or released before June 27, 1950, after serving at least one enlistment, or for a disability incurred or aggravated in line of duty.
5. Certain person who served in the organized military forces of the Commonwealth of the Philippines while in service of the U.S. Armed Forces AND who died on or after April 25, 1951.
6. Certain former member of the Selected Reserves.

Who Is Eligible to Receive the Burial Flag?

Generally, the flag is given to the next of kin as a keepsake after its use during the funeral service. When there is no next-of-kin, VA will furnish the flag to a friend making request for it. For those VA national cemeteries with an Avenue of Flags, families of Veterans buried in these national cemeteries may donate the burial flags of their loved ones to be flown on patriotic holidays.

How Can You Apply?

You may apply for the flag by completing:

VA Form 27-2008, Application for United States Flag for Burial Purposes (See next page).
Available at:

http://www.vba.va.gov/pusb/forms/VBA-27-2008-ARE.pdf.

OMB Control No. 2900-0013
Respondent Burden: 15 Minutes
Expiration Date: 06-30-2021

Department of Veterans Affairs | **APPLICATION FOR UNITED STATES FLAG FOR BURIAL PURPOSES**

PRIVACY ACT NOTICE: VA will not disclose information collected on this form to any source other than what has been authorized under the Privacy Act of 1974 or Title 38, Code of Federal Regulations 1.576 for routine uses (i.e., civil or criminal law enforcement, congressional communications, epidemiological or research studies, the collection of money owed to the United States, litigation in which the United States is a party or has an interest, the administration of VA programs and delivery of VA benefits, verification of identity and status, and personnel administration) as identified in the VA system of records, 58VA21/22/28, Compensation, Pension, Education, and Vocational Rehabilitation and Employment Records - VA, published in the Federal Register. Your obligation to respond is required to obtain or retain benefits. Giving us the veteran's SSN account information is voluntary. Refusal to provide the veteran's SSN by itself will not result in the denial of benefits. VA will not deny an individual benefits for refusing to provide his or her SSN unless the disclosure of the SSN is required by a Federal Statute of law in effect prior to January 1, 1975, and still in effect. The requested information is considered relevant and necessary to determine entitlement to benefits under the law. The responses you submit are considered confidential (38 U.S.C. 5701). Information submitted is subject to verification through computer matching programs with other agencies.

RESPONDENT BURDEN: We need this information to determine eligibility for issuance of a burial flag to a family member or friend of a deceased veteran (38 U.S.C. 2301). Title 38, United States Code, allows us to ask for this information. We estimate that you will need an average of 15 minutes to review the instructions, find the information, and complete this form. VA cannot conduct or sponsor a collection of information unless a valid OMB control number is displayed. You are not required to respond to a collection of information if this number is not displayed. Valid OMB control numbers can be located on the OMB Internet Page at www.reginfo.gov/public/do/PRAMain. If desired, you can call 1-800-827-1000 to get information on where to send comments or suggestions about this form.

IMPORTANT - Postmaster or other issuing official. Submit this form to the nearest VA regional office. Be sure to complete the stub at the bottom.

INFORMATION ABOUT THE DECEASED VETERAN ***(Complete as much as possible)***
(Information provided is considered essential when applying for other VA benefits.)

1. FIRST, MIDDLE, LAST NAME OF VETERAN *(Print or type)*

2. MAIDEN NAME OR OTHER NAME(S) VETERAN USED WHILE ON ACTIVE DUTY *(Print or type)*

3. VA FILE NUMBER

4. SOCIAL SECURITY NUMBER

5. MILITARY SERVICE NUMBER/SERIAL NUMBER

6. BRANCH OF SERVICE *(Check box)*
☐ ARMY ☐ NAVY ☐ AIR FORCE ☐ MARINE CORPS ☐ COAST GUARD ☐ SELECTED SERVICE ☐ OTHER *(Specify)*

7. DATE ENTERED ACTIVE DUTY *(or Selected Reserve)*

8. DATE RELEASED FROM ACTIVE DUTY *(or Selected Reserve)*

9. DATE OF BIRTH

10. DATE OF DEATH

11. DATE OF BURIAL

12. PLACE OF BURIAL *(Name of cemetery, city, and State)*

13. HAS DOCUMENTATION BEEN PRESENTED OR ATTACHED THAT SHOWS THE VETERAN MEETS THE ELIGIBILITY CRITERIA? *(See Paragraphs C, D, and E of the "Instructions")*
☐ YES ☐ NO *(If "No," explain in Item 15, "Remarks" (See paragraph E of the "Instructions"))*

INFORMATION ABOUT THE FLAG RECIPIENT AND APPLICANT

14A. NAME OF PERSON ENTITLED TO RECEIVE FLAG

14B. RELATIONSHIP OF DECEASED VETERAN *(See Paragraph F of the "Instructions")*

14C. ADDRESS OF PERSON ENTITLED TO RECEIVE FLAG *(Number and street or rural route, city or P.O., State and ZIP Code)*

14D. TELEPHONE NUMBER

15. REMARKS

I CERTIFY that the statements made in this document are true and complete to the best of my knowledge. I further certify that the deceased veteran is eligible, in accordance with the attached instructions, for issue of a United States flag for burial purposes, and such flag has not been previously applied for or furnished.

16. SIGNATURE OF APPLICANT *(Sign in INK)*

17. ADDRESS OF APPLICANT *(Number and street or rural route, city or P.O., and ZIP Code)*

18. RELATIONSHIP TO DECEASED VETERAN

19. DATE SIGNED

PENALTY - The law provides that whoever makes any statement of a material fact knowing it to be false shall be punished by a fine, imprisonment, or both.

ACKNOWLEDGMENT OF RECEIPT OF FLAG (ONLY ONE FLAG MAY BE ISSUED FOR EACH DECEASED VETERAN)

20. SIGNATURE OF PERSON RECEIVING FLAG *(Sign in INK)*

21. DATE FLAG ISSUED

22. NAME AND ADDRESS OF POST OFFICE OR OTHER FLAG ISSUE POINT

FOR VA USE

DATE NOTIFICATION FORWARDED TO SUPPLY | STATION NUMBER

VA FORM 27-2008, JUN 2018 SUPERSEDES VA FORM 27- 2008, MAR 2015, WHICH WILL NOT BE USED.

This stub is to be completed by the POSTMASTER or other issuing official. Upon receipt the VA Regional Office will detach and forward it to the appropriate Supply Officer.

NOTIFICATION OF ISSUANCE OF FLAG

DATE FLAG ISSUED | ISSUING POINT TELEPHONE NO. | ADDRESS OF POST OFFICE OR OTHER FLAG ISSUE POINT

SIGNATURE OF POSTMASTER OR OTHER ISSUING OFFICIAL

VA FORM JUN 2018 **27-2008** SUPERSEDES VA FORM 27- 2008, MAR 2015, WHICH WILL NOT BE USED. SEE INSTRUCTIONS

Source: https://www.vba.va.gov/pubs/forms/VBA-27-2008-ARE.pdf

Presidential Memorial Certificates

A Presidential Memorial Certificate (PMC) is an engraved paper certificate, signed by the current President, to honor the memory of deceased Veterans who are eligible for burial in a national cemetery.

Administration: The VA prepares the certificates bearing the current President's signature, expressing the country's grateful recognition of the Veteran's service in the Armed Forces.

Eligibility: A PMC is authorized for Veterans who are eligible for burial in a national cemetery by reason of any of paragraphs (1), (2), (3), or (7) of section 2402(a) of title 38 U.S. Code §112.

Application: An eligible recipient (i.e., next of kin, a relative or friend upon request, or an authorized service representative acting on behalf of such relative or friend) may apply for a PMC by completing a ***VA Form 40-0247, Presidential Memorial Certificate Request Form***. More than one PMC may be requested. To expedite the processing of the claim, please submit the Veteran's military discharge documents and death certificate. Do not send original documents, as they will not be returned.

Form Approved, OMB No. 2900-0567
Expiration Date: Oct. 31, 2020
Respondent Burden: 3 Minutes

Department of Veterans Affairs | **PRESIDENTIAL MEMORIAL CERTIFICATE REQUEST FORM**

RESPONDENT BURDEN: Public reporting burden for this collection of information is estimated to average three minutes per response, including the time to review instructions, search existing data sources, gather the necessary data, and complete and review the collection of information. The obligation to respond is voluntary and not required to obtain or retain benefits. Statutory authority for the Presidential Memorial Certificate (PMC) Program is 38 U.S.C. 112. The information requested is approved under OMB Control Number 2900-0567, and is necessary to allow eligible recipients (next of kin, other relatives or friends) to request PMC.

The National Cemetery Administration does not give, sell or transfer any personal information outside of the agency. The Department of Veterans Affairs (VA) may not conduct or sponsor, and you are not required to respond to this collection of information unless it displays a valid OMB Control Number. Responding to this collection is voluntary. Send comments regarding this burden estimate or any other aspects of this collection of information, including suggestions for reducing this burden, to VA Clearance Officer (005G2), 810 Vermont Avenue NW, Washington, DC 20420. **SEND COMMENTS ONLY.** *Please do not send applications for benefits to this address.*

SECTION I - INSTRUCTIONS FOR COMPLETING VA FORM 40-0247, PRESIDENTIAL MEMORIAL CERTIFICATE REQUEST FORM

Military/Discharge Documents: VA recommends that you attach photocopies of readily available supporting documents so that we can make the determination quickly. Documents may include the most recent discharge document (DD Form 214) showing active duty service records other than for training purposes, or active duty for a minimum of 24 continuous months for enlisted Servicemembers after September 7, 1980; for officers, after October 16, 1981, or the full period for which the person was called to active duty. If you are unable to locate copies of military records, apply anyway, as VA will attempt to obtain records necessary to make a determination.

Name of Veteran: DO NOT include nicknames, military rank or civilian title(s).

Name and Mailing Address of Person Requesting Certificate: Provide the full name and complete mailing address to avoid delays in delivery.

We strongly recommend you complete this form online (http://www.cem.va.gov/pmc.asp) and print and sign before you submit your request.

Complete a new VA Form 40-0247 for each additional address where certificates will be mailed to.

Privacy Act Information: VA considers the responses you submit confidential (38 U.S.C. 5701). VA may only disclose this information outside the VA if the disclosure is authorized under the Privacy Act, including the routine uses identified in the VA system of records, 175VA41A published in the Federal Register.

SECTION II - VETERAN/SERVICEMEMBER INFORMATION

1. NAME OF VETERAN *(First, Middle, Last)*	2. VETERAN SSN OR SERVICE NUMBER OR VA FILE NUMBER *(Required)*

SECTION III - PERSON REQUESTING CERTIFICATE INFORMATION

3. NAME OF PERSON REQUESTING CERTIFICATE	4. MAILING ADDRESS OF PERSON REQUESTING CERTIFICATE
5. HOME OR WORK TELEPHONE NUMBER *(Include area code)*	
6. REQUESTOR EMAIL ADDRESS	7. NUMBER OF CERTIFICATES REQUESTED

SECTION IV - CERTIFICATION AND SIGNATURE

CERTIFICATION: I certify, to the best of my knowledge, that the decedent has never committed a serious crime, such as murder or other offense that could have resulted in imprisonment for life, has never been convicted of a serious crime, and has never been convicted of a sexual offense for which he or she was sentenced to a minimum of life imprisonment.

8. SIGNATURE OF PERSON REQUESTING CERTIFICATE *(Required)*

SECTION V - MAILING ADDRESS AND FAX NUMBER

PLEASE SEND ANY MILITARY DOCUMENTS AND SIGNED FORM TO:

Presidential Memorial Certificates (41B3)
National Cemetery Administration
5109 Russell Road
Quantico, VA 22134-3903

Or

Fax To: 1 (800) 455-7143

(The blocks below are for official use only)

9. CASE MANAGER NAME	10. PMC ID NUMBER	11. CASE MANAGER EMAIL

VA FORM NOV 2017 **40-0247** **ALL VERSIONS OF THIS FORM DATED BEFORE MAY 2013 WILL NOT BE ACCEPTED OR PROCESSED.**

Source: https://www.va.gov/vaforms/va/pdf/va40-0247.pdf

Military Funeral Honors

The Department of Defense (DOD) is responsible for providing military funeral honors. "Honoring Those Who Serve" is the title of the DOD program for providing dignified military funeral honors to Veterans who have defended our nation.

Upon the family's request, Public Law 106-65 requires that every eligible Veteran receive a military funeral honors ceremony, to include folding and presenting the United States burial flag and playing of Taps. The law defines a military funeral honors detail as consisting of two or more uniformed military persons, with at least one being a member of the Veteran's parent service of the armed forces. The DOD program calls for funeral home directors to request military funeral honors on behalf of the Veteran's family. However, the Department of Veterans Affairs (VA) National Cemetery Administration cemetery staff can also assist with arranging military funeral honors at VA national cemeteries. Veterans organizations may assist in providing military funeral honors. When military funeral honors at a national cemetery are desired, they can be arranged prior to the committal service by the funeral home.

Headstones, Markers and Medallions

Regardless of the date of death, the VA will furnish, at no charge to the applicant, a government headstone or marker for the unmarked grave of any eligible Veteran in any cemetery around the world. There is no charge for the headstone or marker itself, however arrangements for placing it in a private cemetery are the applicant's responsibility and all setting fees are at private expense.

The VA furnishes upon request, at no charge to the applicant, a Government headstone or marker for the unmarked grave of any deceased eligible Veteran in any cemetery around the world, regardless of their date of death.

A Government-furnished headstone or marker may be provided for eligible Veterans who died on or after November 1, 1990 and whose grave is marked with a privately purchased headstone. A Government-furnished medallion may be provided for eligible Veterans who served on or after April 6, 1917 and whose grave is marked with a privately purchased headstone or marker.

Flat markers in granite, marble, and bronze and upright headstones in granite and marble are available. Bronze niche markers are also available to mark columbaria used for inurnment of cremated remains. The style chosen must be permitted by the officials in charge of the private cemetery where it will be placed. When burial or memorialization is in a national cemetery, state Veterans cemetery, or military post/base cemetery, a headstone or marker will be ordered by the cemetery officials based on inscription information provided by the next of kin or authorized representative.

Spouses and dependents are not eligible for a Government-furnished headstone or marker unless they are buried in a national cemetery, state Veterans cemetery, or military post/base cemetery.

Note: There is no charge for the headstone or marker itself, however arrangements for placing it in a private cemetery are the applicant's responsibility and all setting fees are at private expense.

To order a medallion claimants should use the form, ***VA 40-1330M, Claim for Government Medallion for Placement in a Private Cemetery***.

Important: Eligible Veterans are entitled to either a Government-furnished headstone or marker, or the new medallion, but not both.

Memorial Headstones and Markers

Memorial headstones and markers, for individuals or groups, are furnished for eligible deceased active duty service members and Veterans whose remains are not recovered or identified, are buried at sea, donated to science, or whose cremated remains have been scattered.

Memorial headstones and markers may also be furnished in national, military post/base, or state Veterans cemeteries to eligible spouses whose remains are unavailable for interment, whether or not they predecease the eligible Veteran.

These headstones and markers bear an *"IN MEMORY OF"* inscription as their first line and must be placed in a recognized cemetery.

Memorial headstones and markers for spouses and other dependents are not available for placement in private cemeteries.

A ***VA Form 40-1330, Claim for Standard Government Headstone or Marker,*** must be submitted to request a burial or memorial headstone or marker.

National Cemetery Administration - Scheduling Update

To: NYSFDA Members
Date: September 17, 2019

We want to share information we received about changes to the system used to schedule services for Veterans and eligible family members at National Cemeteries.

Starting today, Tuesday, September 17, 2019 the National Cemetery Scheduling Office (NCSO) will begin conversion to a **new system for scheduling cases**.

The National Cemetery Administration announced plans to ensure a seamless transition, but calls may take longer as schedulers familiarize themselves with the new system. Full transition should take a "few months," according to the National Cemetery Administration. The change is expected to bring greater flexibility to the process.

To help you prepare for a call to arrange for burial of a Veteran, the National Cemetery Administration is urging Funeral Directors to make use of the "BEFORE YOU CALL CHECKLIST." (See Next Page.)

You can learn more about the National Cemetery Administration's burial and memorial benefits for Veterans and eligible family members on the National Cemetery Administration's **HOMEPAGE** at: https://www.cem.va.gov/.

National Cemetery Scheduling Office
(800) 535-1117

Before You Call Checklist

To help expedite your call to the National Cemetery Scheduling Office (NCSO), please obtain the information listed in the checklist below.

In advance of the call to schedule services, you may also fax discharge or other documents to (866) 900-6417.

Information Type	Information Details	Response
Cemetery Information		
National cemetery requested	Name of cemetery:	
Is this burial a first or second interment *If second (subsequent) interment, previous decedent information is required*	First or second:	
Previous Decedent Information		
Previous decedent's full name	First name, middle name, and last name:	
Previous decedent's social security number	Social security number:	
Previous decedent's date of birth	Date of birth:	
Previous decedent's date of death	Date of death:	
Veteran Information		
Veteran's full name	First name, middle name, and last name:	
Veteran's social security number	Social security number:	
Veteran's date of death	Date of death:	
Veteran's date of birth	Date of birth:	
Veteran's branch of service	Branch of service:	
Military rank	Rank:	
Marital status	Married/divorced/never married/widowed/other:	
Gender of Veteran - Male or Female	Male/female:	
Race of Veteran	Race:	
Decedent Information		
Relationship to Veteran	Self (Veteran)/spouse/child/other:	
Decedent's full name	First name, middle name, and last name:	
Decedent's social security number	Social security number:	
Date of birth	Date of birth:	
Date of death	Date of death:	
Decedent address	Address/state/zip code:	
Home of record in service area	Home within 75 miles of cemetery:	
Decedent Gender	Gender:	
Marital status	Married/divorced/never married/widowed/other:	
Funeral Home Information		
Funeral home name	Funeral home name:	
Funeral home identification number	Funeral home identification number:	
Funeral home address	Address/state/zip code:	
Funeral home contact full name	First name, middle name, and last name:	
Funeral home contact email address	Email address:	
Funeral home phone number	Phone number:	

Fax discharge documents and death certificate of Veteran and prior decedent, as applicable, to (866) 900-6417
Death certificate of previous decedent is required to validate legal marital status, if documents are not available within NCSO records

1
National Cemetery Scheduling Office - Before You Call Checklist
September 2019

Information Type	Information Details	Response
Marital Status and Surviving Spouse Information		
Surviving spouse information	First name, middle name, and last name:	
If no surviving spouse, name of decedent's next of kin	First name, middle name, and last name:	
Relationship to decedent	Spouse/child/other:	
Social security number of spouse	Social security number:	
Date of birth of spouse	Date of birth:	
Veteran status of spouse	Veteran status of spouse:	
Request for set-aside grave	Yes/no:	
Does the Veteran have any adult dependent children, who are mentally or physically disabled	Yes/no:	
Information Type	**Information Details**	**Response**
Adult Dependent Child		
Adult dependent child's full name	First name, middle name, and last name:	
Adult dependent child's social security number	Social security number:	
Adult dependent chiild's date of birth	Date of birth:	
Interment Details		
Type of remains	Casket/urn:	
Liner type	Standard government/private vault:	
Liner size: *Small - 60L x 20W x 18D* *Regular - 86L x 30W x 28D* *Extra Large - 86L x 38W x 28D* *Oversized - 88L x 34W x 27D* *Jumbo - 98L x 44W x 30D*	Small/regular/ extra large/oversized/jumbo:	
Urn dimensions: *Niche size - 9L x13W x18 D*	Dimensions:	
Federal Law Information		
Response to the question *"To the best of your knowledge, has the decedent ever **committed** a capital crime?"*	Yes/no:	
Response to the question *"To the best of your knowledge, has the decedent ever been **convicted** of a sexual offense of which he or she was sentenced to a minimum of life in prison?"*	Yes/no:	
Military Honors Information		
Request for military honors	Yes/no:	
Branch of service requested	Branch of service:	
Request for committal service	Yes/no:	
Emblem of Belief Information		
Request for a religious emblem of belief for the marker	Yes/no/not at this time:	
Selection of the emblem of belief	Selection:	
Scheduling Information		
Method of delivery to cemetery	Funeral home/family:	
Name of individual who is scheduling military honors	Name:	
Preferred date and time of the scheduled service	Date/time:	
Fax discharge documents and death certificate of Veteran and prior decedent, as applicable, to (866) 900-6417 *Death certificate of previous decedent is required to validate legal marital status, if documents are not available within NCSO records*		

2
National Cemetery Scheduling Office - Before You Call Checklist
September 2019

Burial at Sea Program

United States Navy Mortuary Affairs (2016)

Source: https://navylive.dodlive.mil/2015/05/23/honoring-our-shipmates-the-heritage-of-the-military-funeral-and-burial-at-sea/

BURIAL AT SEA (BAS) is a means of final disposition of remains that is performed on United States Navy vessels. The committal ceremony is performed while the ship is deployed. Therefore, family members are not allowed to be present. The commanding officer of the ship assigned to perform the ceremony will notify the family of the date, time, and longitude and latitude once the committal service has been completed.

ELIGIBILITY - Individuals eligible for this program are:

(1) Active duty members of the uniformed services.
(2) Retirees and Veterans who were honorably discharged.
(3) U.S. civilian marine personnel of the Military Sealift Command.
(4) Dependent family members of active duty personnel, retirees, and Veterans of the uniformed services.

HOW TO GET STARTED: After the death of the individual for whom the request for Burial at Sea is being made, the Person Authorized to Direct Disposition (PADD) should contact the Navy and Marine Corps Mortuary Affairs office at 1-866-787-0081 to request a packet and for additional information.

<u>Supporting documents which must accompany this request are:</u>

(1) A photocopy of the death certificate;
(2) The burial transit permit or the cremation certificate; and
(3) A copy of the DD Form 214, discharge certificate, or retirement order.

The Burial at Sea Request Form and the three supporting documents listed above make up the Burial at Sea Request package.

BURIAL FLAG: A Burial Flag is required for all committal services performed aboard United States Naval vessels, except family members, who are not authorized a burial flag. Following the services at sea, the flag that accompanied the cremains/remains will be returned to the PADD. If the PADD does not wish to send a burial flag for the service, a flag will be provided by the Navy for the committal service but will not be sent to the PADD.

CREMATED REMAINS (CREMAINS): Cremains must be in an urn or temporary container (preferably Biodegradable) to prevent spillage in shipping. Recent changes in law prohibit the discharge of plastics at sea. Families are encouraged to have the cremains inurned directly or transferred to a sturdy biodegradable urn at their local funeral home to facilitate burial at sea. Burial at Sea Coordinators at the ports of embarkation are available to field any questions regarding the urns. The cremains, along with the completed Burial at Sea Request package, should be forwarded to the Burial at Sea Coordinator at the desired port of embarkation (listed below). Prior to shipment, it is recommended that a phone call be made informing the coordinator of the pending request. ONLY Priority Mail Express Service is authorized when shipping cremains and it is recommended that Tracking and Signature on Delivery is used to ensure the package is delivered to the correct individual in a timely manner.

INTACT REMAINS (CASKETED): Specific guidelines are required for the preparation of casketed remains. All expenses incurred in this process are the responsibility of the PADD, who will select a funeral home in the area of the port of embarkation. After this selection has been made and notification has been provided to the coordinator, the casketed remains, the request form, supporting documents, and the burial flag are to be forwarded to the receiving funeral home. The coordinator will make the inspection and complete the checklist for the preparation of casketed remains. It is recommended that funeral homes responsible for preparing and shipping intact remains contact the Mortuary Services Office at Navy Casualty in Millington, TN to receive the preparation requirements.

PORTS OF EMBAKATION/COORDINATORS

Norfolk, VA
Commander, Naval Medical Center
ATTN: Code 0210C
620 John Paul Jones Cir.
Portsmouth, VA 23708-5100
Phone: (757) 953-2617\2618

Jacksonville, FL
Officer in Charge
Naval Hospital Branch Clinic
P. O. Box 280148
Naval Station
Mayport, FL 32228-0148
Phone: (904) 270-4285

San Diego, CA
Commanding Officer
Naval Medical Center
Decedent Affairs Code: 09O4
34800 Bob Wilson Drive
San Diego, CA 92134-5000
Phone: (800) 290-7410

Bremerton, WA
Commanding Officer
Naval Hospital Bremerton
Code: 015-BAS/HP01 Boone Road
Bremerton, WA 98312-1898
Phone: (360) 475-4313

Honolulu, HI
Navy Liaison Unit
Tripler Army Medical Center
Tripler AMC, HI 96859-5000
Phone: (808) 433-4709
(808) 577-7590

Questions concerning Burial-at-Sea?
Please call Monday - Friday, 0730-1600 Central Time
Toll Free - 1-866-787-0081
DSN - 882-8576

Source: United States Navy Mortuary Affairs (2016, May 27). Burial at Sea Program. Retrieved from: https://www.navy.mil/navydata/questions/burial.html

BURIAL-AT-SEA
REQUEST/AUTHORIZATION FORM

(please ensure items in **bold** are filled in)

To Whom It May Concern:

This is to certify that I: ______________________________, am the person having the
(Full Name of Requester)

legal right to direct the disposition of the: **Remains / Cremains** of my: ______________.
(Relationship)

______________________, ______________, __________, __________, __________.
(Full Name of Deceased) (SSN) (Service) (Rank) (Status)

I respectfully submit my request for Burial-At-Sea and authorize the committal to sea of the

Remains / Cremains from a Naval Vessel.

The dates of military service were from: ____________ until: ____________, as confirmed

in the attached documentation.

Death occurred on: __________, in: ________________________. The cause of death is
(Date) (City and State)
listed on the death certificate.

If possible, I request the selected religious service be provided during the committal service:

Catholic / Protestant / Jewish / Other (Please Specify) ______________________

I understand, that it is my responsibility to pay all expenses for the remains, to include: preparation and casketing, or cremation and inurnment, plus delivery, to the selected port of embarkation. In the case of casketed remains, I understand I must engage a receiving funeral home in the area of the port, to prepare the casket for committal at sea.

AUTHORIZATION CERTIFICATION

______________________	______________________
(Signature of Requester)	(Signature of Witness)
______________________	______________________
(Printed Name of Requester)	(Printed Name of Witness)
______________________	______________________
(Complete Address)	(Complete Address)
______________________	______________________
______________________	______________________
(Phone Number)	(Phone Number)

GUIDELINES FOR CASKET PREPARATION

WEIGHTING

Add 150 lbs. of weight to the foot-end of the casket to ensure 'feet first' sinking. Sandbags are best. However if lead weights are used, secure them to the inside of the casket to avoid them shifting around and causing excessive noise.

BANDING

The casket is to be banded with a minimum of six (6) nylon or metal bands, at least ¾ of an inch wide. The bands are to be placed: two around the head panel, two around the foot panel, one lengthwise, head-to-foot; and one horizontally around the sides. **NOTE**: Ensure bands are placed under the casket handles to allow continued use of handles.

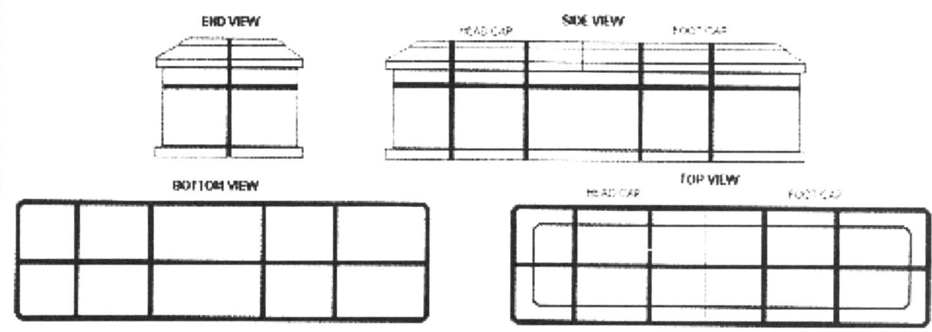

HOLES

A total of 20 holes, 2-inches in diameter, are to be drilled in the casket. There are to be eight holes in the top of the casket, with four in the head panel; four in the foot panel; eight in the bottom; and two in each end.

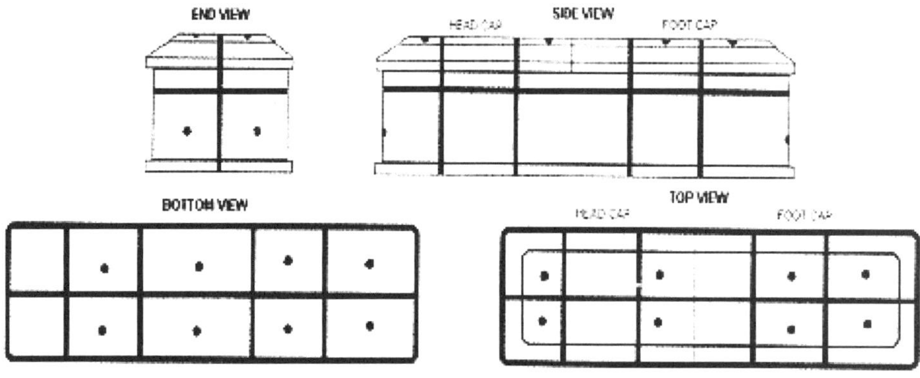

If you require additional guidance for preparation of the casket, please don't hesitate to contact our Navy Mortuary Affairs Office, toll-free at (888) 647-6676, and follow the voice menu.

How Social Security Can Help You When a Family Member Dies

Source: www.ssa.gov

Social Security Administration Publication No. 05-10008 | ICN 451390 | May 2017 (recycle prior editions), Retrieved from: https://www.ssa.gov/pubs/EN-05-10008.pdf.

You should let Social Security know as soon as possible when a person in your family dies. Usually, the funeral director will report the person's death to Social Security. You'll need to give the deceased's Social Security number to the funeral director so they can make the report.

Some of the deceased's family members may be able to receive Social Security benefits if the deceased person worked long enough in jobs insured under Social Security to qualify for benefits. **Contact Social Security as soon as you can to make sure the family gets all the benefits they're entitled to**.

Please read the following information carefully to learn what benefits may be available.

- A one-time payment of $255 to the surviving spouse if they were living with the deceased. If living apart and eligible for certain Social Security benefits on the deceased's record, the surviving spouse may still be able to get this one-time payment. If there's no surviving spouse, a child who's eligible for benefits on the deceased's record in the month of death can get this payment.

- Certain family members **may be eligible** to receive monthly benefits, including:

  - A widow or widower age 60 or older (age 50 or older if disabled);

  - A widow or widower any age caring for the deceased's child who is under age 16 or disabled;

  - An unmarried child of the deceased who is:

    - Younger than age 18 (or up to age 19 if they're a full-time student in an elementary or secondary school); **or**
    - Age 18 or older with a disability that began before age 22;

  - A stepchild, grandchild, step grandchild, or adopted child under certain circumstances;

  - Parents, age 62 or older, who were dependent on the deceased for at least half of their support

  - A surviving divorced spouse, under certain circumstances.

If the deceased was receiving Social Security benefits, you must return the benefit received for the month of death or any later months. For example, if the person dies in July, you must return the benefit paid in August. If received by direct deposit, contact the bank or other financial institution and ask them to return any funds received for the month of death or later. If paid by check, do not cash any checks received for the month the person dies or later. Return the checks to Social Security as soon as possible.

However, eligible family members may be able to receive death benefits for the month the beneficiary died.

Contacting Social Security

Contact us anytime, anywhere is to visit www.socialsecurity.gov. There, you can: Apply for benefits; open a my Social Security account, which you can use to review your Social Security Statement, verify your earnings, print a benefit verification letter, change your direct deposit information, request a replacement Medicare card, and get a replacement SSA-1099/1042S; obtain valuable information; find publications; get answers to frequently asked questions; and much more.

If you don't have access to the internet, we offer many automated services by telephone, 24 hours a day, 7 days a week. Call us toll-free at 1-800-772-1213 or at our TTY number, 1-800-325-0778, if you're deaf or hard of hearing.

If you need to speak to a person, we can answer your calls from 7 a.m. to 7 p.m., Monday through Friday. We ask for your patience during busy periods since you may experience a higher than usual rate of busy signals and longer hold times to speak to us. We look forward to serving you.

SOCIAL SECURITY ADMINISTRATION

Form Approved
OMB No. 0960-0142

STATEMENT OF DEATH BY FUNERAL DIRECTOR

NAME OF DECEASED	SOCIAL SECURITY NUMBER
	FOR SSA USE ONLY
	Please complete the items below, and return the form in the enclosed addressed, postage paid envelope. Your assistance and cooperation are appreciated.

PRIVACY ACT/PAPERWORK ACT NOTICE: The information on this form is authorized by Section 404.715 and 404.720 of the Federal Regulations (20 CFR 404.715 and 404.720). While your response is voluntary, we need your assistance to make an accurate and timely determination concerning the death of the individual named above, and to determine if there are survivors who may be eligible for Social Security benefits.

We may also use the information you give us when we match records by computer. Matching programs compare our records with those of other Federal, State or local government agencies. Many agencies may use matching programs to find or prove that a person qualifies for benefits paid by the Federal government. The law allows us to do this even if you do not agree to it.

Explanations about these and other reasons why information you provide us may be used or given out are available in Social Security Offices. If you want to learn more about this, contact any Social Security Office.

Paperwork Reduction Act Statement - This information collection meets the requirements of 44 U.S.C. § 3507, as amended by Section 2 of the Paperwork Reduction Act of 1995. You do not need to answer these questions unless we display a valid Office of Management and Budget control number. We estimate that it will take about 3.5 minutes to read the instructions, gather the facts, and answer the questions. **SEND THE COMPLETED FORM TO YOUR LOCAL SOCIAL SECURITY OFFICE. The office is listed under U. S. Government agencies in your telephone directory or you may call Social Security at 1-800-772-1213 (TTY 1-800-325-0778).** *You may send comments on our time estimate above to: SSA, 6401 Security Blvd., Baltimore, MD 21235-6401.* ***Send only comments relating to our time estimate to this address, not the completed form.***

1. NAME OF DECEASED		2. SOCIAL SECURITY NUMBER
3. DATE OF DEATH	4. DATE OF BIRTH *(if known)*	5. Check (x) whether the deceased was ☐ Male ☐ Female

6. NAME OF WIDOW OR WIDOWER *(if known)*

7. ADDRESS (No. and Street, P.O. Box) OF WIDOW OR WIDOWER *(if known)*

CITY	STATE	ZIP CODE	TELEPHONE NUMBER (if Available) ( ) - area code

I hereby certify that I am an authorized funeral director and prepared for final disposition the body of the person named above. I understand this statement may be used in connection with an application for Social Security benefits. I declare under penalty of perjury that I have examined all the information on this form, and on any accompanying statements or forms, and it is true and correct to the best of my knowledge. I understand that anyone who knowingly gives a false or misleading statement about a material fact in this information, or causes someone else to do so, commits a crime and may be sent to prison, or may face other penalties, or both.

NAME AND ADDRESS OF FUNERAL DIRECTOR OR FIRM	SIGNATURE OF FUNERAL DIRECTOR OR AUTHORIZED REPRESENTATIVE	
	TELEPHONE NUMBER ( ) - area code	DATE

FOR SOCIAL SECURITY USE ONLY - DO NOT WRITE IN THIS SPACE

DO Processed (Date)

Form **SSA-721** (5-2005) ef (8-2008) Use 1-2004 edition until supply is exhausted

Source: https://www.ssa.gov/forms/ssa-721.pdf

NOTES

Chapter 25 FEDERAL TRADE COMMISSION / OSHA

Federal Trade Commission (FTC)

Excerpt From: Emily Albrecht (2018)

The Federal Trade Commission Funeral Rule went into effect in April 1984 and was revised in July 1994. It requires that funeral providers give consumers accurate, itemized price information and various other disclosures about funeral goods and services.

The Funeral Rule requires disclosure of itemized price information both over the telephone and in writing concerning funeral services and ancillary arrangements offered as well as price lists for caskets and outer burial containers. The Funeral Rule also requires persons arranging a funeral be given a statement of the funeral goods and services selected by that person and the price to be paid for each item.

The Funeral Rule was designed to (1) ensure that consumers receive the information necessary to make informed decisions and (2) lower existing barriers to price competition in the market for funeral goods and services. The Funeral Rule applies to anyone who sells or offers to sell both funeral goods and services. Funeral goods include all products sold directly to the public in connection with funeral services, which are used to care for and prepare bodies for burial, cremation, or other final disposition and to arrange, supervise, or conduct the funeral ceremony or final disposition of human remains.

Pursuant to the Funeral Rule, it is an unfair or deceptive act or practice for funeral providers to:

- Fail to furnish consumers with accurate price information disclosing the costs of each funeral good or service used in connection with the disposition of dead bodies.
- Require consumers to purchase a casket for direct cremations.
- Condition the provision of any funeral good/service on the purchase of any other funeral good/service.
- Embalm the deceased for a fee without permission.

The Funeral Rule prohibits funeral providers from making misrepresentations about the legal/local cemetery requirements for (1) embalming; (2) caskets in direct cremations; (3) outer burial containers; or (4) purchase of any other funeral good or services, that cash advance items are provided to the consumer at the same price as that paid by the funeral provider when that is not the case, or that any funeral good or service will delay the decomposition of human remains for a long-term or indefinite amount of time by setting forth price and information disclosures to ensure funeral providers do not engage in unfair or deceptive acts/practices.

The Funeral Rule gives important rights to consumers when making funeral arrangements. Funeral homes must provide consumers with an itemized general price list at the initiation of an in-person discussion about funeral arrangements, a casket price list before showing consumers any caskets and an outer burial container price list before consumers view grave liners or vaults. The Funeral Rule also prohibits funeral providers from requiring customers to buy any item as a condition of obtaining any other funeral good or service. By requiring the use of itemized prices, the Funeral Rule enables consumers to compare prices and buy only what goods and services they want.

Health and Safety in the Funeral Home

Excerpt From: Marjori Todd & Richard Best (2011)

OSHA

The Federal Occupational Safety and Health Administration (OSHA) is part of the United States Department of Labor, and its mission is to ensure safe and healthful working conditions by setting and enforcing standards and providing training, outreach, education, and assistance. In addition to federal OSHA, there are also some states that have their own approved occupational safety and health programs. However, each state OSHA program must have regulations that are at least as strict as federal OSHA.

Several activities in funeral homes fall under OSHA's General Industry Standards. Of primary importance for worker safety is control of infection and working with hazardous chemicals, such as embalming fluids containing formaldehyde or formalin, as well as many other hazardous chemicals that may be present in the workplace.

OSHA Hazard Communication Standard

The Hazard Communication Standard (29 CFR 1910.1200) was created to ensure that chemical hazards in the workplace are identified and evaluated, and that the information concerning those hazards is communicated to both employers and employees.

General requirements of OSHA's Hazard Communication Standard:

- Provide written Hazard Communication Program specific to our facility. The written program does not have to be long and technical, but it must be in writing.
- Provide master list of all hazardous chemicals used at your facility.
- Ensure that containers of hazardous chemicals are properly labeled.
- Obtain a Material Safety Data Sheet (MSDS) for each hazardous chemical covered by the standard and used at the facility.
- Train all affected employees about the hazardous chemicals with which they work.

OSHA Management/Safety

Information published by IFFCA Magazine

Proper formaldehyde waste disposal

Formaldehyde waste must be stored in a labeled hazardous waste container for proper disposal, or made available for recycling, if practical.

Bloodborne Pathogens: Bloodborne pathogens were the second most frequently cited standard last year.

The key elements of a Bloodborne Pathogens Program include:

- **Exposure determination**. Assess the risks of exposure to bloodborne pathogens (generally in the form of potential contact with body fluids) that employees may encounter at their workplace. List the tasks and location where this contact can occur (e.g. cleaning out the refrigerated storage area).

- **Engineering and work practice controls**. Engineering and work practice controls must be used to eliminate or minimize employee exposure. Some examples of engineering controls include needle handling and disposal procedures, labels and signs, hand washing facilities, and housekeeping procedures.

- **Written exposure control plan**. Policies for protecting employees against exposure to bloodborne pathogens must be in writing. The Exposure Control Plan must be accessible to employees. It must be reviewed and updated at least annually, or whenever new or modified tasks and procedures affect occupational exposure.

- **Labels and signs**. Labels and signs must caution employees where exposure risks exist. Appropriate warning labels must be affixed to containers of regulated waste; refrigerators and freezers that contain blood or other potentially infectious material; and other containers that are used to store, transport, or ship blood or other potentially infectious materials. This does not include public spaces such as crypts or viewing rooms.

- **Personal protective equipment**. When engineering controls do not completely eliminate hazards, personal protective equipment (PPE) must be used. The appropriate PPE must be provided to shield employees from exposure risks. PPE could include gloves, gowns, shoe covers, laboratory coats, face shields or masks, and/or eye protection. It is the employer's responsibility to provide and maintain such equipment at no cost to the employee.

- **Employee information and training**. All employees with occupational exposure must participate in a bloodborne pathogens training program. This training must take place during work hours and must be appropriate to the education level and language of each employee. The person conducting the training must be knowledgeable in the subject matter as it relates to the workplace and be able to answer employee questions.

- **Vaccinations**. Hepatitis B vaccinations must be provided at no cost to all employees who will potentially be exposed as a part of their jobs. These vaccinations must be performed by or under the supervision of a licensed physician or another licensed health care professional according to the recommendations of the U.S. Public Health Service that are current at the time that these evaluations and procedures take place.

- **Post-Exposure evaluation and follow up.** Following a report of an exposure incident, the employer must immediately make available a confidential medical evaluation and follow-up at no cost to the employee. The employer must ensure that all laboratory tests are conducted by an accredited laboratory at no cost to the employee. The employer must obtain and provide the employee with a copy of the evaluating health care professional's written opinion within 15 days of the completion of the evaluation.

- **Recordkeeping**. Maintain records of employee training as well as of injuries and accidents that are related to any bloodborne pathogen exposure in the workplace.

Respiratory protection

Funeral home personnel may need respirators to protect themselves from formaldehyde or other chemical exposures. Exposure must be determined for each chemical, and each respirator's protection level must be adequate for the exposure level.

Before using a respirator, a physician must determine that it is safe for the employee to use one and he/she must be trained on its use and care. ***Your respirator program must be in writing.***

Flammable liquids

In 2012, OSHA updated the Hazard Communication Standard by adopting the Global Harmonization System (GHS) of classification and labeling of chemicals. The Flammable Liquids Standard also was updated to incorporate these changes. Flammable liquids are now classified differently, and labels have changed.

Flammable liquids often used in funeral homes include formaldehyde, cleaning products, alcohols, and aerosols, such as spray paint and WD-40. Even hand gels may be flammable. Additionally, gasoline for vehicles, mowers, and other equipment used for grounds maintenance and propane are flammable.

You may have other flammable liquids used or stored at your facility. Be sure that you have a program that includes safe use and storage of these liquids.

Sources of ignition are common in funeral homes, including open flames or candles, hot surfaces such as a retort, radiator, hot lawn care equipment, or radiant heater.

Your safety program also must include control of ignition sources, a fire plan that identifies the equipment to prevent and detect fires, and the means for fire control should an incident occur. The employer must also provide appropriate fire extinguishers in each location where a fire hazard exists.

NOTES

NOTES

Section VII

TECHNOLOGY & THE FUTURE

- Technology
- Green Burial
- Future Trends

Chapter 26 TECHNOLOGY & THE FUNERAL INDUSTRY

Source: https://rockresearch.com/top-10-views-on-technology/

Author's Note: This chapter is not intended to be a complete and detailed analysis of the many ways that technology can both benefit and be used in the Death Care industry, or more specifically in the role of a Funeral Director. It is intended to show the importance of understanding how technology interacts with this profession, as well as provide some suggestions as to how it can be used. A more detailed analysis is outside of the scope of this book. Additionally, technology changes rapidly and is constantly evolving. As a result, written text can quickly become out of date.

Funeral Service Technology in the 21st Century
By: Candice Giles

"In a world of change, the learners shall inherit the earth, while the learned shall find themselves perfectly suited for a world that no longer exists." Eric Hoffer

"If you want something new, you have to stop doing something old." Peter Drucker

We live in an electronic and technology-saturated society. Smart phones and social media are fully integrated into almost every part of daily life for most people, including people of older generations down to young children. People are used to getting the latest iPhone, android, tablet, smart watch, or hi-def, smart TV. Many homes now have at least one smart device, such as an Amazon Echo or Google Home, that can be interacted with and that can control everything from the thermostat to the lights. Technology use has been increasing across the generations. Millennials, or "Gen Y," are dependent upon technology, but in a recent survey of "Gen Z," young adults and teens ranked the importance or necessity of technology on the same level as air and water (Elmore, 2019). This generation is completely reliant on technology in their daily lives. The newest generation, Gen Alpha, will be even more immersed in technology.

Technology is continually evolving and as a result most industries have had to adapt and evolve as well. The funeral profession is also changing rapidly, as are attitudes around death and dying (Billingham, 2016a). But, is the funeral industry adapting to the modern use of technology? Should funeral directors utilize technology to provide better customer service, especially considering the technology-driven age we live in? The answer is a resounding **YES**. In fact, funeral directors should begin utilizing the ever-evolving technologies available or they risk becoming irrelevant. Nick McCourt (2019) asserts that the most important facet in the death care industry is PEOPLE. He suggests that the correct question funeral directors should be asking themselves is not "should" but, "***How*** can technology be used to improve the ability to care for people before, during, and after the funeral?" The use of technology in the funeral industry is not only important to stay relevant, but it also can result in better and more personalized service for families as they move through the death process.

Megan Kelly (2018a) identifies several ways technology can impact a funeral business, including efficiency and productivity, marketing and merchandising, revenue, personalization, and family experience. McCourt (2019) suggests several ways the funeral industry that can be directly improved through technology use, including speed and efficiency as a business; creating a warm and friendly atmosphere; and focusing on the family by using technology to provide them with what they need before, during, and after they reach out to your funeral home.

These suggestions can be distilled into 4 specific areas of the funeral industry that can be improved through the integration of technology.

1. Running a funeral home business/Customer Service
2. Marketing/Advertising
3. The handling of the deceased/remains
4. The use of technology in planning before, during, and after the funeral/memorial process.

Using Technology to Run a Funeral Home Business

Technology and the latest innovations can help in the running of a funeral home business, as well as improve customer service and interactions with client families. Running a business requires a lot of background work to occur before client interaction even takes place. Disorganization in the running of the business can negatively affect the business, customer service, and the client directly. It is important to consider what problems and issues technology can help with.

The use of single-entry data systems is one specific way that technology has improved the dynamics of running a funeral business. Brandon Meawasige (2017) explains that mountains of paperwork and unorganized records can cause issues, but the implementation of single-entry data systems can allow funeral directors to stop wasting time on paperwork and spend more of it on helping families. There are programs, software, and even businesses that help in the transition from the paper to the computer world.

According to Meghan Kelly (2018a), a funeral home business can make improvements in efficiency and productivity, merchandising, and revenue by embracing technology in the daily running of the funeral home business. She asserts that technology can be one of a firm's greatest resources because it can streamline processes and operations, never needs a day off, reduces paperwork and paperwork errors, and improves time management of busy schedules. All of these factors contribute to an improvement in efficiency and productivity allowing staff to focus on the families. Technology allows more products and services to be showcased without having to have them physically onsite – a zero cost product expansion. Families can view goods and services from anywhere through apps and the funeral home's website. This technology-enabled expansion of options, and how the options are accessed, can lead to growth in revenue. Ibid.

Peter Billingham (2016) outlines a process that can help grow a funeral home business digitally allowing it to last long into the next generation. This process begins with having a desire to innovate. He defines "innovation" as "something original and more effective and, as a consequence, new, that breaks into the market or society." A desire to innovate enables the owner to get past the attitude of "we have always done it this way" and truly begin growing their business. Billingham (2016) argues that a customer-focused approach is absolutely vital to this process. A customer focused approach means thinking of your customer and their needs, not your business and what you offer. Ask what the customer needs, what questions the customer would ask, and seek to answer those questions first.

Billingham's steps can help build a successful and growing digital business:

1. **Allocate Resources** – Going from "the way things have always been" to a modern, technology-assisted business requires not only a shift in attitude, but a flexible and constantly evolving approach. Allocating resources is necessary to adapt technology into customer service, organization of the business, marketing and advertising, in client interactions, and the memorialization process. To be successful, a funeral home owner must be willing to use the staff, time, and finances needed (Billingham, 2016)

2. **Develop a customer-focused website** – The priority of the website is to clearly communicate critical information about your funeral business to a searching audience as quickly and easily as possible. The website should be designed from the perspective of your client and should be clean, functional, and responsive. It should include links to customer reviews, blog posts, and social media profiles. It should also include clear, easy ways to communicate with your funeral home, including phone number, email, Skype/facetime options, text messaging, and online forms (Billingham, 2016a).

3. **Digitize your customer experience** – Billingham (2016b) believes that funeral home businesses must create interactive and memorable digital experiences for their customers, primarily to communicate in every way possible. A website that is easily read on a mobile phone is a must. Giving the customer's ability to instant message or text the funeral home is also an easy and excellent way to reach and engage them. A few more ways he suggests using digital technology to create excellent customer experiences are:

   - An email subscriber list.
   - Downloadable resources and info sheets that provide resources surround death, dying, and the funeral process.
   - The use of social media for obituaries and funeral notices.
   - Online memorials.
   - Using digital technology to accept all forms of payment (PayPal, iPay, Venmo, etc.).

4. **Create customer-focused platforms**. Billingham (2016c) defines a "customer-focused platform" as "any online service that allows you to communicate with your past, existing, or potential customers" (p.2). It is key to have a consistent and clear voice online that builds an awareness and trust of your funeral home. The 4 main platforms that can build your digital/online presence include:

   A. **Email Newsletters** – Create an email list of clients and send them updates, relevant articles, or even a quarterly newsletter. The benefits are that:

      - It keeps your business in their minds.
      - It demonstrates that you are focusing on their needs.
      - It helps you build and maintain an ongoing relationship with clients.

   B. **LinkedIn** – LinkedIn is a social network that enables you to connect with other professionals in your area (both geographically and in your area of expertise). Having a strong LinkedIn profile gives you credibility, strengthens your reputation online, raises your online profile, and build awareness of you and your business.

C. **Facebook** – Facebook and other social media sites are becoming a popular way to memorialize a deceased person online. Many people leave a deceased person's profile/account active and continue to post on it for years after the funeral. Having a Facebook page for your business can enable you to build connections with customers and create awareness of your business. Posting images with encouraging quotes or articles on loss is a good use of this platform.

D. **Twitter** – Twitter is a "microblogging and social networking site that users can send and receive up to 280 characters posts on" (Wikipedia, 2019). Billingham (2016c) suggests several benefits to creating a Twitter account for your business:

- It can raise awareness of your business.
- It can make connections with other businesses.
- It can establish your businesses name in the community.
- It can showcase your business online.

5. **Create content**. According to Billingham (2016d), the primary reason for creating digital content is that it increases the chance of your business being able to provide the solution people need. Digital content can be pictures, images, written text, audio, or videos. It is what you choose to share on your website, social media accounts, and any other online platform you have set up for your funeral home business. Some types of content include:

   - Blog – A blog is a regularly updated website that has information or articles written in an informal or conversational style. For more information on Blogging, see *Blogging 101: What to Write, How Much and How Often* by Welton Hong, at the end of this Chapter.

   - Quote Images – Photographs with uplifting/relevant quotes posted on social media platforms.

   - Infographics – Charts or diagrams that communicate information customers need to know.

   - Podcasting – Digital recordings or broadcasts that cover relevant topics, answer questions, or even involve interviews of people in the industry. Podcast are available to download or stream on a device like a phone, computer, tablet, or even Amazon Echo/Google Home devices.

   - Vlogging – A video post that can result in a deeper connection with the audience. Vlogs can be posted on the businesses Blog, Social Media accounts, or the Funeral Home's YouTube Channel.

6. **Engage with consumers**. Online there is an unending supply of people and business vying for attention through blogs, podcasts, YouTube videos, vlogs, and social media accounts. While potential consumers are using these digital platforms, it is incredibly important to distinguish yourself among the noise. Billingham (2016e) points out that there is a lot of shouting, attention-grabbing, and "look at me" type behavior on these platforms, but little **dialogue**. He argues that the best way to distinguish yourself and your business and make a lasting positive impression, is to engage with people and seek out their impressions and conversation. Comment on other people's posts specifically and kindly. Share your specific thoughts, rather than generic statements or likes, and do so in a positive manner. Reaching out to others can leave traces of you/your business across the internet and leaves positive impressions on the recipients of your comments.

Customer Service

Customer service is another aspect of running a business in which technology can be fully integrated and useful. One of the most important aspects of excellent customer service is communication with clients. The use of various technologies, such as email, websites, mobile apps, blogs, and social media, facilitates faster and better communication with potential clients, allows clients to do more from their own home, and allows for better, more efficient coordination among family members. Technology can also improve communication among employees within the funeral business and collaborative partners in other business that you need to interact with in the funeral process (Kelly, 2016a).

Having an active blog for your funeral home business is a useful, creative, and informative way to improve communication with your clients, improve brand recognition, and improve positive image of your funeral business in the community. Allowing clients to be able to connect with you through email or instant message directly from your website creates easier communication and a feeling of easy access.

Marketing/Advertising

The marketing and advertising methods used by a funeral home business must integrate the newest forms of technology available. Brandon Meawasige (2017) asserts that it is necessary to engage your audience where they spend their time. People of all ages are using the internet and social media, but there are now more millennials than baby boomers in the U.S. This means millennials are increasingly going to be the potential client audience for funeral homes as they start to plan funerals and to make arrangements for their grandparents and parents. As a result, it is vital to use marketing and advertising methods that use social media, forums, YouTube, blogs, mobile apps, and many other online platforms to engage clients. The use of social media and search engines allow funeral homes to reach a much wider market than just their immediate area.

Peter Billingham (2016) contrasts the idea of an “analogue” vs a “digital” mindset in funeral business advertising. If you think: Local newspaper ads, posters in hospitals, the use of local business directories, or pens with your funeral logo on them, then you are operating in “analogue mode” as a business. This is a traditional, pre-internet way of operating a business and Billingham suggests that to continue to operate this way is akin to signing a commitment to “go out of business in 5 years.” A funeral business must ask itself, “Did we do it this way before the internet?” If the answer is yes, then it is time to change to a “digital mindset.” A digital mindset requires the funeral business/director to view all business activities, especially marketing and advertising, through a digital viewpoint that includes social media, Search Engine Optimization, Google AdWords, YouTube, Podcasts, and any other form of online customer engagement.

Society has evolved in many ways in the past several decades that had a direct impact on advertising. When people have questions, they look to Google for the answer. Social media has replaced face -to-face relationships. People are able to record and fast-forward TV and utilize streaming services instead of watching live TV. Most people listen to music through platforms, such as Spotify, Pandora, Apple Music, or Sirius XM in the car. This results in limited exposure to TV and radio commercials. Because of this, social media is now the most effective place to advertise. Kelly (2018) suggests a few importance pieces to successful marketing and advertising, including:

1) Having a great website, which is what customers will find from their Google searches.
2) Integrating social media with the website.
3) Utilizing search engine optimization and/or paid click ads via Google or Facebook.
4) Work on increasing, monitoring, and improving your business’s online reviews. These reviews can be the determining factor in whether a client pursues your funeral home business for both at-need and pre-need.

The Handling of Deceased/Remains

Technology continues to evolve and adapt in how human remains are handled and disposed of. The push toward new technology in this area is partially a result of the movement toward more environmentally friendly, climate-friendly options in the death process. "Tech Changes in the Face of Death," a recent podcast on *Science Friday* (2018), covered some of the newest technologies being developed, including:

- **Alkaline hydrolysis** – Both chemical and biological hydrolysis in which either a chemical or microorganism is used along with water and pressure to break down human remains, instead of the traditional heat used in cremation. **For more information on this, see Chapter 18 Cremation**.

- **Promession** – A system that breaks down human remains using nitrogen and liquid to freeze-dry them. **For more information on this topic, see Chapter 28 Future Trends.**

- **Green Burial** – This is a movement in which people are looking to limit their impact on the environment. There are many options available from burial without embalming, mushroom suits, biodegradable caskets and urns, or using remains to make compost. **For more information on this, see Chapter 27 Green Burial & Chapter 28 Future Trends.**

We will continue to see interesting and creative technologies develop in this area. As a result, the funeral director should be aware of the options, creative in meeting the family where they are at, and able to help them with alternative ways to dispose of their loved one's remains.

The Use of Technology Before, During, and After the Funeral/Memorialization Process

There are many ways that technology can be used before, during, and after the memorization process. The use of computers and online catalogs in planning a funeral can result in a funeral home being able to offer a much wider range of products for clients to view. As an added benefit this results in a more personalized approach for clients. Technology allows for more of the arrangement process to be done online. Clients who live out of town or state can work with a local funeral home to plan a loved one's funeral online. Many funeral homes offer the option to plan and arrange services completely online without ever visiting the funeral home (Marsden, 2012).

The funeral/memorial service itself can be improved with the use of technology. Guests can visit and sign online memorials, obituaries, and guest books. Facebook pages can be turned into life memorial pages for the deceased where people can continue to post and share for years. QR codes can be added to gravestones that can share the deceased's story. Tribute videos can be created and shared online. The funeral can be webcasted/live streamed. This allows family members and friend who live far away to participate in the memorial and grief process. Offering this option is not only good for client families, but it can also spread the name recognition of your funeral home far beyond your town or region.

The ultimate goal of a funeral director is to help families as they move through an immensely difficult time in their life. The newest technologies allow for families to move through the death process in a more intimate, personalized way. It allows for the process to be just a tiny bit easier. Families can create a memorialization process that is unique to the person they lost. In the end, this is the definition a "customer-focused approach."

Digital Innovation Key Areas to Focus On: Technology Solutions Enable Exceptional Customer Service

Excerpts From: D. Ugan (2017)

So, what does your website say about your funeral home? Is it outdated and stodgy? Does it look the same as every other funeral home website, or is it high-tech, innovative, and fresh?

Traditional websites need to be far more than online brochures. They should offer interactive options, such as video testimonials from satisfied customers or explanations of your funeral home's offerings. All websites should be responsive. This simply means no matter what device a person is viewing your website on, whether the standard desktop, a tablet, or a mobile device, the screen changes to fit the format of the device the person is using. This is an important feature as most first encounters with a website occur with a "smart" device.

Websites should also have links between the funeral home website and Facebook page. When a Facebook page links to the website, it provides the customer with more detailed information about your business and drives search engine optimization, which is one small way to help boost your ranking on Google and other search engines. In addition, by posting a link on your website to other social media outlets, you allow your customers to interact more personally with funeral home staff. All of this draws the customer in and personalizes their experience with your funeral home.

Social media is a powerful way to connect with families, to engage with them emotionally, and to allow real-time conversations to occur. When used correctly, it can be one of the most powerful tools in your tool belt.

For social media to be effective, keep a few things in mind:

- **Social media isn't just about obituaries**. While posting obituaries may be the norm on funeral home Facebook pages, make sure you are engaging families by providing more information such as the upcoming Mother's Day memorial service, the community picnic, or helpful ways to heal after the loss of a loved one. Take the opportunity to let the public get to know you and your staff on a more personal level, to see you as individuals. Also take the opportunity to show off your home's unique features or offerings.

- **Provoke interactions with your families**. Provide ways to interact with your families by asking questions like, "What are your favorite childhood memories?" or "What is a favorite recipe that has been passed down to you?" Funeral homes aren't simply a service to bury the dead, they also exist to help those still living celebrate life and carry on. This promotes a more personal connection between you and your target consumer.

- **Respond to comments and respond promptly**. When someone takes time to post a question or comment on your wall, that means that they want to interact with you personally. Make sure you take time to respond to all comments in a timely manner (within minutes to hours, and no longer than 24 hours if possible). This is simply customer service 101.

- **Don't run from controversy**. If you are on social media, you will get negative comments. It is going to happen. But don't run from negativity. Instead, embrace it and address the problem in a way that is friendly and provides a positive resolution. When families see you are willing to resolve problems, it makes your funeral home more authentic and trustworthy. These negative comments can play in your favor. If the person is unreasonable, and as long as it is not a Facebook review of your business, you have the opportunity to delete comments; however, the first response should always be to resolve, not to delete.

Digitizing the Arrangement Process Allows for More Flexibility for Families.

The arrangement process by itself is the foundation of the funeral service and where we spend the majority of our time with families. Traditional paper contracts still work, but why would we use them when we can use an online system to purchase a car or house with minimal interaction? Digitizing the arrangement process benefits everyone by making the arrangement more fluid and by minimizing entry errors. It also allows you to present more options, and it enables the purchaser to commit at a later date and not feel pressured in a vulnerable moment. Digitizing the process is just one more way we can provide superior customer service to families and ensure we gain their trust for the future.

Blogging 101: What to Write, How Much, and How Often

By: Welton Hong (2018)

You should add a blog to your website because:

- A lot of great, interesting content will work perfectly for a funeral home blog.
- You can outsource the writing of the blog if that works better for you.
- You can do the above very affordably, and with great return on investment.
- You can come up with enough content to publish several times a week.
- This is a spectacular way to improve your website SEO, attract and convert visitors, and bolster your reputation both online and locally.

What to Write About

This seems like the trickiest aspect of funeral home blogging, but really, it's not too complicated. The key is to remember that your subject matter doesn't merely have to cover burials, cremations, and related topics. It can also cover a wide spectrum of generally associated subjects.

Some Ideas:

- ***Funeral/Visitation Etiquette***: Instead of one article, this could be a series of posts touching upon aspects of etiquette in detail (what to wear, how to address the family, understanding religious and cultural customs, silencing and putting away your phones, etc.).

- ***Grief Support***: You might have a page of links to resources, but this is another opportunity to provide grief education and support. If you have a relationship with local grief program/support groups, do a post on each. You can even have a local expert do a guest post for you, either paid or for exposure.

- ***Preplanning Services:*** There are easily dozens of considerations for why and how individuals might contract for pre-need services, and each one can be its own post. Don't use this area (or any of the posts) to directly pitch your services. Simply make the posts educational to convey trust, and in time, turn into paid clientele.

- ***Community Service/Involvement:*** If your funeral home does community service, anything from charity events to sponsoring recreational sports teams, this is a perfect place to highlight that. These life-affirming, entirely positive posts also help add diversity to the blog's subject matter.

- ***Death Benefits for Veterans:*** You can get several posts on this subject, which is particularly fruitful if you live in an area with a high aging Veteran population, such as the Colorado Springs or Virginia Beach areas.

- ***Hospice/End-of-Life Care:*** This is another subject with a lot of potential content. A good freelance writer can shape the information in a way that's informational and beneficial without getting too gloomy.
- ***Estate Planning***
- ***Probate Issues***
- ***Power of Attorney***

How Often/How Many Words to Post

You want a post to be long enough to be valuable, so try for close to 400 words. And because blogs need to be updated regularly, post at least twice a week – three times is better, but if you can only reasonable post two, do that. It's much better to have 12 posts a month of 450 words each than five posts a month with 900 words each. And whatever you do, remember that quality is imperative. You need to be as detail-oriented in your posts as you are in your normal day-to-day duties because your blog will reflect how you do business. You should integrate high-performing key words into your post, but always make it sound natural.

Additional Tips for Blog posts

- **Write a Catchy Headline and First Sentence** – Create a headline and first sentence that immediately draws the reader in and makes them want to know more.
- **Open Strong** – Entice your readers with the opener. Research shows that people only read the first few lines of an article before deciding whether or not to keep reading.
- **Make it Easy on the Eyes** – Split up your points by breaking up long paragraphs and using headers when appropriate to separate content into different sections. Use bullet points.
- **Use Images** – The web is a highly visual medium so use relevant images to help tell your story and break up content.
- **Make It Conversational** – Blogging is different from other types of writing, such as essays or reports. Blogging is more social and about community, so it should really feel like a conversation. Avoid technical language, jargon, and industry acronyms.
- **Call to Action** – Every blog article should end with a clear and actionable call-to-action, such as an invitation to comment on your information. Readers are less likely to act on their own initiative, so if you want people to comment or subscribe, you need to invite them to do it.

Why Are You Doing This Again?

I realize that adding a blog to your website might seem like a big investment. Indeed, it will require some distribution of resources, either time or money (or both). But it's worth it. A blog is a powerful tool.

NOTES

Chapter 27

GREEN BURIAL

<u>Green Burial</u> – *Green, or natural burial is a way of caring for the dead with minimal environmental impact that aids in the conservation of natural resources, reduction of carbon emissions, protection of worker health, and the restoration and/or preservation of habitat. Green burial necessitates the use of non-toxic and biodegradable materials, such as caskets, shrouds, and urns (*Green Burial Council, n.d.*).*

Many families are not necessarily looking to write off all traditional options; they simply want to add an original and green aspect to their funeral (Rempen, 2018).

The funeral profession has been mixed in its acceptance of the Green Burial Movement. Although not fully embracing the idea, most funeral homes accept it for what it is – Another change to deal with. Organic foods, hybrid or electric cars, and recycling trash are all part of the green movement. As death care professionals, it is more important than ever to be able to offer consumers green and environmentally friendly options for their funeral arrangements. The growth in demand for green funeral alternatives is only a threat to your traditional business if you choose to ignore it (Ibid).

A green burial is generally considered to be the interment of a body into the soil in a manner that does not inhibit decomposition but allows the remains to decompose naturally. The body is not prepared with chemical preservatives or disinfectants, such as embalming fluid. It may be interred in a biodegradable coffin, casket, or shroud. A natural coffin is made from materials that are readily biodegradable, such as cardboard and wicker. A simple cotton shroud is another option.

A burial vault or outer burial container that would prevent the body's contact with soil is not used. The grave should be shallow enough to allow microbial activity similar to that found in composting. Natural burials can take place both on private land (subject to regulations) and in any cemetery that will dispense with the normal requirement for the use of a vault.

Environmental burial grounds employ a variety of methods of memorialization. Headstones, tributes, and other common markers may be allowed or, in some cases, prohibited, according to local custom. Trees, shrubs, and flowers planted on or near the grave can provide a living memorial. Irrigation, pesticides, herbicides, and synthetic fertilizers may be significantly reduced or eliminated altogether in favor of non-toxic and less intensive plant management.

History

There is an old saying, "everything old is new again." This pertains to green burials. Historically, people were buried in wood coffins or shrouds for hundreds of years. Embalming, steel caskets, and burial vaults did not become customary until the 20th century.

What type of consumer is looking for a green funeral or burial?

According to Martin-Bartsche (2015), there are several types of consumers that see the appeal of natural burial.

- The obvious one is an individual that spent their life living green. They valued actions such as driving a hybrid vehicle, recycling, composting, and/or living a healthy, often outdoor, lifestyle.
- There are consumers that like the simplicity of green burial. These consumers do not see the value in embalming, vaults, and the formality of traditional funerals.
- There are also those that are concerned about their final impact on the environment. They want to give back to the earth in the same way that the earth has given to them during their life. These individuals want their bodies returned to the earth. Many feel as though they took from the earth all their lives – in the form of food, water, shelter – and when they die, they want to return to the earth. It is the ultimate act of recycling. Simplicity and giving back to the earth are key motives for these natural burial clients.

Environmental Impacts

Alex Janin (2016) reports, citing *Scientific American* statistics, that 30 million board feet of casket wood is used annually for burials in the U.S. alone. In addition, each year the U.S. uses 800,000 gallons of embalming fluid, which is traditionally used to preserve a body rather than allow it to decay. Embalming fluid is a toxic fluid that contains a known carcinogen – formaldehyde – which can leach into the soil following burial. Unfortunately, cremations are not much better, emitting 246,240 tons of carbon dioxide into the atmosphere per year in the U.S.

Green Burial and Traditional Funeral Industry

The funeral industry can be slow to adopt new ideas. Signs of discontent are everywhere. If families were happy with modern death care, there would not be new developments, like human composting or pods that contain the body and allow trees to grow out of them. The industry needs to embrace greener options that can work within the current funeral framework.

Some examples of greener options that could be offered are:

- A wicker casket that can be buried in a traditional cemetery, but without a vault.
- Biodegradable and sustainably produced urns for containing cremated remains.
- The option of a live tree with every urn purchase.

It is important to acknowledge the shift in consumer demand toward more green, eco-friendly options, but this does not mean you need to change your entire business into a green one. Without a doubt, the traditional funeral industry is still strong. Families that want a more permanent mahogany casket and full traditional ceremony are still there. The customer is more educated than ever, and they have demands that need to be met. You can position yourself strategically to capture both sets of customers. Position your business to address the needs of green funeral customers, while still providing the excellent traditional funeral services that you have done in the past. Instead of seeing the green movement as a threat, embrace the change and focus on the new opportunities that it brings to your business (Rempen, 2018).

The latest green burial option as of 2020 is human composting, AKA "natural organic reduction." It has been described as an effective and safe alternative to burial and cremation. The body is buried unembalmed and treated with natural substances to speed up decomposition, which can take a few months. The result is that the body is turned to 1 cubic yard of compost/soil, which can be given to the family of the deceased or used to "nourish surrounding land" (Solly, 2019).

NOTES

Chapter 28 FUTURE TRENDS

Source: https://www.foodservicedirector.com/operations/6-trends-shaping-future-foodservice

FUNERAL HOME OF THE FUTURE

Like most other businesses, funeral service is evolving to meet the changing demands of the future. The following is a preview what future trends are emerging.

Move to More Cremation

There has been a continuing and steady increase in the cremation rate. One positive aspect in the cremation drama is that more families are selecting some type of service with cremation.

Approximate Percent (%) of Cremation

	2005	2010	2015	2017	2020	2030
Cremation %	32.3	40.4	51	53	56	71.1
Burial %	61.4	53.3	45.4	42.3	38	23.2

With more funeral homes adding cremation units there will be a continuous and possible increase in attendance at crematory operation certification classes.

Funeral Services

One- or two-day visitation will decrease to one or two hours before the funeral. There will also be an increased number of people requesting no service at all at the funeral home. Instead they will select a memorial service at the church or other facility. There has been and will continue to be an increase in the use of new terminology. Instead of "memorial service" or "visitation," the term "gathering" is growing in popularity. The use of the terms "life celebration" or "remembrance service" are replacing "funerals."

Family Business Losing the Family

According to Phanuef (2016), funeral homes have historically been family businesses, passing down practices and business models from generation to generation. Yet with the wealth of opportunity and variety available to the next generation, we will see fewer family funeral homes.

Gender Issues

Over 67% of students in funeral service programs are female. Female entrants into the profession have steadily increased over the last 20 years. This is predicted to continue in the future.

Casket Use

Due to increased cremation, there has been a decrease in the purchase of traditional caskets and an increase in the use of ceremonial (rental) caskets or alternative cremation containers. Some experts recommend that funeral homes eliminate casket display rooms and instead show caskets on a computer or through catalogs because traditional caskets are less important in funerals.

Cemeteries

Marsden (2014) points out that the future of the cemetery business is tied to funeral service. Cemeteries have also seen a decrease in the bottom line. This changing dynamic has resulted in the sale of fewer graves and outside containers. Cemeteries must change their business plan, marketing, and operations.

A nice story is shared in the industry of a local crematorium in Brazil that is also a public park. People were picnicking, running around a track, flying kites, and just hanging out in the middle of a park filled with little ash mounds. It is truly a place where the living and the dead hang out together. Everyone there seems comfortable, even though there are clearly hundreds of cremated remains everywhere you look. Ibid.

Competition Fuels Industry Change

A funeral home's competitors are not just local funeral homes. Recently the funeral industry has seen an emergence of **"alternative funeral service providers."** These organizations market themselves as a lower cost alternative to traditional funeral homes. They typically offer the services of funeral directors but may specialize in certain services or offer a packaged, **simplified**, or **"no frills"** approach. For example, they may specialize in cremation or offer only graveside services. To control costs, many of these organizations do not own funeral homes. Instead they will rent facilities on an hourly or daily basis as needed.

Green Burial will continue to increase.

Human Composting

In 2019 some states began allowing human composting as a form of funeral disposition. This option is projected to increase in use.

Consolidation

Most businesses in the death care industry continue to be family-owned or small businesses. Over 82% of the roughly 19,000 funeral homes in the country are privately owned. Service Corporation International (SCI) is a publicly traded company based in Houston, Texas. SCI controls nearly all of the 17% of the funeral home industry that is not held by small companies or families. It is estimated consolidation will continue in the future. Consolidators are less interested in small funeral homes that do fewer than 100 funerals a year, however.

Human Resources Management

Retaining and replenishing a high-quality work force remains one of the greatest challenges that funeral home owners encounter. It is estimated that there will be an employee crisis soon. Fewer people enter the profession and some new employees leave once exposed to the reality of the profession. Many of the millennial generation who are replacing the departing/retiring employees will not be as tolerant of some of the challenges, including pay, working hours, schedules, and the need to be "on call."

Regulatory Issues

Review of the FTC's Funeral Rule – The Funeral Consumers Alliance grabbed headlines last year by asking the Federal Trade Commission to require funeral homes to post their prices online. It's unknown whether the FTC will take this request seriously.

Required burial or cremation of fetal remains – Another widely publicized trend that continued last year was the passage of state laws requiring aborted fetal tissue to be buried or cremated. In 2016, 28 states introduced legislation related to disposal of fetal remains. Nine states ratified this legislation, while four states' requirements are on hold pending lawsuits challenging them. In May 2019, the Supreme Court upheld the law requiring the burial or cremation of aborted fetal remains (Williams, 2019).

OSHA fines increased 70% – For the first time in 25 years, OSHA raised its maximum citation amounts for violations to as much as $120,000 each. The agency plans to impose annual increases moving forward.

The future of formaldehyde – A new law gave the EPA authority to ban formaldehyde as a toxic substance. It hasn't announced plans to do so, but growing evidence of its cancer-causing properties suggests that the agency is moving in that direction.

OSHA

The Occupational Safety and Health Agency has been and will continue to be active in the 21st century. Regulations that affect funeral homes include (OSHA Regulations, 2019):

- The Right to Know Law
- Blood borne Pathogens
- Personal Protective Equipment
- Respiratory Protection
- Formaldehyde and Glutaraldehyde
- Eye Face Wash
- Medical First Aid
- Disposal of Hazardous Waste

Online arrangements moved toward the mainstream

A growing number of people respond favorably to the idea of making funeral arrangements, or at least a portion of them, without speaking to a human being. The National Cremation Society-Denver launched a system in which families can opt to make cremation arrangements and pay online. Other companies are developing online systems for traditional funerals. Many funeral homes are now collecting certain information/data from families online.

Financial Restructuring

The increase in cremation has generally caused a decrease in the bottom line of most funeral homes. If this decrease in income continues, funeral directors who have built their business plan on a more historic financial structure will need to develop a new business plan more reflective of the financial reality.

Technology

As in all businesses, funeral homes will depend more and more on technology to improve business operations, arrangements, visitations and the funeral. Keeping up with advancements in websites, record keeping software, streaming of funeral services, improved tribute video options, digital sign boards, and register books will all be necessary to be successful in the 21st century. **For additional information, see Chapter 26: Technology & The Funeral Industry.**

Jacob Terranova (2016) thinks that avatars will become increasingly important in the future of internet memorialization. People will use avatars and holograms to deliver powerful and perhaps personal messages. Some funeral homes may begin using augmented reality to make the cemetery interactive, and provide pop-up videos, favorite playlists, a pop-up collage of favorite pictures, etc. that could be easily accessed via smartphone through image recognition software at the grave or in the funeral home itself. There will be many exciting technologies in the field of memorialization in the future, including:

- **Augmented Reality:** You have probably heard about the Pokémon Go craze. The technology behind it, augmented reality, might have benefits when it comes to remembering the deceased. Augmented reality blends the real world with the virtual world. Google Glass, for example, is a pair of glasses that allows the user to see things like videos, maps, and pictures, while simultaneously looking at their real-world surroundings. How would this work for remembering a loved one? Imagine your relatives are going to visit your memorial plot (it could be a traditional headstone, a special place in a park, or even GPS coordinates to your favorite place). At the memorial plot, with the use of a smartphone, glasses, or other technology, videos, pictures, messages, and stories from yourself or other family members would appear via augmented reality. Ibid.

- **Artificial Intelligence:** Things are starting to sound like science fiction, right? There are companies that are trying to preserve the dead through artificial intelligence, or AI. The idea is to store data of our habits, things like how we interact with people, our thought processes, our likes and dislikes, and our memories – and then use it to create a map of our personality. Ibid.

- **Holographic Images:** Holographic images at funerals is a concept currently being developed. If a person chooses a holographic eulogy, Minardo, the idea creator, will dispatch a camera crew to the home to film several hours of footage. This footage is edited down to a six-minute presentation that's then shared with the funeral home. While six minutes sounds short for a meaningful summering up of a person's life, Minardo says his experience indicates it's a good length. Ibid.

  "If you do this hologram – which is going to be as crisp and alive as you are – you want to do it when you are younger," Minardo says. "Who wants to be remembered the way you look when hospice has you? You want people to remember you 15 to 20 years younger." If the recordings catch on it could also make consumers more interested in pre-planning their services. Ibid.

A Picture is Worth a Thousand Words: Digital Presentation Capabilities Are Worth Even More.

Photo presentations during the funeral service have progressed from the bulletin board format to the digital slideshow. A new entry into the market is ShareLife. ShareLife is a multisensory experience that allows families a unique way to celebrate loved ones using sight, scent and sound. The ShareLife experience includes high-definition motion picture and static image backdrops projected on a large screen. Each family's story and preferences are matched with the theme that best commemorates the loved one, including matching sounds as well and ambient scent provided by a scent projector. Family and friends can see the ocean, hear crashing waves, and smell the salty air. ShareLife brings a loved one's memories to life, and there are a dozen themes to choose from. Digital presentation capabilities offer a new way to memorialize loved ones and care for families (Ugan, 2017).

Memorial Societies

These societies position themselves as consumer organizations whose purpose is to disseminate information. However, many have established relationships with service providers enabling them to offer discount funeral services to anyone who pays a membership fee. Use of the term "society" implies that they are not-for-profit, but that may not be the case.

Social Network Memorials

The article, "Virtual Afterlives Explores the Changing Nature of Rituals, Grieving" (2017) published in *Funeral Service Insider*, reports:

> "In many ways social network memorials more accurately reflect lives than do their distant narrative cousins, obituaries. They are repositories of quips, funny moments and sayings, embarrassing and revealing pictures and passages, songs, and passing thoughts. They are not neatly structured, organized or packaged, and so perhaps they more closely resemble lives as they are: Disorganized, without a clear purpose, full of sudden beginnings and ending, and containing no clearly laid-out path."

We will continue to see a rise in the use of social network memorials because of the reasons above and the continual increase in the creation of online memorial sites and social media usage.

Religion

National research indicates that fewer people are describing themselves as religious with less participation in traditional religious services. A popular description given by these people is that "**they are spiritual, not religious.**" This has affected funerals by more people choosing secular rather than religious services.

Pet Memorialization

There will be more pet memorialization as a complimentary business for funeral homes. This involves options such as starting a pet cemetery, crematory, funeral home, or adding these services to an existing funeral home. **For more information, see the Pet Memorials article on page 468.**

Therapy Dogs

In 2019, the funeral setting began to see an increase in the use of therapy dogs. It is projected that this service will continue to grow at a slow pace.

Work-Life Balance

Our profession's history of long unscheduled working hours and insufficient pay must change. Future employees will not stay in a position that does not compensate them in hours and pay in relation to other professionals. This may cause a change in how some funeral homes operate.

DNA Collection

Compiling a family medical history through DNA collection, can help medical professionals (Funeral Service Insider 2015a):

- Diagnose a medical condition.
- Determine whether you may benefit from preventative measures to lower your risk of a specific disease.
- Decide what medical tests to run as well as what medications to give.
- Identify other members of your family who are at risk of developing certain diseases.
- Calculate your risk of passing certain conditions to your children.
- Selective effective therapies.
- Measure mutation rates over generations, which can predict health problems before they happen.
- Trace ancestry thousands of years back.

Personalization/Memorialization

We will see more event planning as part of the arrangements and offering catering as an option. **For more information, see Chapter 9 Personalization and Chapter 10 Memorial Service, Life Celebration & Gatherings.**

3-D Printing

What is 3-D printing? Simply put, a 3-D printer operates similarly to an inkjet printer, which has an ink cartridge that passes over paper laying down ink. With 3-D printers, a cartridge melts plastic, metal, or other substances and lays it down in three dimensions according to a three-dimensional design fed to the printer by a computer (Martin Bartsche, 2014).

3-D printing has the potential to create personalized keepsakes for families, such as a bust of the deceased face or an urn that looks like the deceased.

In 2010, Cremation Solutions started offering Personal Cremation Urns. The company's tagline states, "Celebrate life in a most personal style and create a perfect replica of that special someone." It is available in two sizes. The "full-sized" Personal Urn stands 11 inches tall and holds the cremated remains of an adult, while the "Keepsake- Sized" Personal Urn is 6 inches tall and holds a portion of cremated remains. Using pictures and special facial recognition software, the technology allows for the creation of a three-dimensional urn in the exact likeness of a loved one.

Source: Photo courtesy of Cremation Solutions

Preserving Tattoos

Source: Photo Courtesy of Save My Ink Forever

There are a couple of companies that now offer families a one-of-a-kind memorial keepsake that will create a lifetime of memories in a dignified manner. Through a proprietary process developed over a two-year period, these companies can offer recovery of skin art and produce a unique and artful keepsake for families.

The skin art industry is becoming more mainstream. This trend will likely continue to increase over the years. Tattoos have meaning and 'tell stories." Families today are looking for ways to memorialize and celebrate the life of a loved one. As a memorial keepsake, skin art, which is recovered at the funeral home through instructions and a removal kit and then sent to the company where it takes approximately a couple of months to dry and preserve the tattoo, display it in a sealed shadow box, and send it to the family. The funeral director is paid to do the removal of the tattoo (Cronin, 2016).

Cremation Alternatives

Alkaline Hydrolysis, which some people called liquid cremation, is being used increasingly. Instead of heat and flames to reduce a body, a heated alkaline liquid is used to reduce the body to bone fragments.

Capsula Mundi Project

Source: https://laughingsquid.com/capsula-mundi-eco-friendly-burial-pods-that-plant-bodies-under-trees-in-egg-shaped-capsules/

Capsula mundi are biodegradable pods that resemble an egg. The deceased's body is encapsulated into a fetal position – the same one in which a human is born – and the pod is sealed. Once the burial pod is placed sufficiently deep inside the earth, a seed is placed above it. This will allow the seed to draw nutrients that will slowly keep seeping out of the decomposing pod. The eco-friendly burial pod, which dissolves a lot sooner in the Earth, are made from renewable and biodegradable materials, including starch plastic and seasonal plants, such as potatoes and corn (Desai 2015).

Promession

According to Chris Raymond (2017), a notable recent innovation in the disposition of human remains comes from a Swedish biologist, Susan Wigh-Masak. Promession has some distinct green advantages over other forms of disposition. Promessa (2019) claims that promession can "combine the best from cremation and burial – taking up less space and giving off less pollution."

Raymond (2017) outlines the promession process. A body is frozen with liquid nitrogen, which crystalizes the body's cells. The brittle form that emerges is vibrated, which causes it to disintegrate. The particles are placed into a vacuum and freeze-dried. Then pollutants and metals can be removed from the fragments and recycled. The remaining powder is just 30% of original body weight. It is placed in a biodegradable container and biodegrades rapidly.

There has been much interest in promession, but it is still in a testing phase and is currently unavailable as a form of disposition (Raymond, 2017). But it may develop further in the future.

Death Suit

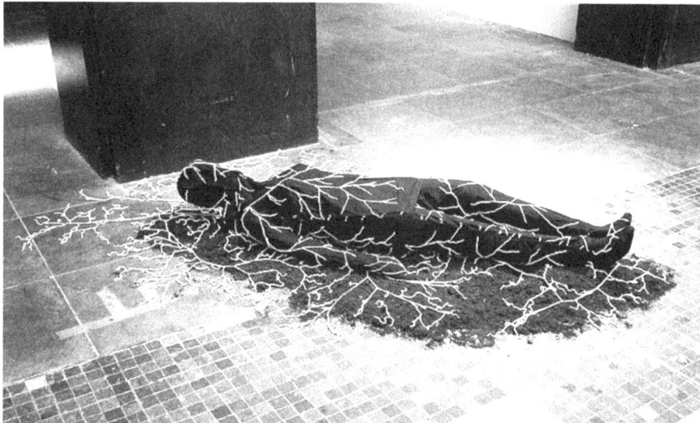

Source: https://www.flickr.com/photos/de_buurman/7216297514

According to Alex Janin (2016), a death suit is **a suit made of mushroom spores which helps decompose bodies sustainably.** The Infinity Burial Suit, a one-piece garment designed to be worn after death, is sewn with mushroom spore-infused thread. The suit is embroidered with a special type of thread infused with infinity mushroom spores. When buried, the mushroom spores act to cleanse the body of many toxins and gently return it to the earth. There are three benefits to the suit:

1. It speeds the return to earth through decomposition.
2. It remediates toxins accumulated over a lifetime.
3. It speeds nutrient delivery back to plants.

The Hollywood actor Luke Perry was buried in a death suit in May of 2019 (Farber, 2019). It was one of his final wishes to be buried in a mushroom death suit and have an eco-friendly burial. Ibid.

Changing Cultures

Funeral homes must adjust to a new generation and, perhaps, a new business model as culture shifts become more apparent, customers become savvier in their end-of-life choices, and religion becomes less of a concern. People will be more inclined to choose the more flexible, cheaper option that better fits faster-paced lifestyles. For many funeral homes, this means a decrease in traditional customers and a shift in perspective. Future funeral directors must be prepared to accommodate all manner of beliefs and practices.

In his article, "Future Trends: Funeral Home of the Future," Jacob Terranova (2016) lists several interesting changes to funeral homes, including:

1. More focus on interior design and architecture

Funeral homes are taking the initiative when it comes to the design and layout of the facility. Funeral directors want families to feel at home. They have fireplaces, big comfortable couches, spacious open rooms with vaulted ceilings, and large windows. Ibid.

2. Multi-event centers

Some funeral directors are thinking outside the box. Why have a funeral home that's just for funerals? Why not incorporate other life events into the mix? Some funeral homes are adopting the practice of hosting different events like birthdays, anniversaries, and even weddings. The idea is to turn the funeral home into a community center for the important milestones of a person's life. Ibid.

3. Wine and dine

Keeping with the one-stop shop concept, funeral homes are installing catering kitchens, banquet halls, reception lounges, and bars. In addition to selling catering packages, some have even gotten licensed to serve and distribute alcohol in their funeral home. They even personalize the catering packages so that a family can enjoy a meal made from recipes of the deceased. Ibid.

4. High-tech, Immersive, and Communal

The funeral home of the future, aided by technology, will provide families with an interactive and immersive ceremony. The integration of massive displays or video walls could be a possibility. These displays are massive and can wrap around more than one wall. Some encompass the whole room. The video walls can display one continuous video or photos and information about the deceased. They could depict a favorite landscape or places the deceased loved to visit. Social tributes posted by family members could show up in real time on the wall. The displays would allow for an interactive and virtual tour of the deceased's life. Ibid.

Source: Terranova (2016)

NOTES

NOTES

Section VIII

SUPPORTIVE READINGS

- Making the Forensic Removal: Assisting with Medical Examiner Transfers
- Watch Out for Bedbugs! Removing Remains from a Home or Long-Term Care Facility
- Dangerous Synthetic Opioids and the First Call
- Changing Our Perspective: Providing Individual Attention to Family Members of Different Generations.
- Narrow Your Focus, Broaden Your Market
- Knowing Who Has Legal Control of the Final Disposition
- What Does the Supreme Court Ruling on Same-Sex Marriage Mean for Death-Care Providers?
- Photographing at a Funeral
- The Pros & Cons of Funeral Webcasting
- The Dual Licensure Debate
- Death Doulas and Funeral Service
- Defining Home Funeral Guides
- Shaking Hands
- Funeral Poverty in the 21st Century
- 8 Reasons to Memorialize with a Monument
- Spring Burials
- How to Fold the Flag
- Organ and Tissue Donation
- Pet Memorials
- Crowd Funding: The Future of Funeral Financing
- Funeral Home Buyer's Guide
- Funeral Insurance Pros, Cons, and Differences
- Servant Leadership

Chapter 29 SUPPORTIVE READINGS

Making the Forensic Removal: Assisting with Medical Examiner Transfers

By: Eric D. Ruggeri (2006)

With all of today's advanced crime solving technology and with everything we have learned about DNA and other forensic sciences in the last 15 or 20 years, one of the most important duties at a crime scene is the safe transportation of the deceased and protection of evidence from a crime scene.

Many funeral homes and mortuaries hold contracts with local medical examiners' or coroners' offices for performing removals of remains from death scenes in addition to their regular funeral service responsibilities. While this service still remains mostly popular with the more rural funeral homes than with urban ones, it is a service performed in some communities that dates back hundreds of years. It may have even started as part of the local funeral home providing the ambulance service for the community.

With all of today's advanced crime solving technology and with everything we have learned about DNA and other forensic sciences in the last 15 or 20 years, one of the most important duties at a crime scene is the safe transportation of the deceased and protection of evidence from a crime scene to the medical examiners' or coroners' facilities for autopsy and further investigation. This is a pretty big responsibility that is sometimes left with the untrained funeral director or their staff assistants when performing a removal for the medical examiner.

One of the most important things we can do when responding to a crime scene is making sure that we do not cause any loss of evidence or the addition of evidence to a potential scene. This is often referred to as cross-contamination. We can curtail this by entering the scene properly attired with shoe covers, hair covers, and our gloves. We also should not smoke, eat, use the bathroom, or use the telephone within a potential crime scene. And when we are done with our personal protective units (PPUs), we do not leave them at the scene. We make sure they are properly disposed of offsite.

It is the investigating law enforcement agency's responsibility to ensure the deceased is transported from the scene correctly. During the removal process, many errors occur when the evidence on the remains is often lost or disturbed between the scene and the morgue. Many of us in the funeral profession have been taught when performing a removal under normal circumstances when the police and medical examiner are generally not involved, such as a house call, we must always turn the body over and transport it on the cot face up. This is done in an attempt to prohibit blood from pooling in the face and hampering the work of the embalmer later during the embalming process and to ensure viewable remains at the funeral.

When doing a forensic removal, the body is always transported in the fashion it was found so that whatever evidence is on and in the body can be properly collected without being destroyed or lost. If the body is found face down on a kitchen floor, it must be transported face down on the removal cot. This can be a difficult decision for funeral directors considering what they have been taught in the past, but when they are assisting in the transportation of remains from a crime scene, they must think and act as an investigator would. Many medical examiners' and coroners' offices have pre-determined policies and procedures that govern how remains are transported to their respective facilities.

Dr. Michael Baden, a board-certified pathologist and former chief medical examiner for New York City, recently discussed in *Evidence Terminology* Magazine where errors just like this had a significant impact in the 1994 O.J. Simpson Case. "When Nicole Simpson's body – which was lying face down – was moved, a lot of very important blood-splatter evidence that was on her back was rubbed off by the time the body made it to the morgue. That happened because, in traditional fashion, the mortuary personnel turned her onto her back when they moved her. And all of that evidence was lost. If evidence had remained intact, they could have probably solved the whole thing very quickly. If it had been O.J. Simpson's blood, that would have been the end of the case. If it had been someone else's blood, that would have been important to pursue. But that evidence never had the chance to be tested."

Once remains are moved at a crime scene or potential crime scene, the signs that indicate how long those remains have been dead are no longer valid because things change during transport. This is where investigators rely on photography and diagramming. The body itself is a crime scene that has to be protected. There might be evidence under the fingernails, there might be DNA, blood, skin, and fibers just to name a few. Each of these things needs to be protected during the transportation process to the morgue. In most suspicious death cases, the hands are often bagged with brown paper bags to protect any evidence on the hands for processing later. The remains also need to be protected from us, those transporting the remains. In the removal process, sometimes we drop our own hair and fibers onto the remains when packaging them for transport. And there are times when trace evidence gets stuck on somebody's uncovered shoe and gets carried away from the scene. We need to be careful where and how we walk.

Selecting what style body bag to use on forensic removals may be dependent upon what type of incident the remains came from. Lightweight body bags, similar to the ones used in hospital morgues, are generally only 7 mil. They are thick and are constructed of a lightweight vinyl material that rips easily in the field, and therefore should be avoided. For death scene calls, it is recommended to use a minimum of 10-12 mil. thickness, higher strength body bag that meets or exceeds OSHA regulation 3130 regarding Universal Precautions. Dual rust resistant zipper pulls and an envelope style zipper opening are also added bonuses in selecting the correct body bag. For decomposition or difficult cases such as water-recovery, a heavier 18 mil. thickness bag with six-to-eight handles should be selected for more comfortable handling during transportation. Selecting a bag that is static-lift tested to a 750-pound capacity by crane or helicopter may be necessary for handling recoveries in rugged terrain. One new item on the market is the forensic body bag with tamper-resistant seals designed to fit body bag zipper pulls to prevent tampering with bag contents. It is important to always carry an assortment of these different body bags in the removal vehicle when responding to forensic removals.

Remember, body bags manufactured with chlorine properties are not recommended for cremation, as they are not environmentally friendly.

Another aspect of this type of removal that may be new to funeral home personnel is the possibility of a high-profile case with news media already on the scene before the funeral director arrives. Remember, it is unprofessional when being summoned by a medical examiner or coroner to advertise the funeral home. Make sure all nameplates in the hearses' windows are removed as well as any cot covers with the name of the funeral home embroidered on them.

In some high-profile deaths, such as a celebrity or dignitary, it may be necessary to temporarily remove the license plates off the vehicle to further alienate the funeral home from being involved with the removal process.

Also, removal personnel should be appropriately attired for the climate and act and drive as professionals. The actions during the removal process could be filed by the local news stations and be broadcasted on the six o'clock news or photographed for the front page of tomorrow's newspaper.

Source: Ruggeri, E.D. (2006, March). Making the Forensic Removal: Assisting with Medical Examiner Transfers. *American Funeral Director*.

Watch Out for Bedbugs! Removing Remains from a Home or Long-Term Care Facility

By: Barb Garrison (2012)

Bedbugs are probably the furthest thing from your mind when removing remains from a private residence or a long-term care center, but you may want to start thinking about what you would do if you encountered the creatures or signs of a bedbug infestation during removal. The last thing you want to do is carry them back to your funeral home or your own home.

There is a plethora of information about bedbugs out there, but one excellent resource is the Central Ohio Bed Bug Task Force's website: http://www.centralohiobedbugs.org. Most of the following information was obtained from this site.

Identification

Bedbugs are small but visible insects. The newly hatched nymph is very pale until it feeds, and then it looks like a tiny droplet of blood. The adult is about the size and shape of an apple seed and dark red to brown in color. It is also as flat as a credit card before feeding. *Interesting fact: Bed bugs can live for a year after consuming a blood meal.*

Signs of an Infestation

The first sign of a bedbug infestation is usually the appearance of bites on the arms, neck, torso, or legs. If you see what appear to be insect bites on the deceased, you may want to consider donning the personal protective equipment recommended below. Clusters of small stains or droplets of dried blood on furniture and bedding may also be found. These stains are the bedbug's fecal droppings. They may be accompanied by shed bedbug skins, because bedbugs shed their outer skin, or molt, as they grow.

How to Avoid Transporting Bedbugs when Making Removals

- Wear disposable shoe covers and tuck your pants into your socks. This may be very difficult to do in the presence of family members, but a few awkward moments could save you a huge headache later. If you don't use shoe covers, designate a pair of shoes specifically for removals, and inspect them before getting into your car or returning to the funeral home. Store your "removal shoes" in a sealed plastic bag until they can be placed in a dryer for 15 minutes.

- If the home is known to be infested with bedbugs, or, if you see evidence of the bugs, don a disposable paper suit (Yeah, I know you're laughing now). If this isn't possible, carry an extra set of clothes with you and change out of your "bedbug clothes" as soon as possible — preferably before getting into your vehicle. Place your clothes in a sealed plastic bag until you can wash them. Wash potentially contaminated clothing in hot, soapy water and dry in a dryer using the highest heat setting. Any clothing or items that cannot be washed or dry-cleaned should be placed in a hot dryer for at least 15 minutes.

- Before making a removal, check with your local health department to see if it keeps a list of homes that it knows are infested with bedbugs. This could help you make an informed decision about whether you should suit up or not.

- Do not sit on sofas, upholstered chairs or beds, and avoid placing any items on upholstered furniture, bedding, or carpeted floors.

- Carry a spray bottle containing 70% solution of isopropyl alcohol. Do a self-check before getting into your vehicle and spray any bedbugs you may find with the solution. Pay particular attention to inside and outside of shoes, lace holes, socks, pant legs, leg area, and around hands and arms.

Remember – Bedbugs have been found in the following establishments:

- Private homes
- Senior housing
- Nursing homes
- Firehouses
- Apartment buildings
- Hotels
- Schools
- Churches
- Movie Theaters
- College Dorms
- Social Service Agency Offices

Let's try to avoid adding funeral homes to the list!!

Source: Garrison, B. (2012, August 26). Watch Out for Bedbugs! Removing Remains from a Home or Long-Term Care Facility? *Ohio Funeral Directors Association*. Retrieved from: http://www.ohio-fda.org/aws/OFDA/pt/sd/news_article/62669/_PARENT/layout_details/true

Dangerous Synthetic Opioids and the First Call
By: William York (2018)

The new emerging threat to first call removal personnel across the country is fentanyl. Fentanyl is a synthetic opioid with a potency 50-100 times stronger than morphine. Due to the high potency and availability, drug users and criminal organizations are increasingly utilizing this dangerous synthetic opioid as an adulterant in heroin and other controlled substances. There is a significant threat to funeral home personnel and first responders who come in contact with fentanyl and fentanyl-related substances through routine activities. Since fentanyl can be ingested orally, inhaled through the nose or mouth, or absorbed through the skin or eyes, any substance suspected to contain fentanyl should be treated with extreme caution. Exposure to a small amount can lead to significant health-related complications, respiratory depression, or death.

Fentanyl-related substances have been identified in powder, pill, capsule, and liquid forms, and on blotter paper. It is possible that illicit fentanyl or fentanyl-related substances could be mixed with other drugs or concealed in innocuous devices, such as nasal spray or eye dropper bottles, in varying amounts and purities, causing unintentional exposure.

With the large number or overdose calls, funeral home personnel should be vigilant when making a removal, transporting, and in the prep room. Trace residues can be found on a decedent's clothing, skin, or personal effects. All overdose-related calls should require a pouch to secure the decedent and personal effects for transport and storage. The minimum PPE — "Personal Protective Equipment" — used on the first call should be nitrile gloves, safety glasses, N95 dust mask, and a disposable paper suit.

Personnel should look for any cyanosis (turning blue or bluish color) of decedents, including the skin or lips, as this could be a sign of fentanyl overdose caused by respiratory arrest. Before proceeding, personnel should examine the scene for any loose powders (no matter how small) and nasal spray bottles, as these could be signs of fentanyl use.

Prep room decontamination should include washing the decedent with a large volume of soap and water, making sure no residues exist on the body. Stretchers should be decontaminated using PPE, soap and water or a disinfectant, and allowed to air dry.

Personal effects should be bagged and handled carefully with gloves, eye protection and dust mask. The bag should note that items have been potentially exposed to fentanyl. Our suggestion when returning such effects back to a family member is to include a documented release reading: "These items may be contaminated with suspected Fentanyl or Opioids." This gives the family member the knowledge of potential exposure.

If an exposure occurs, seek immediate medical attention as fentanyl and fentanyl-related substances can be very fast acting. Contact emergency medical services. Remember, it only takes 2-3 milligrams of fentanyl to induce respiratory depression, arrest, and possibly death. 2-3 milligrams of fentanyl is about the same size as 5-7 individual grains of table salt.

Source: York, W. (2018, April). Dangerous Synthetic Opioids and the First Call. *Funeral Home & Cemetery News.* Retrieved from: http://www.nomispublications.com/NewsPaper/04-2018/

Changing Our Perspective: Providing Individual Attention to Family Members of Different Generations

Excerpts From: Lacy Robbins (2014)

Instead of viewing families as a single unit with a single goal in funeral arrangement, it helps to realize that each person involved in the planning process has his or her own needs, desires, and perspectives on how to best to honor and celebrate the life of their loved one.

In most circumstances, survivors come from different backgrounds and different generations. As such, they have different experiences with their loved one and therefore different expectations in funeral planning. Not only do they have different ideas, but they communicate and process information differently. If our style and approach with each person is the same, we take a great risk in failing to meet expectations and, ultimately, the services we provide with suffer.

Being sensitive to the needs and perspectives of each survivor, individually, can help funeral directors move beyond the ordinary and into the realm of the extraordinary.

Traditionalists

Our first generational survivor group is made up of traditionalists. These are people born before World War II and frequently the spouse of the deceased. Often called the "Greatest Generation," respect is of vital importance to the traditionalist. They have lived long, productive lives and feel they have earned the right to be respected and treated with dignity. One way to accomplish this is to ensure that the traditionalist knows what benefits they stand to receive from investing their time and money in you, your products, and your services.

Consider, for instance, the small actions funeral directors can take to exceed clients' expectations: Extra bookmarks, bottled water during the visitation, additional copies of the tribute DVD at no extra charge, and so on. Your traditionalist client will want to know about these benefits because, at their age, they feel they deserve them. In the context outside of the funeral industry, catch phrases such as "senior discount," "senior days," and "early bird special" appeal to traditionalists because they communicate benefits. Within our industry, words that communicate benefits to traditionalists include: "Value," "security," "quality," and "satisfaction." Always keep in mind: Your word is their bond. Traditionalists will rely heavily on your verbal cues.

When communicating with a traditionalist, always speak clearly, express one idea at a time, and refrain from asking complicated questions. In keeping with the atmosphere of the conference, use slow hand gestures and keep the mood relaxed. Traditionalists will not respond well to a lot of pressure. Instead, they want recommendations from you that have nostalgic and emotional meaning. For example, a photographic montage set to music from their era will bring profound nostalgia and emotional connection for a traditionalist. They enjoy reminiscing about the past, when they were young, in love, starting a family, and feeling good. They like to remember simpler times.

Traditionalists have more life experiences than any other generation, and because of that, they understand the meaning behind their emotions. When they feel an emotional connection to your recommendations, they see value!

Baby Boomers

The next generation among our clientele is the baby boomers born between 1946-1964. This generation couldn't be more different than their parents, the traditionalists. They have active lifestyles and don't think of themselves as "old" in any way. As far as boomers are concerned, 60 is the new 40. Baby boomers are frequently crunched between taking care of aging parents, financially assisting their young adult children, and still working full time. Many are also doing something they never anticipated: Raising their grandchildren.

Baby boomers are consumer savvy and tend to know exactly what they want. They respond well to a funeral director who is friendly and creative, makes the planning process uncomplicated, and does not waste their valuable time. Like traditionalists, your verbal cues are very important. What carries equally are your non-verbal cues. Simply put, baby boomers expect a performance from you. That matters more to them than your age or how many years of experience you have. To elicit that performance, they will press you for details, challenge your recommendations, and ask a lot of questions. Baby boomers are not shy! They know what they want and have high expectations for competence.

In addition to using the right words and body language, one thing you can do that will appeal to baby boomers is package your services – to give them the simplicity and the ease they want when planning a life celebration service. Baby boomers also appreciate themes. Highly individualistic, they will value a funeral tailored to capture the essence of their loved one's life and their own life. A memorable themed funeral represents all aspects of a person's life and is supported by storytelling, ritual, music, pictures, special effects, colors, scents, and tastes. A highly individualized, well-planned, themed funeral will appeal strongly to a baby boomer client.

Finally, boomers tend to be motivated by emotion more than any other generation. Think of ideas and recommendations that will appeal to this emotional side, but always keep it individualized and based on important information the family has shared with you. For instance, if your clients have indicated that their father enjoyed fishing with his grandkids, you might offer ways to honor the legacy in a way that would be meaningful to everyone. When you give a recommendation for your personalization based on experiences the family has had with their loved one, you are motivating them to move forward with that idea.

Gen Xers

Generation X is most often represented at a funeral by the children and, more often, grandchildren of the deceased. Gen X encompasses those born roughly between 1965 and 1981. Generation X is often compared to the so-called "Lost Generation" because they are sandwiched between two much larger and more prominent generations and, thanks to the active, busy lifestyles of their parent or parents, didn't received as much attention growing up. The parallel in the funeral industry is that Generation X is frequently overlooked in the arrangement conference.

Consider that, more often than not, your Generation X clients are not the next of kin, not the informant, and not the ones paying for the funeral service. Their grandparents or parents are typically the ones arranging the service, doing most of the talking, and asking most of the questions.

While Generation X clients may not have a lot of primary involvement in the planning conference, this doesn't mean they aren't paying attention or don't have valuable ideas to add to the discussion. People from this generation tend to be skeptical and sometimes cynical as well, so be sure to use this knowledge to your advantage. Generation X is focused on their immediate family, so try to connect with them on this level by exploring ways in which their children can participate in honoring their loved one or how they might find more time to spend with their adult cousins who are coming from out of town. Grief resources are valuable to Generation X both for themselves and for helping their children cope with what is likely a first experience death. These sorts of things appeal to Generation X because they deal with creating experiences rather than purchasing decisions.

Gen Xers are very independent and full of great ideas. Yet, they often feel that their ideas and desires are overlooked. Tap into this by partnering with them to ensure that their ideas for personalization and participation are executed in a way that will be meaningful and memorable for them.

The extra effort you give in reaching out to Gen Xers will build their confidence and allow you to take a primary role in shaping their overall view of funeral service. Remember, one day in the not-too-distant future, nearly all of the arrangement conferences you conduct will have Gen Xers as the primary decision-making party.

Millennials

Millennials are those born between the early 1980s and 2000. Coming of age in the shadow of the new millennium, they are tech savvy, open-minded, and better educated than previous generations. Older millennials may be present at an arrangement conference, but more often they will be present only in spirit, represented by their parents and grandparents.

In the same way that Millennials in the workplace frequently require a lot of attention, the same is true for Millennials as survivors. Reach out to Millennials by exploring opportunities for them to participate and express their grief in unique ways.

If you do have Millennials at an arrangement conference, be sure to consider their expectations. Chances are, this is their first such conference and likely their first intimate experience with death, so you should be clear with them about what to expect and what their role will be. Ask them questions about their relationship with their loved one and listen to their ideas. Millennials want to feel included and doing so will not only help make the arrangement conference a positive experience for them, but their parents and grandparents will appreciate the effort as well.

Generations Z & Alpha

Generation Z, represents those among your clientele, born in the mid-to-late 1990s to 2010. Generation Alpha are those born in 2010 and are still being born. Many from Generation Z & Alpha are still children and young adults. We know that children grieve differently than adults. Be sensitive to this and encourage parents and grandparents to talk to their kids about death and the purposes of funerals. Have a conversation with your clients about bringing children to the services and emphasize how these services provide the opportunity for everyone to acknowledge the reality of death, honor their loved one's life, and receive emotional support. Children have the same emotional needs as adults and as children age and mature, they will revisit their funeral experiences and begin to find meaning in them.

Teaching younger generations about the traditions and rituals unique to their families, communities, and cultures is crucial in this day and age. Children who are not included in their family's funeral rituals may never understand the importance of taking time to honor loved ones and grieve appropriately. Death is difficult to discuss, and many people feel the need to shield their children from it, but the life lessons that can be taught during this time are invaluable. Ultimately, your clients will have to decide for themselves how involved their children will be in the funeral services, but you should encourage parents to view it as an opportunity for their children to grow and learn.

As with millennials, participation is key for Generation Z. It may be as simple as placing a drawing, note, or memento in the casket. Coach parents on how to prepare their children for the funeral. If parents choose not to bring their children to the services, you must, of course respect the decision. However, even when this happens, there are opportunities for you to advocate on behalf of Generation Z. Give suggestions to the parents for things they can do at home with their children, such as looking through photo albums, telling stories, lighting a candle, or saying a prayer. No one at the arrangement conference knows more about children and grief than you do. You are Generation Z's primary advocate. Help shape their view of the service by providing resources and ideas and taking an active role in their experience at your funeral home.

Every generation is different. Recognizing each person's unique needs, expectations, and ways of communicating can offer a tremendous opportunity to connect with your clients and ensure that everyone feels like that are a valuable part of the planning of the funeral or memorial service.

Understanding each generation as consumers and participants in the funeral experience will enable you to communicate better and, in the end, tailor services that not only capture the essence of the loved one whose life is being celebrated but help everyone feel the emotional connection they seek.

Source: Robbins, L. (2014, April). Changing our Perspective. *The Director.*

Knowing Who Has Legal Control of the Final Disposition

Excerpt From: Poul Lemasters (2016)

If you haven't noticed, the family structure has and continues to change. The days of meeting a family to make funeral/burial/cremation arrangements and dealing with the spouse, 2.5 children, and 1 pet are long gone. Those statistics are a dream or rather a fantasy. Today, when getting an internment authorization form signed, you can expect the spouse, or someone claiming to be a spouse; a live-in girlfriend; 2 stepchildren; and at least one uncle or aunt who happen to also be listed as the Power of Attorney. With so many new acceptable family roles, how does a business know who is responsible?

It is amazing that no matter how many family conflict situations you could ever think of, there are still more situations that haven't been thought of yet. To describe every scenario with a solution would be impossible. However, there are some common problems that many businesses face on a frequent basis. And those are the ones described here.

The focus in this article is on two classes of family members: The spouse and the children. The following issues are a general overview, and do not encompass everything – but, by understanding the basics and the general rule, the arranger and business can at least understand who has the right to control the internment or cremation/disinterment and how to proceed.

The Spouse:

DIVORCE - Probably the most common scenario that a business can be involved with is the divorced spouse. Generally, this is one of the easiest situations as well. When a couple is divorced, then the spouse typically loses the right to control the disposition. Keep in mind that this principle is true for the couple that is divorced. If a couple is in the process of a divorce, then the laws are split. There are some states that specifically address this issue, and many of those states take away the right of disposition from the pending divorced spouse. The flip side of this is that many states do not address the divorce issue and therefore the couple would still be married, and the spouse would still control. And, as far as cemeteries, the divorce may still allow the spouse to retain an interment right.

SEPARATED - Many people assume that the word separated means the period before a divorce. While there are some states that require separation before granting a divorce, be clear that the separation and divorce are two different procedures. Separation, specifically a legal separation, is a court approved order that outlines a spouse's responsibility while the spouses live apart. Unlike divorce, legal separation does not terminate a marriage. It is important to understand that a legal separation requires some declaration from the Court identifying the responsibilities of each spouse. Simply not living together – or simply being separated – does not mean anything when it comes to a spouse's rights.

In regard to a separated couple, the general rule is this: If a couple is separated, as in just living apart, then the spouse is still the spouse and has the authority to control the right of disposition. However, if there is a legal separation, then there is a chance that the spouse will not have the right to control the disposition. There is only a chance, because once again many states do not address a legal separation in the priority of who controls disposition. Unfortunately, it is unlikely that the spouses address control of funeral arrangements in their legal separation order.

COMMON LAW - There are only a handful of states that still recognize common law marriage (Included in this list are Alabama, Colorado, Kansas, Iowa, Montana, Oklahoma, Rhode Island, South Carolina, and Texas). In addition to states that still recognize common law marriages, there are several states that have grandfathered in common law marriage if it was established before a certain date (Georgia – pre-1997; Idaho – pre-1996; Ohio – pre-1991; Oklahoma – pre-1998; Pennsylvania – pre-2005). Despite the very few states that even recognize this type of marriage, there is a common misconception that if two people live together for a certain amount of years – then Voila! We are married. In actuality it doesn't work this way.

Common law marriage takes a few things including, a law that allows it; a significant amount of time living together (No state identifies a magic number); intention of being married; and holding yourself out as married (such as sharing the same last name, using the title husband and wife, or filing a joint tax return). It also takes one more thing – Someone other than the arranger to qualify it as a marriage. Some other states require a court to determine if a couple has a recognized common law marriage, and for purposes of making funeral/cremation arrangements the arranger should expect nothing less. If the couple has not had a court recognize their union as a common law marriage, then at the time of death a probate court can rule on it. Once you have proof that a common law marriage exists, and is recognized in your state, then you can proceed as any other arrangement with the right of disposition going to the spouse.

One more point in regard to common law marriages – While there are instances where a couple can form a common law marriage, there is no such thing as a common law divorce! While a family may try to convince the arranger that the spouse is not in control, because they have lived apart for so long, they "must be divorced by now," remember that a divorce takes a formal action through a court system – there is no common law divorce.

The Children:

STEPCHILDREN - It is common in today's society to deal with the stepchildren. Much like divorce, this is one of the simpler matters to handle when it comes to children. The general rule is that stepchildren do not have equal authority as biological children in regard to controlling the disposition. In some states, stepchildren fall into a lower class or a catch-all class of "any other individuals who are willing to assume responsibility for final arrangements." Keep in mind this authority relates to stepchild and the stepparent. As far as the stepchild and their biological parent, they still have their rights as a biological child. A remarriage does not affect any of their rights as a biological child.

ADOPTED CHILDREN - Compare adopted children to stepchildren. While a stepchild has no rights in their new family but retains all their rights in their original family, an adopted child is generally the opposite. Adopted children generally lose any and all rights to their biological parents, and instead assume all the rights of a child with their adopted parents (Some states like California – of course it's always California – allow adopted children to retain certain rights with their biological parents despite the adoption). Because of the general rule, the business can typically treat adopted children the same as any other child when making arrangements for the deceased parent.

ESTRANGED CHILDREN - The last class of children is the estranged child. Sadly, this has become a more common scenario. The children of the deceased say there is one other child, but that child is estranged from the parent. While this will make life more difficult, it generally does not mean the child is without authority to control the right of disposition. Generally, a biological child is always recognized as such unless the parent gives up legal custody, such as through adoption. While a child may never speak to his parents, the child still has certain rights. In fact, unless the parent specifically disinherits a child, in most states a child will have a right to inherit from their parents.

Handling this situation can become quite difficult. In some states, where majority rules, there may be enough children to provide a majority. However, if there are two children and one is estranged, there is no majority. Some states also have provisions that allow a funeral provider to rely on a limited number of children if after all efforts the other children cannot be located. Either of these options can raise risk and potential liability. The facts of each situation must be considered, and typically the form of procedure will be a business decision.

What to Do?

Based on all the general rules, there is one common element that will solve every scenario – documentation. This is not the same as document, document, document. When you document it means you, the provider, document everything that you do. In these cases, you need documentation. The family must bring you some documentation to prove the relationship.

For example, in the case of legal separation, the family needs to bring in the court order. In the case of an adopted child, the arranger should require the adoption papers. In the case of an estranged child, have the family obtain a court order from probate court stating that all efforts have been employed and the court recognizes that the estranged child has no right in handling the funeral arrangements.

This may seem like a lot of work but, in the words of Samuel Johnson, “What is easy is seldom excellent.” In this age of changing family structure and of course the ever increasingly liability risk associated with cremation, providers must take every precaution available to them. Consider the documentation an extra line of defense. And rest assured, if something goes wrong, you will need every defense available to you.

Source: Lemasters, Poul. (July/August 2016). “Knowing Who Has Legal Control of Cremation”. Southern Funeral Director Magazine.

What Does the Supreme Court Ruling on Same-Sex Marriage Mean for Death-Care Providers?

By: Poul Lemasters (2015)

1. What was this case about?

The case decided by the Supreme Court, Obergefell v. Hodges, was actually a combination of six different state cases from Ohio, Kentucky, Tennessee, and Michigan. All asked their respective states to allow the fundamental right of marriage regardless of sexual orientation.

The lead case was an Ohio case. James Obergefell asked the court to force Ohio to legally recognize his marriage in Maryland (where same-sex marriage was already recognized). The original case involved Mr. Obergefell's desire to handle the funeral arrangements – including burial – of his partner after his partner died from ALS a few months after they were married.

2. Do all states now allow same-sex marriage?

Yes. As of the date of this decision, the Supreme Court now holds that ***all*** states must allow same-sex couples to marry. This decision also holds that ***all*** states must recognize ***all*** marriages regardless of where they occurred.

3. I live in a state where same-sex marriage is already allowed, does this change how I serve my families?

No. If you are in one of the 37 states that already allow same-sex marriage (Alabama, Arkansas, Alaska, California, Colorado, Connecticut, Delaware, Florida, Hawaii, Idaho, Iowa, Illinois, Indiana, Kansas, Maine, Maryland, Massachusetts, Minnesota, Montana, North Carolina, Nevada, New Hampshire, New Jersey, New Mexico, New York, Oklahoma, Oregon, Pennsylvania, Rhode Island, South Carolina, Utah, Virginia, Vermont, Washington, West Virginia, Wisconsin, and Wyoming – plus Washington, D.C.) then this opinion makes no change to your current practices.

4. Should I ask for a marriage certificate from the spouse claiming they are in a same-sex marriage?

No. Unless you have a practice of requiring a marriage certificate from all spouses when they make arrangements at your business, it is not proper and could cause other issues.

5. Does this mean that a spouse in a same-sex marriage is in the top position of someone who is legally able to control the right of disposition?

Yes. As a spouse, they will typically be in the top position to make and control final disposition of the deceased.

Remember that most states allow an individual to appoint or designate an agent who would be above the spouse and would control funeral arrangements. Also, this means that on the death certificate, the same-sex spouse is identified as a spouse – this was the main issue in the original Obergefell case.

6. **What if there is a dispute among the survivors over who is in control?**

   A dispute would be handled the same as any other dispute. If someone challenges the validity of a spouse (same-sex or not) then you – as the provider – have a right to ask for further documentation to prove or disprove the allegations.

   Remember that you can and should slow down in case of any dispute until you are confident about the facts presented and believe you are dealing with the proper decision maker.

7. **Should I stop using the Appointment/Designation of Agent for Final Disposition Form now?**

   No. This form was not created solely for use in a same-sex partnership. It has many uses beyond this, and in fact should still be used regularly to avoid various issues such as confrontations, missing or skipping individuals, and multiple parties wanting to be involved – just to name a few.

Source: Lemasters, P. (2015, August/September). "What Does the Supreme Court Ruling on Same-Sex Marriage Mean for Death-Care Providers?" *ICCFA Magazine*.

Photographing at a Funeral

Excerpt From: Alice Adams (2016)

1. "It is very useful to have photographs of the service if there are relatives living abroad and unable to attend the funeral or cremation service," said English photographer Michael Elton. "Having photos allows you to send them photographs of the day and this, in turn, enables those not attending to feel they were almost there with you."

2. "In this day and time, it seems that everyone has a cell phone with a built-in camera," the director points out," and because taking photos is a lot easier... family members may decide, once they've viewed the decedent, to snap a quick picture to send to an absent family member. But, in most cases, the photos at the visitation, the service, and at graveside are simply a way to save a memory."

3. For a lot of people, it means a great deal to be able to look back on what is a very emotional day when we say goodbye to a loved one for the last time. Having photographs will enable you to reflect on the event at a later date and in your own time.

4. The reasons for a videographer and photographer are to preserve the memories of these special moments in life, but they also serve as a tribute to the person or persons being honored. Yes, pictures of a funeral may bring up sad memories of the final time we saw a beloved family member, but in just as many ways, these images may also serve to help us remember how we memorialized our loved one and the day we celebrated the life they had lived.

Source: Adams, A. (2016, April). Capturing the Final Goodbye. *American Funeral Director.*

Author's Note: I have to admit that back in what you might call the "old days," when I was an apprentice, there was a different perspective on taking photographs at a funeral. I once saw someone taking a picture of the deceased at a funeral. I thought that it was quite weird, even somewhat macabre. I do not feel this way anymore. It may be that with everyone having a cellphone camera it seems like everything and everybody is fair game for being photographed. Then again it may be because I have taken photos of funerals and deceased for many publications and seminars (always with permission of the family). How I feel about it or how you feel about it doesn't really matter. The only thing that matters is how the family you are serving feels about it.

The Pros & Cons of Funeral Webcasting

By: Chris Raymond (2017a)

Modern technology enables anyone with a web camera and a computer, or a video-enabled phone or tablet, to easily shoot and share their videos on the internet, whether streamed live or uploaded post-recording. Many funeral homes are now using this same technology to broadcast funeral services online in real-time.

Advantages of Funeral Webcasting

- Broadcasting a funeral service over the internet enables family members, friends, and loved ones to attend the service virtually if they cannot physically travel to the funeral due to financial, geographic, physical, or other challenges.
- Funeral webcasts can be saved to a CD or DVD, which provides a permanent record of the service that some mourners might wish to view again.
- For those who simply cannot attend the physical funeral service, or even watch it as it is streamed online in real time, funeral webcasts can be accessed and viewed later.
- Online funeral broadcasts can incorporate a real-time “chat” component, enabling remote viewers to communicate with each other during the service to express condolences, or even to speak to those physically attending the funeral, if appropriate.
- A funeral webcast might encourage someone to “attend” (virtually) who might otherwise not participate at all, for whatever reason.
- Attending a funeral service, even virtually, is better than not participating at all in terms of supporting the grieving family and, for the virtual attendee, acknowledging and accepting the reality a loved one has died.

Disadvantages of Funeral Webcasting

- Many people already seek a reason to skip a wake/visitation and/or funeral service, and a funeral webcast might offer a convenient excuse not to physically attend.
- While funeral webcasts typically provide a method to keep such broadcasts private using password-access and secure servers, families might feel concerned about the security of this highly personal event, as well as viewing by unauthorized individuals.
- While some funeral homes provide funeral webcasting at no charge, others charge the family a fee (typically around $150 to $200 for the service), adding to the overall cost of the funeral. In addition, the fee generally includes 30 to 90 days of video access beyond that period.
- Some people, whether among the immediate family or other survivors, might consider broadcasting a funeral service on the Internet disrespectful or in poor taste.

Source: Raymond, C. (2017a, August 9). The Pros & Cons of Funeral Webcasting. Retrieved from: https://www.funeralhelpcenter.com/the-pros-cons-of-funeral-webcasting/

The Dual Licensure Debate

Excerpts From: S. Cronin (2017d)

Rising cremation rates and the difficulty in attracting new employees are among the challenges funeral home operations face. But even as fewer families are having their loved ones embalmed, more states are moving to make learning such skills a mandatory requirement for licensing.

Currently, 30 states and the District of Columbia require funeral directors to have a single license that ensures they are trained in funeral directing and embalming, according to the National Funeral Directors Association. Nineteen states require separate licenses for funeral directors and embalmers. That's a big change from just four years ago, when – according to the NFDA – 22 states and the District of Columbia had a single license and 27 states had dual licenses. Colorado is the sole sate that requires no mandatory licensing.

Despite this shift, some leaders in funeral service say that if there is a change to licensing in the future, it should increase adoption of dual licensing. Will that change occur? It's hard to say, the experts concede. Currently there is groundswell demanding revisions to licensing.

"As we progress through the next 10 years and the pool of qualified people becomes smaller, you are going to see more states go to two licenses," said Bob Arrington, immediate NFDA past president and owner of Arrington Funeral Directors in Jackson, Tennessee. "I think different people are suited for different paths, and we should give them the opportunity to pursue them."

But funeral service is facing challenges. And challenges frequently bring change. "Where are the future funeral directors coming from?" asked Robert M. Fells, executive director and general counsel for the International Cemetery, Cremation and Funeral Association. "Certainly, dual licensing would be a real boon to that goal of attracting more people."

Fells has heard the joke that working in funeral service wouldn't be bad, if it weren't for the fact that you had to deal with dead bodies. Like most jokes, that one contains its share of truth, he said. "People hear what a funeral director does, and they think, 'hmmm, that's interesting,' but then they learn you have to be trained in embalming and they lose interest," Fells said.

"You are turning away a great deal of people who could be a real boon for the industry," Fells added. "You shouldn't take someone who just wants to be a funeral director and say, 'No, you also have to be an embalmer.'"

Arrington, whose state uses dual licensing, agrees. Single licensing programs, he said, exclude more than just those who are squeamish about embalming. The additional cost and study time required to obtain a license covering both funeral directing and embalming can discourage those interested in entering the field. Many people attracted by the idea of helping families and planning funerals have no interest in learning embalming skills or doing embalming work, Arrington said.

This is particularly true for older workers who are considering a mid-life career switch but don't want to go back to school for years to do it. "You're telling them, 'You have to spend money and invest time in something you rarely, if ever, are going to do," he said.

The same logic, he added, applies to people who wish to pursue a career in the prep room and have no interest in dealing with families or planning services. Why do these people, who Arrington concedes are few in number, have to be licensed as funeral directors?

In addition, obtaining a funeral director's license often leads to people, after becoming familiar with the business, to pursue their embalming license, as well, Arrington added.

Trends Bring Change

Changes in funeral customs and funeral service operations are reducing the demand for trained embalmers, said Douglas "Mack" Smith, executive secretary of the Kansas State Board of Mortuary Arts, which oversees that state's dual licensing system.

Rising cremation rates mean that there is less demand for embalming. Consolidation by large companies that operate several funeral homes served by a centralized preparation facility means that each funeral home no longer needs to have a staff trained to embalm. "There is always need for embalming, that will never go away. But the question is how many embalmers do you need?" Smith asked.

"I'm seeing a definite increase in funeral directors only," he said. "Sometimes those people have a change of heart and go back and get the second license. Other times, they realize it will be to their professional benefit to have both." Among the benefits is that the embalming license is necessary for those who might decide to go work in a single-license state.

Source: Cronin, S. (2017d, April). The Dual Licensure Debate. American Funeral Director, p. 34-39.

Death Doulas and Funeral Service
By: Cole Imperi (2017)

What is a Death Doula?

When most Americans hear the word "doula," they probably think about birth – not death. Birth doulas or midwives have been around since the 1980s and are now an accepted option available to mothers navigating the journey of pregnancy, the process of delivery, and post-birth adjustment. Death doulas, also commonly called "End-of-life guides" or "death midwives," play a similar role to birth doulas: They help individuals and their families navigate the end-of-life journey in a nonmedical way.

"A death doula is someone who acts as a guide and a companion to a dying person and their family through the end phase of an illness. This work starts as much before the last days of life as possible, goes through the final dying process, and continues into the early time of grieving for the family," says Henry Fersko-Weiss.

"The first part of the doula's approach centers on helping a dying person explore the meaning of their life, tell the story of what is important to them for others to hold on to, and plan for how the last days should look."

A Budding Profession

As of 2016, the death doula movement is well-established and steadily growing. This emerging profession has been covered by major publications, including a front-page article in the New York Times. "Between INELDA (International End of Life Doula Association) and I, together we have taught well over 1,000 people to do this work," Fersko-Weiss said. This does not include the numerous other doula trainings available in the United States, nor does it include individuals who began work in this profession without any training at all. The New York Open Center in New York City (which houses the Art of Dying Institute) has been offering death doula courses and trainings since 2008.

"Our end-of-life doula workshop is one of our most consistently popular programs. Our students are quite diverse. Roughly 50-55% are end-of-life care professionals, including nurses, chaplains, counselors, social workers, psychologists, and bereavement specialists at various stages of their careers. The other 45-50% are laypeople."

Two Professions, One Family

The death-care profession is beginning to see death doulas involved with funeral arrangements. In some areas, it is understood that death doulas can provide home funerals for a family in addition to the end-of-life services they also provide. Some death doulas do, in fact, provide home funerals and effectively use the funeral home for body-specific services only. On the other hand, some do not. As the death doula profession is very young, its scope has not yet been clearly defined. And this presents a number of challenges.

"Death doulas are filling the nonreligious ceremony space – among others – that people are searching for. While the reality is that many funeral directors are ready and able to offer services to all people – religious and nonreligious, or any other format – the perception does not match. People are searching for answers, and this movement is providing them," said Poul Lemasters Consulting, a death-care-specific consulting company.

Where is the line drawn between the work of the death doula and the work of the funeral director? Or, can the two overlap?

"If a funeral director knows a dying person and family are using doulas, they should make an effort to understand the legacy work that might be occurring, as well as the feeling in the space around the dying person, and the rituals that might have been planned. I also see a need to make sure that the doulas we train engage directly with the funeral director before the death to make them aware of the work they are doing and to see how they might work together more consciously toward achieving the kind of after-death experience the family wants. Of course, conversations like this would have to be OK'd by the family," Fersko-Weiss said.

Challenges

The death doula movement is not going away. The death-care profession is not going away. The families – the people both professions are designed to serve – will continue to diversify, expect quicker service, and demand more options for personalization. Not to mention that the country is looking at an uptick in deaths based on U.S. Census Bureau projections as the baby boomer generation ages.

"Funeral providers have and will continue to face liability. The issue is where do death doulas fall in the space of funeral providers? As a death doula, providing services that are not funeral specific, they are probably free from many issues. But the line is blurry, and becoming blurrier," Lemasters said. "As death doulas offer more services, crossing over into the funeral world, they run the risk of being governed by state and federal regulations. Keep in mind, this is a very new area and is under some scrutiny among state and federal governments. There is talk that the definition of a provider needs to be examined to govern people that offer services to help families even though they are not a funeral director. If these areas change, death doulas could face regulations." Perhaps the biggest challenge is a lack of education – funeral directors are not trained or educated on what a death doula is or does unless they seek it out, and death doulas are, generally speaking, not trained on death-care law, the Funeral Rule, or licensing and regulations.

Further complicating matters, the death doula movement itself does not have clearly defined edges.

"INELDA has established a certification program that we hope will become recognized broadly as the standard for this emerging field," Fersko-Weiss said. "As of now, there is no outside organization that can establish an industry-supported certification or licensing process. But we firmly believe that a professional level certification is essential for establishing the legitimacy of the death doula profession. We have established a base-level certification that involves taking our doula training class, providing proof of experience in acting as a doula following the class, evaluations, references, singing off on a code of ethics and a scope of practice, written presentation demonstrating how they are interacting with the dying and their families, and finally a written exam.

Source: Imperi, C. (2017, January). Death Doulas and Funeral Service. *American Funeral Director*, p.46-50.

Defining Home Funeral Guides

Excerpts From: Lee Webster (2017)

When home funerals started popping up in places they hadn't been for decades, funeral directors confessed to being a bit baffled, and some took it personally. A common response was, "We have a homelike setting right here. Families can bring whatever they want. We can do home funerals right in our funeral homes, right?"

Unfortunately, no. For those who want a relaxed, family-centered vigil in their own home, nothing will substitute. Still, some find it comforting to keep a loved one home for just a brief time and then partner with a professional for the rest of the necessaries. For many, the idea of inviting a professional into the home is less about saying no to their help and more about saying yes to absorbing the reality in their own time and in their own way.

Why Home Funeral Guides?

So why home funeral guides? After all, they're not professionals and they're probably strangers, too. What is it that appeals to families about home funeral guides? And why would families need them? How do home funeral guides fit into the growing movement of end-of-life volunteers and consultants that include advance directive planners, end-of-life guides and doulas, celebrants and more?

The simple answer is that most Americans have lost touch with the practical realities of caring for their own dead. They seek someone who is versed in the law and can teach the finer points of natural, non-invasive body care without all the conventional funeral fanfare. But among the more compelling reasons to call a home funeral guide may be the desire for a more integrated, authentic experience, one which home funeral guides are uniquely qualified to contribute to at the invitation of the family.

Char Barrett, the first president of the National Home Funeral Alliance and a licensed funeral director with 12 years of experience providing home funeral services, has witnessed first-hand what a home funeral guide delivers that a licensed funeral director can't or won't.

"Home funeral guides fill a niche in after-death care that is structurally difficult for most funeral directors to meet," she said. "The very premise of a home funeral is that it takes place within the comforting, familiar and deeply personal space of a family's home. This is the space within which home funeral guides excel, because their orientation is that of guiding families, in the reality of their homes, through all of the messiness of life when death is on the doorstep."

Barrett went on to describe the obstacles some families face. "There may be tight spaces, young children or pets under foot, dirty dishes in the sink, a needy distant relative on the phone and piles of unattended papers and mail that need to be swept aside just to have a place to meet and discuss plans for a home funeral," she said. "Many times these meetings are conducted within a context of high anxiety and emotions, not to mention fatigue, where the dying (or recently dead) loved one lies in a hospital bed nearby. Being present to the family's reality while also delivering knowledgeable guidance is where a home funeral guide delivers his or her highest value."

Out of legal and functional necessity, funeral directors operate from a very different professional and business-like aura when they are in charge. In contrast, home funeral guides lend a less formal, more organic feel to the experience, keeping the responsibility – and privilege – of caring for their own squarely in the family's hands. As Barrett observed, "Merging these two worlds is where home funeral guides can be a valuable bridge supporting a family in need."

What Are Home Funeral Guides?

Elizabeth Knox, who served as NHFA president from 2012 to 2014, said it best: "Home funeral guides are not warmer, fuzzier funeral directors." It has never been the intention for guides to take the place of professionals – that would defeat the purpose entirely.

Home funeral guides are educators, first and foremost. Guides focus on relaying the legal regulations of their state and region to families as they navigate the steps, including body care, paperwork, transportation, and other aspects that the family may choose to undertake themselves. Guides may charge for educational or consultative services, but the majority of their time is volunteered.

The NHFA got out in front of this conundrum early on, developing the NHFA Code of Ethics, Conduct and Practice and working with the Federal Trade Commission on the publication Essentials for Practicing Home Funeral Guides. The booklet clearly delineates what guides can and cannot charge for, and under what conditions they are subject to The Funeral Rule.

Families call guides when someone dies because they know they will get the information that empowers them so they can act quickly when necessary. They also call for the simple reason that this is a person with experience who will know what has to happen next. Home funeral guides do a lot of hand holding and confidence building. The families, after all, are themselves both the givers and receivers of all that occurs during a home funeral.

Source: Webster, L. (2017, May). Defining Home Funeral Guides. *American Funeral Director*, p. 44-48.

Shaking Hands

By: Ralph L. Klicker, Ph.D.

I really enjoy the custom of shaking hands. In years past I might have thought it was a male bonding thing. However, I enjoy it just as much now that women are shaking hands as well. My enjoyment of shaking hands must have started when I was a teenager working at a funeral home where the funeral directors shook hands with everyone.

A handshake, according to Wikipedia (2017), is a "short ritual in which two people grasp one another's like hand. In most cases it is accompanied by a brief up and down movement of the grasped hands."

The history of the handshake has not been absolutely determined. It is thought to have started as a gesture of peace in medieval times. When a man extended his arm with an open and empty hand it signified that he did not have a weapon and was not going to harm you. There is archeological evidence that shaking hands was practiced in ancient Greece as far back as the 5th century BC. There is also a depiction of two soldiers shaking hands on a 5th century funeral stile at the Pergamon Museum in Berlin (Thomas, 2009).

<u>The handshake is commonly done when you are</u>:

- Introduced to someone for the first time.
- Seeing someone you haven't seen in a long time.
- Offering congratulations.
- Expressing gratitude.
- Completing a business agreement.
- The host or hostess is greeting their guests.
- As a guest greeting your host or hostess.
- Saying goodbye to a friend or business associate.
- Responding to someone who extends his or her hand to you.
- Making a bet with another person.
- When involved in a sport or other competitive activity.

Mastering the Handshake

Stand near the person you want to shake hands with. Leave three or four feet between the two of you. You should both be able to comfortably extend your arms to shake hands. If you stand too close, you may come across as creepy. If you stand too far away, they may think that you don't want to shake hands.

- Use good posture when shaking someone's hand. This will make you look more confident.
- If you're sitting, rise before shaking someone's hand.

Extend your right hand. Using the right hand is generally considered proper etiquette. Reach halfway toward the person with your thumb extended upward and your fingers pressed together. Lean toward the person and maintain eye contact to show that you're interested in shaking their hand.

- Smile while you extend your hand, otherwise you may come across as aggressive.
- Look the person in the eyes while shaking his/her hand.
- If the person's right hand is injured, offer your left hand instead.

Grasp hands. Grasp the middle of the person's hand so that the webs of your thumbs are touching. Use a firm grip but be careful not to squeeze too hard. Try to mirror the pressure that the other person applies.

- Your fingers should be completely curled around the other person's hand.
- Don't grab the end of the person's fingers. Otherwise you'll shake their limp fingers instead of shaking their hand.

Pump hands two or three times. As you grasp the other person's hand, bend your elbow to lift your hands up and down. Do this two or three times with a small and precise movement.

- Avoid swinging hands in a large back-and-forth movement.
- Don't pump hands more than three times as this may come across as creepy.
- Hold the handshake for 2-3 seconds.

Release hands and lean back. After you finish shaking hands, release the other person's hand and return to your original position. As this point, you can politely break eye contact. However, continue smiling as you talk to appear friendly.

- Resist the urge to wipe your hand after a handshake. The other person could be offended.
- The person of higher authority or age should be the first one to extend a hand.

Adaptations to the Traditional Handshake

- Related to the handshake but more casual, some people prefer the "fist bump." Typically, the fist bump is done with a clenched hand. Only the knuckles of the hand are typically touched to the knuckles of the other person's hand. Like a handshake, the fist bump may be used to acknowledge a relationship with another person. However, unlike the formality of handshake, the fist bump is typically not used in formal business settings or to seal a business deal.

- Another adaptation that I particularly like is greeting an old friend with a strong hug instead of a handshake. The hug can also follow the handshake.

- Closely related to the hug and often performed by sports figures is the grasping of each other's hands together while simultaneously pressing opposite shoulders together.

Other adaptations to the handshake that express closeness and sincerity include:

- Placing the left hand over the two hands that are shaking.
- Placing the left hand on the right upper arm of the person whose hand you are shaking.

If you extend your hand but the other person does not see it, don't panic, it happens to everyone. Just bring your hand down and wait for another opportunity. To help in avoiding this situation:

- **Do not** offer a handshake if the other person is engrossed in a conversation with someone else.
- **Do not** approach someone from the side with your extended hand – it is hard to see.
- **Do not** give what is known as a "crushing handshake." This can be painful and is generally considered to be an exhibition by the person doing the crushing to show his strength and dominance over the other person.
- **Do** verbally greet the person first to get their attention, and then offer your hand. If you know the person's name, use it.
- If your hand is sweaty, wipe it dry on your pants or skirt.

Funeral Poverty in the 21st Century

Excerpts From: Sara J. Marsden (2014a)

With the considerable population we have of low-income families that are struggling to make ends meet month to month, it comes as no surprise that we are entering an era of what is being termed "funeral poverty." That is, there are more and more families simply unable to meet funeral costs when a family member dies.

How does funeral poverty affect families?

A traditional funeral costs $7,360.00 (NFDA, 2019), an amount which does not take into account cemetery costs, meaning the full cost of a burial is more likely to reach over $10,000 in many cases. How can a family on low-income find $10,000 in a short space of time to cover funeral costs? What about life insurance or a burial fund, you may ask? Well, there was a time when people did carefully put aside a few dollars per month into an appropriate policy or fund, but unfortunately this acknowledgement and provision for immortality no longer features so strongly in our culture.

How has this funeral poverty crisis crept up on us?

Funeral poverty is an unexpectedly potent indicator of the combined impact of recession, austerity, low wages, and an insecure job market. This situation has been creeping upon us slowly as more families have fallen upon hardship or are struggling just to put food on the table. Many families have already maxed out all possible credit opportunities, and the reality is that lending for a funeral (or funeral finance) is not so easy to get. The lack of open discussion about death and end of life planning, the economy, and the breakdown of nuclear families and communities are all contributing factors in why we now face a funeral poverty crisis. As families have become extended and transient, the responsibility for who should pay for a family member's funeral can come under contention.

How is this funeral poverty crisis affecting the funeral industry?

The funeral poverty issue in the United States needs to be acknowledged by the funeral industry, and the industry (as a whole) needs to re-align itself. Many families simply cannot afford a $7,360 outlay for a funeral these days and they are demanding lower cost options. As a result, we have witnessed a huge shift to cremation, as a much lower cost disposition alternative. A simple cremation can be performed for under $1,000 in many areas of the U.S.

The funeral industry is already beginning to see declining profits as the cost of the average funeral case decreases, and more families choose cremation. But this is but the tip of the iceberg! The funeral industry as a whole maintains a position where they are now accepting that cremation is here to stay but see their role as one to 'educate' the funeral consumer in how to befittingly create a cremation memorial. There is a belief that incremental sales (upselling, as it is known in the industry) can still help them to add revenue to a basic cremation case.

The reality that we see and hear about is that more families are seeking out an alternative that does not involve funeral home services. Natural, or green, burials have experienced something of a revival as families explore the alternative of a simple burial without a casket, burial vault, or embalming. There is an increased interest in DIY Funerals, where the family makes all the cremation or burial arrangements themselves, file the paperwork, and transport the deceased to the crematory or cemetery in their own vehicle. However, the most common way that families are dealing with funeral poverty is to opt for the most basic cremation option – a direct cremation. A direct cremation can be conducted in many cities for less than $800.

This is a huge reduction in case value to a funeral home when a family opts for a low-cost direct cremation and no additional services. There are some funeral businesses that recognized what was happening and altered their business plan to meet this demand. You will find a low-cost cremation provider in most cities, and these are the guys that (quietly) understand what is happening in their industry. These are going to be the businesses that ride out the funeral poverty storm!

Funeral homes have always tried to work with their client families regarding paying for a funeral. In the good old days, a funeral could go ahead before the family had paid in full, but this rarely happens these days. Today more funeral homes find themselves in the position of having to negotiate payment terms with a family who has requested the funeral home's services before realizing the implications of the cost. Bad debt has always been an issue for funeral businesses, and some funeral homes have been willing to take on charitable cases for the goodwill and community recognition it gains. But this growing funeral poverty issue is causing funeral businesses to re-work their policies on bad debt and funeral contracts. Even state and county authorities are re-writing policy on indigent burials, as more families seek out public assistance to meet the cost of a funeral. Some states have axed financial assistance, whilst others have reduced it significantly, dealing with all their indigent deaths by direct cremation.

An indigent burial program used to cater to those poor individuals who had no family or had been in state care. Today authorities are finding that even those with no family can be left for the state to dispose of when family walk away without the means to attend to a funeral and the costs attached.

How can we tackle the problem of funeral poverty?

Funeral poverty is already an issue, but it is going to become a crisis if we do not try and avert it. How can we tackle it? We need to ensure affordable options ARE available, and that those families that need them KNOW they are available. We need to address this in a bigger way to get the message across to millions of struggling Americans. People need to know there are cheaper ways of arranging a funeral. They need re-assurances that it is not undignified or disrespectful to arrange something simple and inexpensive.

Source: Marsden, S. (2014a, October 29). Funeral Poverty in the 21st Century. *U.S. Funerals Online*. Retrieved from: http://www.us-funerals.com/funeral-articles/funeral-poverty-in-the-21st-century.html#.XWVzJ-hKg2w

8 Reasons to Memorialize with a Monument
By: Quincy Memorials (2018)

1. Cremation Has Options

Cremation is a method of preparing a body and does not take the place of a funeral service or a proper monument. A person may choose to be cremated, but that does not mean he or she does not wish to be honored and memorialized. Cremated remains can still be buried in a family plot, interred in a family columbarium, or placed in a communal columbarium or garden.

2. A Monument Says "Their Life Mattered"

A monument serves as an everlasting tribute to a life well lived and a life worth remembering. It is a representation of that person and how he or she lived. It is a final gift. Monuments can be custom made and personalized to honor and depict that person to please the departed and family.

3. Monuments Bring Families Together.

Monuments provide a peaceful focal point for families who wish to visit and be with their loved one. Cemeteries are permanent, tranquil places where you can feel comfortable visiting without judgement.

4. Monuments Are Forever

Monuments serve as a focal point for cemetery visits and as a permanent record for future generations and genealogy.

5. Memorialization is a Healthy Part of the Grieving Process

Psychologists say that remembrance practices, from the funeral or the memorial service to permanent memorialization, serve an important emotional function for some survivors by helping to bring closure and allowing the healing process to begin. Providing a permanent resting place through traditional internment or cremation is a dignified treatment of a loved one's mortal remains, and it fulfills the natural desire for memorialization.

6. Memorialization is In Our Nature.

Monuments and memorialization have been part of every society as far back as we have records.

7. Monuments Can Remind Us of What Never Dies

Granite is symbolic, it is everlasting, much like the love that was shared by and toward your loved one.

8. Prevent Regrets

Some people have regretted scattering the cremated remains of a loved one. Consider a memorial in a permanent and accessible place where survivors and descendants can visit and remember a loved one. If you still wish to scatter the remains of a loved one, consider scattering half of the remains and burying the other half in a family plot or interring them in a cremation memorial or columbarium.

Source: Quincy Memorials (2018). 8 Reasons to Memorialize with a Monument." *Quincy Memorials Info. Center.* Retrieved: https://www.quincymemorials.com/info-center/importance-of-memorialization/

Spring Burials

By: Ralph L. Klicker, Ph.D.

One of the unique aspects of death care in states that experience extreme cold and snow in winter is the custom of not burying the deceased in the winter, but rather placing them temporarily in holding until spring. Not all cemeteries follow this custom, and it is usually smaller rural cemeteries that do.

Freezing water temperature and large accumulations of snow can cause the ground to freeze extremely hard as deep as 3-6 feet. This makes it extremely difficult and even impossible for cemeteries that do not have the proper equipment to dig graves. The ice and snow can make it dangerous to try to drive on the narrow road of the cemetery, and the snow can make it impossible to find grave sites.

Cemeteries can close as early as November and not open again until April or May. These cemeteries have storage buildings to hold the casketed remains during this time. The design of these storage buildings varies from chapel-looking structures to an area in a building with other uses. Most are separate, unheated structures that can actually slow down decomposition during the storage time.

Funeral services conclude at the funeral home or church. Families usually do not accompany the casketed remains to the storage area. In the spring, the cemetery notifies the funeral home or family when spring internments begin. Families differ in the amount of participation they desire in spring burials. Some want the complete committal service and will invite family and friends to attend. Others do not participate at all.

A small percentage of families request a viewing before burial. The author has seen many stored remains that could be viewed with a minimal amount of work by the funeral director. The most common post-mortem conditions are dehydration, discoloration, eye and lip separation, and mold growth. Mold growth is more common the longer the remains stay in storage during warmer temperatures and if flowers were inside the casket.

Families have different emotional responses to spring burial. It more often has a negative effect if the family has not had experience with the custom. Funeral director Richard Putman did a study of spring burials while in college and found the following responses:

- Whether they were familiar with the custom or not, most families would rather not have had to deal with it.

- Along with normal grief reactions, some experienced more stress. One respondent was devastated and felt she had let the deceased down by not being able to complete the internment at the time.

- The most common emotion was frustration because they feared the emotional scars that should be healing by spring would now be reopened. It's as if the grieving process is interrupted and must be restarted again.

- Some people were upset to think of the deceased lying there in sub-zero temperatures and experiencing all of the negative effects of the cold, wind, and snow.

- Some experienced relief because they felt they did not have to deal with the death now but could put it off until later. They did not feel rushed and felt they were given extra time to adjust before final internment.

- Spring burials are often considered disruptive by funeral directors. Not only do they have to conduct business as usual, but now have this additional work. The larger the number of spring burials a funeral home has, the more disruptive it is.

How to Fold the Flag

By: Veterans Flag Depot (2019)

The following are the correct steps in folding an American Flag at a funeral.

STEP 1

To properly fold the Flag, begin by holding it waist-high with another person so that its surface is parallel to the ground.

STEP 2

Fold the lower half of the stripe section lengthwise **over** the field of stars, holding the bottom and top edges securely.

STEP 3

Fold the Flag **again** lengthwise with the blue field on the **outside.**

STEP 4

Make a triangular fold by bringing the striped corner of the folded edge to meet the open (top) edge of the flag.

STEP 5

Turn the outer (end) point inward, parallel to the open edge, to form a second triangle.

STEP 6-12

The triangular folding is continued until the entire length of the flag is folded in this manner.

STEP 13

When the flag is completely folded, only a triangular blue field of stars should be visible.

Source: Veteran's Flag Depot (2019). Flag Presentation Protocol and Flag Folding. Retrieved from: https://www.Veteransflagdepot.com/flag-presentation-protocol-and-flag-folding/

Organ and Tissue Donation

By: Ralph L. Klicker, Ph.D.

Source: donatelife.net

The Federal Routine Referral Act requires hospitals to notify the Organ Procurement Organization (OPO) and tissue and eye banks of all deaths or impending deaths of their patients. If the patient is eligible to be a donor, the family has to be given the opportunity to approve the donation of organs, eyes, or tissues. Funeral directors are affected by the donation process in two major areas. The time it takes for the family to be contacted can delay removal of the deceased. If consent is given for a donation, there is extra time and work involved with the embalming. Most funeral directors realize that the lifesaving or enhancing benefits of donation outweigh the inconvenience it causes.

According to Donate Life America (2019), there are about 113,000 people waiting for an organ transplant. Too few organs are donated each year. As a result, 22 people die each day waiting for a transplant.

Why is the donation rate so low?

- Lack of knowledge about the critical need for organ donors. People have little knowledge about any aspect of donation and transplantation.
- Fears and misconceptions about the donation process. The knowledge people do have often comes from television, which often portrays donation in a negative manner.
- Lack of family discussion leading to low consent rates – If family members know what each member's views on donation are, it makes the decision easier at the time of death.

What is an Organ Procurement Organization (OPO)?

An OPO is a non-profit organization designated by the federal government to coordinate activities relating to organ retrieval (procurement) in a designated area. OPO activities include evaluating potential donors, discussing donation with surviving family members, arranging for surgical removal and transport of donated organs, and educating the public about the need for donation.

What is a Tissue Bank?

An organization that coordinates the activities relating to tissue procurement for transplantation.

What is an Eye Bank?

An organization that coordinates the activities relating to eye procurement for transplantation.

Who Can Be an Organ Donor?

Those of any age may be eligible to donate organs, if they have been declared dead by neurological criteria referred to as **"BRAIN DEATH"** and their organs are being temporarily maintained by receiving oxygen through a ventilator (breathing machine). In certain situations, organs can be recovered for transplantation after a person's breathing and heartbeat have stopped. This is called donation after cardiac death.

Who can be a tissue donor?

Most individuals who have died as a result of either "cardiac" death, in which the heart stops beating, or "brain" death, in which all brain functions is lost, can be eligible to be a tissue donor.

Who cannot be an organ or tissue donor? (medical contraindications)

Organ and/or tissue donors for transplantation cannot have a communicable disease such as HIV or certain malignancies (cancer) or a disease affecting the function of the organs to be donated. They may, however, be eligible for research.

BRAIN DEATH VS. CARDIAC DEATH

What does "brain death" mean?

Brain death means there is no blood flow or oxygen being delivered to the brain. When this occurs, the brain cells die within minutes. This cell death is permanent and therefore is not reversible. A brain-dead patient's organs, such as the heart, lungs, kidneys, pancreas, intestines, and liver can be kept functioning for a limited time by providing oxygen through a ventilator (breathing machine). Unless damaged by disease or injury, these organs may save the lives of others through transplantation.

Common Causes of "Brain Death"

- Stroke
- Drug overdose
- Head trauma
- Brain injury due to loss of oxygen
- Brain tumor without metastasis

How is "Brain Death" Determined?

"Brain death" is determined through a series of tests, including the assessment of the individual's ability to breath on his/her own and the determination of the lack of blood supply to the brain.

What is the difference between "brain death" and "coma?"

While brain death is the death of the brain (and therefore the individual), a coma is a condition in which there is a disruption of some of the brain's functions resulting in the loss of consciousness. Coma can be permanent or temporary. In this situation, the part of the brain that controls breathing (brain stem) is still functioning. Therefore, the patient can breathe on his/her own, although many coma patients may need help from a ventilator to breathe. Patients in a coma sometimes regain consciousness and recover some or all of their brain functions. However, brain death is permanent, and patients will not recover.

Once "brain death" occurs, why does the heart continue to beat?

The heart has its own pacemaker independent of the brain. The oxygen supplied by the ventilator will allow the heart to continue to beat.

Does the body of a brain-dead patient sometimes begin to deteriorate even if the patient is on respiratory support (ventilator)?

The deterioration and failure of many organs begins soon after brain death despite being supplied with oxygen.

Would removing the respiratory support from a patient be the same as not giving him or her all possible chances for survival?

No. When a patient is brain-dead, the brain will never recover. Respiratory support only keeps the heart beating to supply the vital organs with oxygen. There are no clinically documented cases where a patient was declared brain-dead and later restored to normal life. The recorded time of death is when the patient is declared brain-dead, not when the heart actually stops beating after ventilation is removed.

Since a brain-dead patient may be placed on a ventilator (meaning he or she is being provided with oxygen via machine), the heart, with its own pacemaker, continues to beat and pump the oxygenated blood to the body's organs. This will temporarily keep the organs and tissues functioning and suitable for transplant.

On the other hand, when cardiac death occurs, the patient's heart stops beating. His/her organs go without oxygen and lose their ability to function. This person is not able to donate organs but may donate tissue.

WHAT SOME FUNERAL DIRECTORS SAY ABOUT DONATION

Most funeral directors support organ donation even though it may mean more time spent in embalming. If funeral directors do have complaints, it is usually with tissue donation, such as bone and skin. Their concerns are usually twofold:

1. Some directors feel the extensive nature of the process is mutilating the body.
2. Some directors feel that the donation agency does not accurately explain the extensive nature of the tissue removal process.

Pet Memorials

By: Ralph L. Klicker, Ph.D.

The author and his Soft-coated Wheaten Terrier "Dooley".

A growing body of research into the human-animal bond clearly reveals that animals play an important role in the lives of their owners. Animals can provide companionship, unconditional love, and even health benefits, such as lowering blood pressure, stress, and anxiety. To put it simply, in many households, pets are considered family members. There was never a clearer example of this than in Hurricane Katrina. Millions of television viewers around the world saw people who would not evacuate the flood area because rescuers would not allow their pets to come along. For those who left their pets, we heard the anguish of their guilt and grief.

There is a growing trend in funeral service to encourage funeral homes to offer memorialization services to bereaved pet owners. By offering this option, funeral homes can provide emotional comfort to grieving families and provide an economic benefit to their business. Funeral home owners are not leaping into this area in large numbers. A survey of funeral homes by *American Funeral Director* magazine showed that 75% of respondents did not offer services for pets and 34% said they never plan to enter the market.

The potential market is staggering. According to the American Pet Products Manufacturers Association (2019-2020):

- 67% of households own pets, which equals 84.9 million homes that own pets
- 63.4 million own dogs
- 42.7 million own cats
- 5.7 million own birds
- 5.4 million own some other small animal
- 4.5 million own reptiles

APPA (2019) also reports that more than 75 billion dollars are spent on pets annually! The pet funeral industry is estimated to be making over 100 million dollars a year in revenue.

Around 15% of funeral home owners are now offering pet services (Stone, 2016). Schaal (2007) advises that the services that can be offered are removal, care and grooming (not usually embalming), viewing/visitation, music, and receptions. The key to success in the pet death care industry is not to limit the perception of what pet owners truly desire, but to embrace the possibilities that mirror their love and affections for their special companion.

We understand that losing a pet is difficult. Our separate pet crematory allows us to offer cremation services, exclusive to pets, so your pet can receive the same dignity all beloved family members deserve.

ANDERSON
FUNERAL HOME
123 Any Street • Mahnomen
(123) 456-7890

Source: Adfinity Ad cannot be duplicated without permissions from Adfinity.

Crowdfunding: The Future of Funeral Financing

By: L. Howard-Fusco (2016)

Crowdfunding [kroud-fuhn-ding]: The act of seeking money from a large number of people which has recently exploded on the internet.

Many people now turn to social media or a growing network of internet platforms dedicated to crowdfunding in order to finance life's milestones and challenges. The practice has been used to pay the medical bills of sick children and subsidize weddings and adoptions.

It turns out crowdfunding is also finding a place in funeral service and its influence could grow in the future.

"Along with medical, education, emergencies, volunteerism and sports, the funerals, memorials, and tributes category is among our most popular," said Kelsea Little, media director at GoFundMe, a crowdfunding site that has allowed thousands of people to raise more than $1.25 billion since launching in May 2010. "It's much more common these days for friends and family to be the ones raising funds for funerals and memorials."

For example, on GoFundMe.com alone, there are often more than 22,000 open funeral, tribute, and memorial campaigns at one time, with an average funeral campaign raising about $2,200, and an average individual donation amount of $65.

Desiree Vargas Wrigley, CEO and co-founder of GiveForward, said, "What I think crowdfunding does is makes people feel they are a part of the grieving process. They leave a donation to help and can write something about the person who passed."

Funeral directors are also beginning to see its growing popularity, as more of the families they serve turn toward the practice. "I think it's a great tool for both families and funeral homes," said one owner and funeral director. "A lot of families are struggling in this day and age. If family and friends know they need assistance, it fulfills a lot of needs."

While it's usually free to create and share an online fundraising campaign, the platform that a campaigner chooses makes its money by charging credit card payment processing fees and commissions that often add up to 10% of the amount donated. For example, GoFundMe will automatically deduct a 5% fee from each donation as well as a processing fee of about 3%, for a total of 8% on every donation; GiveForward charges 7.9%, plus 30 cents per transaction. But since the fee are deducted automatically at the time of donation, the campaigner is never billed, which appeals to cash-strapped families.

Some funeral directors set up campaigns for families; it's good that someone else can set up the fund-someone that is not in the middle of all the chaos and can help the family.

Unfortunately, crowdfunding is plagued by stories documenting the risk donors take in giving to dishonest people who are only out to falsely play on people's heart strings for personal financial gain. The websites acknowledge this risk and warn donors to proceed with caution. "We're often asked how a donor can tell the authenticity of a personal cause found on GoFundMe," the company posts under it's "Safety and Security" guidelines. "Unfortunately, there is no way to 100% guarantee that a user's GoFundMe donation page contains accurate or truthful information.

Source: Howard-Fusco, L. (2016, March). Crowdfunding: The Future of Funeral Financing? *American Funeral Director.*

Funeral Home Buyer's Guide

Article By: Live Oak Bank (2018)

So You're Ready to Purchase a Funeral Business? Here's How to Make it Happen!

Becoming a business owner is a great achievement both personally and professionally. As a small business lender who specializes in funeral home financing, we want to help you prepare for ownership. This guide outlines what you should consider and prepare when acquiring a funeral home.

CHOOSING THE RIGHT FUNERAL HOME

When it comes to funeral home acquisitions, we typically see two scenarios: a key employee purchases the funeral home where he or she currently works; or a current funeral home owner or director purchases an outside funeral home. Deciding which option is best for you greatly depends on your current circumstances and opportunities. Examine the business trends and operations and market trends to determine if it is the right fit for you.

Business Trends and Operations

When acquiring a funeral home, you want to make sure it is the right fit for your personal and business goals. Consider the following questions to determine if the business you are acquiring is a good fit:

- Is the business growing? If not, can you identify and implement improvements?
- Will the business support your current lifestyle? The business will be your source of income.
- Is the business located in a place where you will be happy living?
- Do you have a similar leadership style and philosophy to the current owner? As the new owner, you can make improvements, but an understanding of the former owner's leadership style can help you ease any apprehension from the staff.

Market Trends

Many of the business trends will be driven by market trends, so it is important to understand the demographics in the area as well as trends in funeral service.

- What are the demographics of the area?
- What competition do you face in your local community?
- Is the local population growing?
- What is the cremation rate? How quickly is it rising?
- Does the cremation rate and cremation service charge justify the addition of a retort?

PREPARING FOR OWNERSHIP

CREATING A BUSINESS PLAN

As you prepare to purchase the funeral home business, you will need to write a business plan. The business plan is your blueprint for success. It will help you think through decisions as you approach

ownership and will serve as a guide once you are in the day-to-day operations. You will also share your business plan with your lender, business partners and key employees.
Be clear and thorough when writing your business plan. Include a formal title page, and make sure your writing is grammatically correct. Make an accurate and professional representation of your capabilities and objectives.

Your business plan should include the following six components:

I. EXECUTIVE SUMMARY

The Executive Summary introduces you and your business venture to readers and is often the first impression they receive of your project. This section should be concise, providing the "what, why, and how" of your undertaking, but also compelling enough to persuade lenders and others that your acquisition plan is viable. You may want to tackle the Executive Summary last, as much of the information for this section is extrapolated from the rest of your business plan.

Your Executive Summary should include:

- Business Overview – Provide a brief overview of the funeral business, your background in the profession, and the specific services you will offer. Describe where your funeral home will be located and the area's demographics. If you are expanding your current funeral home, describe the benefits this expansion will bring to your business and the community.

- Mission Statement – Outline your business philosophy and rationale for your funeral home. Define your goals and where you expect to be in five or ten years.

- Financing Requirements – Summarize the amount of capital you will need to achieve your acquisition or expansion goals.

II. BUSINESS DESCRIPTION

The Business Description goes into greater detail about the structure of your business, your qualifications for managing the funeral home, and your business resources. This section explains why you have the personal know-how and professional means to build long-term success.

Include the following in your Business Description:

- Professional History – Describe your professional experience to date, such as your business background, any professional experience in the funeral home industry, and where and when you attended school, degrees earned, and any related courses taken.

- Management Team and Key Personnel – Identify the principals who are ultimately responsible for the financial performance of your funeral home, your key team members and their roles, and any professional advisors who will be instrumental in providing input and guidance.

- Organizational Structure – Define the legal entity for your business (Sole Proprietorship, LLC, etc.) and ownership details.

III. MARKET RESEARCH

A certain amount of research is required to ensure the local market for your funeral home has the appropriate demographics and income to support your business. The Market Research section demonstrates to your lender that you understand your community and that you have considered the competition in this area.

The Market Research section should include the following:

- Market Description – Describe who lives in the community surrounding your funeral home and what sort of growth or changes are predicted for this area over the next five or ten years.

- Target Customer – Describe the ideal customer or family for your business, including age and income level. Consider the mix of pre-need versus at-need services. If the community based on the Market Description above does not match the type of funeral service you plan to provide, you may want to reconsider the location of the business you are acquiring.

- Competitive Analysis – Define the other businesses in your local market, how many are funeral homes, what kind of services do they offer, and what their advantages and disadvantages are.

- Competitive Advantage – Finally, define the competitive advantage your establishment offers that your competitors do not – for example, the types of services, the variety and range of your cremation offerings, location, price point, etc.

IV. MARKETING PLAN

This section allows you to be a bit more creative as you describe the marketing activities you will use to create visibility for your funeral home and support ongoing business growth.

Be sure your marketing plan is realistic and addresses the following issues:

- *Approximately how much are you budgeting for marketing activities during the first year or two?*

- *How will you set yourself apart from the competition? For example, will you offer special events or sponsor community events?*

- *How will you attract families from the surrounding area and be at the top of your guests' minds when they have a future need for their family?*

- *What is your marketing mix – the balance between print and television advertising, referrals, social media, and other channels of marketing?*

V. OPERATIONS

The Operations section of your business plan details the day-to-day needs and functions of your funeral home, demonstrating that your future success is based on well-thought-out ideas about how you intend to run your business. Include the following:

- Location and Premises – Describe in detail the location of your funeral home, why you chose it, and whether you will own or lease the space. Detail the equipment and inventory necessary now and in the future, whether the equipment will be owned or leased, and who your major suppliers will be. Describe the visibility of your funeral home to surrounding foot and vehicle traffic.

- Days and Hours of Operation – Describe the days and hours you will be open and how you will handle holiday and after hours calls.

- Staffing – Outline any staffing changes that will occur after the acquisition. Define the roles of staff members, compensation, and personnel policies.

VI. FINANCIAL FORECAST

For most business owners, the Financial Forecast is the most challenging section to complete. For your lender, it is the most important. The financing package you receive is based on the numbers in your financial forecast, so it is critical to make these calculations as accurate as possible. Work with your CPA or financial advisor to ensure your forecast is viable and reflects the business accurately.

Your forecast should include:

- Income and Cash Flow Projection. The financial projection should cover at least 36 months of operation of your funeral home. Your projected income is based on service costs per week and will likely grow over time. Your cash flow is the difference between your gross income and your operating expenses and overhead.

- Capital and Operating Expenses. These are the total funds needed to acquire and operate your new or expanded funeral home. Try to be as specific and realistic as possible. Include loan payments, staff salaries, rent, utilities, supplies, and other minor expenses. It is better to be conservative and overestimate your budget.

- Project Financing. Detail how much you need in financing to your funeral home and consider your preferred terms. Include any personal or investor funds that will be contributed to the project. Include purchase price details, such as real estate value and whether the transaction will be an asset or stock purchase.

SETTING GOALS

Whether your objective is to run a small, profitable funeral home or become a leading funeral home in your region, the only way to ultimately control the outcome of your business goals is to plan for it. Set realistic goals quarterly that will help you reach your ultimate goal.

Goals may include the following:

- Growing revenue by 5-10%
- Reducing your Cost of Goods Sold
- Offering new cremation products and service offerings
- Creating an effective marketing plan
- Adding a reception center, memorial garden, and crematory

SETTING A BUDGET

As a business owner, you will need to set a budget. Develop a budget for projected income and expenses. At a minimum, your budget should include operating expense, inventory, staffing, business savings, and your salary. Working with an accountant or consultant who specializes in funeral service can help you set an appropriate budget.

FINANCING THE PURCHASE

To successfully acquire a funeral home, you will likely need financing. Historically, seller financing was the primary method to complete the transaction, but today buyers have financing options through financial institutions. As the buyer, you will work directly with the lender to receive the funds to purchase the funeral home. Ultimately, a lender will base an approval on the funeral home's financial strength — the ability for the business to service all new and existing business debt including new owner's salary and the buyer's personal credit.

Initial qualifications of the borrower include:

- *Three years of funeral home experience*
- *Funeral Director's license*
- *No bankruptcies*

You will then work with your lender to complete the following requirements:

FINANCIALS

- Three years of business tax returns
- Year-to-date (YTD) income statement and current balance sheet
- Comparable income statement and balance sheet from previous year
- Projections for at least the first three years under new ownership.

If you have plans to acquire a funeral home, we hope this guide aides in your success. Please do not hesitate to contact our team with any questions. Our goal is to partner with you to make your dreams of ownership a reality.

CONCLUSION CHECKLIST

- Staffing plan:
  - *Will existing employees remain on staff once you own the business?*
  - *Will you need to hire additional staff?*
- Identify new expenses upon acquisition (refer to "Creating a Business Plan") such as:
  - *Marketing*
  - *Renovations*
  - *New Equipment*

- Call volume for past three years and year-to-date (YTD) interim call volume, including cremation percentage

- Market share and competition overview

- Pre-need Insurance & Trust backlog and amount converted to at-need volume for past three years

- Letter of intent (LOI) stating:

  1. Purchase price
  2. Stock or Asset Purchase
  3. Portion of purchase price allocated to:
     - *Real estate intangible business assets (goodwill)*
     - *FF&E (Furniture, Fixtures, & Equipment)*
  4. Seller Carry (if applicable)
     - *The rate of the seller note is at the buyer and seller's discretion. The seller carry must be on full standby with no principal or interest payments to be made for the life of the SBA loan. Seller note cannot exceed 5% of the required equity.*

The financial information will be used by Live Oak Bank to qualify the acquisition opportunity. We understand this acquisition is an important event for both you and the current owner, which is why we do our best to structure the deal to benefit both parties. Our goal is to work with you to simplify the loan process and help ensure a smooth ownership transition.

CONCLUSIONS

If you have plans to acquire a funeral home, we hope this guide aids in your success. Please do not hesitate to contact our team with any questions. Our goal is to partner with you to make your dreams of ownership a reality.

Source: Live Oak Bank (2018, January 18). Funeral Home Buyers Guide. Retrieved from: https://www.liveoakbank.com/wp-content/uploads/2018/01/18-LOB-DC-AcquisitionGuide-digital.pdf

Funeral Insurance Pros, Cons, and Differences

By: Gail Rubin (2015)

Many Americans don't have the financial self-control to actually save money in the bank to pay the costs associated with their eventual demise. Just look at the popularity of online funeral fundraising pages and memorial fund car washes for proof. That's why there's insurance.

There are big differences between funeral insurance – also known as burial insurance – and those big insurance policies that cover a family's finances should the main breadwinner die. Many people don't know the difference between those life insurance policies, pre-need funeral insurance, and final expense insurance. This article can help explain the differences.

TIME IS NOT ON YOUR SIDE

Many Americans think their group life insurance policy from work will pay for a funeral. Well, yes, it can – eventually. That's assuming they even have such an insurance policy – many don't.

Many don't realize the money from a life insurance policy doesn't become available until an official death certificate for the insured person is issued by the state. Then it can take weeks or even months to process the claim.

Some families who count on life insurance to cover funeral expenses have to scramble to cover expenses right after someone dies. They might access personal savings, credit cards, borrow from family and friends, or take a bridge loan through the funeral home, known as an assignment.

Think about it – could an average person's credit limit handle a charge of $8,000 to $15,000 for the products and services of a funeral home or cemetery? Think of the points, the miles, if you could! Funeral homes and cemeteries won't bury or cremate a loved one without some kind of payment up front.

Some life insurance companies offer expedited payment of death benefits, reduced from months or weeks to days, but that's through group life insurance offered through employers. What are the options if you don't have such benefits?

There are two types of funeral insurance: Prepaid funeral insurance issued through a funeral home and final expense insurance offered by independent insurance agents.

PRE-NEED INSURANCE

PROS

- Funeral homes and cemeteries will offer a "price lock-in" at current rates, so the costs remain covered even if the person dies many years later.

- Most policies are portable if you move, you can take the money in the policy and apply it at another funeral home. Make sure this is an option!

- One the policy is paid up and the information is on file, all it takes is a phone call from the family to have everything taken care of the way the deceased had planned.

- If the funeral home is bought by another company or goes out of business, your money is still protected in the insurance policy.

- Any excess funds left over after the funeral expenses are paid get returned to the family tax-free.
- Pre-need funeral insurance is available to anyone in any medical condition.

CONS

- A funeral home policy doesn't usually cover cemetery expenses – that requires a separate cemetery burial insurance policy or additional funds.
- If you move and apply the funds in the policy at a different funeral home, the "price lock-in" benefit does not apply – you pay the current rates at the new funeral home, which may be much more expensive then when the policy was purchased.
- Pre-need insurance may not cover all the expenses outside of the funeral home's control when the insured actually dies.
- If the policy owner does not pay all the premiums, all benefits – and funds – are lost.

FINAL EXPENSE INSURANCE

Final expense insurance is a small whole life policy that typically ranges from $3,000 to $50,000 in benefits. This insurance is designed for those over 50 years of age, and it can be issued to people with various health conditions. These policies are sold by independent insurance agents representing companies such as Aetna, MetLife, Mutual of Omaha, New York Life, and Transamerica.

PROS

- You name the beneficiary who receives the fund and carries out your final wishes. Secondary and tertiary beneficiaries can also be names.
- The funds can be used for any kind of expenses, including funeral costs. The money can cover a big life celebration event, airfare for dispersed family members to gather, and outstanding bills that need to be paid.
- As a whole life policy, final expense insurance builds cash value over time through affordable monthly payments that don't increase, and the benefit doesn't expire like term policies do.
- Most final expense insurance policies have a simple applications process with no medical examination required and claims are paid quickly.
- Final expense insurance policies can also be used as a charitable giving vehicle to support non-profit organizations and worthy causes.
- Policy holders can borrow against the cash value of the policy, and proceeds from insurance are tax-free to the beneficiaries.

CONS

- You rely on the beneficiary to carry out your funeral plans, which they may or may not do.
- Funeral costs will continue to rise, and a final expense policy does not "lock-in" current prices at a funeral home.
- Since a final expense policy pays a fixed amount, depending on how far in the future the insured dies, the policy may not cover all funeral expenses.
- Those with certain illnesses or medical conditions will pay more in premiums, and they may not be insurable.

Whether a client decides to use pre-need funeral insurance or final expense insurance depends on several factors:

- Current state of health, age, and income.
- What funeral plans entail – it's best to have an idea before shopping around!
- Are there family or friends who will carry out the client's last wishes?
- How many local funeral homes are competing for business?
- Does the client plan to stay in the current location, or is a move to another town in the future?

Take all these factors into consideration before choosing pre-need funeral insurance or final expense insurance.

Source: Rubin, G. (2015, December). Funeral Insurance Pros, Cons, and Differences. *Mortuary Management Magazine*.

Servant Leadership

By: Ralph Klicker, Ph.D.

"A good objective of leadership is to help those who are doing poorly to do well and to help those who are doing well to do even better." Jim Rohn, American Entrepreneur

What is Servant Leadership?

Robert K. Greenleaf first coined the phrase "servant leadership" in his 1970 essay, "***The Servant as a Leader***." However, it's an approach that people have used for centuries.

In servant leadership, you consider the needs of your staff before you consider your own. You acknowledge other people's perspectives, give them the support they need to meet their work and personal goals, involve them in decisions where appropriate, and build a sense of community within your team. This leads to higher engagement, more trust, and stronger relationships with team members and other stakeholders. It can also lead to increased **innovation.**

Servant leadership is a leadership philosophy in which the main goal of the leader is to serve. This is different from traditional leadership where the leader's main focus is the thriving of their company or organization. A servant leader shares power, puts the needs of the employee first, and helps people develop and perform as highly as possible. Servant leadership inverts the norm and puts the customer service associates as a main priority. Instead of people working to serve the leader, the leader exists to serve the people. As stated by its founder, Robert K. Greenleaf, a servant leader should be focused on, "whether those served grow as persons? Do they, while being served, become healthier, wiser, freer, more autonomous, more likely themselves to become servants?" When leaders shift their mindset and serve first, both they and their employees' benefit. The employees acquire more personal growth under this type of leadership. Additionally, the organization grows due to increased commitment and engagement by the employees.

10 Characteristics of Servant Leaders

1. **Listening** — You'll serve people better when you make a deep commitment to listening intently to them and understanding what they're saying. Give people your full attention, take notice of their body language, avoid interrupting them before they have finished speaking, and give them feedback on what they are saying.

2. **Empathy** — Servant leaders strive to understand people's intentions and perspectives fully. They see the situation through the eyes of the other person and are able to "walk in their shoes."

3. **Healing** — This characteristic relates to the emotional health and "wholeness" of people. It involves supporting them both physically and mentally. It also means creating and maintaining a supportive work environment.

4. **Self-Awareness** — This means understanding oneself and the impact one has on others.

5. **Persuasion** — Servant leaders use persuasion, rather than authority, to encourage people to take action. They also aim to build consensus in groups, so that everyone supports the decisions made.

6. **Conceptualization** — This characteristic relates to your ability to "dream great dreams," so that you look beyond day-to-day realities to the bigger picture. Servant leaders seek a balance between short-term and long-term goals and outlooks.

7. **Foresight** — Servant leaders have the ability to foresee future outcomes associated with a current course of action of situation. They are able to trust their own intuition. If intuition is telling you something is wrong – listen to it!

8. **Stewardship** — Stewardship is about taking responsibility for the actions and performance of your team and being accountable for the role team members play in your organization.

9. **Commitment to Growth of People** — Servant leaders are committed to the personal and professional development of everyone on their teams.

10. **Building Community** — Servant leaders build a sense of community within their organization. They take steps to actively build relationships and connections among the members of their team. This creates a culture and sense of community. You can do this by providing opportunities for employees to interact with one another across the company. For instance, you could organize social events, such as team lunches and barbecues, design your workspace to encourage people to chat informally away from their desks, and dedicate the first few minutes of meetings to non-work-related conversations.

Conclusion

Servant leaders are likely to have more engaged employees and enjoy better relationships with team members and other stakeholders than leaders who do not put the interests of others before their own. Encouraging people to take responsibility for their work and reminding them of their contribution results in better success for the organization. You are a servant leader when you focus on the needs of others before you consider your own. This is a long-term, foundational approach, rather than a technique that you adopt for specific situations. It can be used with other situational and specific leadership styles.

Resources

Spears, L.C. (2010). Character and Servant Leadership: 10 Characteristics of Effective, Caring Leaders. *The Journal of Virtues ad Leadership*, Vol. 1, Issue 1, p.25-30.

NOTES

Section IX

APPENDIX

REFERENCES

Adams, A. (2016, April). Capturing the Final Goodbye. *American Funeral Director*.

The African Seeds of Scouting (n.d.). The Ashanti Campaign. Retrieved from: http://www.scouting.org.za/seeds/ashanti.html.

Albrecht, E. (2018, November 12). A Detailed Analysis of How Funeral Homes Are Complying with the FTC Funeral Rule. *Funeral Service Insider*. Retrieved from: http://www.bpmlaw.com/wp-content/uploads/2018/11/A-Detailed-Analysis-of-How-Funeral-Homes.pdf.

Albrecht, E.A. (2017, July). Million Dollar Mistake. *American Funeral Director.*

Albrecht, E.A. (2017a, December) Pulling Back the Curtain: Risk Management Strategies for Dealing with Third Party Crematories. *American Cemetery and Cremation*, p. 28-30.

Allen, M. (2017, October 11) *Nine Tips for Connecting with Funeral Shoppers*. Retrieved from: https://goldenrulefh.wordpress.com/2017/10/11/nine-tips-for-connecting-with-funeral-shoppers/.

American Bar Association (2012, October 23). *Protection for LGBT Employees Under Title VII of the 1964 Civil Rights Act*. Retrieved from: https://www.americanbar.org/publications/human_rights_magazine_home/human_rights_vol31_2004/summer2004/irr_hr_summer04_protectlgbt/.

American Board of Funeral Services Education (2000, July). Funeral Merchandising Syllabus.

American Funeral Director (2016, February). 8 Tips to Succeed at a Job Interview. *American Funeral Director*, p.14.

American Pet Products Association (2017-2018). AAPA National Pet Owners Survey. Greenwich, CT: *American Pet Products Association*; Retrieved from: https://americanpetproducts.org/Uploads/MemServices/GPE2017_NPOS_Seminar.pdf.

American Pet Products Association (2019-2020). *Pet Industry Market Size and Ownership Statistics*. Retrieved from: https://www.americanpetproducts.org/press_industrytrends.asp.

Andrews, J. (2014, July 30). *The Difference Between Funerals and Celebrations of Life*. Retrieved from: http://funeralcostshelp.co.uk/difference-funerals-celebrations-life/.

Australian Funeral Directors Association (2018, March). *So You Want to Be a Funeral Director: A Guide for School Leavers and New Entrants into the Funeral Industry.* Retrieved from: https://afda.org.au/wp-content/uploads/2018/03/So-you-want-to-be-a-funeral-director.pdf.

Baklarz, M. (2004, January). Focusing on Service as a Marketing Strategy. *Yellow Book News.*

Bartsche, P.M (2014, June). Thinking Out of the Box. *American Funeral Director*, p. 20-24.

Bartsche, P.M. (2014, September). Marketing Roundtable. *American Funeral Director*, p.58-62.

Bartsche, P.M. (2015, June). Green Roundtable. *American Cemetery and Cremation*, p. 30-32.

Bartsche, P.M. (2015a, August). Casket Personalization: Making your Mark. *American Funeral Director*, p. 28-31.

Bartsche, P.M. (2015b, October). Vaults Roundtable. *American Funeral Director*, p. 88, 90.

Bartsche, P.M. (2016, January). Roundtable Answering Services. *American Funeral Director*.

Bartsche, P.M. (2016a, February). A New Option, Right Choice Cremation. *The Director*, p. 31.

Bartsche, P.M. (2016b, May) Building Pre-need Success. *American Funeral Director*, p. 22.

Bartsche, P.M. (2016c, August). Celebrating a Life with Mountain Dew. *American Funeral Director*, p. 38.

Bartsche, P.M. (2016, November). The Cremation Business Blueprint for Death-Care Professionals. *American Cemetery & Cremation*, p. 28.

Bartsche, P.M. (2017, January). Urns Roundtable. *American Funeral Director*, p. 68-71.

Bartsche, P.M. (2017a, July). Roundtable. *American Funeral Director*.

Batesville (n.d.) *Creating a Meaningful Funeral*. Retrieved from: https://www.batesville.com/helping-families/meaningful-service/#1473872372015-f76caa85-d18d.

Beebe, W.H. Jr. (2016) Three Things Every Funeral Director Must Do…Without Fail. *The Forum,* p. 42.

Berwald, A. (2011, November). Top 10 Things to Consider When Dealing with Funeral Shipping. *The Southern Funeral Director*, p.32.

Billingham, P. (2016, May 10). How to Develop A Digital Strategy for Funeral Directors. *Death Goes Digital Blog*. Retrieved from: https://www.deathgoesdigital.com/blog/digital-strategy-funeral-directors-1-allocate-resources.

Billingham, P. (2016a, August 2). Is There Any Place for Innovation in the Funeral Industry Today? *Death Goes Digital Blog*. Retrieved from: https://www.deathgoesdigital.com/blog/digital-strategy-funeral-directors-innovation.

Billingham, P. (2016b, May 24). This is How to Create A Customer Experiences for Your Funeral Business That Will Make You Memorable. *Death Goes Digital Blog.* Retrieved from: https://www.deathgoesdigital.com/blog/digital-strategy-funeral-directors-3-customer-experience.

Billingham, P. (2016c, June 1, 2016). Who is the Hero of Your Funeral Business? *Death Goes Digital Blog*. Retrieved from: https://www.deathgoesdigital.com/blog/digital-strategy-funeral-directors-4-platforms.

Billingham, P. (2016d, June 7). This is a Proven Way to Make Your Funeral Business Thrive Online. *Death Goes Digital Blog*. Retrieved from: https://www.deathgoesdigital.com/blog/digital-strategy-funeral-directors-5-create-content.

Bloomquist, B. (2015, August 27). *4 Ways Aftercare Can Help Grow Your Funeral Home Business*. Retrieved from: https://www.homesteaderslife.com/blog/4-ways-aftercare-can-help-grow-your-funeral-home-business.

Boots, C. (2015, March/April). Caskets To-Let. *Funeral Business Advisor*, p.66-68. Retrieved from: http://viewer.zmags.com/publication/f086dc2a#/f086dc2a/67.

Boroff, D. (2014, May 19). Six Superheroes Serve as Pallbearers for Funeral of 5-Year-Old Boy Who Died of Cancer. *New York Daily News*. Retrieved from: https://www.nydailynews.com/life-style/superheroes-serve-pallbearers-funeral-5-year-old-boy-article-1.1797827.

Boxley, J. (2017, April) Charting a Course for Success and Creative Event Planning. *The Director*.

Brown, B. (2015, September). 6 Tips for Creating an Effective Community Outreach Program. *American Cemetery & Cremation.*

Brown, J. (2002, June 13). Help New Employees Ease into Their Positions. *Death Care Business Advisor.*

Campbell, Anita (2018, December 26). What is Owned, Earned, and Paid Media. *Small Business Trends.* Retrieved from: https://smallbiztrends.com/2013/08/what-is-owned-earned-paid-media.html.

Canadian Animal Health Institute (2017, January 23). *Latest Canadian Pet Population Figures Released.* Retrieved from: https://www.canadianveterinarians.net/documents/canadian-pet-population-figures-cahi-2017.

Callaghan, J. (2015, March 30). *The 3 Keys to Marketing Your Funeral Home in a Changing Industry.* Retrieved from: http://www.funeralsuccess.com/2015/03/the-3-keys-to-marketing-your-funeral home-in-a-changing-industry/.

CANA (2017, July 18). *Asking the Right Questions: Interviewing Families with an Event Planner Mindset.* Cremation Association of North America. Retrieved from: https://www.cremationassociation.org/blogpost/776820/280873/Asking-the-Right-Questions-Interviewing-Families-with-an-Event-Planner-Mindset.

Canine, J. (2002, Sept.) The Funeral Professionals Role in the Greif Process: What You Can do to Help. *American Funeral Director.*

The Cemetery Handbook, 2nd Ed. (1946). Madison, WI: Park & Cemetery Publishing Co.

Clark, C. (2006, September). Little Acorns. *The Director.*

Cohen, H. (2011, August 8). *30 Branding Definitions.* [Blog Post]. Retrieved from: https://heidicohen.com/30-branding-definitions/.

Cozine, W.A. (2017, April). The First and Last Word in Funeral Service. *The Director.*

Crawford, C. (n.d.) *Ethical issues in today's funeral industry.* Retrieved from: http://smallbusiness.chron.com/ethical-issues-todays-funeral-industry-62750.html.

Creedy, A. (2012, January). Narrow your focus, Broaden your market. *The Director*, p.24, 26-28.

Cremation Association of America (2018). *2018 Annual Statistics Report.* Retrieved from: www.cremationassociation.org/pages/IndustryStatistics.

Cremation Resource (2019). *How is a Body Cremated?* Retrieved from: http://www.cremationresource.org/cremation/how-is-a-body-cremated.html.

Cremation Resource (2019a). *How is Cremation Done?* Retrieved from: http://www.cremationresource.org/cremation/how-is-cremation-done.html.

Cronin, S. (2016, April). Preserving Personal Art. *American Funeral Director*, p. 26-28.

Cronin, S. (2016, October) Green Roundtable. *American Funeral Director*, p. 98-100.

Cronin, S. (2016a, August). Pre-need Roundtable. *American Funeral Director,* p. 67.

Cronin, S. (2017). Jake Johnson's Advice for Aspiring Funeral Home Owners. *Funeral Service Insider.*

Cronin, S. (2017a, December) Witnessing Rooms Give Cremation Families Options. *American Cemetery and Cremation*, p. 24-26.

Cronin, S. (2017b, August) Pre-need Roundtable. *American Funeral Director*, p. 74.

Cronin, S. (2017c, August). Somewhere on a Beach. *American Funeral Director*, p. 46-47.

Cronin, S. (2017d, April). The Dual Licensure Debate. *American Funeral Director*, p. 34-39.

Darby, R. (2015, July). 4 Things Families Don't Know about Cremation. *American Funeral Director*, p. 56.

Darby, R. (2016, June). Give the Families You Serve Peace of Mind. *American Funeral Director*, p. 52-53.

Darland, T. (2015, May). Optimizing Business Opportunities with Different Family Types. *American Funeral Director*, p. 59.

Dawson, F. (2015). *Transformational Funeral Service: Gaining a Competitive Edge – A Funeral Director's Guide*. Somerset: UK, Haynes Creative Publishing.

Dean, K. (2017, January). Let's Chat. *Funeral Home and Cemetery News.*

Dearborn Financial Publication (1996). *Life and Health Insurance Principles and Practices (3rd Ed).* Southfield, MI: Dearborn Financial Institute.

Defort, E.(2017, April). The "Wow" Factor vs. the "Whatever" Factor. *The Director.*

Desai, A.N. (2015, March 2). *Burial Pods: Biodegradable Coffins Could One Day Replace Depressing Cemeteries with Lush Green Forests*. Retrieved from: www.inquisitr.com/1888594/burial-pods-biodegradable-coffins-could-one-day-replace-depressing-cemeteries-with-lush-green-forests/.

Devaney, M. (2016, July/August). Creating an Atmosphere of Choice for Cremation Families. *Southern Funeral Director Magazine*, p. 22-25.

Donate Life (2019). Retrieved from: http://donatelife.net.

DNA Memorial (2017, September 18). *How Technology is Disrupting the Funeral Industry*. Retrieved from: http://linkedin.com/pulse/how-technology-disrupting-funeral-industry-dna-memorial.

The Director (2015, January). Http://www.nfda.org.

Ellis Funeral Homes (n.d.). *Funerals vs. Celebrations of Life*. Retrieved from: https://ellisfuneralhomes.com/funerals-vs-celebrations-of-life.html.

Elmore, T. (2019). *Six Defining Characteristics of Generation Z*. [Blog Post]. Retrieved from: https://growingleaders.com/blog/six-defining-characteristics-of-generation-z/.

EPA (2018, March 12). *Burial at Sea*. The United States Environmental Protection Agency. Retrieved from: https://www.epa.gov/ocean-dumping/burial-sea.

Examples of Personalization Options (2017). *Cremationist Magazine*, Volume 53, No. 2.

Farber, M. (2019, May 4). *Luke Perry was Buried in Eco-friendly "Mushroom burial suit" According to Daughter*. Retrieved: https://www.foxnews.com/entertainment/luke-perry-mushroom-burial-suit.

Filhaber, D. (n.d.). How Many Times Does Someone Need to See Your Ad Before They Buy? *International Cemetery, Cremation, and Funeral Association.* Retrieved from: https://iccfa.com/2016/04/20/how-many-times-does-someone-need-to-see-your-ad-before-they-buy/.

Filhaber, D. (2016). *Lead Generation Made ~~Easy~~ Easier*. Scotts Valley: CA, CreateSpace Independent Publishing Platform.

Fowler, J. (2015, February 15). *8 Imaginative Ways to Personalize a Funeral*. Retrieved from https://www.myasd.com/blog/8-imaginative-ways-personalize-funeral .

FTC (2015, January 9). Trade Regulation Rule Concerning Cooling-Off Period for Sales Made at Homes or at Certain Other Locations 2015. *Federal Trade Commission. Fed. Reg. Vol. 80, No. 6. 16 CFR Part 429.*

Funeral and Memorial Information Council (FMIC) (2015). *New Study Shows Americans Recognize the Role of Memorialization in Healthy Healing Following the Death of a Loved One*. Retrieved from: https://www.famic.org/famic-study/.

Funeral Cost Help (2019). *The Difference between Funerals and Celebrations of Life*. Retrieved from: https://funeralcostshelp.co.uk/blog/difference-funerals-celebrations-life/.

Funeral Home and Cemetery News. (2017, September). Available at: http://www.nomispublications.com/onlinenews.aspx.

Funeral Service Insider (2014). Kates-Boylston Publications. Retrieved from: https://kates-boylston.com/funeral-service-insider/.

Funeral Service Insider (2014, November 3). Kates-Boylston Publications. Retrieved from: https://kates-boylston.com/funeral-service-insider/.

Funeral Service Insider (2015). Rental caskets take center stage as the cremation rate climbs. Retrieved from: https://kates-boylston.com/funeral-service-insider/.

Funeral Service Insider (2015a, March 9). Why Preserve DNA?

Funeral Service Insider (2016, January 18). Retrieved from: https://kates-boylston.com/funeral-service-insider/.

Funeral Service Insider (2016c, June 13). Biggest Frustrations for Management in Hiring: Management Complaints. Retrieved from: https://kates-boylston.com/funeral-service-insider/.

Funeral Service Insider (2016, April 4). Marketing Survey Shows Online Tactics Becoming More Important (2016, April 4). Retrieved from: https://kates-boylston.com/funeral-service-insider/.

Funeral Service Insider (2017, November 6). Retrieved from: https://kates-boylston.com/funeral-service-insider/.

Funeral Service Insider (2018, November 5). Retrieved from: https://kates-boylston.com/funeral-service-insider/.

Funeralwise (2019). *Honoring the Deceased with a Memorial Donation*. Retrieved from: https://www.funeralwise.com/etiquette/donations/

Funeralwise (2019a). *A Guide to Sending Funeral Flowers*. Retrieved from: https://www.funeralwise.com/etiquette/flowers/

Garrison, B. (2012, August 26). Watch Out for Bedbugs! Removing Remains from a Home or Long Term Care Facility? *Ohio Funeral Directors Association*. Retrieved from: http://www.ohio-fda.org/aws/OFDA/pt/sd/news_article/62669/_PARENT/layout_details/true.

Glawe, L. (2006, June). "Can-Do" Media Coverage. *The Director*.

Gould, G. (2015, April). Understanding the Consumer's Perspective. *The Director*, p. 64-65.

Goldade, J. (2017, March 28). *Making the Most of Your Funeral Flowers*. Retrieved from: https://www.frazerconsultants.com/2017/03/making-the-most-of-your-funeral-flowers/.

Green Burial Council (n.d.). *What is Green Burial?* Retrieved from https://greenburialcouncil.org/home/what-is-green-burial/.

The Guardian (n.d.). Undertaker Uses Newspapers for Coffins. *The East London and West Essex Guardian*. Retrieved from: http://www.guardian-series.co.uk/.

Handy, A. (2012, February 13) *House Transfers*. Retrieved from: http://theothersideoffunerals.blogspot.com/search?updated-max=2012-02-15T20:55:00%2B11:00&max-results=10&start=87&by-date=false.

Harbeson, J. (n.d.). *What's More Important: Products or Services?* Retrieved from: https://theforesightcompanies.com/whats-more-important-products-or-service/.

Harris, J. (1999). *Chocolat*. UK: Doubleday.

Haas, A. (2018, January 28). Life is for Sharing, Beginning to End. *The Buffalo News*.

Heart in Diamond (2018, November 5). *Funeral & Cremation Costs Compared*. Retrieved from: https://www.heart-in-diamond.com/cremation-diamonds/burial-cost-future.html.

Heppell, R. (2015, July). Creating the Best Funeral Home Ads. *Mortuary Management Magazine.*

Homesteader Life Company (2017). How Satisfied are You with Your Decision to Prearrange Your Funeral? Retrieved from: https://www.homesteaderslife.com/.

Hong, W. (2018, June). Blogging 101: What to Write, How Much, & How Often. *American Funeral Director.*

Howard-Fusco, L. (2016, March). Crowdfunding: The Future of Funeral Financing? *American Funeral Director.*

Hsieh, T. (2010). *Delivering Happiness: A Path to Profits, Passion, and Purpose.* New York, NY: Grand Central Publishing.

Hyams, C. & Troxler, J. (2012, November). Behave Yourself on LinkedIn. *Texas Funeral Director.*

Imperi, C. (2017, January). Death Doulas and Funeral Service. *American Funeral Director*, p.46-50.

Isard, D. (2014, January). The Floodgates: Dan Isard Argues Against the Guarantee – Again. *American Funeral Director*, p. 44-48.

Isard, D. (2015, January). Aftercare, Outreach, and Pre-Need: The Next Frontiers. *Canadian Funeral News*, p. 31-33.

Isard, D.M. (2017, July). The Past, Present & Future of Cremation. *American Funeral Director*, p. 46-47.

Janin, A. (2016, February 9). *This 'Death Suit' Makes Burials Eco- and Wallet-Friendly.* Take Part, Participant Media. Retrieved from: http://www.takepart.com/article/2016/02/09/death-suit-makes-burials-eco-wallet-friendly.

Joachim, J. (2014, March 4). *The Ugly Truth: Baby Boomer's Thoughts on Funeral Service*. Retrieved from: http://blog.funeralone.com/news/unly-truth-baby-boomers-thoughts-funeral-service.

Katz, B. (2017, August 11). Cremation Rates Reach All-Time High in U.S. *Smithsonian Smart News.* Retrieved from: https://www.smithsonianmag.com/smart-news/cremation-rates-reach-all-time-high-us-180964478/.

Kelly, M. (2018, May 29). Strategic Marketing in 2018. *Funeral Business Advisor Magazine*. Retrieved from: https://funeralbusinessadvisor.com/strategic-marketing-in-2018/funeral-business-advisor.

Kelly, M. (2018a, September 10). Technology in the Funeral Industry. *Funeral Business Advisor Magazine.* Retrieved from: https://funeralbusinessadvisor.com/technology-in-the-funeral-industry/funeral-business-advisor.

Koth (2015). Handling a Customer Service Complaint.

Kubasak, M. (2015, August) Accountability on Arrival. *American Funeral Director*, p. 80-81.

Kuhnen, C. (2016, September 1). *Telephone Funeral Price Shoppers*. Retrieved from: http://www.nomispublications.com/blogdetail.aspx?id=466 Funeral and Cemetery.

Kuhnen, C. (2017, January). There's More to It. Advance Funeral Planning. *Funeral Home & Cemetery News*, p. A6.

LeBlanc, A.B. (2019, February 11). Bogati Urns Founder: Make Urn Selection More than Just a Sale. *Funeral Service Insider*.

Lemasters, P. (2015, August/September). What Does the Supreme Court Ruling on Same-Sex Marriage Mean for Death-Care Providers? *ICCFA Magazine*.

Lemasters, P. (2016, July/August). Knowing Who Has Legal Control of Cremation. *Southern Funeral Director Magazine*.

Live Oak Bank (2018, January 18). *Funeral Home Buyers Guide*. Retrieved from: https://www.liveoakbank.com/wp-content/uploads/2018/01/18-LOB-DC-AcquisitionGuide-digital.pdf.

Lucas, S. (2013, August 30). *How Much Employee Turnover Really Costs You*. Retrieved from: https://www.inc.com/suzanne-lucas/why-employee-turnover-is-so-costly.html.

Marsden, S.J. (2014, October 15). *An industry in change: How cremation is becoming the nation's preferred funeral option*. Retrieved from: http://www.us-funerals.com/funeral-articles/how-cremation-is-becoming-the-nations-preferred-choice.html#.WY8cw1GGM2w.

Marsden, S. (2014a, October 29). Funeral Poverty in the 21st Century. *U.S. Funerals Online*. Retrieved from: http://www.us-funerals.com/funeral-articles/funeral-poverty-in-the-21st-century.html#.XWVzJ-hKg2w.

Mayeroff, B. (2014, August 29). *Funeral Processions Should be Outlawed*. Retrieved from: http://www.chicagonow.com/where-beer-whiskey-flow/2014/08/funeral-processions/.

McCourt, N. (2019, June 16). *How Funeral Homes Stay Competitive with Technology*. Retrieved from: https://mksh.com/how-funeral-homes-stay-competitive-with-technology/.

McRae, O. (2004, August). A History of the American Cemetery. *American Cemetery Magazine*.

Mintel (2015, July 13). "Nearly 70% of Americans Shop Online Regularly with 50% Taking Advantage of Free Shipping." *Mintel Press Office*. Retrieved from: https://www.mintel.com/press-centre/technology-press-centre/nearly-70-of-americans-shop-online-regularly-with-close-to-50-taking-advantage-of-free-shipping.

Mittenzwei, M. W. (n.d.). What is in Your Selecting Room? Personal Leadership. *The World of Funeral Service*, p. 41.

MyMajors (2019). *Morticians, Undertakers, and Funeral Directors Career*. Retrieved from: https://www.mymajors.com/career/morticians-undertakers-and-funeral-directors/.

National Cemetery Administration (2019, September 25). *Burial Benefits*. Retrieved from: http://www.cem.va.gov/cem/burial_benefits/index.asp.

Nelson, B. & Economy, P. (2010). *Managing for Dummies*. Hoboken, NJ: John & Wiley Sons, Inc.

New Jersey Funeral Directors Association (2012, April). Police Will Issue Tickets to Funeral Processions. *The Forum*, p. 14.

New York Times (2021, April 6). Coronavirus in the US: Latest Map and Case Count. Retrieved from: https://www.nytimes.com/interactive/2020/us/coronavirus-us-cases.html.

New York Times (2021, April 6). Coronavirus World Map: Tracking the Global Outbreak. Retrieved from: https://www.nytimes.com/interactive/2020/world/coronavirus-maps.html.

NFDA (2016). Consumer Awareness & Perception Study. National Funeral Directors Association.

NFDA (2016a). The FTC Cooling-Off Rule. *National Funeral Directors Association, CPC Program*, p. 29.

NFDA (2017, July 18). Increase in Cremation Impacts the Way Families Honor Loved Ones Lives. *National Funeral Directors Association News Release*. Retrieved from: http://www.nfda.org/news/media-center/nfda-news-releases/id/2511/nfda-cremation-and-burial-report-shows-rate-of-cremation-at-all-time-high.

NFDA (2019). *Frequently Asked Questions (Shipping Remains)*. National Funeral Directors Association. Retrieved from: http://www.nfda.org/resources/operations-management/shipping-remains/united-states-shipping-regulations/frequently-asked-questions.

Newbern, S. (2015, December). Precautions to Prevent Calamity. *Mortuary Management*, p. 6.

Neptune Society (2015, September 9). *Next of Kin and Same Sex Marriage*. Retrieved from: https://www.neptunesociety.com/cremation-information-articles/next-of-kin-and-same-sex-marriage.

O*NET (2019, August 6). *Details Report for 39-4031.00 Morticians, Undertakers, and Funeral Directors*. O NET Online. Retrieved from: https://www.onetonline.org/link/details/39-4031.00.

OSHA Regulations That Affect Funeral Homes (2019). Granger, Inc. Retrieved from: https://www.grainger.com/content/qt-funeral-home-regulations-280.

Patch Spotlights (2018, June 14). *Funeral Director Jeffery M. Dames Discusses Traditional Funerals*. Retrieved from: http://www.patch.com/illinois/joliet/funeral-director-jeffery-m-dames-discusses-traditional-funerals.

Phaneuf (n.d.). *Changing Landscape: Funeral Homes of the 21st Century*. Retrieved from: https://phaneuf.net/blog/changing-landscape-funeral-homes-in-the-21st-century.

Planningafuneral.com (2008). *After Funeral or Cremation Gathering*. Retrieved from: http://www.planningafuneral.com/afterfuneral.aspx.

Promessa (2019). *Ecological Burial*. Retrieved from: http://www.promessa.se/.

Prothero, S. (2001). *Purified by Fire- A History of Cremation in America*. Los Angeles, CA: University of California Press, p. 47-50.

Prothero, S. (2002, September). A History of Cremation. *American Funeral Director*.

Quincy Memorials (2018). *8 Reasons to Memorialize with a Monument*. Quincy Memorials Info Center. Retrieved from: https://www.quincymemorials.com/info-center/importance-of-memorialization/.

Ramsey, S. (2017, September 13). *The Under Achiever: Mentor or Terminate? Part 2*. Retrieved from: https://goldenrulefh.wordpress.com/2017/09/13/the-under-achiever-mentor-or-terminate-part-2/.

Raymond, C. (2017a, August 9). *The Pros & Cons of Funeral Webcasting*. Retrieved from: https://www.funeralhelpcenter.com/the-pros-cons-of-funeral-webcasting/.

Raymond, C. (2017, December 15). *What is Promession and how does it work?* Funeral Help Center. Retrieved from: https://www.funeralhelpcenter.com/what-is-promession-and-how-does-it-work/.

Rempen, K. (2018, May). Staying Competitive in an Increasingly Green Industry. *American Cemetery & Cremation*, p. 4.

Rental Caskets: Alive and Well (2015, August). *American Funeral Director*.

Reid, T (2005, August). Branding Your Funeral Home. *The Director.*

Rietow, R. (2015, January 7). *26 Awesome Funeral Personalization Ideas to Try*. Retrieved from: http://blog.funeralone.com/funeralone-products/life-tributes/personalized-funeral-ideas/.

Robbins, L. (2014, April). Changing Our Perspective. *The Director*.

Rohling, D. (2012, September). Question for Today. *Funeral Home & Cemetery News*, p. A28.

Rubin, G. (2015, December). Funeral Insurance Pros, Cons, and Differences. *Mortuary Management Magazine*.

Ruggeri, E.D. (2006, March). Making the Forensic Removal: Assisting with Medical Examiner Transfers. *American Funeral Director*.

Science Friday (2018, August 31). *Tech Changes the Face of Death*. [Podcast]. Retrieved from: http://www.sciencefriday.com/segments/tech-changes-the-face-of-death/.

Schaal, S. (2007, February). Pet Loss Services. Mentally Positioned to Succeed Part 1. *American Funeral Director*.

Secking, S. (2005, September). The Community Mausoleum- A Brief History. *American Cemetery Magazine*.

SESCO (2006, May). Customer's Top 10 Requirements. *The SESCO Report*. Retrieved from: https://sescomgt.com/sesco-report.

SESCO (2014, October). What Do Employers Want from Their Employees? *The SESCO Management Consultant's Report*. Vol. MMXIV, Issue 7, p. 1-2. Retrieved from: https://sescomgt.com/sesco-report/2014/10.

SevenPonds.com (2019). *Planning a Memorial Service*. Retrieved from: http://www.sevenponds.com/after-death/planning-a-funeral-or-memorial-service.

Sevenponds.com (2019). *After Death: Planning a Funeral or Memorial Service*. Retrieved from: http://www.sevenponds.com/after-death/planning-a-funeral-or-memorial-service.

Sizemore, W. (2017, March). 4 Signs It's Time to Jumpstart Your Pre-need Program. *American Funeral Director*, p.48-50.

Solly, M. (2019, April 23). Washington Becomes First State to Allow 'Human Composting' as a Burial Method. *Smithsonian Magazine Online*. Retrieved from: https://www.smithsonianmag.com/smart-news/washington-first-state-allow-burial-method-human-composting-180972020/.

Spears, L.C. (2010). Character and Servant Leadership: 10 Characteristics of Effective, Caring Leaders. *The Journal of Virtues ad Leadership*, Vol. 1, Issue 1, p.25-30.

Stansbury, G. (2015) Searching for the Beautiful Question: Pre-Need. *Dodge Magazine, Winter Edition*, p. 25-28. Retrieved from: https://issuu.com/ddawebdesign/docs/winter_2015_dodge_magazine.

Starks, J. (2015, June). Properly Managing Cremated Human Remains: Identification Verification Procedure. *American Cemetery & Cremation*, p. 4-6.

Starks, J. (2017). Protecting Your Families and Business. *Funeral Home and Cemetery News*.

Starks, J. (2017a, October). From the First Call to Release: Chain of Custody with Cremation. *ICCFA Magazine*, p.46,48.

Starks, J. (2017b, September). Dignified Speech – 21st Century Vocabulary. *Funeral Home and Cemetery News.*

Statista (2019). Number of Internet Users from 2017-2023. *Statista.* Retrieved from: https://www.statista.com/statistics/325645/usa-number-of-internet-users/.

Strohofer, M. (2012, September). Five Top Trends in Casket Merchandising. *American Funeral Director*, p. 60-62. Retrieved from: www.scribd.com/document/360481103/ICCFA-magazine-october-2017.

Strohofer, M. (2012, September). Five Top Trends in Casket Merchandising. *American Funeral Director*, p. 60-62.

Stone, Z. (2016, January 27). The Pet Funeral Industry Makes 100 million in Profit. *The Hustle.* Retrieved from: https://thehustle.co/pet-funerals-in-2016-make-100-million-dollars.

Swisher, D. (2018). Social Superstar: How to Show off Your Best Self to a Potential Employer on Social Media. *Career Planners: First Time Job Keepers Guide*. Retrieved from: https://www.horizonhospitality.com/wp-content/uploads/2018/02/First-Time-Jobseekers-Guide.pdf.

Sugars, B. (2014, April 22). *Ten Principles of Leadership*. Retrieved from: http://angiefairbanks.actioncoach.com/2014/04/22/ten-principles-of-leadership-by-brad-sugars/.

Terranova, J. (2016, July 20). *Future Trends: Funeral Home of the Future*. Retrieved from: www.frazerconsultants.com/2016/07/future-trends-funeral-home--of-the-future/.

Terranova, J. (2017, March 28). *Are Funeral Processions Becoming Too Dangerous?* Retrieved from: https://www.frazerconsultants.com/2017/03/are-funeral-processions-becoming-too-dangerous/.

Thomas, C. (2009, August 27). *Handshake – Priest and Two Soldiers, 500BC*. Pergamon Museum Berlin (SK1708). Picasa Web Albums. Google.

Todd, M. & Best. R. (2011, January 1). Health and Safety in the Funeral Home. *The Director*. Retrieved from: http://duncanstuarttodd.com/health-and-safety-in-the-funeral-home/.

Trimarchi, M. (2009, January 15) How Natural Burial Works. Retrieved from: http://science.howstuffworks.com/environmental/green-science/natural-burial.htm.

The True Professional. (2014, October). *The SESCO Management Consultants Report. Vol. MMXIV, Issue 7*, p. 2-3.

Ugan, D. (2017, June). Digital innovation key areas to focus on; technology solutions enable exceptional customer service. American Funeral Director, p. 22-24.

United States Department of Veterans Affairs (2018, October). *Burial and Plot Internment Allowance*. Veterans Benefits Administration. Retrieved from: https://www.benefits.va.gov/BENEFITS/factsheets/burials/Burial.pdf.

United States Navy Mortuary Affairs (2016, May 27). *Burial at Sea Program*. Retrieved from: https://www.navy.mil/navydata/questions/burial.html.

United States Postal Service (2014, October). *How to Ship & Packages Cremated Remains. Publication 139.* Retrieved from: https://about.usps.com/publications/pub139.pdf.

Van Beck, T. (2016, November 15). The Vital and Active Role of the Funeral Professional. *Funeral Home and Cemetery News.*

Van Beck, T. (2017, December). Keys to Service. *Funeral Home and Cemetery News*.

Van Beck, T. (1994). *Cemetery History Book*. The Lowen Group.

Van Buren, A. (2007, April 4). Mourner Who Pays Respects is Asked to Buy Something Else. *Dear Abby.* Retrieved: https://www.uexpress.com/dearabby/2007/4/4/mourner-who-pays-respects-is-asked.

Veteran's Flag Depot (2019). *Flag Presentation Protocol and Flag Folding*. Retrieved from: https://www.Veteransflagdepot.com/flag-presentation-protocol-and-flag-folding/.

'Virtual Afterlives' Explores the Changing Nature of Rituals, Grieving (2017, January 30). *Funeral Service Insider*, p. 1, 5-6.

Watts, J. (2009, November). Code of Ethical Cremation Practices. *Watt's Funeral Homes-Ask the Director.* Retrieved from: http://wattsfuneralhomesaskthedirector.blogspot.com/2009/11/code-of-ethical-cremation-practices.html.

Webster, L. (2017, May). Defining Home Funeral Guides. *American Funeral Director*, p. 44-48.

Weigel, J. (2015, November). 10 Tips to Create Press Releases that Get Published. *American Cemetery & Cremation*, p.6.

Wikipedia (2017, February 26). *Handshake*. Retrieved from: https://en.wikipedia.org/wiki/handshake.

Wikipedia (2019, November 20). *Twitter*. Retrieved from: https://en.wikipedia.org/wiki/Twitter.

Wikipedia (2019, October 24). *VLOG*. Retrieved from: https://en.wikipedia.org/wiki/Vlog.

Wilde, C. (2013, December 21). *21 Tips for Aspiring Funeral Directors*. Retrieved from: http://www.calebwilde.com/2013/12/21-tips-for-aspiring-funeral-directors.

Williams, M.J. (2005, September). Viewing without Embalming. *The American Funeral Director.*

Williams, P. (2019, May 28). *Supreme Court Upholds Indiana Abortion Law Requiring Fetal Remains to be Buried or Cremated*. NBC News. Retrieved from: https://www.nbcnews.com/politics/supreme-court/supreme-court-upholds-indiana-abortion-law-requiring-fetal-remains-be-n1010736

Wolfelt, A. (2014, February 4). Teaching the Way. *The Director.*

Wolfelt, A.D. (2015, February) Helping Families Make Transformations Through Choices, Not Decisions. *The Director.*

Worldometer (2020, June 22). COVID-19 Coronavirus Pandemic. Retrieved from: https://www.worldometers.info/coronavirus/

Yearsley, D. (2014, April 8-11). The Mausoleum Checklist: Smarter Planning and Car. *ICCFA Convention.* Retrieved from: https://www.ensureaseal.com/sites/default/files/best-practices checklist.pdf.

York, W. (2018, April). Dangerous Synthetic Opioids and the First Call. *Funeral Home & Cemetery News.* Retrieved from: http://www.nomispublications.com/NewsPaper/04-2018/.

YourTribute (2015). Memorialization. Retrieved from: http://www.yourtribute.com/end-of-life/memorialization/.

INDEX

NOTES

NOTES